D0072377

Interactive Digital Narrative

The book is concerned with narrative in digital media that changes according to user input—Interactive Digital Narrative (IDN). It provides a broad overview of current issues and future directions in this multi-disciplinary field that includes humanities-based and computational perspectives. It assembles the voices of leading researchers and practitioners like Janet Murray, Marie-Laure Ryan, Scott Rettberg and Martin Rieser. In three sections, it covers history, theoretical perspectives and varieties of practice including narrative game design, with a special focus on changes in the power relationship between audience and author enabled by interactivity. After discussing the historical development of diverse forms, the book presents theoretical standpoints including a semiotic perspective, a proposal for a specific theoretical framework and an inquiry into the role of artificial intelligence. Finally, it analyses varieties of current practice from digital poetry to location-based applications, artistic experiments and expanded remakes of older narrative game titles.

Hartmut Koenitz is Assistant Professor of Mass Media Arts in the Grady College of Journalism and Mass Communication at the University of Georgia, USA.

Gabriele Ferri is a Postdoctoral Researcher in the School of Informatics and Computing at Indiana University Bloomington, USA.

Mads Haahr is Lecturer in the School of Computer Science and Statistics at Trinity College Dublin, Ireland.

Diğdem Sezen is Assistant Professor in the Faculty of Communications at Istanbul University, Turkey.

Tonguç İbrahim Sezen is Assistant Professor in the Faculty of Communication at Istanbul Bilgi University, Turkey.

Routledge Studies in European Communication Research and Education

Edited by Nico Carpentier, Vrije Universiteit Brussel, Belgium and Charles University, Czech Republic, François Heinderyckx, Université Libre de Bruxelles, Belgium and Claudia Alvares, Lusofona University, Portugal.
Series Advisory Board: Denis McQuail, Robert Picard and Jan Servaes

http://www.ecrea.eu

Published in association with the European Communication Research and Education Association (ECREA), books in the series make a major contribution to the theory, research, practice and/or policy literature. They are European in scope and represent a diversity of perspectives. Book proposals are refereed.

Interactive Digital Narrative

History, Theory and Practice

**Edited by
Hartmut Koenitz, Gabriele Ferri,
Mads Haahr, Diğdem Sezen
and Tonguç İbrahim Sezen**

Routledge
Taylor & Francis Group

NEW YORK AND LONDON

First published 2015
by Routledge
711 Third Avenue, New York, NY 10017

and by Routledge
2 Park Square, Milton Park, Abingdon, Oxon OX14 4RN

Routledge is an imprint of the Taylor & Francis Group, an informa business

© 2015 Taylor & Francis

The right of the editors to be identified as the authors of the editorial material, and of the authors for their individual chapters, has been asserted in accordance with sections 77 and 78 of the Copyright, Designs and Patents Act 1988.

All rights reserved. No part of this book may be reprinted or reproduced or utilised in any form or by any electronic, mechanical, or other means, now known or hereafter invented, including photocopying and recording, or in any information storage or retrieval system, without permission in writing from the publishers.

Trademark notice: Product or corporate names may be trademarks or registered trademarks, and are used only for identification and explanation without intent to infringe.

Library of Congress Cataloging in Publication Data

Interactive digital narrative : history, theory, and practice / edited by Hartmut Koenitz, Gabriele Ferri, Mads Haahr, Digdem Sezen and Tonguc Ibrahim Sezen.
    pages cm. — (Routledge studies in European communication research and education ; 7)
Includes bibliographical references and index.
    1. Digital storytelling. 2. Interactive multimedia. 3. Narration (Rhetoric)
    4. Digital media—History. I. Koenitz, Hartmut, editor. II. Ferri, Gabriele, editor.
    III. Haahr, Mads, editor. IV. Sezen, Digdem, editor. V. Sezen, Tonguc Ibrahim, editor.
QA76.76.I59I549 2015
006.7—dc23   2014046169

ISBN: 978-1-138-78239-6 (hbk)
ISBN: 978-1-315-76918-9 (ebk)

Typeset in Sabon
by codeMantra

Printed and bound in the United States of America by Publishers Graphics, LLC on sustainably sourced paper.

Contents

Foreword

Nick Montfort

The essays in this collection further our understanding of how computers can narrate responsively and in profoundly new ways. While the articles are organised into those emphasising the historical, the theoretical and the practical, the editors have helpfully identified ways to also read across the three sections by following common threads. In addition, many essays deal quite substantially with two or all three aspects.

Consider a few of the ways in which these three categories overlap: Scott Rettberg's 'historical' essay on the American hypertext novel documents his 'practical' experience as an author of *The Unknown*; Marie-Laure Ryan develops her 'theoretical' discussion with reference to the 'history' of play-fields in digital games; Janet Murray situates her 'theoretical' discussion by considering a rich 'history' of women and their boyfriends in interactive and noninteractive media; Nicolas Szilas draws on his system-building practice to 'theorise' highly interactive digital narrative; and those whose work appears in the practice section have informed their system-building and art-making with an awareness of both history and theory. While this book is organised according to whether history, theory and practice are stressed—and it needs to be somehow organised—these are not exclusive silos, and they are not shown to be. Rather, they are the bases from which connections are made. The work the authors and editors have done moves us beyond the popular chant of "theory and practice," which really does nothing but juxtaposes these two without explaining their relationship, to actually connect them, and history as well, allowing all three to inform one other.

A FIELD IN FORMATION

Having noted the above, this collection is also important because of how it reveals a lack—not any lack inherent in this particular project overall, or in any essay, but rather something that is incomplete in this intellectual area, which is still in the process of coalescing into a field. This nascent field has framed but not solved its initial conceptual problems. That is part of what makes it exciting. This book, after all, is not a festschrift for a body of work that has essentially been concluded, but it is an important part of the foundation for those of us still establishing major ideas, directions and practices.

A sign that this is not a well-established and fixed field is that those of us in this area have not yet agreed on its name. *Interactive digital narrative*, whether in short form (IDN) or long, is in certain ways similar to *intelligent narrative technologies* (the name of a workshop series), *interactive drama* (pioneered by Oz Project participants but also taken up by David Cage), *interactive storytelling* (the name of a conference series and considered so conventional that it is abbreviated to IS in Chapter 12), and *narrative games* (a term often used at the Game Developers Conference, for instance, although it appears only in passing in this book). These different terms suggest their own different emphases and connections—to artificial intelligence or narrative theory, or traditions and theories of drama, or ludic interaction and videogaming—while, at the same time, the people working under these banners, and others, do truly share many common assumptions, use many similar techniques, and are often informed by each other's work.

At certain points, developing some sort of neologism to serve as a standard term can be extremely valuable. A new name can serve to productively expand some concept, defined by previous terms, that is now seen to be too narrow. This happened in different ways with both cybertext and electronic literature, two categories that have rich intersections with each other and with interactive digital narrative. These two terms were also successful because they hearkened back to a relevant history and foundation (-text, literature), contextualising the field they described and grounding it in known cultural practices, while also embracing recent changes and the future cyber-, electronic).

While this type of naming activity can be valuable, and may eventually be important, there seems to be no need to immediately unify everyone's name for this activity or field, or to standardise on a single term, old or new, for all that we do. *Interactive digital narratives* is a fine term, existing alongside several that are slightly different, because it too makes connections to well-known aspects of culture, to history, while also looking forward. It gathers together academic work from a wide variety of disciplines and from the practice of artists, writers and game-makers within and beyond industry. Certain other terms—as long as they aren't attempts to retrench and to wall off and ignore relevant, related work—can be fine, too, and can show how many different perspectives are involved in the same enterprise, or at least, very similar enterprises.

Yes, there are some related activities that would seem to be left out of IDN strictly interpreted: Interactive digital poetry and art that is nonnarrative, story generation systems that are noninteractive, live interactive drama experiences that may be scripted and rule-based but are enacted by people without the use of computers. Of course, some focus is always needed for conversation and progress. The existence of other, related fields simply suggests to me that this diversity in names is a good thing and can allow researchers and practitioners to make different connections at different times.

That is, our diversity of names, and the use of IDN here, is productive. These are not serving as exclusive decrees; rather, they facilitate intersections and connection, just as the conjunction of history, theory and practice do.

A MATTER OF GOALS AND IDEALS

Since there is no need to create history/theory/practice intersections or to worry ourselves about establishing a single standard name for the whole field and everything related, what needs to change in IDN?

The urgent question for interactive digital narrative is what it truly aspires to. What are its goals? How does it seek to change or maintain society? Is it here to reassure us or provoke us? In this sense, it is time to refine our associations, to discern, and to distinguish, even as we celebrate intersections in other ways.

Will the work that we are doing end up as a (possibly profitable) extension of the worst properties of current media—as with "The Family" in Ray Bradbury's *Fahrenheit 451*, in which the numbed Mildred Montag reads a script to characters on three wall-sized displays, becoming ever more enthralled? In such a scenario, which is participatory although not truly interactive, the absence of fourth wall is hardly what is important—no matter that Mildred bemoans having only three walls installed. The real issue is that the system provides a sort of engagement, immersion and ability to play along in superficial ways, without offering any true agency, any new aesthetic vision or any new philosophical or political concept.

Our field doesn't lack passion and enthusiasm on the part of researchers, theorists and artists who seek to dig into every possibility. But, why are we doing this?

What this field needs now is to become a movement, or perhaps more than one if there is no single common cause. Is IDN out to bust up the game industry and fundamentally change it, or does it seek to simply buttress what exists? Is it supposed to be pure entertainment or something beyond that? Does it care more about empowering the disenfranchised or about training the military, and does the answer to this question depend upon how much funding is available for each option? Is it about human nature and our cultural world, or a distraction from them? Is IDN fashion, always seeking to set and follow trends, or can it open a chasm to the timeless? Is it a pleasing but meaningless salve to soothe workday aches or a way to model a better society?

Something I have heard Scott Rettberg speak about is that electronic literature is a migration rather than a movement. This description is inclusive, and it too connects the past with the future, as there is somewhere to migrate from (print literature) and new possibilities of where to migrate to (the digital medium). It means that people do not have to have a common artistic vision or shared goals at the highest level to discuss their experiences and learn from one another. Whether this is precisely true of the related field called IDN or not, IDN is certainly *more* a migration than a movement. The migrants may come from a wider or at least different variety of disciplines and practices, but it is the arrival at user-controlled computational narrative, not the underlying drive, that defines this field.

A CHOICE POINT: ENTERTAINMENT OR UTOPIA?

People making videogames, interactive TV, interactive story generators and all manner of other interactive narrative experiences on computers can consider themselves in the same field—the same migration—and they would be correct. But people who have opposite answers to these questions I have posed—some trying to retrench and focus entirely on earnings, some trying to innovate and make progress toward new cultural developments and understandings—may not be in the same field. They certainly aren't in the same movement.

The technologies to model a utopia may not be the same ones needed to entertain, or, at least, the intersection of these may be slight and not very interesting. Let me suggest that people need to communicate, collaborate, and be empowered with an understanding of computation to use interactive digital narrative as a way of designing a new society or ameliorating social ills. They have to be builders, makers and coders, rather than just being given an experience. Working toward such a goal involves collective thought, deliberation and consciousness on the part of the interactors. Mildred Montag did not need any of this in order to feel a part of her video narrative and to be entertained. The techniques that entertained her, we have to imagine, were very different. It was a fundamentally different design problem.

The community of writers using Twine, an effective and straightforward hypertext creation tool, one that is free software and outputs HTML for the Web, provide one example of a more movement-like group. While authors seem glad to be part of the interactive fiction (IF) community (the former participate in and do well in its annual competition, and the creator of Twine is an IF author), the work they do is radically different as a writing practice and as interactive design. Recent Twine work strongly focuses on issues such as cultural desolation, personal identity, alienation, and lack of choice much more thoroughly than has been done in parser-based interactive fiction, even though individual parser-based works have treated these themes.

One might try to locate the difference between Twine production and parser-based production (most of which is done using the Inform 7 system) in particular aspects of writing style, in Inform 7's ability to accept input and understand typed user commands, or in the choice of themes. Perhaps the most significant distinction is that Twine authors are more allied in terms of what they want to accomplish. They create unusual fantasy worlds of the sort that appear in other digital work, but theirs cut into personal and cultural questions in obvious and jarring ways. They are often seeking to do work that is personally or politically meaningful, to provoke the reader into understanding other people's cognition, emotion, and experiences.

If the Twine community agrees with my (outsider) assessment or something like it, they might realise that although it's good to trade tips and technical tricks with other Twine users, it isn't the development tool, but their more abstract goals, that unite them as a group. They might join with others working in different sorts of IDN and other sorts of poetic, narrative, and digital development. They might decide that someone writing a Twine game that is, for instance, a humorous Choose-Your-Own-Adventure parody aimed only at laughs isn't really part of their movement, while a digital poet working with a different system could be.

The more retrograde and more aspirational types of IDN can, of course, both exist, and there can be groups, even large and organised ones, working in both of these ways. But as people in the field determine who to conference with and collaborate with, they should both consider the particular valence of IDN being undertaken, as well as think about who the others are, or would be, in their movement. I am not suggesting that we shun those with different goals, but rather take the opportunity to form alliances based on deep values and principles, noticing where we have already done so, and reaching out across different practices and media.

The essays in this book show that IDN has tremendous capability and is continuing to excel. As someone compelled to learn more about this field, while you read and learn from what is included here, consider, please, how this capability will be used. Consider in what direction you would like to move the field, and what you and like-minded researchers and artists—in your movement—can do to help it progress.

Acknowledgments

The editors would like to give their sincere thanks to the ECREA book series editors, especially Nico Carpentier, for their positive critique and helpful advice during the formative period of this volume, as well as their support in seeing this work to completion.

The editors are also grateful for Benjamin Larkin, whose outstanding abilities in copy-editing and proofreading were crucial for the readability of this volume.

1 Introduction

Perspectives on Interactive Digital Narrative

Hartmut Koenitz, Gabriele Ferri, Mads Haahr, Diğdem Sezen and Tonguç İbrahim Sezen

1. AN OPPORTUNITY AND A CHALLENGE: VISION AND STATE OF THE ART OF IDN

Interactive Digital Narrative (IDN) connects artistic vision with technology. At its core is the age-old dream to make the fourth wall permeable; to enter the narrative, to participate and experience what will unfold. IDN promises to dissolve the division between active creator and passive audience and herald the advent of a new triadic relationship between creator, dynamic narrative artefact and audience-turned-participant. Within this broad vision of fully interactive narrative environments through the use of digital technologies, IDN aggregates different artistic and research directions from malleable, screen-based textual representations to the quest for virtual spaces in which human interactors experience coherent narratives side by side with authored narrative elements and synthetic characters.

The IDN vision is as much about narrative and control as it is about balance. Indeed, the quest for the right artistic measure, for equilibrium between agency and a coherent, satisfying experience, might be the ultimate challenge of the field. Yet, the artistic challenge does not exist in isolation and is joined by technological and analytical challenges. IDN is a truly interdisciplinary field, which includes scholars and practitioners with backgrounds in multiple disciplines: from literary studies to computer science and fine art. While guiding visions have been described, sometimes even heralded, in various forms for quite some time—for example, the image of Alice entering the rabbit hole or Borges' infinite labyrinth in the form of a novel—it is only with the advent of computer technology that its realisation seems possible, and constant developments in computer technologies seem to put them ever closer to our reach. Indeed, digital media has radically changed the way narrative content is being created, shared, experienced and interpreted.

In her seminal work *Hamlet on the Holodeck* (1997), Janet Murray notes that digital media is inherently procedural and participatory, referring to the capacity of computers to execute a series of commands and react to user input. While procedurality affords digital creators the expressive power to define initial conditions and rules under which an interactive work executes and reacts to input, IDN bestows cocreative power on its users through interaction and therefore reshapes the relation between creator, work and audience in a way that far surpasses aspects of interpretation and reader-response theory, but whose exact extent is a subject of scholarly debate. The complex relation between authorial control and the power of interactive agency is therefore an underlying topic in all three parts of this collection of essays, which focus on history, theory and practice.

While IDN has been an artistic practice and a topic of scholarly inquiry for more than two decades, it is still in its infancy compared to other narrative forms like the stage drama, the printed book or the moving image. As a technical and artistic challenge and opportunity, advances in the IDN field depend on the combined effects of developments in different parts within the greater field. However, progress in these different areas has historically been uneven. For example, graphical representation has seen rapid improvements from the humble beginnings as text on the screen to current cinematic-quality 3D depictions driven by simulations of highly realistic physics. Whilst the progress in graphics and physics is no less than astonishing, the same cannot be said for the larger challenge of creating specific narrative forms to produce compelling and captivating experiences: in this regard, the pace of development has been unsteady and slow. The virtual environments used for many contemporary interactive narratives are realistic, dynamic and feature high fidelity in terms of their visual presentation and physical mechanics. However, the narratives and characters they host remain shallow, static and lacking in believability, dramatic engagement and narrative development in comparison.

Indeed, while clearly eclipsed in visual presentation, the strong narrative of early titles like *Zork* (1982) holds up well even today. Maybe this fact should not surprise us, as resources for work on improving the graphical representation have been more readily available than for the more artistic problem of narrative development, spurred originally by the US Air Force's interest in convincing visuals for flight simulators (Myers, 1998). Research in IDN ideally combines technical development and advances in artistic expression, as well as the expansion of analytical perspectives; and historically, it has been difficult to find resources for such interdisciplinary projects. Funding, however, is only one aspect of the problem. Cinematic visualisation and real-world perceptions provide an ideal to aspire to for graphical representations. A comparable, shared goal on the side of narrative development and resulting form is elusive. Janet Murray's proposal of the 'Holodeck' (Murray 1997), an imaginary future form of entertainment first depicted in the TV series *Star Trek: The Next Generation* that immerses its audience in a dynamic, reactive narrative, has perhaps been rejected more often (Ryan, 2001; Aarseth, 2004; Spector, 2013) than it has been tacitly embraced (Mateas, 2001; Nitsche, 2008). Other visions, like constructive hypertext or interactive drama, share this fate. However, while the absence of a canonical set of narrative structures specific to IDN can be problematic, the lack of a unanimously shared vision also represents an opportunity because it provides space for experimentation and creative license to create new forms.

If the defining artistic moment of the book was the advent of the novel in the 17th century[1] and of film was the invention of montage (Eisenstein, 1949), a similar breakthrough is still elusive in IDN, and maybe there never will be a comparable moment in this field. Instead, we might see existing design modes (e.g., third-person versus first-person perspective, modes of audience participation and novel narrative structures) grow into mature artistic conventions applied in a conscious way by a new generation of authors. A possible defining milestone for IDN might even be the emergence of a consistent group of practitioners, IDN auteurs or *cyberbards*, to use Murray's term (1997), who feel more confident with the notion of relinquishing some of their authorial control to users, players and interactors, and see themselves not as the creators of singular visions, but as designers of expressive potential.

Analytical perspectives have developed considerably since the 1980s, when the first scholars with backgrounds in design and the humanities became interested in the topic. Where early treatments of the topic focused on the comparison to older narrative practices, later works have become increasingly more focused on specific aspects like space (Jenkins, 2004; Nitsche, 2008; Ryan, in this Volume), on the particular manifestations (Montfort, 2003), specific theoretical concepts (Koenitz, 2010) and the connections to larger frameworks (Ryan, 2006; Koenitz et al, 2013a) and most recently on particular theoretical aspects (Bruni and Baceviciute, 2013; Mason, 2013; Ferri, 2013). Amongst this much needed focus, scholars in this field are also engaged in a meta-reflection on the defining characteristics of IDN (Murray, 1997; Aarseth, 1997, 2012; Juul, 2011; Eskelinen, 2012; Mateas, 2001; Ryan 2001, 2006; Frasca, 2003b; Crawford, 2004; Koenitz et al., 2013b). A particular example of this discussion emerged in the early 2000s with the advent of computer game studies as a discipline. In that debate, narrative-oriented and game-oriented approaches were framed as a dichotomy, painting games through the simulative aspects as a "radically different alternative to narratives as a cognitive and communicative structure" (Aarseth 2001). A group of game studies scholars (Aarseth, 2001, 2004; Juul, 1999; Eskelinen, 2001; Frasca, 2003a), opposing narrative-centric views, adopted the name of *ludologists*; and thus the discussion is often referred to as the 'narratology vs. ludology debate.' The very first ludological perspectives not only opposed the use of narratological concepts to describe video games but, in their early forms, also described interactive narrative as practically impossible: "computer games [are] simply not a narrative medium" (Juul, 1999, p. 1). Jesper Juul's argument conflated two claims; notions derived from narratology—or related disciplines—are not effective to read games, and games cannot convey narratives. The first claim followed from the need to legitimise game studies as an independent academic discipline, thus defining it by contrast with others and establishing its own vocabulary. This was a move understood by Stuart Moulthrop (2003) as a necessary "defensive maneuver (sic)," however at the cost of an "alarmingly narrow" point of view, one that carries the danger of creating "conceptual blind spots" (Jenkins, 2004). As game studies became a recognised academic discipline in the following years, a gradual softening of perspectives finally allowed Janet Murray to pronounce the end of the debate (Murray, 2005). The second claim about the constitutive dichotomy between play and narration—although retracted by Juul himself (2001)—today remains influential, especially in the professional practice of game design where gameplay and narrative are often seen as opposing parameters. In this vein, game designer Ralph Coster, for example, defines narrative in contrast to gameplay: "The commonest use of a completely parallel medium that does not actually interact with the game system is narrative" (Koster, 2012). He categorises the narrative parts of a game experience as linear, noninteractive and in the sole function of rewarding players.

Even after years of research and discussion, the coupling of narration and interaction can still spark provocative debates that require our attention. Therefore, the practical and ontological analogies and differences between interactivity and narration warrant further academic inquiry. Likewise, the relationship between static and procedurally generated narratives calls for more attention. In this respect, a more holistic view of IDN, foregrounding how digital means enable interactive forms of narrative, could also contribute to the ludological discussion.

2. A DIVERSE AND VIBRANT FIELD

This volume covers a diverse and vibrant field that has continually grown since the late 1970s, from the first text-based Interactive Fiction to such forms as Hypertext Fiction, Interactive Cinema, Interactive Installations, Interactive Drama and Video Game Narrative.

The book is structured in three parts. The first part is historical and addresses how forms of IDN emerged over the years as distinct phenomena and how the transformations of digital media shaped the current forms. Scott Rettberg examines hypertext novels and poems, offering an historical perspective on their technical development and literary fruition, while Chris Hales describes the historical development of interactive cinema with a focus on the impact of digital technology on this form of IDN. Finally, Udi Ben-Arie and Noam Knoller offer a diachronic perspective on the userfacing aspects in IDN, foregrounding the aesthetic, experiential and hermeneutic dimensions.

The book's second part is theoretical. Theoretical enquiry into IDN started with adaptations of established narratological perspectives, for example neo-Aristotelian poetics (Laurel 1986, 1991; Mateas, 2001), post-classical narratology (Ryan, 1999, 2001), African oral traditions (Jennings, 1996;

Harrell, 2007) and French post-structuralism (Montfort, 2003). In recent years, scholars have started to look beyond narratology to understand the changes in narrative modalities afforded by IDN. Also, particular aspects, such as spatiality, have come to the forefront of analytical work. The editors introduce this section with an overview of these earlier approaches before the book's second part presents a range of current theoretical perspectives. First, Gabriele Ferri proposes a common ground for narrative theory of IDN by reexamining the similarities and differences with unilinear storytelling. Hartmut Koenitz argues for a theoretical approach that is specific for IDN based on cognitive science and cybernetics, while Marie-Laure Ryan discusses spatial representations as a key topic in interactive narratives. Janet Murray analyses dynamics of relationships in literature and discusses their application as a schema for IDN, before Nicolas Szilas in the final theoretical chapter offers a critical perspective on the role of Artificial Intelligence in developing a future, better form of digital narrations.

The book's third part is concerned with practice. When a new medium appears, early practitioners often engage with it first by extending existing practices. In this way, early film was used to show theatrical performances. Eventually these modes of extension lead to distinct practices. As the written text became more than a collection of printed pages in the form of the novel, and film became more than a theatrical performance through montage, it is no longer adequate to relegate IDN practices to the fringes of a perspective centred on narrative in long-established media forms. The third part of the book is intended to examine the wide range of current practices and the emergence of IDN as a distinct phenomenon. Ulrike Spierling begins this part of the book with a chapter that emphasises the importance of user interface design for the IDN experience, as well as its implementation in practice. Scott Rettberg describes current practices in electronic literature, while Sandy Louchart, John Truesdale, Neil Suttie and Ruth Aylett report on research and implementations of emergent narrative, based on autonomous intelligent virtual characters. Andreea Molnar and Patty Kostkova ask how story-based learning is transformed by the encounter with truly malleable narrative. Mads Haahr analyses examples of location-based games that position digital narrative elements in the real world, and Diğdem Sezen examines video game poetry. Martin Rieser puts the spotlight on distinctly artistic uses of IDN, while Tonguç Sezen's chapter on remakes alerts us to the fact that IDN has already reached a self-reflective state.

In addition to reading the book's three parts in a linear order, the reader can also follow specific trajectories across the whole volume, for example on IDN and the human-computer interface (Knoller and Ben-Arie, Szilas, Spierling, Haahr, Rieser), on literary aspects (Rettberg, Murray, Diğdem Sezen), transformation of existing fields and self-reflective practices (Hales, Rettberg, Molnar and Kostkova, Tonguç Sezen), novel theoretical approaches (Ferri, Koenitz), spatial aspects (Ryan, Haahr, Rieser) and critical/practical perspectives on the role of artificial intelligence (Szilas, Louchart et al.).

As the development of procedural media progresses, the powers and abilities of readers as interactors and authors as procedural creators are constantly being shifted and rebalanced. Since we are aware of the continuous advances in the IDN field, a companion website at www.gamesandnarrative.net/idn-book will provide a space for further discussion. IDN enhances the experiential dimensions of human expression, with multimodal manifestations, procedural generation and novel structures. Furthermore, technical and artistic advances in interactive narratives open epistemological questions that require constant theoretical attention. As this volume attests, the development—in every dimension—is continuous and shows no signs of slowing down. And herein might lie the lasting attraction of the field—to further human expression by applying a range of human faculties, from the invention of digital technology to the continuous development of hardware and software to artistic treatment and critical reflection.

NOTE

1. Cervantes' *Don Quixote* (1605) can be seen as the foundation of the modern novel (Riley, 1962).

REFERENCES

Aarseth, E. (1997) *Cybertext: Perspectives on Ergodic Literature*. Baltimore: Johns Hopkins University Press.
Aarseth, E. (2001) Computer game studies, year one. *Game Studies*. 1(1).
Aarseth, E. (2004) Genre trouble. *Electronic Book Review*. 3.
Aarseth, E. (2012) A narrative theory of games. In *Proceedings of the International Conference on the Foundations of Digital Games*. New York: ACM.
Blank, M. and Lebling, D. (1980) *Zork I*. [Interactive fiction]. Cambridge, MA: Infocom.
Bruni, L. E., and Baceviciute, S. (2013) Narrative intelligibility and closure in interactive systems. In: Koenitz, H., Sezen, T. I., Ferri, G., Haahr, M., Sezen, D. and Çatak, G. (eds.) *Interactive Storytelling: 6th International Conference, ICIDS 2013*. Heidelberg: Springer.
Crawford, C. (2004) *Chris Crawford on Interactive Storytelling*. New Jersey: Pearson Education.
Eisenstein, S. (1949) *Film Form: Essays in Film Theory*. New York: Harcourt Brace.
Eskelinen, M. (2001) The gaming situation. *Game Studies*. 1(1).
Eskelinen, M. (2012) *Cybertext Poetics: The ritical Landscape of New Media Literary Theory*. New York: Continuum. C.
Ferri, G. (2013) Satire, propaganda, play, storytelling, notes on critical interactive digital narratives. In: Koenitz, H., Sezen, T. I., Ferri, G., Haahr, M., Sezen, D. and Çatak, G. (eds.) *Interactive Storytelling: 6th International Conference, ICIDS 2013*. Heidelberg: Springer.

Frasca, G. (2003a) Ludologists love storties, too: Notes from a debate that never took place. In *Proceedings of the DIGRA 2003 Conference.*

Frasca, G. (2003b) Simulation versus narrative. In: Wolf, M. J. P. and Perron, B. (eds.) *The Video Game Theory Reader.* New York: Routledge.

Harrell, D. F. (2007) GRIOT's tales of haints and seraphs: A computational narrative generation system. In: Harrigan, P. and Wardrip-Fruin, N. (eds.) *Second Person: Role-Playing and Story in Games and Playable Media.* Cambridge, MA: MIT Press.

Jenkins, H. (2004) Game design as narrative architecture. *Electronic Book Review.* 3.

Jennings, P. (1996) Narrative structures for new media: Towards a new definition. *Leonardo.* 29(5). pp. 345–350.

Juul, J. (1999) *A Clash Between Game and Narrative: a Thesis on Computer Games and Interactive Fiction.* MA Thesis. Institute for Nordic Languages and Literature, University of Copenhagen.

Juul, J. (2001) Games telling stories. *Game Studies*, 1(1), 45.

Juul, J. (2011) *Half-real: Video Games Between Real Rules and Fictional Worlds.* Cambridge, MA: MIT Press.

Koenitz, H., Haahr, M., Ferri, G., and Sezen, T. (2013a) First steps towards a unified theory for interactive digital narrative. In: Pan, Z., Cheok, A. D., Mueller, W., Iurgel, I., Petta, P., and Urban, B. (eds.) *Transactions on Edutainment X.* Heidelberg: Springer.

Koenitz, H., Haahr, M., Ferri, G., Sezen, T., and Sezen, D (2013b) Mapping the evolving space of interactive digital narrative—From artifacts to categorizations. In: Koenitz, H., Sezen, T. I., Ferri, G., Haahr, M., Sezen, D., and Çatak, G. (eds.) *Interactive Storytelling: 6th International Conference, ICIDS 2013.* Heidelberg: Springer.

Koenitz, H. (2010) Towards a theoretical framework for interactive digital narrative. In: Aylett, R., Lim, M. Y., Louchart, S., Petta, P., and Riedl, M. (eds.) *Interactive Storytelling: Third Joint Conference on Interactive Digital Storytelling, ICIDS 2010.* Heidelberg: Springer.

Koster, R. (2012) *Narrative Is Not a Game Mechanic.* Available at: http://www.raphkoster.com/2012/01/20/narrative-is-not-a-game-mechanic/.

Laurel, B. (1986) *Toward the Design of a Computer-Based Interactive Fantasy System.* PhD Thesis. Drama Department, Ohio State University.

Laurel, B. (1991) *Computers as Theater.* Reading, MA: Addison-Wesley.

Mason, S. (2013) On games and links: Extending the vocabulary of agency and immersion in interactive narratives. In: Koenitz, H., Sezen, T. I., Ferri, G., Haahr, M., Sezen, D., and Çatak, G. (eds.) *Interactive Storytelling: 6th International Conference, ICIDS 2013.* Heidelberg: Springer.

Mateas, M. (2001) A preliminary poetics for interactive drama and games. *Digital Creativity.* 12(3). pp. 140–152.

Montfort, N. (2003) *Twisty Little Passages: An Approach to Interactive Fiction.* Cambridge, MA: MIT Press.

Moulthrop, S. (2003) Stuart Moulthrop's response. *Electronic Book Review.* 3.

Murray, J. (1997) *Hamlet on the Holodeck: The Future of Narrative in Cyberspaace.* New York: The Free Press.

Murray, J. (2005) The last word on ludology v narratology in game studies. In *Proceedings of the DiGRA 2005 Conference.*

Myers, B. A. (1998) A brief history of human-computer interaction technology. *Interactions*, 5(2), 44–54.

Nitsche, M. (2008) *Video Game Spaces. Inage, Play, and Structure in 3D Worlds.* Cambridge, MA: MIT Press.

Riley, E. C. (1962) *Cervantes's Theory of the Novel.* Oxford: Clarendon Press.

Ryan, Marie-Laure(1999) Immersion vs. interactivity: Virtual reality and literary theory. *SubStance*, 28(2). pp. 110–137.

Ryan, Marie-Laure(2001) *Narrative as Virtual Reality: Immersion and Interactivity in Literature and Electronic Media.* Baltimore: Johns Hopkins University Press.

Ryan, Marie-Laure(2006) *Avatars of Story. Narrative Modes in Old and New Media.* Minneapolis: University of Minnesota Press.

Ryan, Marie-Laure (2001) Beyond myth and metaphor—The case of narrative in digital media. *Game Studies.* 1(1).

Spector, W. (2013) Holodeck: Holy grail or hollow promise? *Gamesindustry International.* [online] August 31. Available at: http://www.gamesindustry.biz/articles/2013-07-31-holodeck-holy-grail-or-hollow-promise-part-1.

Section I
IDN History

Introduction

A Concise History of Interactive Digital Narrative

Hartmut Koenitz, Gabriele Ferri, Mads Haahr, Diğdem Sezen and Tonguç İbrahim Sezen

The first part of the book is concerned with the history of Interactive Digital Narrative (IDN). Its intention is to serve as a concise historical account of the development of IDN from its beginnings to recent works by means of representative and influential examples. The identification of distinct historical phases is problematic, given the many parallel developments in the field, for example of hypertext fiction and graphical adventure games. Therefore, we identify trajectories based on form—in the sense of particular visual and physical manifestations. The three evolutionary trajectories identified here—text-based, cinematic/performative and ludic/experimental—represent major facets of IDNs. The trajectories traced here are not meant to be mutually exclusive the same artifact might easily be related to several of them.

Text-based examples constitute the first trajectory, from the very first IDN artefact originating in the 1960s, to Interactive Fiction games in the late 1970s and Hypertext Fiction in the early 1990s, leading to their recent resurrection in the Versu platform in 2013. The second trajectory adds an audio-visual dimension that partly remediates aspects of cinema and performance, and examples in this group range from interactive movies over multi-linear TV shows to experimental art installations. This trajectory also shows the strong interests of *avant-garde* artists in the expressive use of interactive technologies. Finally, the third trajectory encompasses video games and experimental forms that feature complex narrative design. This last trajectory traces examples that benefitted most from recent advances in technology—better visual representation, more advanced AI and increased storage capacity.

1. TEXT-BASED EXAMPLES: FROM *ELIZA* TO INTERACTIVE FICTION AND HYPERFICTION

The beginnings of IDN can be traced back to the computer program *Eliza*, created as an experiment in artificial intelligence (AI) in 1966 by Joseph Weizenbaum. *Eliza* took the form of a program that emulates a Rogerian therapist; it responds to a user's textual input by adopting simple but effective techniques of parsing and pattern matching. For example, *Eliza* could reply to sentences like "I'm depressed much of the time" with "I am sorry to hear you are depressed" (Weizenbaum, 1966). *Eliza's* ability to sometimes sustain surprisingly compelling dialogues marks a significant milestone for the use of computers as an expressive narrative medium. *Eliza's* considerable impact at the time (Murray, 1997, pp. 69–70) was also due to the still largely unchallenged belief in the abilities of AI in 1966, and therefore users interacting with *Eliza* were more disposed to accept the premise of a computer program as an intelligent therapist. With this work, Weizenbaum became the first successful author of an IDN experience by finding the right balance between procedurality (the rules behind *Eliza's* responses), agency (allowing natural language input) and scenario/role (therapy session and patient) that played into the belief system of his contemporaries (AI as capable of intelligent conversations).

Adventure (Crowther, 1976) is the next seminal piece in the IDN tradition that marks the beginning of the Interactive Fiction (IF) genre. *Adventure* allowed players to explore a fictional world set in a large cave that is rendered to the players in the form of textual descriptions and subject to interaction through the entry of textual commands such as "go north," "pick up sword" or "fight troll with sword." The basic mechanics of *Adventure* consisted of problem solving, combining objects, dialogues and spatial exploration. *Adventure's* considerable success would reach into the commercial realm, as the American company Infocom famously expanded this framework in the following years. Their first product, *Zork I* (Blank and Lebling, 1980), broke new technical ground as programmers applied techniques like object orientation, demons and states to create a dynamic fictional universe (Murray, 1997, p. 78). IF successfully integrated complex narrative with puzzles and riddles that not only control the revelation of the narrative (Montfort, 2003a, p. 3) but also generates narrative through the players' typing of words.

Michael Joyce's *Afternoon, A Story*—first shown in 1987 and subsequently published in 1991—constitutes one of the earliest pieces of Hypertext Fiction (HF, sometimes also abbreviated as Hyperfiction), another text-based IDN subgenre that was particularly active until the mid-1990s. Michael Joyce and Jay Bolter, cocreators (with John B. Smith) of the HF authoring tool *Storyspace*, clearly position HF as a new form of highbrow literature in contrast to IF:

> Interactive fiction has already existed for some time in the form of computerized adventure games. ... Admittedly the text of the current games is simple-minded, but the method of presentation is not. ... This method of presentation can now be applied to serious fiction.
>
> (Bolter and Joyce, 1987)

Whilst the other examples discussed so far originated within research labs in computer science, HF works from the very beginning were created by authors like Michael Joyce and Douglas Cooper who had already published traditional books before picking up HF. These creators aimed at overcoming the limitations of the printed book by embracing digital media and turning readers into participants, which Murray terms *interactors* (Murray, 1997). The interactor of HF as envisioned by Bolter and Joyce is no longer the passive consumer of a finished work but instead is given an active role in constructing meaning.

HF relies on the principles of segmentation and linking, as authors produce screen-sized segments, or *lexias*, and connect them with different types of hyperlinks. Interactors traverse the story by selecting links, unveiling new lexias, or returning to the ones already visited. Such repeated visits—called *multivalence* by hypertext theorist Mark Bernstein (2000)—constitute a design strategy specific to HF, where the meaning of particular lexias change upon revisitation, as the interactor gains additional insights. The success of this strategy depends on the complexity and depth of the particular narrative. In Michael Joyce's *Afternoon, A Story* (1991), multivalence is particularly successful, as the interactor slowly gains a better understanding of the unreliable narrator's narrative by traversing more than 500 lexias connected by over 900 links regarding the life-changing event of witnessing a car accident, the protagonist's failure to provide help and his consequent psychosis.

Another design strategy in HF is in the equivalence between content and structure: for example, a fragmented narrative like *Afternoon* is presented in fragmented pieces and the associative connections as links. In Shelly Jackson's *Patchwork Girl* (1995), the protagonist herself is literally patched together from body parts of deceased women. This narrative strategy sets the stage for a fragmented narrative, exploring the main character as well as the lives of the donors.

After years of relative obscurity, Interactive Fiction recently seems poised for a return to the spotlight in the form of Versu (2013), a project that originated with Linden Labs, the developer of *Second Life*. Versu merged text-based narrative with advanced artificial intelligence methods and expressive graphics. The project aims to create a platform for procedural textual narrative and hopes to attract authors by offering a specific authoring tool and a business model for distribution. The first examples—narratives set in a Jane Austen-inspired Regency era and the Roman Empire, respectively—by renowned interactive fiction writer Emily Short received positive reviews.[1]

2. FROM INTERACTIVE CINEMA TO INTERACTIVE PERFORMANCES

Interactive Cinema is an umbrella term for works and experiments combining cinematic experiences and interactivity, dating back to the 1967 experiment *Kinoautomat* created by Radúz Çinçera for the Czechoslovakian pavilion at the Montreal World Fair. The movie *One Man And His World* was stopped at several points during the presentation, and the audience was asked to make a decision. Depending on the answer, the projectionist exchanged the lens cap between two synchronised film projectors (see Naimark, 1998).

The *Kinoautomat* therefore required a human intermediary to execute the audience's choices, and direct interaction between an interactor and a cinematic experience was not possible until the late 1970s when MCA/Phillips, Pioneer and RCA introduced the laser disc system which allowed random, direct access to every point in a video via a computer interface. With this technology, the Architecture Machine Group at MIT created the *Aspen Moviemap* (1978), which enabled an interactor to virtually explore the town of Aspen in Colorado, USA by using a touch screen interface to control a running video of a drive through the town. The interactor could click on the facades of houses along the way to access additional material, such as interior shots, historical images, menus of restaurants and video interviews with inhabitants. In the following years, many other applications combining video and interactivity were explored. Of these, *A City in Transition: New Orleans 1983–86* (Davenport, 1987), a multimedia experience providing access to narrative video and other content, stands out as a particularly refined piece. Glorianna Davenport, a pioneer in the area of interactive documentaries, focused her work on a massive urban development effort on a strip of New Orleans Mississippi river embankment in connection with the 1984 world fair.

The terms *Interactive Movie* and *Interactive TV* have also become associated with experiments in interactive films for the cinema and television, respectively. In 1991, Oliver Hirschbiegel created *Mörderische Entscheidung* (Murderous Decision), a crime story broadcast on two TV channels simultaneously, each one presenting the same story from the perspective of a different character and allowing the audience to interact by zapping between the channels with an ordinary remote control. Hirschbiegel experimented with several narrative strategies to adapt his story for interactivity—for example, cueing interactors to switch channels by reducing the amount of information given (Weiberg, 2002), but also making sure that information essential for understanding the story was given on both channels. An empirical study about the experiment (Kirchmann, 1994) suggested that the narrative "worked best when both versions showed the same information from different points of view" (Weiberg, 2002), for example when both main characters were present in the same space and their views were represented similarly. Conversely, the moments in which the representation diverged (for instance, when one of the two characters was depicted as intoxicated) proved more problematic for the audience.

In the following years, the same concept was reelaborated in the Danish experiment *D-Dag* (Kragh-Jacobsen, Levring, Vinterberg and von Trier, 2000), showing four different narratives on separate channels plus additional channels presenting the directors' commentary, for a total of seven options. The framing narrative for *D-Dag* was a bank robbery on New Year's Eve of the new millennium in which the noise from the celebratory fireworks was used to mask the explosion needed to break into the bank.

Interactive video installation pieces combine video segments with algorithmic rules and a level of interactive control by the audience or a live performer. Historically, the majority of artists came to this field through a gradual process, often by starting to use computers as control devices for noninteractive work before exploring the potential of user participation. For example, the artist Toni Dove started using computers to synchronise slide shows in her 1990 work *Mesmer: Secret of the Human Frame*. Her first interactive piece *Archeology of a Mother Tongue* (1993) is a virtual reality murder mystery (Dove, n.d.) that combines interactive computer graphics, laserdisc video, and slides with interactive sound (Dove, n.d.). The interactor controls the environment by using a small camera to look around a virtual reality environment and a data glove to touch virtual objects. As an untrained interactor might be overwhelmed by the technology involved, Dove often uses a trained tutor to interact with her pieces (Bonin, 2001). What Dove explores in her art pieces is the sensation of walking around in a movie, of actually being inside of a narrative space (Jennings, 1995) and also the powerful experience of a physical action [that] produces a response in video and audio (Jennings, 1995).

A particularly interesting piece is *Wheel of Life* (1993), jointly directed by Glorianna Davenport and Larry Friedlander. The large-scale installation was created around the idea of representational spaces for the different elements of water, earth, fire and space as symbols for both the circle of life and the evolution of life on Earth and beyond. Each space contained video screens and projectors, a sound system, light installations and interactive objects. What sets *Wheel of Life* apart from other examples is its three-way interaction: the piece augments the usual interaction between a computer program and a human interactor by including a second interactor. Individual spaces were designed for interaction between a *guide* controlling the space on a computer display from the outside and an *explorer* experiencing the space from within:

> Together they had to discover how to navigate through a world that responded mysteriously to their actions; the explorer's task was to decipher the rules and narratives governing each area, while the guide sought to help the explorer by using the computer to manipulate the images, lights and sounds in the area.
>
> (Davenport and Friedlander 1995)

Toni Dove's latest work, *Lucid Possessions* (2013), is a contemporary ghost story centred on a programmer whose advanced skills make her a target for being possessed by ghosts. Beyond this narrative frame, the piece explores the state of identity in a dichotomous relationship between the virtual and the real on the backdrop of our ever-increasing presence in the virtual world of social networks. In technical terms, the work combines actors and musicians, robots, custom computer hardware and real-time motion-tracking technology in an on-stage performance. The artist becomes an interactor in the dynamic presentation by means of a gesture-based interface, controlling the presentation of video clips. *Lucid Possessions* is a compelling example of the expressive potential of IDN in the hands of an artist.

3. VIDEO GAME NARRATIVES AND
EXPERIMENTAL FORMS

We conclude this overview of the historical evolution of IDN by noting several important examples of narrative video games and experimental forms. Following in the footsteps of the early text-based narrative games, graphic adventure games helped to diffuse and popularise IDN, pioneered by the *King's Quest* series, the first of which appeared in 1984.

The *Monkey Island* series of games (1990–2010) is a paradigmatic example in its combination of narrative and game elements. The game places the interactor in the role of a hapless pirate who has to overcome many difficult challenges to prove himself to the pirate establishment while winning the heart of his love interest, the governess of a pirate municipality. The series featured a rich narrative and became famous for its humour and irony. The flow of the narrative is intertwined with puzzles requiring funny, improbable solutions, such as freeing a prisoner by melting the iron bars of his cell with a very potent drink. Advancement in the narrative becomes the reward for puzzle solving, often in the form of noninteractive cut scenes that follow major accomplishments. The *Monkey Island* series is exemplary for keeping a balance between puzzle-solving and narrative development—establishing a consistent style and setting many canonical conventions still in use today.

Myst (1993) continues the adventure game tradition in terms of spatial exploration and puzzle-solving, but it also introduces a highly atmospheric visual representation seen from a first person perspective. The interactor finds her/himself on an island that contains abandoned buildings and mysterious machinery and is left to explore a highly detailed and evocative world. The game was not only an aesthetic milestone but also a convincing example of embedded narrative (Jenkins, 2004) through narrative-infused encounters. More recently, *Gone Home* (2013) applies the same underlying strategy. The game places the interactor in the role of a student returning from an exchange year abroad, only to find the family home empty and the parents and sibling gone. By exploring the house and its contents—the furniture, notes from the inhabitants, audio cassettes and other personal items, the interactor patches together the narrative of her sister's disappearance and the parent's attempt to resurrect their marriage.

Although not a commercial success, *The Last Express* (Mechner, 1997) is remarkably innovative for its integration of narrative, game and exploration. This game casts the interactor in the role of a passenger investigating a murder aboard the Orient Express from Paris to Constantinople on the eve of World War I. Space and time play a central role in this piece, as many events take place simultaneously and provide a variety of narrative paths. By moving through the train, the interactor assembles a particular narrative composed by the conversations he/she overhears and the events he/she witnesses. The game runs in 6x accelerated real time and presents the player's current location on a map. This use of temporality and location helps to enhance the player's sense of immersion and precludes exhausting the limited amount of possible narratives easily, as the interactor can only be in one location at any given time. The train's stops in stations provide a natural means to structure the narrative into chapters, which make the amount of possible combinations more manageable by folding back to a shared backstory.

The second half of the 1990s saw an important technical development in the advent of 3D representations in video games. The 3D game engines gave interactors the ability to roam free in the designed spaces, but they also removed a measure of control from the creators, which has important implications for narrative design.

The influential game *Blade Runner* (1997) uses a 3D depiction and is set in the same world of the movie of the same name by Ridley Scott. The interactor is cast in the role of a police officer whose job it is to find and kill replicants, illegal synthetic humans that are so much like their natural counterparts that they are almost impossible to distinguish. The game confronts the interactor with strong moral choices that affect the outcome of the narrative. For example, the protagonist can decide to go over to the outlaw side and fight alongside with the replicants; try to restore his reputation by hunting down synthetic humans; or simply leave the city and the fighting behind. These decisions eventually lead to thirteen different endings, variations of the three main outcomes based on the interactor's earlier choices. *Blade Runner* eclipses many other narrative games in the variety of narrative paths that lead to alternative endings, in contrast to the singular successful completion of *Monkey Island*. A key narrative element that enables enhanced variety and deep engagement with the character is the ability to switch sides, as the police officer may turn into an outlaw and gain an obviously different perspective. In this way, the game invites the interactor to explore moral ambiguities in the *Blade Runner* narrative, for example the corruption of police officers and the ethics behind killing replicants.

Fahrenheit (2005), also known as *Indigo Prophecy* in North America, contains the narrative of ritualistic murders in New York City in an imagined year 2009 and combines a 3D real-time rendered gameworld with cinematic elements in the form of screen montage and transitions. In addition to a well-formed multilinear narrative, *Fahrenheit* is especially relevant for the unusually high degree of narrative control given to the interactor over three different characters in a single game session. This interesting mechanic results in novel narrative experiences, for example when two user-controlled characters work against the third who is also managed by the interactor.

The critically acclaimed *The Walking Dead* (2012) is an adventure game in the setting of the TV series of the same name, which depicts a post-apocalyptic world after a zombie outbreak has befallen the United States. The narrative design requires the interactor to make difficult, morally ambiguous choices, such as which of the other characters to save. These decisions are coupled with a feedback system that succeeds in making the choices meaningful and memorable for the interactor. In tandem with a rich narrative world, the game creates a compelling IDN experience, which is indicative of the development in the adventure game genre. The focus on narrative feedback is a productive direction for future work.

The Last of Us (2013) pairs the player in the role of a middle-aged man with a 14-year-old girl on a journey through a dark, postapocalyptic world that is full of deadly enemies. The narrative design is carefully crafted so that the interactor builds a connection with the teenage sidekick through many dialogues and a slow change in behaviour, signalling growing trust. This emotional connection helps give the narrative depth and creates an immersive experience to the point that some players felt that the fighting scenes represented a distraction. *The Last of Us* is an outstanding example of a satisfying narrative experience that not only enhances the shooter genre but also works as a stand-alone design.

Finally, we discuss IDN experiments in the form of interactive drama and hybrid forms. This combination of drama and interactivity has been introduced to the digital realm in the late 1980s by the OZ project at Carnegie Mellon University. Influenced by Brenda Laurel's neo-Aristotelian approach to interactive narratives (Laurel, 1986, 1991), research in the OZ group focused on related Artificial Intelligence (AI) techniques and their concrete implementation. Interactive drama was conceptualised as a combination of presentation, virtual characters and a drama manager component to preserve coherence and advance the narrative. Based on this conceptual framework, the OZ group produced two implementations: *Lyotard* (Bates, 1992), a text-based experiment that simulated a house cat, and *Edge of Intention* (Loyall and Bates, 1993), a graphical experiment that contained an animated avatar (called *Woggle*) plus other autonomous agents in different roles. Michael Mateas later continued the research on interactive drama with his collaborator Andrew Stern by working on *Façade* (Mateas and Stern, 2003, 2005a, 2005b). This interactive experience cast the interactor in the uncomfortable position of witnessing a couple on the verge of a break-up, in a "dramatically interesting, real-time 3D virtual world inhabited by computer-controlled characters." (Mateas and Stern 2003) The narrative development in the work is dynamic and leads to various consequences. Stuck between two arguing partners, the interactor of *Façade* faces an implicit choice between helping them to face their issues and stay together or siding with either of the characters and potentially leading to a break-up. *Façade* adopts several strategies to engage the interactor in the unfolding narrative: a finite space (the couple's small apartment), the uncomfortable but familiar situation of a fighting couple, the continuous real-time flow of events and the audible answers of the virtual characters work together to create immersion. *Façade* exemplifies the kaleidoscopic nature of interactive narratives (Murray, 1997), as the system can produce a wide variety of different narrative paths leading to more or less satisfying finales; in the best version, interactors may experience a powerful sense of agency by saving the couple's marriage. Unfortunately, this ending is hard to reach for a variety of reasons, some due to technical limitations but also because of particular design decisions, especially the advancement in real-time, which affords the interactor very little time to make decisions. Nevertheless, *Façade* remains the most complete interactive drama in the tradition of the OZ project—Mateas and Stern's piece has received considerable acclaim and was praised as a critical breakthrough. Mateas has, since then, continued his work in *Prom Week* (2012), an IDN piece that recreates the social situations in a high school class in the week leading up to the prom.

As interactive media matures, some authors have consciously begun to cross over conventions, applying foreign design strategies to produce ambiguous artefacts. Adam Cadre's IF *Photopia* (1998) is a work that presents interleaving narrative strands of the events leading up to a car accident, the exploration of an alien planet and a surreal world in which the interactor can fly. However, this IF presents spatial and textual exploration and emerges as a segmented narrative with hyperlinks substituting standard IF commands and creates an interesting hybrid between IF and HF. Natalie Bookchin's *The Intruder* (1999) turns a short story by Jorge Luis Borges into an interactive experience by requiring the interactor to play several rudimentary video games in the style of classic titles like *Pong* or *Space Invaders*. Both Cadre's and Bookchin's pieces offer a glimpse of possible future design directions that transgress traditional boundaries within Interactive Digital Narrative and are a testament to the vitality of this field for future experiments. A case in point is *Device 6* (2013), a work that continues in the same vein of genre crossover by mixing textual presentation reminiscent of HF with animated audio-visual elements. In this interactive thriller, the screen text is arranged spatially and serves as both narrative manifestation and map. *Save the Date* (2013) pushes the boundaries of narrative on a different level. The premise of the game initially seems straightforward, as the interactor is given a range of options on how to arrange a dinner date; however, the task quickly becomes problematic because the love interest invariably gets killed. In addition, the game changes the epistemological dimension by representing the interactor's memory in successive sessions. Yet, even with the added knowledge of previous failed attempts, a satisfying narrative ending remains elusive and the interactor ultimately faces a choice between two unsatisfying alternatives—either to give up on the date or to end the game before disaster strikes. In that sense, *Save the Date* presents a considerable challenge to our established sense of narrative.

Interactive Digital Narrative, in its manifold forms, has come a long way since *Eliza* and *Adventure*. Works like *The Walking Dead, Gone Home*, but also *Ludic Processions* and *Device 6,* are testimony of an established field. And yet, there are no signs of stagnation on this creative frontier for narrative expressions. Great things are yet to come.

NOTE

1. See for example http://www.whatmobile.net/2013/03/07/app-review-versu-the-choose-your-own-adventure-app/,http://www.148apps.com/reviews/versu-review/ and http://storycade.com/mobile-blood-laurels/

REFERENCES

Adams, E. (2014) *Fundamentals of Adventure Game Design*. San Francisco: Peachpit Press.

Bates, J. (1992) *The Nature of Characters in Interactive Worlds and the Oz Project*. Technical Report CMU-CS-92-200, Department of Computer Science. Pittsburgh, PA: Carnegie Mellon University.

Bates, J., Loyall, A. B. and Reilly, W. S. (1992) Integrating reactivity, goals, and emotion in a broad agent. In *Proceedings of the Fourteenth Annual Conference of the Cognitive Science Society*. New York: Lawrence Erlbaum.

Baudrillard, J. (1983) *Simulations*. New York: Semiotext(e).

Bernstein, M. (1992) Contours of constructive hypertexts. In *Proceedings of the 1992 Hypertext Conference*. New York: ACM.

Blank, M. and Lebling, D. (1980) *Zork I*. [Interactive fiction] Cambridge, MA: Infocom.

Bolter, J. D. and Joyce, M. (1987) Hypertext and creative writing. In *Proceedings of the 1987 Hypertext Conference*. New York: ACM.

Bonin, V. (2001) *Toni Dove*. [Online] Available at: http://www.fondation-langlois. org/html/e/page.php?NumPage=226

Bookchin, N. (1999) *The Intruder*. [Interactive narrative] Available at: http://bookchin. net/projects/intruder.html

Cyan, (1993) *Myst*. [video game] Brøderbund.

Coover, R, (1992) The end of books. *New York Times Book Review*. June 21. 1. pp. 23–25.

Crowther, W. (1976) *Adventure*. [Interactive fiction].

Davenport, G. and Friedlander, L. (1995) Interactive transformational environments: wheel of life. In: Barrett, E. and Redmond, M. (eds.) *Contextual Media: Multimedia and Interpretation*. Cambridge, MA: MIT Press.

Davenport, G. (1987) New Orleans in transition, 1983–1986: The interactive delivery of a cinematic case study. In *Proceedings of the International Congress for Design Planning and Theory, Education Group* Conference. Boston, MA.

Dove, T. (1990) *Mesmer: Secret of the Human Frame*. [interactive installation].

Dove, T. (1993) *Archaeology of a Mother Tongue*. [Interactive installation].

Dove, T. (2013) *Lucid Posessions*. [Interactive installation].

Dove, T. (n. d.). [Project description of "Archeology of a mother tongue"]. Retrieved March 12, 2009 from http://www.tonidove.com/

Evans, R. and Short, E. (2013) *Versu*. [Interactive Narrative Platform].

Fauth, J. (1995) Poles in your face: The promises and pitfalls of hyperfiction. *Mississippi Review*. 6.

Fullbright Company (2013) *Gone Home*. [Video game] Fullbright Company.

Jackson, S. (1995) *Patchwork Girl*. [Interactive fiction] Watertown: Eastgate Systems.

Jenkins, H. (2004) Game design as narrative architecture. In: Harrigan, P., Wardrip-Fruin, N. (eds.) *First Person: New Media as Story, Performance, and Game*. Cambridge, MA: MIT Press.

Jennings, P. (1995) Interpretation on the electronic landscape: a conversation with Toni Dove. *Felix: a Journal of Media Arts and Communication*. 2(10).

Joyce, M. (1991) *Afternoon, a Story*. [Interactive fiction] Watertown: Eastgate Systems.

Kirchmann, Kay (1994) Umschalten erwünscht? Wenn ja, von wem? Ergebnisse einer Studie zu Ästhetik und Rezeption des ersten interaktiven. *TV-Spiels des Deutschen Fernsehens Arbeitshefte Bildschirmmedien*. 48. pp. 23–60.

Kragh-Jacobsen, S., Levring, K., Vinterberg, T., von Trier, L. and Ehrhardt, B. (2000). *D-Dag*. [Interactive movie].

Laurel, B. (1986) *Toward the Design of a Computer-Based Interactive Fantasy System*. Doctoral Thesis. Drama Department, Ohio State University.

Laurel, B. (1991) *Computers as Theatre*. New York: Addison Wesley.

Loyall, A. B., and Bates, J. (1993) Real-time control of animated broad agents. In *Proceedings of the Fifteenth Annual Conference of the Cognitive Science Society*. Boulder CO: Lawrence Erlbaum.

Mateas, M., and Stern, A. (2003) Integrating plot, character and natural language processing in the interactive drama Façade. In *Proceedings of the 1st International Conference on Technologies for Interactive Digital Storytelling and Entertainment (TIDSE-03)*.

Mateas, M. and Stern, A. (2005a) Structuring content in the façade interactive drama architecture. In: Young, R. M. and Laird, J. (eds.) *Proceedings of the First Artificial Intelligence and Interactive Digital Entertainment Conference (AIIDE 2005)*. Menlo Park, CA: AAAI Press.

Mateas, M. and Stern, A. (2005b) *Façade*. [Software] Available at: http://www.interactivestory.net/

Mateas, M. (1997) *An Oz-Centric Review of Interactive Drama and Believable Agents*. Technical Report CMU-CS-97-156, Department of Computer Science. Pittsburgh, PA: Carnegie Mellon University.

Mechner, J. (1997) *The Last Express*. [Video game] Brøderbund.

Montfort, N. (2003a) *Twisty Little Passages: An Approach to Interactive Fiction*. Cambridge, MA: MIT Press.

Montfort, N. (2003b) *Toward a Theory of Interactive Fiction*. Available at: http://nickm.com/if/toward.html

Moulthrop, S. (1992) *Victory Garden*. [Interactive fiction] Watertown: Eastgate Systems.

Murray, J. (1997) *Hamlet on the Holodeck: The Future of Narrative in Cyberspace*. New York: The Free Press.

Naimark, M. (1998) Interactive art—Maybe it's a bad idea. In: Leopoldseder, H., and Schšpf, C. (eds.) *Cyber Arts 1998 International Compendium Prix. Ars Electronica*. Berlin, Heidelberg: Springer.

Naughty Dog (2013) *The Last of Us*. [Video game] Sony Computer Entertainment.

Paper Dino Software (2013) *Save the Date*. [Video game] Paper Dino Software.

Quantic Dream (2005) *Farenheit*. [Video Game] Atari.

Rand, A. (1971) *Night of January 16th*. New York: New American Library.

Simogo (2013) *Device 6*. [Video game] Simogo.

Telltale Games (2012) *The Walking Dead*. [Video game] Telltale Games.

Weiberg, B. (2002) *Beyond Interactive Cinema*. Available at: http://keyframe.org/txt/interact/

Weizenbaum, J. (1966) ELIZA—A computer program for the study of natural language communication between man and machine. *Communications of the ACM*. 9(1). pp. 36–45.

Westwood Studios (1997) *Blade Runner*. [Video game] London: Virgin Interactive.

2 The American Hypertext Novel, and Whatever Became of It?

Scott Rettberg

The 1990 Eastgate publication of Michael Joyce's *Afternoon, A Story* earned hypertext fiction a place within institutionalised literary culture. Robert Coover's 1992 essay "The End of Books" announced hypertext fiction as a challenge to traditional conceptions such as narrative linearity, the sense of closure, and the desire for coherence. While some theorists, such as George Landow, praised hypertext for instantiating poststructuralist theory, others, such as Sven Birkerts in *The Gutenberg Elegies* (1994), regarded it with strong concern. The publication of more hypertext fictions such as Stuart Moulthrop's *Victory Garden* (1991) and Shelley Jackson's *Patchwork Girl* (1995) resulted in a small, dedicated interest community. However, no paradigm-shifting rise in interest took place. The independent publication of hypertext novels on the World Wide Web such as Robert Arellano's *Sunshine '69* (1996), Mark Amerika's *Grammatron* (1997), and William Gillespie, Frank Marquardt, Scott Rettberg and Dirk Stratton's *The Unknown* (1998) briefly revitalised the networked fictional form before it was eclipsed in the first decade of the 21st century by a range of other digital narrative forms.

1. HYPERTEXT FICTION BEFORE THE WEB

During the 1990s, as the personal computer became a fixture of everyday life in offices and homes, writers and academics became interested in exploring the potential of hypertext as a genre for narrative fiction. During the early 1990s in particular, the form seemed to offer great promise as a logical literary follow-on both to late 20th-century poststructuralist theory and to general shifts in late 20th-century fiction writing, especially in the United States, towards postmodern narrative structures that contested prior conventions of linearity, closure and immersive reading.

For what was in retrospect a quite brief period during the late 1980s and early 1990s, what Robert Coover (1999) referred to as the Golden Age of literary hypertext, writers working in dedicated hypertext systems such as Hypercard, the Intermedia system at Brown University and, most importantly, *Storyspace*, explored the potential of hypertext for narrative fiction.

Enough writers were working in the form during this period, and their works garnered enough critical attention that we can speak of these hypertext fictions as a group—what some of have called 'The Eastgate School'—named after the publisher responsible for publishing and distributing most of the early works of hypertext fiction.

Hypertext was first conceptualised by Theodore Holm Nelson (1965) in his paper "A File Structure for the Complex, the Changing, and the Indeterminate" when he introduced the term "to mean a body of written or pictorial material interconnected in such a complex way that it could not conveniently be presented or represented on paper." In his "No More Teachers' Dirty Looks" (1970), Nelson followed up with a more expansive definition of hyper-media as "branching or performing presentations which respond to user actions, systems of prearranged words and pictures (for example) which may be explored freely or queried in stylized ways." Among the types of hypertexts he discusses in that essay, which focused on the potential uses of hypermedia in new systems that could potentially revolutionise education, are discrete hypertexts which "consist of separate pieces of text connected by links." The majority of hypertext fictions published during the 1980s and 1990s would fit within this rubric though, as Noah Wardrip-Fruin (2004) argued, this conception of hypertext as *chunk-style* linked nodes is somewhat narrower than hypermedia as Nelson originally envisioned it. The postmillennial turn in electronic literature towards a broader use of media-rich texts, more complex uses of generativity and other computational processes, and deeper engagement with network-specific communication technologies and styles of writing better represents the broader range of hypertext and hypermedia as conceptualised by Nelson than either the first-generation hypertext fictions published by Eastgate or the second-generation works published on the Web.

During the 1980s, digital writing experiments, including long-form hypertext fictions such as Judy Malloy's pioneering hyperfictional narrative database *Uncle Roger* (1986),[1] were distributed on bulletin boards such as the WELL.[2] Interactive fiction developed separately from hypertext fiction, emerging from a different cultural context. The text-parser-based form of interactive digital writing that began with *Colossal Cave Adventure* by Will Crowther and Don Woods (1976) saw commercial success during the 1980s with Infocom titles such as the *Zork* series before graphic computer games swallowed the market in the late 1980s. As Nick Montfort documents in his *Twisty Little Passages* (2003), an amateur community developed around the form shortly thereafter, enabled by group effort and the release of free programming languages, authoring and reading environments such as TADS (in 1987) and Inform (in 1993). Though there were substantial literary and aesthetic achievements in interactive fiction, outside of a few outliers,[3] it was not until the publisher and software developer Eastgate Systems began publishing hypertext fiction in 1987 that literary critics began to significantly engage with electronic literature.

The novelist Robert Coover played an important role in bringing these experimental fictions to the notice of a broader public, most notably in his 1992 *New York Times Book Review* essay "The End of Books," which introduced hypertext fiction to a broader literary audience. The essay describes the ways that the hypertext form poses challenges for writers, and readers accustomed to conventional narrative forms, including assumptions about linearity, closure and the division of agency between the writer and reader. Coover focused on the disruptions that hypertext caused to narrative linearity, its interruption of "the tyranny of the line" (1992). Coover noted that in hypertext, the narrative structures of fictions are foregrounded and become a predominant concern: "The most radical new element that comes to the fore in hypertext is the system of multidirectional and often labyrinthine linkages we are invited or obliged to create."

Coover identified a core tension for fiction writers working in hypertextual forms in the "conflict between the reader's desire for coherence and closure and the text's desire for continuance, its fear of death." He asked: "If the author is free to take a story anywhere at any time and in as many directions as she or he wishes, does that not become the obligation to do so?" Coover's essay on hypertext remains a key summation of the affordances and opportunity costs of hypertext for fiction writers. Forms such as the short story and particularly the novel have a deep, if not intrinsic, relationship to the limits and constraints of print. Whatever belief one has of the function of fiction, most stories or novels strive to reduce, distil and make comprehensible an experience or perception of the world. The role of the fiction writer is both to provide a particular perspective on human experience and to select and enliven some narrative possibilities while eliminating others. The form of the book—such that each page requires more paper and each word more ink—pulls the writer towards economy, restraint, and limitation while the form of hypertext, offering multiple pathways, limitless text and multiple medial modalities, pulls authors towards exploration and expansiveness.

The potential uses of hypertext links in a narrative fiction are multifarious, ranging from offering the reader conscious plot choices in a choose-your-own-adventure style, to establishing multiple lines of narrative or multiple character perspectives on the same set of events, to serving as any kind of footnote-style reference, to poetic or linguistic play between words or scenes in a narrative.

In Michael Joyce's *Afternoon, A Story* (1989) we saw the hypertext link used in all of these various ways in the story of a man in a state of breakdown after a car accident in which his son may or may not have been killed. The fragmented and disrupted nature of the narrator's psychological and emotional state finds an objective correlative in the hypertextual form of the narrative. The narrative of *Afternoon* centres on the various overlapping relations and conflicts between the main narrator Peter, his ex-wife Lisa, her lover Wert (Werther), Lolly and Nausicaa.

There is no need to provide a close reading of *Afternoon* here—as it is the most cited work of electronic literature,[4] and ample discussions of the work are available elsewhere. However, we can highlight a few formal aspects of the work. The first is that the work is playing a great deal with indeterminacy and a sense of loss and confusion. The reader can follow a default path, but there are also typically several links on a given node of the story. Joyce, however, chose not to make those links visible to the reader. Instead, he encouraged readers to seek out 'words that yield'—that is, to click on given words that seem to be particularly evocative, and to see if the system will respond. This indeterminacy extended to the narrative voice. Though the main perspective is that of Peter, selecting some nodes will pull the narrative into the perspective of one of the other characters. These switches are not always clearly marked in a way that would make the perspective immediately clear to the reader. Another notable aspect of the work is its very clear use of modernist techniques and tropes. The work is thick with intertextual references: to the *Odyssey*, to James Joyce's *Ulysses*, to Goethe's *Werther*, to the Grimm brothers, to Tolstoy and to Pynchon. Formally, the text is also diverse. Following links takes the reader from interior monologues and musings to dialogues to poems and lists. The fact that the text as a whole echoes the breakdown state of the main character is yet another modernist gesture. We encounter Peter's interior state through the form of the work in a similar way to encountering the stream-of-consciousness narration in, for example, Virginia Woolf's *To the Lighthouse*.

Michael Joyce's *Afternoon* is, in short, a 'writerly' work of modernist fiction developed in *Storyspace* software. While the material form of the work is digital, its DNA is clearly a strand of the experimental writing traditions of the 20th century. We can see very clear relationships between the work and antecedent print works. While it is not accidental that the work is presented in hypertext form, Joyce's gravitation towards experimenting with hypertext was driven by the fact that the fragmented, nodal style of *Storyspace* software, the tentative, indeterminate, searching way that the reader encountered the interface, and the various models of interconnectivity available in *Storyspace* were particularly well-suited to the form of the story he wanted to tell.[5]

Joyce's *Afternoon* is an exclusively text-based hypertext—it included no images or other multimedia assets. Compared to many contemporary works, it also had very limited use of computation, including links, some limited 'yes/no' text parsing, and guard fields that limited access to some nodes until other nodes had been visited. Writing on the first hypertext experimentalists in his *Literary Hypertext: The Passing of the Golden Age*, Coover (1999) notes that:

> [E]arly experimental writers of the time worked almost exclusively in text, as did the students in our pioneer hypertext workshops at Brown University, partly by choice (they were print writers moving tentatively

into this radically new domain and carrying into it what they knew best), but largely because the very limited capacities of computers and diskettes in those days dictated it.

Coover noted that these constraints were also empowering. The writers working with hypertext in the 1980s and 1990s were not primarily focused on manipulating images or animations or complex programming tasks, but were instead mostly working with words, lines, texts and scenes, just as any other writer of the time would have been. They were working within a computational environment that offered new ways of remedying narrative techniques largely derived from the canon of modernist and postmodernist fiction that preceded them. Though the majority of the hypertext systems available at the time did allow for some use of visual media and other media assets, text was clearly the dominant mode of expression.

The majority of the hypertext fictions published by Eastgate during the late 1980s and early 1990s similarly emerged from a clearly literary heritage. The two other most-frequently cited works of this period, *Patchwork Girl* by Shelley Jackson (1995) and *Victory Garden* by Stuart Moulthrop (1991), were each novel-length works of deeply intertextual postmodern fiction.

Patchwork Girl, Jackson's inventive retelling of the *Frankenstein* story from the perspective of the female monster, wore its postmodernism on its sleeve. In the tradition of American literary postmodernism, *Patchwork Girl* is a self-conscious text, by turns intertextual, polyvocal and expressly concerned with poststructuralist questions of identity. Five sections of the hypertext novel—the journal, story, graveyard, crazy quilt, and the body of the text—each used different material structures and stylistic conventions. A more visual thinker than Joyce, Jackson both used some limited imagery— woodcut images of a female body and a man's skull—and took advantage of the visual layout features of *Storyspace* software to produce visual user interfaces. The reader of *Patchwork Girl* participated in navigating the work in acts of pastiche. Assembly of different types of texts occurs throughout the work. In the 'crazy quilt' section of the text, for example, Jackson stitches together quotations from Jacques Derrida's *Disseminations*, Donna Haraway's "A Cyborg Manifesto," Mary Shelley's *Frankenstein*, L. Frank Baum's *The Patchwork Girl of Oz*, Barbara Maria Stafford's *Body Criticism* and the *Storyspace User's Manual*. The first draft of *Patchwork Girl* was originally produced for one of theorist George Landow's courses at Brown University, and throughout the novel, we can see how Jackson was testing the waters, using both fiction and a new writing technology she was encountering for the first time to represent and deconstruct theories of identity.

Both *Afternoon* and *Patchwork Girl* were extensive hypertexts, including a good deal of writing—according to Raine Koskimaa, 539 lexia (text spaces) were in *Afternoon* and 323 were in *Patchwork Girl*. Though *Afternoon* includes *A Story* in its somewhat humble title, both are clearly of such length and narrative development that they are properly considered novels. Stuart Moulthrop's 1991 *Victory Garden* included 933 lexia. The most Borgesian of the hypertexts published by Eastgate Systems, *Victory Garden* extensively experimented with the multilinear possibility space of hypertext fiction. Taking its cue from Borges' story "Garden of Forking Paths," *Victory Garden* uses hypertext to explore narrative structures: multiple potential outcomes of given storylines, changes in perspective on given events, chronological jumps and flashbacks, and different forms of reading cycles (for instance, narrative loops that vary on recursion). Set during the first Gulf War and centred on a group of characters living in a university town, the novel in a broad sense is about the reception of war filtered through contemporary academic, popular and media culture. In one lexia of the work, "All of the Above," Moulthrop summarised Borges' story: "In all fictional works, each time a man is confronted with several alternatives, he chooses one and eliminates the others; in the fiction of Ts'ui Pen, he chooses—simultaneously—all of them." *Victory Garden* is perhaps the single experiment in the hypertext canon that attempted to do just that. As Koskimaa notes, "*Victory Garden* is clearly pointing towards the kind of hypertext fiction which, because of its size, is theoretically and practically, inexhaustible." Just as an event such as a blitzkrieg war unfolding both in the lived experiences of soldiers and civilians abroad and on multitudes of cable television screens and other networked media outlets is in some sense fundamentally unknowable as a totality, Moulthrop was providing us with a textual analogue in his fiction. As in the other two examples, Moulthrop's novel included a great variety of different types of textual materials and was intertextual in relation to several works of print literature—Borges's fiction and Thomas Pynchon's novels serve as touchstones and make cameo appearances. Moulthrop also integrated images and maps as navigational apparatuses to aid movement through the text.

In discussing the early hypertext fictions, I have cited the three most referenced works, all of which were produced in the *Storyspace* platform. It is important to emphasise that during this time Eastgate also published works in other platforms, such as John McDaid's *Uncle Buddy's Phantom Funhouse* (1992), authored in Hypercard, and later M.D. Coverley's *Califia* (2002), produced in Toolbook. The degree to which platform is important in determining categories or genres of electronic literature is open for debate. It is clear that particular constraints and affordances of operating systems have aesthetic effects. While the stories and styles of *Afternoon*, *Patchwork Girl* and *Victory Garden* were radically different in content and in many qualities of style, the writing and reading platform of *Storyspace* set common material limits and possibility spaces for the authors using it and the readers encountering the works in the platform.

The other important aspect to consider is that, as a publisher, Eastgate was participating in an evolving literary culture that was trying to establish itself. Eastgate advertised itself as the publisher of serious hypertext fiction—perhaps in an attempt to differentiate itself from 'text adventure' publishing enterprises or the emerging market of games. The social and critical apparatus is important. Publishing both software and literary works, Eastgate was partially modelled after the type of serious small press publishers that popularised modernist literature during the 20th century, and partly modelled on contemporary software companies. Theorists such as George Landow, Terry Harpold, Jane Yellowlees Douglas and others were foregrounding the connections between hypertext narratives and postmodern theory, just as later theorists such as N. Katherine Hayles emphasised the materiality of these text-machines in their media-specific context and their relation to the idea of the posthuman.

For a brief period, there was a concerted if in retrospect somewhat desperate attempt to carve a niche for hypertext fiction within the boundaries established by the print literary context and traditions—and for a while this made sense. At the time, most software was sold and distributed as distinct packaged objects, which could be sold by mail order or in stores. Thus, it was sensible for a publisher of literary works for the computer to think along the lines of a traditional publishing model, in which programs could be treated like individual books, and the author/publisher relationship situated in a similar fashion to that of print literature. There were some real benefits to this sort of apparatus. The early hypertext movement had a sort of spiritual home at Brown University and its digital writing workshops, a house publisher in Eastgate, and a school of critics gathering around its creations. Though their works were diverse in terms of content, the participating authors had similar literary heritage and stylistic concerns and were similarly steeped in modernist and postmodernist 20th-century American print literature. The digital writing workshops at Brown emerged from a long tradition of embracing literary experimentation, and Robert Coover himself is of course one of the pivotal figures in postmodern fiction and an avid experimenter with narrative form who had long played with expansions and perversions of the storytelling apparatus.

By the mid to late 1990s, new models of publishing, communicating and interacting in network culture were already beginning to evolve, and this small press model of selling and distributing hypertext fiction would become obsolete before it was ever widely adopted. The World Wide Web came along and brought with it significant changes. The market benefits of selling computer programs on floppy discs or CD-ROMs were soon trumped by the practical benefits of distributing work instantaneously to the global network.

Sadly, though most of the Eastgate hypertext fictions are still "in print," in the sense that they can be bought on physical CD-ROM, few of them can be read on contemporary operating systems. The technical challenges of updating individual works to make them operable with new versions of the Mac OS, for example, have proven to be too much for Eastgate to handle. In other cases, such as that of *Uncle Buddy's Phantom Funhouse*, the whole platform (Apple's Hypercard) is no longer supported. After teaching the

Eastgate hypertexts for more than a decade, I can no longer use them in the curriculum of my electronic literature classes, except as a past reference. They no longer work on any of the computers I own or those available in our university labs. Short of setting up a dedicated lab with old computer equipment (as Dene Grigar at Washington State University and Lori Emerson at University of Colorado Boulder have done), the classic hypertexts are now difficult to access and operate. While critics and archivists have provided valuable references that to an extent document and describe these works, it is not sufficient to read *about* works of e-lit. Students need to be able to access the primary texts themselves.

The short history of electronic literature has proven that works produced and distributed in nonproprietary, open-access and/or open source platforms, and using open standards, have tended to have a longer shelf life than works produced using proprietary software. If a software developer is purchased by another company or goes out of business, the platform itself can cease to be operable. If a publisher holds on to copyright but ceases to release updated versions of the work to operate with contemporary operating systems, then even the authors themselves cannot release their work in an operable format. One hopes that the list of hypertexts published by Eastgate Systems will soon be made available again in a more accessible and durable way, so that their important list of early hypertext fictions will not be lost to contemporary and future readers.

2. HYPERTEXT NOVELS OF THE LATE 1990s

After Tim Berners-Lee's development of the World Wide Web in 1989–91, the release of the Mosaic Web browser in 1992 and its commercial cousin Netscape in 1994, the World Wide Web was by the mid-1990s emerging as a new playground, distribution platform, and online community for hypertext authors. Though the proprietary *Storyspace* platform actually offered more hypertext authoring features than did simple HTML, the extensibility of the Web (allowing for other standards and platforms to plug in to its architecture) and its capacity as an open global distribution network had an irresistible pull for hypertext authors eager to reach an audience beyond the community that had developed around *Storyspace* and other proprietary platforms. During the late 1990s a number of substantial novel-length works of hypertext fiction were published on the Web, where they could encounter new audiences and for a time, some notoriety, if never mainstream commercial success.

Judy Malloy moved her *Uncle Roger* and other 'narrabase' writing projects to the Web in 1995. A wave of hypertext fictions written for the Web followed for the next five years; they were hypertexts written and distributed on the Web in a network-specific context. One could consider this period, however brief it was, as a second wave or renaissance of hypertext fiction.

At the time of its initial release in 1996, Robert Arrellano's *Sunshine '69* was one of the first hypertext novels written specifically for the Web, and it remains one of the best attempts to tell a coherent but multilinear and polyvocal story in the distractive environment of the network. *Sunshine '69* is a historical hypertext novel that attempts to encapsulate the zeitgeist of the 1960s by tracking events in the lives of nine characters from June through December 1969, concluding with the Altamont festival held on 6 December 1969. Arellano based his fiction loosely on historical fact. At different points in the novel, the reader can encounter a bird's-eye view of the historical events in 1969, and the work includes a bibliography of the nonfiction sources that Arellano sampled from. While the novel references historical fact, Arellano uses that context as a background for a largely metaphoric tale of corrupted visions. In the novel, Mick Jagger makes a deal with Lucifer that results in the tragedy at Altamont, and LSD is transformed from a substance for utopian mind-expansion into a sinister market commodity.

The characters of *Sunshine '69* are sketched very quickly as cartoonish types—in one section of the hypertext, a page including a cartoon drawing of a suit and a character sketch represents each individual character. The flatness of the characters helps Arellano to avoid the problem of slowly developing characters in a novel that could be read in thousands of possible orders. The drawings don't include any faces—as if to underscore that these characters should be understood not as individual human beings, but as stereotypes, fictional personalities representative of the cultural forces at play in the novel.

The cast of characters of *Sunshine '69* includes Alan Passoro, a Hell's Angel, hired for security at Altamont; Lucifer; the Glimmer Twins, Mick Jagger and Keith Richards of the Rolling Stones; Ali a.k.a. Ronald Stark, a shady agent provocateur with connections to the CIA; Meredith Hunter, a young African-American hipster from South Berkeley; Orange Sunshine, alternatively a hippie girl-next-door and a brand of LSD; Norm Cavettesa, a discharged Vietnam veteran; and Timothy Leary, one of the leading advocates of experimentation with hallucinogenic drugs.

Arellano freely mixed real people with fictional characters. Leary, Jagger and Richards, real people in the world outside the novel, are also icons who represent cultural movements. Hunter and Passoro are real people who did not become icons: Hunter was the 18-year-old murdered at Altamont, and Passoro was the Hell's Angel who stabbed him. The other characters were presumably fictional.

Real events, adapted from nonfiction texts, are juxtaposed with imagined events to create an alternative history and to underscore the idea that all histories are narrative constructs. In the context of the novel, the characters who really lived through the events, or who died as a result of them, are no more or less real than those imagined by the author to represent flower children, government spies or allegorical evil.

A particular innovation of *Sunshine '69* was the diverse range of navigational options it presented to the reader, in addition to the in-text hypertext link. In the absence of the reading conventions of the book, authors of nonlinear fiction can provide readers with other navigational tools to guide them. These tools can be as simple as the alternate reading order that Julio Cortazar provides the reader of his *Hopscotch* (1966), or they can make more elaborate use of the multimedia capabilities of the computer. Once the readers get past the animated Flash introduction to the work, each screen of the novel has four buttons linking to 'Calendar,' 'People,' '8-Track' and 'Map.' Each button links to a different navigational apparatus, so that readers can navigate by character, chronologically, according to musical selections, or by a map.

Mark Amerika's *Grammatron* (1997) was another expansive work of hypertext and hypermedia narrative. Emerging from the context of the Alt-X online publishing network and Mark Amerika's then-popular "Amerika Online" column,[6] *Grammatron* retells the *Golam* myth in digital form. The work centres on Abe Golam, a pioneering Net artist who creates the Grammatron, a writing machine. The creature becomes a kind of combinatory monster, wherein all texts recombine. Throughout the work, Golam searches for his second half—a programmer, Cynthia Kitchen, who could provide the missing link to another dimension of digital being.

Grammatron included more than 1,000 text elements (some of them scripted and some randomised), thousands of cross-links between nodes of the text, many still and animated images, a background soundtrack and spoken word audio. *Grammatron* was pushing toward a *Gesamtkunstwerk* mode of hypertext writing and was as much a philosophical exploration of network consciousness as it was a novel. It was also situated specifically as *Net Art*. Amerika made a conscious move to position himself in an art world context in this and in later work. *Grammatron* was received as one of the first significant works of Net Art and was embraced within the art world context, having been exhibited at the 2000 Whitney Biennial.

With *Grammatron*, we can see several strands that would become more marked in later years, including the move away from a specifically literary audience and an openness towards other cultural contexts, such as conceptual art and performance. *Grammatron* also marked a shift from hypertext *per se* towards hypermedia, in which text is one of many media elements. This multimodal shift became even more pronounced in subsequent years, particularly with the rise of Flash as an authoring platform in the late 1990s and early 2000s.

William Gillespie, Frank Marquardt, Scott Rettberg and Dirk Stratton's *The Unknown* was the co-winner[7] of the 1999 trAce/ AltX competition (Gillespie et al. 1999). A comic novel, it begins with the premise that the hypertext novel is itself a promotional stunt for a printed book, an anthology of experimental poetry and fiction. The hypertext is the story of the eponymous authors' book tour, which takes on the character and excesses of a rock tour.

As *The Unknown* authors tour venues across the USA and abroad ranging from small used book stores to the Hollywood Bowl, they have encounters with literary and cultural celebrities ranging from Newt Gingrich to William Gaddis, from Marjorie Perloff to John Barth, from Terry Gilliam to Lou Reed. Complications develop, as one of the protagonists becomes a cult leader before becoming a human sacrifice; another becomes a mean and withdrawn social outcast; and another becomes a heroin addict enamoured of celebrity and its excesses. As their fame reaches its apex and a Hollywood blockbuster is made of their hypertext fiction, things generally fall apart. A picaresque novel with classic elements of a road trip novel, *The Unknown* freely mixes writing styles and forms ranging from prose to poetry, credit card statements to freshman composition writing assignments, pastorals to corporate typing tests. Many scenes of *The Unknown* are parodies or tributes to other writers: Scenes are written in the style of Jack Kerouac, Edgar Allan Poe, Cormac McCarthy, Nelson Algren, Kathy Acker and many other notable American authors.

Like many of the other hypertexts discussed, *The Unknown* tended toward expansiveness and embraced excess. As the project was written and distributed, the authors kept writing and adding new material for several years after the novel was first published on the Web and announced. While the main component of *The Unknown* is a fictional narrative, a 'sickeningly decadent hypertext novel,' the work also included several other lines of content including documentary material, 'metafictional bullshit,' correspondence, art projects, documentation of live readings and a press kit (Gillespie et al. 1999).

As the project progressed and after it had won an award, the authors toured in person to a variety of venues and performed interactive readings of the work in jacket and tie, ringing a call bell every time a link appeared on the page, encouraging readers to interrupt and shout out a link to follow whenever they encountered one they found particularly toothsome. The majority of these readings were recorded in audio and/or video, and those recordings integrated into the given page of the hypertext, so that readers could listen to the authors reading the text. These travels also provided further material and settings for writing. *The Unknown* was thus both a novel and a work of performance writing and in some respects also a constraint-driven writing game. Like *Sunshine '69*, *The Unknown* made extensive use of hypertext links to cross-link scenes of the novel and provided other indices and apparatuses for navigation. The links were used in a variety of different ways. Sometimes they were used to guide the reader to the next section of a narrative sequence, sometimes to provide further referential information and other times according to a more whimsical logic: for example every time the word 'beer' appears it is a link taking the reader to another scene in which beer is mentioned. Readers can follow the links into the spiralling web of stories, or they can navigate via a "people" index of celebrities and literary figures in the novel, a list of bookstores in which reading scenes took place, and a map of the USA, each providing links to episodes based on location. The different lines also each have their own index. By including a series of web documentaries about the making of *The Unknown*, documentation of readings and performances, a press kit of links to popular media reviews of and scholarly articles about *The Unknown* as well as correspondence between the authors, *The Unknown* gestures toward a totalising encyclopaedic hypertext form. It is a novel that attempts to fully integrate its own publishing and critical apparatuses. As the authors' statement published in the *Electronic Literature Collection, Volume Two* (only half-jokingly) attests, *The Unknown* "attempts to destroy the contemporary literary culture by making institutions such as publishing houses, publicists, book reviews and literary critics completely obsolete" (Rettberg et al. 2011).

As was the case for the majority of the other hypertexts mentioned, *The Unknown* had a number of metafictional characteristics, including a number of asides on writing in the form itself, which are included in the "metafictional bullshit" nodes of the text. In the node "Hypertext is/are Electronic Space" William Gillespie, for example, mused in Deleuzian fashion:

> Hypertext, to put it clearly, is a mapping of a text onto a four-dimensional 'space.' Normal grammars, then, do not apply, and become branching structures anew. Fragments, branches, links ... The word is glowing and on a screen. It is electronic and cannot be touched. It has been copied over thousands of times and reverberates through virtual space.[8]
>
> (Gillespie et al. 1999)

Reflection on the form of hypertext seems an almost inevitable outcome of writing a hypertext novel. As writers first encountered digital environments, the works they produced were narratives or poems and expressions of ideas, but they are also always explorations and experiments. Hypertext fictions are often field notes as much as they are fiction.

3. CONCLUSION

One of the virtues of the World Wide Web is that it is an extensible platform. Authors developing work for the Web are not restricted to HTML, nor are they restricted to simple link-and-node hypertext. As the 1990s ended, many of the authors who first produced hypertext narratives in *Storyspace* or in HTML began to develop works in other platforms, such as Flash, which allowed for more extensive use of animation and other multimedia. As more and more devices, such as smart phones, locative devices, iPads and other tablets began to proliferate, there was also a shift away from works designed specifically for the desktop computer and towards types of narratives suited to these new environments. While it would not be accurate to say that the hypertext novel was completely abandoned by the first decade of the 21st century, it is the case that link-and-node hypertext would no longer be the dominant mode of literary experimentation in digital media. In my other chapter in this volume, "Posthyperfiction: Practices in Digital Textuality," I will provide examples of how hypertext has provided a basis for other emergent narrative forms within an increasingly diverse range of experimentation in narrative for digital media.

NOTES

1. Uncle Roger was first published in serial form on Art Com Electronic Network and then programmed in BASIC and distributed on the *ACEN Datanet*. She then published a web version of the work in 1995.
2. Jill Walker Rettberg's *Electronic Literature Seen from a Distance: The Beginnings of a Field* provides an excellent introduction both to the scene from which the Eastgate writers emerged and other less-chronicled early electronic literature communities, such as the one that formed on the WELL.
3. Mary Ann Buckles 1987 UC San Diego Ph.D. dissertation *Interactive Fiction: The Computer Storygame "Adventure"* was the first book-length academic work on the form.
4. See Rettberg 2013 "An Emerging Canon? A Preliminary Analysis of All References to Creative Works in Critical Writing Documented in the ELMCIP Electronic Literature Knowledge Base" for data and analysis of critical citations of works of electronic literature.
5. Of course, Michael Joyce didn't simply run across some software that he liked. He took part in its development. Storyspace was initially developed by Michael Joyce with Jay David Bolter and John Smith.
6. http://www.altx.com/amerika.online/
7. With the series of multimedia poems *Rice* by geniwate.
8. http://unknownhypertext.com/hypertext.htm

REFERENCES

Amerika, M. (1997) *Grammatron*. [online] Available at: http://www.grammatron.com/index2.html
Arellano, R. (1996) *Sunshine '69*. [online] Available at: http://www.sunshine69.com
Birkerts, S. (1994) *The Gutenberg Elegies: The Fate of Reading in an Electronic Age*. Boston: Faber and Faber.
Cortázar, J. (1966) *Hopscotch*. New York: Pantheon Books.
Coover, R. (1992) The end of books. *The New York Times Book Review*, June 2. [online] Available at: http://www.nytimes.com/books/98/09/27/specials/cooverend.html
Coover, R. (1999) *Literary Hypertext: The Passing of the Golden Age*. [online] Available at: http://nickm.com/vox/golden_age.html
Coverley, M. D. (2002) *Califia*. Watertown, MA: Eastgate Systems.
Crowther, W. and Woods, D. (1976) *Colossal Cave Adventure*.

Gillespie, W., Marquardt, F., Rettberg, S., and Stratton, D. (1999) *The Unknown.* [online] Available at: http://unknownhypertext.com

Jackson, S. (1995) *Patchwork Girl.* Watertown, MA: Eastgate Systems.

Joyce, M. (1990) *Afternoon, A Story.* Watertown, MA: Eastgate Systems.

Koskimaa, R. (2000) *Reading Victory Garden: Competing Interpretations and Loose Ends in Digital Literature: From Text to Hypertext and Beyond.* Ph.D. University of Jyväskylä. Available at: http://users.jyu.fi/~koskimaa/thesis/thesis.shtml

Malloy, J. (2014) *Uncle Roger.* [online] Available at: http://www.well.com/user/jmalloy/uncleroger/partytop.html

McDaid, B. (1992) *Uncle Buddy's Phantom Funhouse.* Watertown, MA: Eastgate.

Montfort, N. (2003) *Twisty Little Passages.* Cambridge: MIT Press.

Moulthrop, S. (1991) *Victory Garden.* Watertown, MA: Eastgate.

Nelson, T. H. (1965) Complex information processing: a file structure for the complex, the changing and the indeterminate. *Proceedings of the ACM*, pp. 84–100.

Nelson, T. H. (1970) No more teachers' dirty looks. *Computer Decisions*, September. Rpt. In: *The New Media Reader.* Cambridge: MIT Press, pp. 309–338.

Rettberg, S. (2013) *An Emerging Canon? A Preliminary Analysis of All References to Creative Works in Critical Writing Documented in the ELMCIP Electronic Literature Knowledge Base.* [online] Available at: http://elmcip.net/sites/default/files/files/attachments/criticalwriting/emerging_canon_s_rettberg.pdf

Rettberg, S., Gillespie, W., Stratton, D., and Marquardt, F. (2011) The unknown. In: Borras, L., Memmott, T., Raley, R., and Stefans, B. (eds.) *Electronic Literature Collection*, Volume 2 (February 2011) Available at: http://collection.eliterature.org/2/works/rettberg_theunknown.html

Walker Rettberg, J. (2012) Electronic literature seen from a distance: The beginnings of a field. *Dichtung Digital* 41. [online] Available at: http://www.dichtung-digital.org/2012/41/walker-rettberg/walker-rettberg.htm

Wardrip-Fruin, N. (2004) What hypertext is. In *Proceedings of the Fifteenth ACM Conference on Hypertext and Hypermedia*, New York: ACM, pp. 126–127.

3　Interactive Cinema in the Digital Age

Chris Hales

Interactive cinema was pioneered in a predigital age, and despite the inherent linearity of projected film and the need for special equipment to allow audiences to make choices or respond, early interactive films implemented both story-branching and parallel narrative structures. The arrival of digital technology to the audiovisual arena led not just to a reinterpretation of these two structures but also to the creation of new forms of the interactive film that were not possible before.

This chapter analyses the methods, structures and techniques for designing and delivering interactive films and investigates how these have been explored in various projects from the 1960s to the present day, demonstrating how several identifiable models of interactive cinema are directly related to the underlying technologies which have created them. The evolution of the interactive film will be traced through three distinct technological phases: a film-based phase centred on fictional entertainment, a period in which Human-Computer Interaction (HCI) and nonlinear narrative were the central issues, and an online phase founded more on participation, collaboration and personalisation.

1. INTRODUCTION

The interactive film has a relatively recent history, dating in a functional form back to 1967, the year in which the Oxford English Dictionary records the first use of the term *interactive* in the human-to-computer sense (in an IEEE journal). The development of interactive cinema has inevitably been shaped by evolving technologies, since it requires a nonlinear audiovisual delivery system as well as an interface technology to allow choices to be made, making it a type of special format cinema. There has been a lack of consistent terminology and few interactive films have ever achieved widespread acclaim or public recognition. The earliest terms employed included *kinoautomat, audience participation film* or *decision cinema*; in the mid-1990s the term *interactive movie* came to mean a particular type of pixel-based computer game interspersed with passive filmed sequences (typified by *Wing Commander III* of 1994); and in the era of social media audiences can interact by collaborating and personalising what very often remains a linear film. Historically, it is possible to identify three phases of interactive cinema. An early phase was centred on dramatic narrative issues and entertainment. Then in the 1980s and 1990s the genre became dominated by HCI considerations and flavoured by the academic discussion of game versus narrative; and in the post Internet phase, interacting can mean participation in the development of the narrative and/or augmentation of the story content (often across a variety of media) by a social community rather than individual direct manipulation of premade content locked into the product itself.

This chapter discusses systems with integrated interaction that can change what happens next during a viewing, and an interactive film will be understood as a representation of primarily prerecorded moving-image sequences, the display of which can be affected by the audience or a performer. The terms *user* and *audience* will be employed to refer to those attending the playout of an interactive film—others have struggled to find more applicable terms, examples include *vuser* (Seaman, 1999), *viewser* (Roach, 1995; Daly, 2010), *participant* (Feingold, 1995), and *doer* (Davenport and Bradley, 1997). Where the spectatorial aspect of viewing has particular significance, the term *interactive cinema* will be used.[1]

Whether fiction or nonfiction, art or game, interactive films require moving image content in the form of prerecorded sequences—as opposed to real-time manipulation of video, which will not be discussed here. Most popularly, these sequences are filmed as live action using real cameras and actors and locations, although this is by no means obligatory—for example in their category of interactive film in *Remediation*, Bolter and Grusin (1999) take as case studies the games *Myst* and *The Last Express*, both of which are composed of synthetic or graphical imagery. Nevertheless, it is hardly surprising that the majority of interactive films use enacted drama, not only because fiction film is a dominant mode of audiovisual culture in contemporary society but also because to creators it represents the greatest chance of catching public attention and achieving financial success. Interactive cinema started as an entertaining means to add novelty to the traditional fiction film in a predigital era in which facilitating audience interaction was much more difficult to achieve than today.

2. THE EARLY DAYS

Interactive cinema got off to a false start in 1961 with William Castle's film *Mr. Sardonicus,* which was advertised as featuring a 'Punishment Poll.' This was a gimmick that enabled audience members to hold up a piece of paper printed with an image of a fist with thumb sticking out, which could be held either thumbs up or thumbs down before the final reel of the film was shown in order to decide whether the Sardonicus character should be pardoned or, as described in the film, 'made to suffer, and suffer, and suffer.' Although the elements of what we might now call an interface were there (the thumb visualisation was intuitive, the paper sheet could be used for both 'yes' and 'no' votes, and the feature was inexpensive). Castle had neither the budget nor inclination to find any technical solution to show each of the two potential endings, and the poll was in fact a simulation. According to Castle's biography (Law, 2000) only the 'suffer' ending was made and shown every time, Castle being seemingly content with the Punishment Poll as a gimmick to attract curious audiences.[2]

Originating in Czechoslovakia, and almost certainly without influence from the Punishment Poll, *Kinoautomat* was the world's first interactive cinema designed to facilitate greater engagement with the theatrical audience. It debuted during the six months of Expo '67 in Montreal where it garnered much publicity and entertained 67,000 visitors. Although it was the brainchild of Radúz Činčera, the project was a collaboration among numerous talented individuals on all fronts. It involved live actors performing in tandem with a projected nonlinear film entitled *One Man and His House* in a custom-built 123-seat cinema with a red and green push button box attached to every seat. At several times in the performance audiences were offered a choice of two narrative alternatives and could push either button to indicate their choice, the sequence corresponding to the majority vote being subsequently projected. *Kinoautomat* employed an apparatus that was more ingenious than innovative; it was based on electromechanical-analogue technology. Wires running from the seats converged into a panel of telephone-style relays that tallied votes and fed signals to an illuminated scoreboard. The projection room had three synchronised 35mm projectors running simultaneously for the main film, and at the moments of choice two additional 16mm projectors were directed to the sidewalls. Additionally, a shutter system showed either of two competing film segments, the narrative structure being a recombinant one in which both possible options converged their story arcs to the same point.[3]

Kinoautomat was scaled up in size and shown at Expos in 1968 and 1974 and had a season in Prague in 1971, but no change in technology advanced the concept. In 1981, at the Portopia exhibition in Kobe, a new film was presented using the same basic hardware, but by then a fundamentally new technology had arrived which proved revolutionary for the interactive film: the laserdisc.[4] Conventional film projection had a final roll of the dice just as laserdisc was taking hold in the early 1980s with fledgling systems that used special (retrofittable) lens/shutter assemblies that could show either of two films printed in split-screen on conventional 35mm film, or that utilised two projectors.[5] In 1983, a film called *Goodbye Cruel World* was shown on this system (named 'Reactivision' and 'Choice-A-Rama') and described in *Inc.* magazine as follows:

> At various points in the less than compelling plot, a comic appears on screen to offer the audience four choices about which way the story line should go. The audience whoops and hollers to indicate its preferences, while a multicolored electronic totem pole at the screen's side

registers the level of their appreciation. The choice that registers highest on the pole is threaded into the projector, and the film continues.

(L.M.S., 1984)

Although the shift away from film projection was inevitable, this remains historically significant in that it represents the first time that a public interactive cinema screening made significant use of another emerging technology, the microcomputer—in this case arranged to detect and respond to input from an external microphone.

3. A REVOLUTION OCCURS

The early 1980s heralded a fundamental new era in which creators could for the first time experiment with a nonlinear delivery system for video footage, a 30cm diameter optical disc known as a videodisc or laserdisc,[6] while simultaneously benefitting from continuing advances in desktop computer technology. The laserdisc remained in use until the late 1990s when it was superseded by another optical disc, this time offering digital video—the DVD. The essential qualities of laserdisc were that it offered reasonable video quality, which could be accessed nonlinearly, was a consumer product (although it never reached high market penetration), and could be adapted for a computer interface enabling custom-made interactive installations, games and exhibits. Fiction film inevitably continued its flirtation with the nonlinear, some of the earliest commercially available discs being murder-mystery dramas/games[7] that were often played as social events hosted as parlour games by the small number of households that actually owned a laserdisc player. By 1995, Interfilm was projecting the laserdisc-encoded films *Mr Payback*, *Ride for Your Life* and *I'm Your Man* into small cinema rooms with seats equipped with 3-button joysticks that could be used at certain moments to cast a vote—almost a facsimile of the staging of *Kinoautomat*, which ironically was still being shown at that time in its final incarnation (*Cinéautomate*) at Futuroscope.[8] What was truly revolutionary about laserdisc was that it immediately opened up the interactive film to genres other than fiction. One of the first explorations of the true nonlinear potential of laserdisc was *The Aspen Movie Map* (MIT Machine Architecture Group, 1979–81), which organised filmed car journeys around the grid-like streets of Aspen into a navigable entity, with additional factual detail available when the façade of certain buildings had been reached. This matrix structure of video scenes could never have been possible with earlier technologies. The MIT group involved in its creation included Michael Naimark, who subsequently produced numerous videodisc installations that allowed navigation of filmed geographical territories in pursuit of what became known as *surrogate travel* or a *movie map*.[9] In the field of media art, Lynn Hershmann was an early adopter of laserdisc technology: her *Lorna* installation (1979–1984) described itself onscreen as "the world's first interactive video art disc game," although it was clearly designed for the art gallery rather than the gaming arcade. In 1990 the first computer arcade game to cost a dollar a play was the live-action *Mad Dog MacCree* (American Laser Games) which caused a brief sensation because it offered image quality (scenes filmed with costumed actors in a Wild West film set) that was far superior to pixel or vector-based products on the market at the time.[10] The game consists almost entirely of laserdisc video sequences shown on a large monitor, the player standing a metre or so away from the screen and shooting with a model revolver at the filmic image of on-screen actors playing evil gunmen who appear in unexpected places at unexpected times.

The arrival of laserdisc opened up a new area of exploration in at least one other area, that of experimental film and video—the exploration of the nature of the moving image in its own right. One of its most notable early proponents was Grahame Weinbren whose writings, as well as whose own works such as *Sonata* (early 1990s) and *The Erl King* (1983–86, with Roberta Friedman), elevated the analysis of interactive cinema into higher aesthetic territory. Weinbren explained the importance of this early nonlinear video delivery technology thus:

> It is 1981. They show me a videodisc. They explain what it is and how it works. And I realize that the language, the possibilities, the significance of cinema is forever changed.
>
> (Weinbren, 1997)

Weinbren outlined his vision of interactive cinema, a cinema based on the interweaving of strong narrative strands, in his seminal essay "In the Ocean of Streams of Story" (Weinbren, 1995). He was, however, by no means alone in striving to discover the ramifications of the 'Revolution of Random Access' as it was taking place; experimental filmmaker Malcolm le Grice, for example, was using microcomputer technology to examine cinematic nonlinearity, although his interest did not extend to an examination of interactivity in its own right.[11]

4. A PROLIFERATION OF INTERFACES

There is an interesting visual device employed in Weinbren's *Sonata*— achieved with custom programming assistance from his brother Jon—when, towards the end of the film, it is possible to move one's finger horizontally across the represented surface of the film causing a real-time 'wipe' between two competing video streams. Technically speaking, this highlights two other factors that were also being investigated in the 1980s and 90s: the utilisation of unusual or intuitive physical interfaces as a means of user choice and the custom-coding of computer software to create bespoken solutions.

In many cases the interface technology already existed and was appropriated to the demands of the interactive film: *The Aspen Movie Map*, *The Erl King* and *Sonata* all originally used touchscreen;[12] *Lorna* used a handset remote; *Mad Dog McCree* used an optical gun; and Interfilm used joysticks. The fact that so many of these devices were better suited to personal choice and expression rather than group interaction was reflected in a noticeable dip in interest in the latter which only seemed to pick up once the Internet was fully established (and in this case the large audience groups were online and not physically co-present). Other than Interfilm, a notable exception to examining group interaction was the *Cinematrix* system (Carpenter, 1993–4) using computer vision to detect response from audiences holding reflective handheld wands as input devices.

With more and more interface hardware becoming available as well as the means to deliver video nonlinearly, the missing part of the puzzle was a system to process the inputs and control the outputs—a role for which the personal computer was ideal, even though it was not until the mid-90s that affordable computers could deliver acceptable-quality video in their own right. Computers could also remember audience activity and could exhibit random behaviour; hence the interactive film began to appear a little more intelligent and unpredictable. For most of the 1980s it was more or less essential to have assistance from programmers and technical specialists, but Apple's HyperCard introduced in 1987 allowed creators a certain amount of autonomy since it required limited programming ability to use its inbuilt high-level language HyperTalk to control video delivery from a laserdisc player or from hard disk. Luc Courchesne, originally studying in the MIT Film/Video section and joining the MIT Media Lab at its inception in 1985, used the HyperCard-HyperTalk-laserdisc triumvirate for a series of highly influential interactive film installations ranging from *Portrait One* (1989) to *Landscape One* (1997). After HyperCard, other so-called authoring software began to appear (such as Macromedia Director) and desktop computers began to do away with the need for laserdisc players by using their own proprietary digital video file formats such as Apple's QuickTime technology (1991).

5. CENTRES OF GRAVITY

The MIT Media Lab opened in 1985, followed by the founding of Glorianna Davenport's Interactive Cinema (IC) research group. Coincidentally or not, Luc Courchesne recalls the first systematic use of interactive in the cinematic context occurring around the same time: "What we then called 'polylinear storytelling' or 'reconfigurable video' was renamed shortly after 'interactive video'" (Courchesne, 2002). IC opened enquiry to all relevant aspects of interaction with visual narrative, not only producing innovative projects and technologies but publishing (and publicising) widely and running an active academic programme. Importantly, IC was influenced by the documentary rather than the dramatic narrative tradition. *Contour*, developed in 1995 for *Boston: Renewed Vistas*, was a generic interface enabling users to custom-ise their viewing of a themed database of documentary video material, and *Jerome B. Wiesner: A Random Walk through the Twentieth Century* (1995) extended the concept to the web, then in its infancy, allowing the database not only to be manipulated in a browser but to be augmented via online contri-butions. Carol Strohecker's *A Different Train of Thought* (Strohecker, 1986) showed the potential of the interactive film in creating a personal type of video narrative based on autobiographical experiences and self-expression—an approach that would later become commonplace once technological improvements and cost reductions democratised the means of production. In this work small icons, functioning as hyperlinks, appear occasionally under the main video representation—a device that became a frequent design ele-ment of later products (IC's *Elastic Charles* of 1988–89 called them *micons*) including the Korsakow authoring system launched in 2000 which itself became particularly popular for use with nonfictional video content.[13]

As well as pioneering the use of video databases and keywords, the algo-rithmic control of disparate media elements was investigated at IC and the term *emergent narrative*[14] was brought to prominence by Tinsley Galyean in his doctoral thesis of 1995.[15] This concept leads to a whole branch of interactive cinema continuing to the present day in which the algorithm-database plays a major role, an important proponent being Marsha Kinder with the *Labyrinth Project* (1997). Lev Manovich's *The Language of New Media*, with its discussion of database cinema and assertion that "the new media object consists of one or more interfaces to a database of multimedia material" (Manovich, 2001, p. 227), further popularised the concept and his installation *Soft Cinema*[16] represents a classic example.

Although in 2004 the IC group at Media Lab broadened into Media Fabrics, the ZKM in Karlsruhe has continued to nurture—amongst other projects—interactive cinema, not least through the numerous artist-in-residence projects it has supported along with cutting-edge technical assis-tance and equipment. The ZKM Media Museum still displays key works by Courchesne, Hershman and Naimark described earlier. Other specialist cen-tres have more recently been founded, in particular the iCinema Centre for Interactive Cinema Research at the University of New South Wales, which was directed by Jeffrey Shaw from 2003 until 2009.

6. CHANGING FORMATS

The 1990s passed as a technology interregnum, as laserdisc faded to obscu-rity and other optical disc formats came and went until the DVD became a universal standard, whilst at the same time the Internet became widespread and Apple's QuickTime technology brought video to the desktop computer where it could be stored on ever-cheaper hard drives.[17] There was a lot of discussion of interactive television at this time, with little to show in terms of actual products except for some television dramas created with multiform plots and shown simultaneously on two or more channels.[18] A notable exception is *Akvaario*, identified by Manovich as an early example of database narrative.[19] Video CD (created in 1993) was the first format for fitting a film on a 120mm disc, whilst Philips CD-I technology spawned *Voyeur* and *Voyeur II* interactive film games during its short existence. Domestic games consoles were offering full-motion video (FMV), *Night Trap* (1992–1994) being one of the first games consisting almost exclusively of live-action filmed footage and *The X-Files Game* (1999) one of the last.[20] As processor power increased, the limitations to gameplay of using prerecorded video sequences made such games anachronistic, but not before the term *interactive movie* had been used to describe the mid-1990s fad of computer games in which gameplay was interspersed with passive, live-action filmed sequences.

Several factors came together in the early 1990s to bring the creation of interactive films within the range and budget of the average desktop computer user. The advent of QuickTime technology, combined with fast hard drives on which to store the video files, brought digital video to the home computer, and although the size and quality was originally highly limited, it improved steadily.[21] One could film with a domestic camcorder, digitise the sequences, manipulate and edit them with commercially available video editing software, and add interactivity/nonlinearity using multimedia authoring software such as HyperCard, Supercard and Director. A new type of production arose, often experimental or with a personal touch, made with modest means, typified by projects such as *HyperCafé* (Balcom, Smith and Sawhney, 1996) and Chris Hales' 1995 touchscreen installation film *The Twelve Loveliest Things I Know*.[22] Interactive filmmaking could then be taught in hands-on fashion at moderately equipped higher education establishments,[23] which had themselves seen an expansion of degree courses specialising in new media and interaction. Opportunities also increased to exhibit finished work in specialised festivals and other events. CD-ROM discs, offering data storage and distribution of 650MB, proved a useful format for these individual creators, and the Artist CD-ROM became a discrete and recognisable genre of new media art.

The most durable delivery mechanisms for video that emerged during the 1990s were the DVD and Internet. The former had the potential for interactivity built into its specification—on-screen menus allow choices to be made to switch to a different scene, and angles can be used to select from sequences running in parallel scenes. Nevertheless, few commercially available DVD titles have been specifically made as interactive films. *Tender Loving Care* and *Point of View* (Aftermath Media, 1998, 2001) were trailblazers; both were structured as video episodes interspersed with on-screen questionnaires. Bernard Perron (2003) conducted a systematic study of the former title, analysing in depth the activity required from a user in order to complete the interactive experience. *Switching* (Oncotype, 2003) provided 140 minutes of fiction material organised as intersecting video loops in a structure that its makers described as a *Noodlefilm*[24] because every distinct video sequence is hyperlinked to other video sequences throughout its temporal duration. *Late Fragment*, coproduced by The Canadian Film Centre and National Film Board of Canada in 2007 and *Über Life* made in Serbia in 2010 also stand out as purpose-made interactive films produced for DVD. The fact is that whereas a large proportion of commercial DVD (and Blu-ray) titles do offer interactive features, these are separate entities and not an integral part of the main film. Developments in interactive filmmaking have instead, in the 21st century, mostly occurred due to the growth in capability of the Internet, the arrival of new devices and platforms, and a growth in the range and sophistication of interface technology.

7. A NEW CENTURY

Although bandwidth limitations restricted the use of video in the early days of the Internet, by the mid-2000s video was commonplace on the web and the video-sharing website YouTube started operations in 2005. Advertisers were quick to harness online video. *The Subservient Chicken* (2004), for instance, allowed users to type in commands to an on-screen video of a man in a chicken suit who could perform around 300 prerecorded actions. Although the experience was far from seamless and there was no depth to the nonlinear structure, it resulted in numerous imitations and variations. By 2011, the Land Rover brand was advertising online with a short interactive film entitled *Being Henry*, the endings of which were portraying a vehicle customised in a way that reflected the choices made by the user whilst traversing the branching structure. Fiction filmmaking has asserted its interactive online presence with examples such as *The Outbreak*,[25] a zombie survival film of 2008, and *Crimeface*, a Webby Award winner of the same year. In 2008, YouTube extended its functionality to allow annotations to be positioned on video content—essentially acting as hyperlinks to other YouTube videos—making the creation of a branching interactive film a trivial operation requiring few specialised skills. Although traversing an interactive film made in this way is highly anticinematic and lacks flow due to the continual presence of the YouTube visual interface, more interactive films (however simple in structure and content) are being implemented here, and they are being made by a wider profile of creators than have ever before made history in the field.

Interactive music videos have become a burgeoning online presence and now range from annotated YouTube branching narratives (such as "The Streets" *Computers and Blues* music album of 2011) to those using crowdsourcing (such as *The Johnny Cash Project*[26]) or incorporating personal data obtained by voluntary upload or taken from webcam, Twitter and Facebook accounts, or even Google Maps.[27] Interactive web documentary has also emerged after the mid-2000s as a distinct genre, although it is usually analysed in terms of its collaborative and cross-media characteristics rather than its directly interactive ones. In fact there is no longer any simple definition of what constitutes an interactive film, as audiences may be active in other ways than selecting from premade content. A popular YouTube activity is to post homemade remixes or reinterpretations of video content uploaded by others, and more structured projects such as Perry Bard's *Man with a Movie Camera: the Global Remake*[28] (2007) invite their communities to upload personal material to achieve a defined yet malleable creative goal. Henry Jenkins recognised this as "a shift from real-time interaction toward asynchronous participation" (Jenkins, 2006, p. 59), whilst Kristen Daly proposes a "Cinema 3.0: The Interactive-Image," in which films "put the viewer to work" (Daly, 2010, p. 86) with "interaction in the form of user-participation and interpretation" (Daly, 2010, p. 82). Perhaps the key issue then is that interactivity itself has changed, and "should no longer be defined by a specific formal language prescribed by the vocabulary of the 1990s. Today, most of all, it is a set of strategies that can be situated in multiple contexts. ..."[29]

Developments in technology have inevitably broadened the range of devices that can be harnessed as interaction technology and as media viewing platforms. Projects that might previously have stood out by utilising an unusual physical interface are now no longer special. The field of physical computing—characterised by microcontroller boards such as Arduino—enable electronic sensors to be employed to detect all manner of user activity. Michael Lew's *Office Voodoo* (Lew, 2003) permits two users to each shake and squeeze a voodoo doll figurine to control the interplay between two office workers portrayed onscreen. Biofeedback data was used by Pia Tikka in the multiscreen fiction film installation *Obsession* (Tikka, 2008) to control the playback of video sequences from a database under the control of an algorithm informed by a study of the writings of Sergei Eisenstein. British company MyndPlay[30] has produced several short branching-narrative films aimed at entertainment or personal well-being that are controlled by input from commercially available EEG brainwave headsets. Game console interfaces such as the Wiimote and Kinect can recognise physical gestures, and the touchscreen—previously a somewhat neglected and technically limited interface—is standard on many devices and can detect sophisticated actions and multiple touches, as explored in the *Touching Stories* package of short interactive films commissioned for the iPad in 2010.

Although dedicated interactive cinema theatres have never been widely established, interaction for large groups of co-present audience members has benefited from the growth in personally owned mobile devices and from cheaper and easier-to-use technologies and software techniques. Short, interactive screenings have occasionally been used to entertain (and usually advertise to) audiences awaiting the main feature in a traditional cinema environment. Between 2003 and 2009, "Cause and Effect" toured a programme of short interactive films, each with a different interaction mode, using inexpensive technology that could be carried in a rucksack and installed in freeform spaces.[31] Audiences need no longer be instructed to turn off their mobile devices at the cinema: phone calling has been used in the *Last Call* (2010) (although only one audience member could exert influence), a text message may be used to convey a choice or combination of choices, and smart phones allow interaction via online access. Web-based audience response systems can now utilise mobile phone, Twitter and the web to allow audience groups to vote and express themselves in real time using their personal devices. Despite these advances in technology, if all the audience can do is vote to choose by majority what happens next, then the creative potential of the interactive film will have changed little since *Kinoautomat* in 1967. Those projects that find a more imaginative correlation between the on-screen story and the activity required by the audience (often using ingenious interaction modes) undoubtedly offer more engaging experiences, the technique itself having been described as 'movie as interface.'[32]

8. CONCLUSION

Interactive cinema has never become mainstream partly because the terminology used to describe it has been varied and the technology required to deliver it has been under constant change, creating a lack of homogeneity. Although suitable platforms for interactive cinema are now widespread, the experience of interactivity has become a daily necessity, and the possibility to interact to change the representation of a film is no longer the novelty that it once was. Hyperlinked YouTube branching films are proliferating, and more people now possess devices that can record video than ever before. An interactive film is no longer the recognisably distinct item that it once was. It has blended into a wider range of phenomena and now requires a much broader definition, which includes personalisation and collaboration. Audiences have the potential to contribute to the filmic content itself, not just how it is finally manipulated.

Developments in technologies have necessarily been a major factor in the evolution of interactive filmmaking and it is possible to identify a film-based phase, a laserdisc (and subsequently CDROM and DVD) phase, and the rise of the personal computer and the Internet. QuickTime technology was also important in making it possible for modestly equipped individuals to enter the arena of interactive filmmaking. A huge variety of inexpensive electronic devices can now be used as interface technology, and interactive film shows can easily be staged without the need to construct special cinemas.

On a final note, there is now the sense that interactive cinema is aware of—and actively preserving—its history, in tune with a wider interest in new media history and media archaeology. *Kinoautomat* of 1967 has been researched, reconstructed and released on DVD, and reperformed in cinema theatres. The importance of preserving the functionality of projects—made relatively recently but with archaic technological requirements—has become recognised and acted upon. Several historically important installations such as Weinbren's *The Erl King* are being preserved or emulated so that the original use can be accurately experienced in perpetuity (Weinbren, n.d.). Interactive Cinema now has a secure history—what the future holds is a branching narrative that has yet to be traversed.

NOTES

1. One of the pioneers of interactive laserdisc artworks, Grahame Weinbren, uses this term more or less exclusively, and it was the name of an influential research group at MIT Media Lab.
2. Castle used gimmicks in other films that have some relevance to nonlinear narrative. For example, *13 Ghosts* (1960) had different visual representations according to the use of a 'Ghost Viewer' (containing coloured filters) given to audience members.
3. Additional detail on *Kinoautomat* can be found in Nico Carpentier (2011), *Media and Participation: A site of ideological-democratic struggle,* Bristol/Chicago: Intellect, pp. 276–308.
4. Činčera was involved in two more *Kinoautomat*-type projects, the *Cinelabyrinth* (Expo'90, Osaka) and the *Cinéautomate* (which ran at the Futuroscope theme park in France from 1991 until 1996), and both of these projects used laserdisc with video projection.
5. US patent 4,591,248 was applied for in 1983 and granted in 1986 for a 'dynamic audience-responsive movie system' using two projectors and a 'changeover shutter mechanism' and with audience response measured at various moments in the film by the level of samples taken from a microphone near the audience.
6. Numerous variations and trade names exist, but this chapter will use the generic term 'laserdisc.'
7. *MysteryDiscs* featuring fictional detective Stew Cavanaugh appeared in 1982 and 1983.
8. *I'm Your Man* was subsequently released on DVD and marketed with a video trailer that naively proclaimed it to be "the first ever interactive movie that lets you choose the storyline".
9. Examples are Naimark's *Karlsruhe Moviemap* of 1991, which was based on the Karlsruhe tram network and *See Banff!* of 1994 based on footpaths in a National Park.
10. There were precedents such as *Dragon's Lair* (1983), but *Mad Dog McCree* was arguably the most well-known. Different sequels to *Mad Dog McCree* have been produced, depicting different settings and time periods. Upgrades to the arcade

machines were indeed easily performed by swapping the laserdisc, repainting the housing, and changing the model of revolver.

11. Le Grice's *The Chronos Project* (1995–97) structured 60 hours of video footage into a categorised database from which multiple readings were generated, but was not designed with audience interactivity in mind.

12. Weinbren also experimented with unusual input devices: for example hanging wooden frames embedded with infra-red sensors that captured the motion of the user's outstretched finger and, for March (1997), a metal ramp that detected the user's position.

13. Further information at http://www.korsakow.org/about

14. The term 'emergent' was probably in general use at that time in Media Lab and alumnus Bill Seaman used the term 'emergent meaning' in his later doctoral thesis (1999) at University of Wales/CaiiA.

15. Page 27 of Galyean's *Narrative Guidance of Interactivity* introduces the concept: "If any narrative structure (or story) emerges it is a product of our interactions and goals as we navigate the experience. I call this 'Emergent Narrative.'"

16. Installation created by Lev Manovich with Andreas Kratky. First exhibited in 2002 at the Center for Art and Media at Karlsruhe (ZKM) as part of the seminal 'Future Cinema' exhibition curated by Peter Weibel and Jeffrey Shaw.

17. There were, and are, plenty of other digital video formats; however, since the Macintosh was quickly adopted by the creative community, Quicktime had more significant influence and impact.

18. Examples include *Murderous Decisions* (Germany, 1991), *Noodles and 08* (Sweden, 1996) and *D-Dag* (Denmark, 1999–2000).

19. Manovich, *The Language of New Media*, pp. 318–319. *Akvaario* accessed a database of 5000 video scenes and was broadcast on the Finnish national YLE1 channel during March 2000 for six nights a week, from four to seven hours each night, totaling 130 broadcast hours. Viewers could call to any of four different telephone numbers to influence changing the scenes being broadcast.

20. Hyperbole Studios were, for a while, considering making their trademarked 'VirtualCinema' software engine (used to create *The X-Files Game*) available for other developers.

21. In the mid-1990s it was necessary to purchase expensive plug-in video boards in order to work with good quality video; it was only a matter of time before these boards became unnecessary.

22. In 1996 the film was published on CD-ROM as *LAB002 Twelve* by Research Publishing and was probably the first Artist CD-ROM conceived and created entirely as an interactive film.

23. The author of this article, Chris Hales, has taught over 150 short workshops internationally, themed on the creation of interactive films, with the first taking place in 1997.

24. http://www.switching.dk The user need only press the ENTER button on the DVD remote (or click the mouse) whenever they feel so inclined to make a change.

25. http://www.survivetheoutbreak.com Numerous low budget interactive zombie films are available online (including on YouTube), the horror genre seeming to be particularly suited to branching narrative and hence frequently chosen by filmmakers.

26. *The Johnny Cash Project*, dir. Chris Milk, technical dir. Aaron Koblin, 2011.

27. An example is *The Wilderness Downtown* (2010, dir. Chris Milk, technical dir. Aaron Koblin), which requests the user's hometown address before generating a multiscreen audiovisual experience including corresponding Google Map and Street View imagery. The *Tackfilm* (2009), promoting Swedish Television Licenses, and *Take This Lollipop* (Jason Zada, 2011) are other examples of customisation.
28. http://dziga.perrybard.net/
29. From the Interactive Art Jury Statement, Ars Electronica, May 2013. *Cyberarts 2013: International Compendium – Prix Ars Electronica.*
30. http://www.myndplay.com
31. Elaborated on in Hales (2007).
32. Elaborated on in Hales (2006).

REFERENCES

Ars Electronica (2013) *Cyberarts 2013: International Compendium—Prix Ars Electronica.* Ostfildern: Hatje Cantz Verlag.

Balcom, D., Sawhney, N., and Smith, I. (1996) Hypercafe: Narrative and aesthetic properties of hypervideo. In *Proceedings of Hypertext '96, Seventh ACM Conference on Hypertext.* New York: ACM Press.

Bolter, J. and Grusin, R. (1999) *Remediation. Understanding New Media.* Cambridge, MA: MIT Press.

Carpenter, L. (1994) *Cinematrix, Video Imaging Method and Apparatus for Audience Participation.* U.S. Patents 5210604 (1993) and 5365266 (1994).

Carpentier, N. (2011) *Media and Participation: A Site of Ideological-Democratic Struggle.* Bristol UK/Chicago, USA: Intellect.

Courchesne, L. (2002) The construction of experience: Turning spectators into visitors. In: Zapp, A. and Rieser, M. (eds.) *Cinema/Art/Narrative.* London: BFI.

Daly, K. (2010) Cinema 3.0: The interactive-image. *Cinema Journal.* 50(1). pp. 81–98.

Davenport, G. and Bradley, B. (1997)The Care and feeding of users. *IEEE Multimedia.* 4(1). p. 8.

Feingold, K. (1995) OU: Interactivity as divination as vending machine. *Leonardo.* 28(5). pp. 399–402.

Galyean, T. A. (1995) *Narrative Guidance of Interactivity.* PhD diss., Massachusetts Institute of Technology.

Hales, C. (2006) *Rethinking the Interactive Movie.* PhD diss., University of East London/SMARTlab.

Hales, C. (2007) Emergent audience behaviour: Observations of social interaction within physically co-present audiences attending a live interactive filmshow. In: Lugmayr, A., Lietsala, K., and Kallenbach, J. (eds.) *MindTrek 2007 Conference Proceedings.* pp. 31–36.

Jenkins, H. (2006) *Convergence Culture: Where Old and New Media Collide.* New York: New York University Press.

Law, J. W. (2000) *Scare Tactic. The Life and Films of William Castle.* San Jose/New York/Lincoln/Shanghai: Writers Club Press.

Lew, M. (2003) Office voodoo: A real-time editing engine for an algorithmic sitcom. In *Proceedings of SIGGRAPH 2003.*

L.M.S. (1984) Reel money. *Inc. magazine*. May 1984. Available at: http://www.inc.com/magazine/19840501/6541.html

Manovich, L. (2001) *The Language of New Media*. Cambridge, MA: MIT Press.

Perron, B. (2003) From gamers to players and gameplayers. The example of interactive movies. In: Wolf, M. and Perron, B. (eds.) *The Video Game Theory Reader*. New York/London: Routledge.

Roach, G. (1995) Into the vortex. *New Scientist*. pp. 30–33.

Seaman, W. C. (1999) *Recombinant Poetics: Emergent Meaning as Examined and Explored Within a Specific Generative Virtual Environment*. PhD diss., University of Wales/CaiiA.

Strohecker, C. (1986) *Electronic Collage: the Videodisc and Interactive Narrative*. MSc diss., Massachusetts Institute of Technology.

Tikka, P. (2008) *Enactive Cinema: Simulatorium Eisensteinense*. Helsinki: University of Art and Design Helsinki.

Weinbren, G. (1995) In the ocean of streams of story. *Millennium Film Journal*. 28. pp. 15–30.

Weinbren, G. (1997) *The Digital Revolution is a Revolution of Random Access*. Available at: http://www.numeral.com/articles/weinbren/telepolis/telepolis.html

Weinbren, G. (not dated) Emulating the Erl King. *Art In-Sight*. 14. Available at: http://grahameweinbren.net/GW_Papers/Emulating%20the%20ErlKing.html

4 The Holodeck is all Around Us—Interface Dispositifs in Interactive Digital Storytelling

Noam Knoller and Udi Ben-Arie

1. INTRODUCTION: THE FOUR INTERFACE DISPOSITIFS

The landscape of digital media has recently been undergoing a rapid and radical shift. Ever since the mid-1970s, our communication with computers has been mediated by a more or less standard and dominant interface paradigm: the personal desktop computer (PC) and, since the mid-1980s, the multimedia PC with its WIMP GUI.[1]

In contrast, over the last few years we have become entangled in a ubiquitous web of computer gadgetry that is quite different from the desktop PC: from mobile devices with multi-touch screens to voice-command-operated GPS systems and from Nintendo Wii's sophisticated controllers to the Xbox Kinect's gesture-based, controller-free paradigm. Labs around the world continue to develop and test even more interface technologies, from tangible displays that explore embodiment and materiality (Wiberg et al., 2012) to brain-computer interfaces that effectively bypass (the rest of) the body (Gilroy et al., 2013).

This trajectory of increasingly rich interfaces calls for a reexamination of Interactive Digital Narrative's heritage and current practice in relation to the interface. This diachronic perspective also highlights an important difference between the quite stable apparatus (as the interface is known in cinema studies) of film and television, compared to the digital apparatus, which appears to be evolving so rapidly that it disrupts the development of stable schemata of communication (Bordwell, 1985) between authors and audiences. To better understand the development, we propose looking at the history of human-computer interfaces as a series of 'interface dispositifs' forming around specific interface technologies (which we call 'apparatuses').

The terms *dispositif* and *apparatus*, originating in two strands of French thought in the 1970s, are often intermingled when translated into English. In this chapter, we propose to adopt an analytic distinction between the two. Baudry's analyses of cinema (1974, 1975) identify in it an arrangement of three elements: the basic apparatus (*appareil de base*), which is composed of the essentially perspectival equipment for recording and screening moving images; of continuity film editing which sutures its cutting to remain transparent; and of the screening condition in which the spectator is seated in a darkened space, positioned or 'dispositioned' as a voyeur. So, what we have here is a system composed of cinematic hardware, cinematic language and a very specific body posture. Analogously, in this chapter, the term *apparatus* will refer to computer technology and its relation to the user's body and psychology. This use is similar to Agamben's definition of an apparatus as anything that can "capture ... gestures, behaviors, opinions, or discourses of living beings" (Agamben 2009, p. 18).

Our usage of the term *dispositif* follows Foucault (1980), referring to the wider social, cultural, ideological and aesthetic elements that organise knowledge and power relations, which surround and condition the apparatus. According to Foucault, a dispositif is "a thoroughly heterogeneous ensemble consisting of discourses, institutions, architectural forms, regulatory decisions, laws, administrative measures, scientific statements, philosophical, moral and philanthropic propositions" (Foucault, 1980, p. 194) as well as the relations between these heterogeneous elements, which ultimately serve a dominant strategic function at a given historical moment "of responding to an *urgent need*" (Foucault, 1980, p. 195, italics in the original).

It is with this analytical pair that we propose to trace a history of human-computer interfaces. It allows us to examine interfaces both as specific hardware devices that afford specific languages and relations with bodies and as a technological embodiment or response to urgent needs, cultural, sociopolitical tendencies or dispositions.

Dispositifs do not follow discrete and linear trajectories of development. They are constantly changing assemblages of unstable elements and relations, and as such they gradually and unevenly transition one into the other with periods of overlap and superimposition. In the four interface dispositifs we identify, the same types of constitutive relations remain significant for our analysis of works of IDN: (1) the interface-relation between the apparatus and the body which defines, to use Rancière's term, a distribution of the sensible[2] (Rancière, 2004); (2) the effect of this primary relation on narrative structures and communicative storytelling processes; and (3) the dispositif: the dynamic social forces, in their ideological, political or economic manifestations that condition these two relations in order to respond to an urgent need.

Throughout this chapter, we will also refer to Interactive Digital Narrative (IDN) works on a narratological level. Since there are many competing sets of terminology using similar terms in different senses, we wish to clarify the specific set we use. According to Rimmon-Kenan (2002, p. 3–4), out of the three aspects of classical narratology—story, narration, text—the text is the only aspect directly accessible to the reader: "It is through the text that he or she acquires knowledge of the story (its object) and of the narration (the process of its production)" (2002, p. 4). This terminology needs some adjustment to account for the user's contribution to the IDN text. The text of any work of IDN thus incorporates the interface. The story becomes a *storyworld*, able to generate multiple versions, implemented at run-time as local discourses (instead of narrations). Each time a user interacts with the text, one local discourse is generated, and the user decodes one version of the storyworld. Whereas in linear narrative media every 'reading' would produce the same discourse (although every reader would interpret it differently); in IDN, each session might produce a different one, disclosing a different version of the storyworld resulting from different "userly performances" (Knoller, 2012) of the text through the interface. The meaning of the work thus ultimately resides in the logic connecting userly performance to the permutations in the global discourse (the set of all possible local discourses).

2. PRE-PC DISPOSITIF

The computer user before the advent of the PC was a specialised operator, engineer or scientist. Early computers were not interactive since processing times were too slow to allow computer output to become synchronous with the operator's actions. The operator's bodily performance consisted of a series of temporally discrete visits to a computer terminal either to input data and execute a single program using punch cards or to collect printed output. Although a small number of computer-based games were developed as soon as displays appeared, this apparatus did not give rise to any storytelling experiences that we are aware of. However, a need (urgent or not) for the involvement of audiences in determining plot development and outcomes began taking preliminary shape in several traditional media. Already in 1935, Ayn Rand's Broadway play *Night of January 16th* invited audience members to perform jury duty on the theatre stage, uttering their own unscripted text, thereby affecting the verdict and determining the play's ending. In book form, several types of "multiform stories" (Murray, 1997, p. 30) were realised, such as the branching 'choose your own adventure' genre, which gave the reader a menu-like range of page numbers to read on. On television, we can mention Hirschbiegel's *Murderous Decision* (1991), discussed in the introduction to this section.

The first interactive[3] movies appeared in the 1960s. William Castle produced *Mr. Sardonicus* in 1961, followed six years later by Radúz Činčera's audience-voting apparatus *Kinoautomat* (1967—see Chapter 3 in this volume). These early works highlight both the need for, and the complexity of, involving audiences in shaping the discourse. While Castle solved the problem of complexity by faking,[4] Činčera both constructed a customised technical apparatus and created a solution on the level of discourse, with the two possible choices always converging again at the next decision point.

However, none of these participatory works can be considered fully interactive because books, cinema and television do not possess interfaces efficient and convenient enough for interaction with their readers or viewers; and while theatre can afford interaction with a select group of audience members, its collective experience cannot afford personal and distinct agency for each individual and cannot afford individual story presentations in response to userly performance.

3. THE PC DISPOSITIF

The apparatus of the personal computer was ergonomically designed for a single user sitting at a desk using a few fingers to control software applications that mainly appear as visual and textual. The PC era was the era of the individual, intellectual worker of Engelbart's original vision (2001). The *personal* computer's canonical applications were primarily meant to help users become intellectually or cognitively productive (gaming and other home-oriented applications followed suit). The design of the PC, while allowing some naturalistic connection (through the mouse) between the user's bodily movement and operations inside the computer, essentially stresses the cognitive and intellectual over the embodied and affective, the individual over the social and the visual over the other senses.

Interestingly, while videogames were also always created for the PC, the gaming industry, quite early on, developed its own set of interface devices, such as force-feedback actuators inside joysticks, steering wheels and other composite controls that, unlike the cognitive and quite disembodied PC, did address more of the player's body. These innovations did find a market, responding to a more or less *urgent need,* but they had not yet infected the more common apparatus of the PC.

3.1 Agency and the PC Dispositif

By the time PCs eventually became mass market in the early 1980s, they were shrouded in a sanguine emancipatory discourse, which focused on the computer's interactivity as extending the user's agency. The field of HCI, which emerged in the late 1970s, embraced this ideology (Carroll 2009). Commenting on the implications of this move on interactive art, Kristine Stiles and Edward Shanken (2010) try to demystify this notion of agency. According to their account, throughout the 1970–80s, interactive media art increasingly became a sophisticated marketing vehicle for hardware producers. An ideology of interactivity and agency was born, co-opted by commercial concerns, according to which "the augmentation of individual agency—however superficial—offered a veneer of imagined personal control to consumers" (Stiles and Shanken, 2010, p. 83). While in its fullest sense, agency is the ability to act in the physical and social world we inhabit (Stiles and Shanken 2010, p. 87; Knoller, 2012), the agency offered by the PC was limited to the user's power to interact with representations within it. The personal computer was not (yet) a social tool (it would be repurposed for this in the network dispositif—see below), and certainly not a physical one.

It is against this background that Murray's definitive *Hamlet on the Holodeck* (1997) is set. For Murray, and certainly for most of the IDN research community that was deeply inspired by her book, agency became the primary property, pleasure and design goal of the field.[5] Murray's definition of agency as the "satisfying power to take meaningful action and see the results of our decisions and choices" (1997, p. 126) is followed by a comparison to participatory folk dances, which sheds some light on the more specific origins of this concept:

> On the ballroom dance floor, we can at most influence our partner, but the musicians and the rest of the dancers remain relatively unaffected. ... When things are going right on the computer, we can be both the dancer and the caller of the dance. This is the feeling of agency.
>
> (Murray, 1997, p. 128)

The *feeling* of agency, according to Murray, is one of being in command, rather than merely influencing (let alone being influenced or controlled). This control-device experience of having "the entire dance hall ... at our command" (Murray, 1997, p. 128) is still closely linked to an aesthetic of productive applications and even the pre-PC origins of HCI in control engineering.

Interactive Storytelling on the PC took on several forms, as the apparatus evolved its powers of (audio-)visual representation and computational simulation. Interactive Fiction (IF) represents the first generation of PC-based storytelling (see introduction to Part I of this volume). The innovativeness of this genre lies in the fact that, unlike the book, the user can navigate locations, pick up and manipulate objects and converse with characters—all by typing text commands.

However, the affordances of the command-line interface do not communicate to the user the actual constraints of the seemingly natural-language command set. There is no menu of possible commands to choose from and no clear choice to be made, so players are invited to guess which natural language words might function as commands in the system. This produces a challenging (but at the time evidently fascinating) experience of simulated navigation through an imperceptible space. However, the experience breaks down every time the system fails to understand the user's syntax or commands. In order to understand how to act or navigate, the user ultimately had to refer to a (paper-based) manual. Hypertext literature (see Chapter 2 in this volume), which represents the second major genre of interactive storytelling, posed similar challenges to comprehension because the user could not know where following a hyperlink might lead.

In the second half of the 1980s, the PC apparatus went through a first qualitative shift with the addition of the mouse to its hardware interface and the standardisation of the Graphical User Interface (GUI) and the iconic WIMP (Windows, Icons, Menus and Pointer) paradigm. As CPUs and graphics cards became faster, the PC's powers of audio-visual representation and simulation made 3D representation of space possible, but 3D navigation and especially fine manipulation of 3D objects never became mainstream, probably because the capabilities of the PC's hardware input devices fell short of it because the 2D, single-point mouse does not afford detailed 3D manipulation. The representation on the screen reached new heights of perceptual realism, which the apparatus did not allow the user's body to inhabit.

Michael Mateas and Andrew Stern's *Façade* (2005) is a canonical example of IDN for the late PC apparatus.[6] *Façade* attempts to tell a coherent and compelling story, manage a dynamic and responsive narrative presentation, afford natural-language dialogue, express emotion through AI-driven characters and allow navigation in a 3D representation. This attack on several fronts seems to have stemmed from a desire to approximate, as much as possible on the PC apparatus, the Holodeck[7] experience envisioned by Murray. As in Interactive Fiction (IF), *Façade* allows the user to influence the story-world, but in contrast, it makes ample use of the main software-interface paradigms of the late PC apparatus. The arrow keys allow navigation; a (sort of) command-line interface affords typed dialogue and communication with the main characters; the mouse allows picking up objects and executing actions (hug, kiss, or caress). And while IF had already achieved real-time performance by the computer, *Façade* demands the same of userly performance. If the user hesitates to provide input, the story continues regardless.

Most of the academic research on interactive storytelling, from the *OZ Project* (1992) until rather recently, took place within this PC dispositif.[8] Outside of academic research, artists and media designers had been exploring and experimenting with nonstandard interfaces for storytelling. We will discuss some of these examples in the last section. Hazarding a gross generalisation, under the conditions of the PC dispositif, the human body did not receive much attention, and most of the energy and innovation was directed at understanding, representing and simulating narrative and narration and presenting interactive storyworlds within the display and interaction affordances of the PC.

4. THE NETWORK DISPOSITIF

With the advent of the web in the mid-1990s, the role of computers in society changed. The network changed personal computing by gradually making it more social, and human-computer interactions became more about relations and communication.

At first, the network connected only stationary computers, using narrow bandwidth mainly for nonsynchronous and textual communication (email, forum, turn-taking-based chat). As bandwidth expanded, synchronous and multi-modal communication (music, VOIP [Voice over Internet Protocol], video sharing, video-chat) became normal. According to Jan Bordewijk and Ben van Kaam, networked communication can follow four patterns (Bordewijk and van Kaam, 1986) based on a matrix premised on who issues information and who controls it: a centre (broadcaster, corporation, government) or the consumer. In *allocution*, the centre controls both. In *conversation*, the consumer controls both. In *consultation*, the centre issues the information but the consumer controls when and where to access it. In *registration*, the consumer issues the information and the centre controls it. Registration, on the web, is a form of automated surveillance, in the disciplinary sense discussed by Foucault (1977). This adds another dimension to the notion of userly performance, expanding the invisible audience (Boyd, 2007) of such performances to a global (or rather a multinational) scale.

The network dispositif does not change much at the apparatus level: it is still a PC and the body is positioned in a similar way. The significant change is in social interaction, in the rising dominance of the pattern of conversation.

In the web documentary game *Fort McMoney* (2013) the web facilitates what film and TV's linear paradigm and even the PC apparatus could not have achieved: a participatory networked activity and a communal simulation. The work creates a dynamic, interactive simulation of a virtual city named Fort McMoney, which represents and semi-simulates the actual Canadian city of Fort McMurray. At the apparatus level, the text is constructed from documents and interviews, incorporating the game strategy of city simulation. The user can affect the discourse, choosing which character or area to explore.

Fort McMoney is a unique combination of a serious game and social participation, inviting us to influence the outcome through two main methods—debating and voting. In the first method, users debated on a Twitter feed that is embedded in the discussion area on the website. Thus, *Fort McMoney*'s text intertwines documentary material, the creators' design, and the participating community's opinions. In the second method, the players influence the parameters of a virtual city by voting. In the beginning, the virtual city's indicators—inhabitants, home prices, homeless population and a few others—reflect actual indicators. As the project unfolds, the virtual city reflects the collective outcomes of thousands of userly performances. *Fort McMoney* is characteristic of the network dispositif's power to enable collaboration between three authorities—author, computer system, and the user—all taking part (in different levels and degrees) in creating the text through mediated social interactions and distributed decision-making.

At the level of the dispositif, players learn about the oil industry's power and influence, compared to the virtual community's opinion and will. Like other video games, *Fort McMoney* is also value-laden (Brey, 2008, p. 379), but unlike most games it promotes values of community, discussion, democracy and open government. Clearly, the creators are critical of the oil industry and probe its power, but their interface promotes diverse opinions through open discussion and voting. Still, agency is not equally distributed. Players with higher 'influential points' accumulated through playing have more leverage in decision-making. Likewise, the authority level of users is not the same as that of the creators. The user's authority is limited and confined to the creator's authorial design (Ben-Arie, 2009, p. 158).

5. POST-PC DISPOSITIF

The Post-PC dispositif is the one we have entered into relatively recently, with the popularisation of touch-screen-based mobile devices. It is different from the previous two dispositifs in that it cannot yet be named metonymically after an underlying technical apparatus. On that level, the current dispositif is a "heterogeneity without a norm" (Jameson, 1991, p. 17) of apparatuses and several vectors of change. Some of the vectors are a continuation and intensification of trends from the previous dispositifs. However, several other vectors of change, although they may have been in the making for many years, are now converging together and entering mainstream use.

5.1 The Bodily Turn

The first of these vectors is 'the bodily turn.'[9] Already in 1997, Frank Biocca called this vector "progressive embodiment" (1997), "the steadily advancing immersion of sensorimotor channels to computer interfaces through a tighter and more pervasive coupling of the body to interface sensors and displays" (1997). Biocca highlighted the implications of the coupling of body with technological extensions and called it the "cyborg's dilemma:"

> The more natural the interface, the more human it is, the more it adapts to the human body and mind. The more the interface adapts to the human body and mind, the more the body and mind adapts to the nonhuman interface. Therefore, the more natural the interface, the more we become unnatural, the more we become cyborgs.
>
> (Biocca, 1997)

Under the post-PC dispositif, we see a rapid acceleration and dissemination of interface technologies such as the multi-touch interfaces of tablets and smartphones, the integration of accelerometers, geo-location and other sensors into mobile devices and the current generation of game controllers that afford gestural interaction, either via controllers (as in the Wii-mote) or through tracking (as in the Kinect).

A relevant case study for this first vector is Toni Dove's *Artificial Changelings* (1995–2000). Dove's interactive movie installation tracked the viewer's location on four zones of the floor in front of a large screen, which determined relations between the viewer and the movie's protagonist. It also tracked the user's bodily movements using motion-sensing technology. Bodily movement had a range of effects: triggering character speech, changing the emotional tone of the sound environment or moving the character's body (Dove, n.d.). Dove's aim was to create an experience in which "the viewer haunts the movie as traces of their movement appear in the character on the screen." In an interview, Dove explained that her motivation was to explore embodiment in relation to technology because: "the explosion of interest around issues of the body is related to that anxiety about the disappearance of the body within the technical sphere" (Jennings, 1995). Dove's installation is an exploration of the apparatus potentials of embodiment, which begins to articulate some of the wider dispositif-related questions arising from this apparatus, including (in her linking of body movement and emotional tone) the next vector.

5.2 The Affective Turn

The second vector is partly based on the first, and can be termed the *affective turn*. A range of hardware devices and software paradigms are able to capture more of these embodied aspects of userly performance that were not considered relevant for the PC's intellectual worker and to extract the user's emotional or affective states.

Several interactive storytelling projects have used this approach: *Office Voodoo* (Lew, 2003) used accelerometers embedded in dolls to input affective user gesture information to a drama management engine. The project used two dolls, each affecting the mood states of one of two characters in a video-based office sitcom. The dolls could be manipulated by two users—itself an interesting deviation from the PC dispositif; while most consoles afford two colocated players, games usually afford competition rather than expressive dialogue. The authors have used a similar approach using gestures on a touch screen to harness a user's affective gestures to affect the mood of a storyteller character (Dekel et al., 2003; Knoller, 2004). While mainstream gestural interaction on tablets and smartphones is essentially semantic (replacing menu commands), both early projects attempted to afford affective, expressive user input.

Several later affective projects use more advanced forms of physiological interfaces to drive story experiences. These include *Heartbeats* (2004), Pia Tikka's *Enactive Cinema* approach (2008) and *Unsound—Thief in the Night* (2011). Enactive cinema, specifically, is an interesting case for our discussion of agency because its interactivity is passive: it does not rely on intentional userly performance but rather on involuntary physiological responses.

A special case that bucks the vector of the bodily turn is that of projects that use Brain Computer Interfaces (BCI) such as *Parkour Heroes* (2012), Alexis Kirke's *Many Worlds* (2013)[10] and *Pinter* (Gilroy et al., 2013). BCI apparatuses, from the consumer-grade Emotiv helmet to functional magnetic resonance imaging (fMRI), also support both active and passive strategies. The active strategy uses BCI as yet another way to engage users in interactive environments, whereas the passive strategy attempts to achieve narrative adaptation (Gilroy et al., 2012) according to individual physiological or brain activity data.

5.3 Ubiquity and Cross-Device Integration

A third vector is the ubiquity and increasing integration of computing devices: this makes it possible to integrate user experiences across platforms and devices, what Henry Jenkins (2006) has called "media convergence," which now also extends computation to nondigital objects through embedded sensors, RFID chips, QR codes or designated IP addresses (the Internet of things) and imbues space and nondigital objects with layers of data that can be accessed through geo-location-based services and augmented reality. At the same time, such services can, and often do, register and store traces of the user's own geo-location and interactions. This vector also changes the relation between computing and bodies, unshackling the user from the desktop and allowing computational experiences to proceed across space and time. *Fort McMoney* makes use of this affordance: it is possible to access it through multiple devices and platforms.

5.4 Prediction by Attentive Interfaces

A fourth vector is the increasing use of algorithms that predict userly performance, and it is exemplified by the transition from relatively straightforward functions such as auto-completion of search term entries and auto-correction of typing to suggestive 'cards' on smartphone that push functionalities the user might need but has not asked for. This vector is the software manifestation of a combination of a rhetoric of usability and an *urgent need* to structure and guide userly performance, which will be explored more fully in the next vector. A good example of the rhetoric of usability is the following claim made a decade ago: "AUIs (Attentive User Interfaces) may measure and model the focus and priorities of their user's attention. They structure their communication such that the limited resource of user attention is allocated optimally across the user's tasks" (Vertegaal, 2003). This is the sanguine language of the PC dispositif. However, in the post-PC present, the vector is often that of an increasing agency of algorithms, taking their own initiative in their interaction with humans, or more precisely act here as proxies to fulfil the urgent needs (marketing requirements) of their proprietors.

5.5 The User Experience Economy

Whereas the first four vectors describe changes in the apparatuses, the fifth vector, which binds these together, exists at the level of the dispositif and describes the business and economic concerns that organise them. This vector can be seen in the shifting focus in the design of digital artefacts from interface design—centring on the artefact through interaction design that involves the mainly cognitive processes of interaction—to a totalising 'user experience' design. This can be seen as a response to an *urgent need*—the economic demand of an 'experience economy,' itself a late stage of postindustrial economies (moving on from an economy based on either goods or services). This vector also reframes our discussion of agency.

Whereas Engelbart's vision of computing was designed to create value for an intellectual worker, the business models of corporations involved in the manufacture and sale of post-PC devices, software and media content depend not just on the production side but rather on manufacturing demand for (the consumption of) products, services and experiences. This is evident in the interface design of tablets and smartphones, which are not ergonomically suitable for prolonged typing, for instance. Their role in the experience economy seems to be as experiential devices for the consumption rather than the production of media experiences, from e-books to music (videos) to gaming and, recently, interactive storytelling apps.

Edward Bernays, Sigmund Freud's American nephew, revolutionised the world's economy by applying his uncle's theories in the service of business through advertising (Curtis, 2002). By appealing to deep human desires and associating the purchasing of specific products with the satisfaction of these desires, Bernays created the psychological engine driving consumerism. However, this engine requires constant updating as consumers become savvier about advertising tactics and resist them. Business models thus hinge on updating and optimising this psychological engine to help advertisers manufacture desires that motivate demand and drive advertisement revenues.

Through increased powers of registration (or *capture*, to use Agamben's (2009) term) built into the operating systems of our various integrated devices and the corporate walled gardens (and apple orchards) that have come to dominate the post destination-web Internet (Rossiter and Zehle, forthcoming), the gardeners now have much greater powers. They accumulate big data made up of all aspects of our userly performance, construct interfaces and build algorithms, the underlying logic of which is to guide our desires towards faster, more relevant fulfilment, ideally culminating in purchasing decisions. A good illustration of that is a recent patent granted to Google for emotion detection by a gaze-tracking camera mounted on glasses. According to this patent, emotions are inferred from pupil dilation and can be correlated with the object the user is gazing at, producing information that "includes the tendency of a given advertisement to draw user gazes or to hold the user gazes" and "the tendency of a given advertisement to evoke an emotional response" (Neven, 2013). This data can be registered and correlated with data from other users and sold (in anonymised and batched form) as analytical information to advertisers. This is experience design, offering users a better experience, offering up optimised users.

Since, in accordance with the third vector, these devices are not confined spatially or temporally, they can afford consumption anytime, anywhere. They have many more opportunities to structure userly performance itself in many more contexts—and these contexts therefore are permeated with the active, demanding presence of these devices. As Agamben predicted: "He who lets himself be captured by the cellular telephone apparatus—whatever the intensity of the desire that has driven him—cannot acquire a new subjectivity, but only a number through which he can, eventually, be controlled" (Agamben, 2009, p. 21, quoted in Zehle, 2012, p. 345).

5.6 Agency and the Post-PC Dispositif

The post-PC dispositif requires an optimised user who is willing to perform gestures and allow these to be captured. It requires a more affective and less cognitive subject, a communicator, a consumer, a player rather than a producer; a performing user.

How much individuality is left in this user whose every intentional utterance and action, as well as every unintentional corporeal expression, is captured by an interface, registered in databases, compared with all others and normalised to a scale (thereby undergoing homogenisation)—and then fed back in an attempt to discipline and optimise userly performance towards proper consumerist behaviour? How much agency is there in a user whose unconscious and subconscious desires (those that motivate decisions and actions) are manufactured by empowered advertisers?

The notion of a user whose agency is premised on decisions and choices is thus no longer in sync with the current dispositif. It is PC gone mad. We may briefly be led to narcissistically believe that we command this strange 7 to 10 inch dance hall with our gesticulating fingertips, but in fact it is also we who are controlled. Because post-PC apparatuses can predict the user's intentions (and in the future, perhaps, even desires) before they actually become intentions, and because they can detect our emotions and take initiative (and because the dispositif mandates this as socially legitimate and economically desirable), current interfaces progressively subvert the notion of user agency altogether. Human-computer interaction now often takes place at the initiative of computers, whose algorithms try to predict userly performance and contain agency and free will within controllable margins of error (Nunes, 2010), promising to enhance user experience.

6. CONCLUSION: IDN IN THE POST-PC DISPOSITIF

What are the implications of the new relations of the post-PC dispositif on IDN?

First, the proliferation of apparatuses and storytelling methods has undermined traditional schemata of communication between authors and audiences. This remains a challenge to authors who have to factor into their interface design and storytelling methods the disruption of the user's comprehension due to the fact that the user has to comprehend, at the same time, both the apparatus and the storyworld.

Second, a new understanding of user agency in IDN has to take into account that intentionality in the form of decisions and choices is only part of what is relevant in userly performance. The unintentional, subconscious and unconscious aspects of userly performance, which have become part of the relationship between humans and computers in the experience economy, need to be dealt with critically also in IDN theory and practice.

Finally, with a media dispositif that can respond to our location and gestures, predict some of our behaviours, intentions, emotions, needs and desires; where the media are watching (and registering) our userly performance as much and even more than we are watching them; and where the representation of space is now spilling out of the computer/screen and into the physical world, fusing reality and artificiality, meshing bits and atoms and allowing story experiences to cross platforms and embed themselves into everything in our surroundings; with this dispositif, the Holodeck is not a future version of the white cube gallery or the black auditorium cinema. It's already here, and it's all around us.

NOTES

1. WIMP—Windows, Icons, Menus and Pointers; GUI—Graphical User Interface.
2. The distribution of the sensible is the way modes of perception are established and then condition places and forms of participation in a common world.
3. This term is applied here anachronistically.
4. According to Bruce Kawin (1984), Castle only pretended to count the votes, always declaring the outcome to be against the villain.
5. For an extended discussion, see (Knoller, 2010, 2012).
6. An augmented reality implementation of *Façade* was attempted later (Dow et al. 2006) but must remain outside the scope of this chapter.
7. On the 1987 TV series *Star-Trek the Next Generation*, the Holodeck depicted a fully immersive and interactive holographic simulation that offered an individually tailored narrative experience.
8. There were a few exceptions, such as Aylett et al.'s use of a CAVE system for *FearNot!*
9. This was the title of the 2010 inauguration symposium of Amsterdam University's Interface studies group at the now defunct Dutch Institute for Media Arts http://mediasculptures.o94.at/?p=868
10. *Many Worlds'* interface combines physiological response signals and brain activity measurements.

REFERENCES

Agamben, G. (2009) *What is an Apparatus? and Other Essays*. Stanford: Stanford University Press.

Aylett, R. S., Louchart, S., Dias, J., Paiva, A., and Vala, M. (2005) 'FearNot!—An experiment in emergent narrative. In: Panayiotopoulos, T. et al. (eds.) *Intelligent Virtual Agents*. Heidelberg: Springer Verlag.

Bates, J. (1992) *OZ project*. [Computer Program]. Pittsburgh: School of Computer Science, Carnegie Mellon University.

Baudry, J. L. (1975) Le Dispositif. *Communications*. 23(1). pp. 56–72.

Baudry, J. L. and Williams A. (1974) Ideological effects of the basic cinematographic apparatus. *Film Quarterly*. 28(2). pp. 39–47.

Ben-Arie, U. (2009) The narrative-communication structure in interactivenarrative works. In: Iurgel, I. A., Zagalo, N., and Petta, P. (eds.) *Interactive Storytelling*. Heidelberg: Springer Verlag.

Biocca, F. (1997) The cyborg's dilemma: Embodiment in virtual environments. *Journal of Computer-Mediated Communication*. 3(2). pp. 12–26.

Bordewijk, J. L. and Van Kaam, B. (1986) Towards a new classification of tele-information services. Reprinted in: Wardrip-Fruin, N. and Montfort, N. (eds.) (2003) *The New Media Reader*. Cambridge, MA: MIT Press.

Bordwell, D. (1985) *Narration in the Fiction Film*. Madison, WI: University of Wisconsin Press.

Boyd, D. (2007) Why Youth (heart) Social Network Sites: The role of networked publics in teenage social life. In: Buckingham, D. (ed.) *MacArthur Foundation Series on Digital Learning—Youth, Identity, and Digital Media Volume*. Cambridge, MA: MIT Press.

Brey, P. (2008) Virtual reality and computer simulation. In: Himma, K. E. and Tavani, H. T. (eds.) *The Handbook of Information and Computer Ethics*. Hoboken, New Jersey and simultaneously in Canada: John Wiley and Sons.

Bristow, N. and Morrison, G. (2011) *Unsound*. [Biosuite Film]. Belfast, UK: Filmtrip.

Carroll, J. M. (2009) Human computer interaction—a brief intro. In: Soegaard, Mads, and Dam, R. F. (eds.) *The Encyclopedia of Human-Computer Interaction*. Aarhus, Denmark: The Interaction Design Foundation.

Castle, W. (1961) *Mr. Sardonicus*. [Cinema]. USA: Columbia Pictures.

Curtis, A. (2002) *The Century of The Self*. Happiness Machines. [Documentary Feature] London, UK: BBC.

Činčera, R. (1967) *A Man and his Home*. [Kinoautomat Film]. Expo '67, Montreal.

Dekel, A., Knoller, N., Ben-Arie, U., Lotan, M., and Tal, M. (2003) One measure of happiness—A dynamically updated interactive video narrative using gestures. In: Rauterberg, M. et al. (eds.) *Human-Computer Interaction INTERACT '03*. Amsterdam: IOS Press and IFIP.

Dove, T. (1995–2000) *Artificial Changelings*. [Interactive video installation]. RotterdamInternational Film Festival, Rotterdam, the Netherlands.

Dove, T. undated online video documentation of Artificial Changelings. http://tdove.lucidpossession.com/ac1.html

Dow, S., Mehta, M., Lausier, A., MacIntyre, B., and Mateas, M. (2006, June). Initial lessons from AR Façade, an interactive augmented reality drama. In *Proceedings of the 2006 ACM SIGCHI International Conference on Advances in Computer Entertainment Technology* (p. 28). ACM.

Dufresne, D. (2013–2014) *Fort McMoney*. [Online interactive video-game]. Available at: http://www.fortmcmoney.com

Engelbart, D. C. (2001) Augmenting human intellect: a conceptual framework (1962). Packer, R. and Jordan, K. *Multimedia. From Wagner to Virtual Reality*. New York: W.W. Norton & Company, pp. 64–90.

Foucault, M. (1977) *Discipline and Punish: The Birth of the Prison*. Translated from the French by A. Sheridan. New York: Vintage.

Foucault, M. (1980) The Confessions of the Flesh. In: Gordon, C. (ed.) *Power/knowledge: Selected Interviews and Other Writings*. New York: Pantheon.

Gilroy, S., Porteous, J., Charles, F., and Cavazza, M. (2012) Exploring passive user interaction for adaptive narratives. In: *Proceedings of the 2012 ACM International Conference on Intelligent User Interfaces*. Lisbon, Portugal, 14–17 February 2012. New York: ACM, pp. 119–128.

Gilroy, S. W., Porteous, J., Charles, F., Cavazza, M., Soreq, E., Raz, G., Ikar L., Or-Borichov, A., Ben-Arie, U., Klovatch I., and Hendler, T. (2013) A brain-computer interface to a plan-based narrative. In *Proceedings of the Twenty-Third International Joint Conference on Artificial Intelligence*. Beijing, China, 3–9 August 2013. AAAI Press, pp. 1997–2005.

Jameson, F. (1991) *Postmodernism, or the Cultural Logic of Late Capitalism*. Durham: Duke University Press.

Jenkins, H. (2006) *Convergence Culture: Where Old and New Media Collide*. New York: NYU Press.

Jennings, P. (1995) Interpretation of the electronic landscape: Conversation with Toni Dove. *Felix*. [Online] 2(1). Available at: http://www.e-felix.org/issue4/electronic.html

Kawin, B. (1984) An outline of film voices. *Film Quarterly*. 38(2). pp. 38–46.

Kirke, A. (2013) *Many Worlds*. [Interactive Film]. First Performed 23rd February. Peninsula Arts Contemporary Music Festival, Plymouth University, Plymouth, UK.

Knoller, N. (2004) InterFace portraits: Communicative-expressive interaction with a character's mind. In *Proceedings of the 1st ACM Workshop on Story Representation, Mechanism and Context*. New York, 15th October 2004. New York: ACM, pp. 63–66.

Knoller, N. (2010) Agency and the art of interactive digital storytelling. In: Aylett et al. (eds.) *Interactive Storytelling*. Heidelberg: Springer Verlag.

Knoller, N. (2012) The expressive space of IDS-as-art. In: Oyarzun et al., (eds.) *Interactive Storytelling*. Heidelberg: Springer Verlag.

Lew, M. (2003) *Office Voodoo*. [Algorithmic Film]. Media Lab Europe, Dublin.

Mahi, A. (2011) *Parkour Heroes*. [Computer Program]. MyndPlay 2.1. London: MyndPlay.

Mateas, M. and Stern A. (2005) *Façade*. [Computer Program]. Portland, OR: Procedural Arts.

Murderous Decision (1991) ARD and ZDF.

Murray, J. (1997) *Hamlet on the Holodeck: The Future of Narrative in Cyberspace*. New York: Simon & Schuster/Free Press.

Neven, H. (2013) *Gaze Tracking System*, US patent 8,510,166.

Nunes, M. (2010) Error, noise, and potential: The outside of purpose. In: Nunes, M. (ed.) *Error, Glitch, Noise and Jam in New Media Cultures*. New York and London: Continuum.

Portugaly, O., Talithman D., and Younger, S. (2004) *Heartbeats*. [Interactive Video Installation]. WRO 05—International Media Art Biennale, Wroclaw.

Portugaly, O., Talithman D., and Younger, S. (2005) *Jumping Rope*. [Interactive Video Installation]. Ars Electronica, Linz.

Rancière, J. (2004) *The Politics of Aesthetics: The Distribution of the Sensible*. London: Continuum.

Rand, A. (1935) *Night of January 16th*. [Play]. First Produced 16th September, 1935. Ambassador Theatre, New York.

Rimmon-Kenan, S. (2002) *Narrative Fiction: Contemporary Poetics*. London and New York: Routledge Taylor and Francis.

Rossiter, N., and Zehle, S. (forthcoming 2014) Toward a politics of synonymity. In: Parker M., Cheney G., Fournier V. and Land C. (eds.) *Routledge Companion to Alternative Organization*, New York: Routledge.

Stiles, K. and Shanken, E. A. (2010) Missing in action: Agency and meaning in interactive art. In: Lovejoy, M., Paul, C., and Vesna, V. (eds.) *Context Providers:*

Conditions of Meaning in Digital art. Bristol, UK and Chicago, USA: Intellect Books.

Tikka, P. (2008) *Enactive Cinema: Simulatorium Eisensteinensis*. Helsinki: Series of University of Art and Design.

Vertegaal, R. (2003) Attentive user interfaces. *Communications of the ACM*. 46(3). pp. 30–33. New York: ACM.

Wiberg, M., Ishii, H., Dourish, P., Rosner, D., Vallgårda, A., Sundström, P., Kerridge, T. and Rolston, M. (2012) "Material interactions"—From atoms and bits to entangled practices. In: *CHI EA '12*. Austin, Texas, USA, 5–10 May 2012. New York: ACM.

Zehle, S. (2012) The autonomy of gesture: of lifestream logistics and playful profanations. *Distinktion: Scandinavian Journal of Social Theory*. 13(3). pp. 340–353.

Section II
IDN Theory

Introduction

The Evolution of Interactive Digital Narrative Theory

Hartmut Koenitz, Gabriele Ferri, Mads Haahr,
Diğdem Sezen and Tonguç İbrahim Sezen

The hybrid nature of interactive digital narratives—as narratives and procedural digital entities on software executed on computers—poses considerable challenges for analysis and categorisation. A further complication lies in the rapid evolvement of the underlying technologies for creation and dissemination as computing technology has developed dramatically in a very short time compared to the technologies fundamental for other forms of expression. The diverse characteristics of IDNs, their relatively young age as an academic subject and their continuous technical progress have made it difficult to formulate a shared theoretical approach. Furthermore, the hybrid nature of IDN deeply affects analysis and understanding as technical progress and theoretical advancement are intrinsically connected, and every perspective on this field needs to consider both components.

Several theoretical perspectives have been advanced in the past decades proposing different models to conceptualise IDNs: in this introduction, we will briefly trace some of the principal approaches formulated in the past years. To give structure to our initial overview, we isolate two theoretical topics traversing the entirety of the IDN field. As a first step, we will examine how in the 1980s and early 1990s several scholars debated on the most adequate formal model—from Aristotle, to Propp, to African storytelling—as a template for digital narratives. In the second half of this exploration, we will briefly retrace, beginning from the late 1990s, the ongoing discussion of the relationship and compatibility (or lack thereof) between the notions of narrativity and digital media.

FROM THE POETICS TO ARTIFICIAL INTELLIGENCE

As IDN began to be recognised as a subject suitable for academic research, one of the first issues to be addressed was the need for other better-known objects and theoretical approaches to compare with IDNs. Brenda Laurel's metaphor of "computers as theatre" (Laurel, 1986, 1991) has been one of the first and most discussed proposals in this sense. In the cultural and academic context of the 1980s and 1990s, Laurel stood at a peculiar crossroads, with a Ph.D. in theatre and performance studies but also with experience as practicing designer in the interactive digital industry, including the Atari Research Center, and as the editor of the first comprehensive Human-Computer Interface (HCI) guidelines for the Macintosh computer at Apple Computer, Inc. The variety of her competences helped her to identify several common traits between theatrical performance and HCI, and to introduce the study of these practices amongst scholars in the humanities. As she approached the relatively new field of IDN, Laurel chose to elaborate on a theoretical framework with its roots in Aristotle's Poetics—a well-known resource for practicing scriptwriters and drama scholars. Her seminal work *Computers as Theatre* (1991) begins by identifying similarities between theatrical authorship and HCI design before introducing a set of classically-inspired analytical categories. In synthesis, her proposal draws a parallel between producing a dramatic representation and authoring an interactive narrative—the theatrical stage is related to the computer screen, the script to the computer programme and the dramatic action to the experience of using computer software and hardware. Laurel's purpose was threefold: first, she proposed the metaphor of computers as theatre as an analytical framework; secondly, she tried to turn her descriptive system into operative guidelines for designers; and finally, she set guidelines as a criterion for evaluating the effectiveness of the user experience in an interactive system. The compelling nature of the "computers as theatre" metaphor and its interdisciplinary openings make it a foundational element for IDN studies. In addition to its theoretical contributions, Laurel's dialogue with different scholarly backgrounds and her introduction of narrative to a still predominantly technical field made it a seminal—albeit sometimes contested—text.

Laurel's theoretical work became one of the foundations for research in interactive drama at Carnegie Mellon University. Eventually, Michael Mateas (2001) expanded on this foundation to better accommodate the notion of agency. While agreeing with Laurel about the adequateness of the Poetics for describing noninteractive dramatic structures, Mateas foregrounds the description and practical implementation of agency in the phenomenological sense of affecting significant changes in the virtual world. To do so, he reinterprets the Aristotelian categories in terms of material and formal cause, aiming at a more prescriptive and structured model for agency. Interactors experience agency when the dramatic elements that are made available in the plot and that motivate the characters' actions are commensurate with the material constraints offered by the audio-visual, figurative elements of the system. In other words, the narrative elements offered to the user during an interactive experience should be coherent with the material opportunities for actions offered by the system. Vice versa, an imbalance between the two sides of this proportion results in a decrease in agency.

However, theoretical and prescriptive models inspired by Aristotle's Poetics were not unanimously accepted as other scholars also explored different possibilities. For instance, Pamela Jennings (1996) remarked how the Aristotelian framework consisted principally of rules for convenience and brevity in communicating ideas; this is a desirable rhetorical effect if an author wished to encourage linearity but, she argued, not a good model for interactive art. On the contrary, traditional African storytelling often adopts cyclical models and makes use of a different type of cause-effect relationships, with numerous crises and peaks and more than one climax. Furthermore, these folk traditions also accommodate interaction with the audience in the form of call and response and in terms of the narrator's reaction to the environment. For these reasons, Jennings judged the characteristics of African oral storytelling to be more coherent with the actual interaction patterns between humans and computers and, therefore, more suitable as a general theoretical model for IDN. More recently, Fox Harrell has argued along the same lines in his application of African diasporic orality traditions in his interactive poetry system *GRIOT* (2007). Harrell draws explicit parallels between the interactive nature of oral storytelling and the procedural affordance of IDN.

A third model, originating from the formalist study of folk tales was particularly influential in shaping computational approaches to storytelling. In his prominent work *The Morphology of Folktales* (1928), Russian folklorist Vladimir Propp documented a canonical structure of narrative functions appearing in similar order across several texts collected in a corpus. Commenting on the implications of his discovery, the Russian scholar was the first to mention how it would be conceivable to produce mechanically an infinite number of stories (Propp, 1928, p. 118). In the following decades, formalist narratology inspired several efforts at studying and actually implementing credible storytelling machines. Attempts at programming algorithms that recombine sets of narrative functions date back to the early 1960s and—much later, with the advent of more advanced artificial intelligence (AI) techniques—paved the way for contemporary story management software. The first report of a concrete attempt towards automatic story generation software is Alan Dundes (1965), Propp's first American translator, who details the work of his colleague Joseph Grimes implementing a rudimentary computer program capable of randomising sets of Proppian functions and recombining them to construct new storylines. Grimes' algorithm operated by randomly pairing characters and narrative functions and then concatenating them following the canonical order described by Propp in Russian folk tales. In this way, narrative emerges as the result of a computational process; however, user-facing interactivity does not yet enter the picture, leaving such systems outside the realm of IDN. In general, the earliest systems were simple recombinatory algorithms that could assemble and evaluate narrative sequences against different sets of guidelines. Although rudimentary, Grimes and Dundes' program was the first of a long series; in the following decades, several researchers iterated in the same concept and produced prototypes including *Talespin* (Meehan, 1976), *Universe* (Lebowitz, 1983), *Starship* (Dehn, 1989) and *Minstrel* (Turner, 1992). These first-generation generative systems created short written narratives every time the software was executed. Such texts, while formally adhering to Proppian morphology, could not be mistaken for genuine tales without first being radically rewritten and paraphrased, but they marked a very significant milestone for the practical application of narrative theories.

Aristotle and Propp might seem, at a first glance, quite distant from computer-mediated interactive digital narratives, but their theoretical frameworks have been productively adopted in IDN. Of course, relying on theoretical perspectives developed in the past has both positive and negative consequences. On the one hand, the reference to accepted theoretical authorities helped legitimise the subject and provided an accessible common ground with scholars from established fields of study. On the other hand, the continuous reference to established theories comes at the danger of foregrounding only the similarities with legacy forms, obscuring the view for original characteristics of IDNs and slowing the research on specific theoretical frameworks for interactive narratives.

THE TROUBLED RELATIONSHIP BETWEEN NARRATIVE AND INTERACTIVITY

How does the quality of being a narrative relate to interactivity? Is narrativity somehow media-specific, or is it a common trait to several expressive forms and practices? Earlier in this introduction, we discussed how the first scholars approaching the field of IDN tried to establish some comparability with established media. From the early 1990s onward, the tendency to trace IDN back to legacy forms diminishes. More researchers began to perceive interactive experiences not as ancillary but as at least worthy of separate consideration as phenomena within the space of narrative forms (Bolter, 1990; Landow, 1992), if not as fully autonomous entities (Murray, 1997). If this step in the evolution of IDN seemed to close some issues—as comparisons with more traditional forms were no longer dominant—it in fact opened another problematic point: if interactive narratives were to become an independent field, which relationship should exist between the two core concepts?

Like Brenda Laurel, Janet Murray, another key figure to examine for understanding the theoretical context surrounding IDNs, also combines a technical background with a strong grounding in the humanities, having worked as a systems programmer at IBM before earning a Ph.D. in English Literature from Harvard University. She describes how, while teaching at MIT, students showed her *Eliza* and *Zork*, and this experience made her realise the possibilities for storytelling in the new digital medium. A strong proponent of the relevance of interactive literary works, Murray believes that new developments in IDN might allow the emergence of innovative narrative forms. This perspective finds its most accomplished expression in her work *Hamlet on the Holodeck* (Murray, 1997). Through the metaphor of the *holodeck*—a fictional advanced entertainment technology from the Star Trek universe, which envelopes its audiences in believable dynamic narrative experiences—the book analyses the distinctive features of a fully interactive and immersive storytelling system. The holodeck metaphor and the related concept of cyberdrama are important in their argumentative function, as a speculative perspective from which to survey the landscape of digital media. In this way, Murray identifies four essential properties of computers as a narrative medium—procedural, participatory, spatial and encyclopaedic—valid for the description of both the hypothetical holodeck and today's systems. Procedurality refers to the ability to execute algorithmic rules independently, as digital media can enact realistic behaviours evaluating complex cause-and-effect sequences and simulating real-world phenomena. The participatory affordance describes the ability of computers to offer meaningful responses and create an interactive process that integrates the player/interactor. The spatial affordance describes the use of spatial metaphors to represent information and traverse the experience. Finally, the encyclopaedic affordance refers to digital media's ability to organise, index and retrieve vast amounts of information, allowing for unprecedented depth and breadth of narrative treatment.

If we compare ordinary linear texts and a hypothetical cyberdrama running on the holodeck, the four above-mentioned characteristics constitute the principal differences between the two. In particular, interactive experiences follow a procedural, flexible schema: what is enacted and represented does not follow strict predetermined scripts but complex sequences of conditional instructions. Procedural authorship refers to the practice of creating complex rule sets along with narrative contents. The art and craft of the "cyberbard" (Murray, 1997) is to find a balance between narrative content, methods to guide the interactor's engagement and freedom to explore the interactive system.

The compatibility between narrative and interaction, taken for granted until the end of the 1990s, was put into question by a newly-founded discipline named *ludology*. While the term *ludology* appears as early as 1982— as reported by Jesper Juul (2000)—it is the usage in the late 1990s that is specifically attributed to the study of games, in particular electronic ones, by Espen Aarseth (1997), Gonzalo Frasca (1999) and Markku Eskelinen (2001). The first publications of the ludological movement took a strong stance in opposition to the theoretical positions we have traced so far, marking a clear difference between narrating and interacting. As a formalist discipline, ludology specialised in the study of rule-based competitive elements specific to electronic play. Since its origin, ludology defined itself by opposition, emphasising its formal nature and its radical departure from neo-Aristotelian and neo-Proppian approaches. Amongst the first scholars to adhere to the ludological movement, Markku Eskelinen was especially critical of importing theoretical contributions from other fields, finding them inadequate for addressing the specific characteristics of play. One of the fundamental objectives of early ludological perspectives was eliminating narrative components from the analysis of digital interactions: "laying any emphasis on studying these kinds of marketing tools is just a waste of time and energy" (Eskelinen, 2001, p.4). The study of interactive and ludic experiences—argued Eskelinen—could not emerge as an autonomous discipline if it kept relying on notions such as narration, which he deemed too hastily imported into the field and a colonisation effort from literary studies that had to be rejected. To put it differently, the first ludologists sought the legitimisation of Game Studies as a fundamental objective by affirming its academic relevance and, most of all, theoretical independence. For these reasons, the ludological school has consistently criticised the use of literary, theatrical or film-based approaches for unduly shifting the focus away from the fundamental characteristics of digital play (rules and competition) to an analysis of its ancillary—or even absent—narrative components.

Reexamining the first decade of ludological theory and its polemic against narrative-focused game studies, it is quite surprising that semiotic and narratological contributions were almost completely absent. The American narratologist Marie-Laure Ryan (2001, 2004, 2006) constitutes a notable exception, as she is one of the most effective interlocutors in the debate, dispelling claims regarding the incompatibility between storytelling and interaction. Reacting to the ludological critiques of naive neo-Aristotelian and neo-Proppian narrative models, Ryan accepts some distinctions between storytelling and digital interactivity but, unlike ludologists such as Aarseth and Eskelinen, envisions a transmedia narratology instead of founding a new discipline. She proposes to revise the notion of narrative as a cognitive phenomenon that emerges during the interpretation of narrative texts and that is not necessarily linguistic, static and linear, expanding classical narratology—as theorised by Chatman (1978) and Prince (1987). This interpretation of narrative texts extends beyond the traditional boundaries of verbal texts and thus opens the discipline to the analysis of syncretic, audio-visual, interactive systems such as computer games and other digitally-mediated narrative experiences. Two argumentative moves frame this expansion. The first consists of revising the theoretical understanding of the concept of story, leading to broader boundaries for narrative and fiction; the second refutes some early ludological objections against the relevance of literary theory in relation to interactive practices. In transmedia narratology, narrativity is understood as a cognitive construct, a mental diagram detailing events, actors and the relationships between them. A story, in this sense, constitutes a cognitive representation in the same way a narrative text is but—unlike the latter—is not encoded in material signs and is not expressed in a tangible substance. Therefore, narrative discourses may be distinguished from other nonnarrative ones by the ability to evoke stories in an interpreter's mind. Following Jannidis' (2003) understanding of narrative discourse as a fuzzy set, Ryan prefers evaluating 'storiness' rather than distinguishing between stories and nonstories as binary categories. In this sense, storiness might be understood as a scalar property with increasingly stricter requirements from marginal cases to prototypes. This revised definition considers narrative to be every semiotic object—verbal or not—capable of evoking specific cognitive effects in its interpreters' minds. In other words, Ryan is proposing to separate linguistic phenomena from the quality of being a narrative, understood as a sort of cognitive template at work in many different media, including IDNs.

In the second part of this theoretical overview on the different approaches to IDN, we retraced the main perspectives on the relationship between being a narrative and being interactive. While earlier academic descriptions of such systems took for granted the compatibility of interaction and narration, we described how such connection is not automatic. Janet Murray proposes an enthusiastic approach towards interactive narratives, describing their potential and foreseeing an exciting future for this field while the early ludological movement called into question the relevance of narrative for interactive practices. Markku Eskelinen's first contributions explicitly rejected the relevance of any application of narrative in the analysis and practice of HCI. In the following years, the ludological position has changed significantly, moving towards a more inclusive stance. As a synthesis between these positions, we have finally presented Marie-Laure Ryan's proposal of narrativity as a cognitive construct, applicable indifferently to linear, interactive, verbal or other types of narrative artefacts. While the period of fundamental debates might be over, the constantly evolving field of interactive digital narrative presents opportunities for analytical treatment and novel approaches for years to come.

REFERENCES

Aarseth, E. (1997) *Cybertext*. Baltimore (MD): Johns Hopkins University Press.

Bolter, J. D. (1990) *Writing Space: The Computer in the History of Literacy*. Hillsdale, NJ: Lawrence Erlbaum Associates.

Chatman, S. (1978) *Story and Discourse*. Ithaca, NY: Cornell University Press.

Dehn, N. (1989) *Computer Story-Writing: The Role of Reconstructive and Dynamic Memory*. Ph.D. Thesis. New Haven, CT: Yale University.

Dundes, A. (1965) On computers and folktales. *Western Folklore*. 24. pp.185–189.

Eskelinen, M. (2001) The Gaming Situation. *Game Studies*. 1(1).

Frasca, G. (1999) Ludologia kohtaa narratologian. *Parnasso*, 3. English translation Ludology meets narratology: Similitudes and differences between (video) games and narrative. Available at: http://www.ludology.org

Harrell, D. F. (2007) GRIOT's tales of haints and seraphs: A computational narrative generation system. In: Wardrip-Fruin, N. and Harrigan, P. (eds.) Second Person: Role-Playing and Story in Games and Playable Media. Cambridge: MIT Press.

Jannidis, F. (2003) Narratology and the narrative. In Kindt, T. and Meister, J.C. (eds.) *What Is Narratology*. Berlin: de Gruyter.

Jennings, P. (1996) Narrative structures for new media: Towards a new definition. *Leonardo*. 29(5). pp. 345–350.

Juul, J. (2000) What computer games can and can't do. In *Proceedings of the Digital Arts and Culture Conference (DAC)*. Bergen: DAC.

Landow, G. (1992) *Hypertext: The Convergence of Contemporary Critical Theory and Technology*. Baltimore, MD: Johns Hopkins University Press.

Laurel, B. (1986) *Toward the Design of a Computer-Based Interactive Fantasy System*. PhD Thesis. Ohio State University.

Laurel, B. (1991) *Computers as Theatre*. New York: Addison Wesley.

Lebowitz, M. (1983) Creating a story-telling universe. In *Proceedings of the 8th International Joint Conference on Artificial Intelligence*, pp. 63–65.

Mateas, M. (2001) A preliminary poetics for interactive drama and games. *Digital Creativity*. 12 (3). pp. 140–152.

Meehan, J. (1976) *The Metanovel: Writing Stories by Computer*. PhD Thesis. New Haven, CT: Yale University.

Murray, J. (1997) *Hamlet on the Holodeck*. New York: Simon & Schuster/Free Press.

Prince, G. (1987) *The Dictionary of Narratology*. Lincoln, NE: University of Nebraska Press.

Propp, V. J. (1928) *Morfologija skazki*. Leningrad: Academia.

Ryan, M.-L. (2001) *Narrative as Virtual Reality: Immersion and Interactivity in Literature and Electronic Media*. Baltimore, MD: Johns Hopkins University Press.

Ryan, M.-L. (ed.) (2004) *Narrative Across Media. The Languages of Storytelling*. Lincoln, NE: University of Nebraska Press.

Ryan, M.-L. (2006) *Avatars of Story*. Minneapolis, MN: University of Minnesota Press.

Turner, S. (1992) *Minstrel: A Computer Model of Creativity and Storytelling*. PhD Thesis. University of California.

Weyhrauch, P. (1997) *Guiding Interactive Drama*. PhD Thesis. Carnegie Mellon University.

5 Narrative Structures in IDN Authoring and Analysis

Gabriele Ferri

1. CHALLENGING NARRATIVITY

The issues of narrativity and textuality have been discussed at large in literary criticism, narratology, semiotics and related disciplines, but the diffusion of Interactive Digital Narratives (IDNs) has recently challenged these concepts. In this respect, the field of IDN is fragmented and chaotic, with no agreement on whether, and how, such notions should be applied to interactive narrations. I will argue that a closer look at poststructuralist and pragmatist narrative theories can help in constructing a shared understanding and that, more generally, a framework based on semiotic categories is especially well-suited for creating an epistemological common ground between the multitude of approaches in this field.

Heading in the same direction as other current works, the perspective offered here understands IDNs as software-based systems that produce different outputs each time a user interacts with them. This particularity sets them apart from other types of noninteractive objects that remain stable across multiple manifestations. Leaving to others (Koenitz, 2015, this volume) the general description of the subdivision between a user-facing instance and a computer-oriented backend, this chapter will focus on contextualising some specific features of IDNs within a broader semiotic theory. Semiotics does not aim at making the already fragmented field of IDN even more complicated. On the contrary, I will argue how it is fit for supporting a multidisciplinary view of IDN by providing categories and analytical tools that are programmatically abstract, logical and media-independent. This chapter will focus on three main issues:

1 The notion of textuality is problematic when applied to IDN. Its revision will be split into two terms: a structuralist narrative semiotics will provide a model broad enough to accommodate the variable outputs of IDNs, and the more flexible notion of the interactive matrix will describe, at a logical level, the system preceding the enunciation of all actual outputs.

2 Different readings of 'being a narrative' and 'having a narration' raise theoretical issues, fragmenting the IDN field and disrupting the potential

for mutual understanding. Are IDNs narrative experiences? If so, how do they differ from linear narrations? A poststructuralist semiotic notion of narrativity as a shared model, valid across interactive and noninteractive systems, will help overcome this impasse.

3 Digital media artefacts seem to follow a variety of structures in their narrative development. Some are designed on Aristotelian models, others are based on folk tales, and yet others are much more experimental. Attempting to find a single, common Canonical Narrative Schema seems to crystallise the field. Instead, a flexible pragmatist framework will be proposed to accommodate a multitude of potential narrative schemas.

1.1 General Foundations for IDN

The semiotic framework for IDN detailed here aims at creating a theoretical common ground based on general, abstract and logical principles. Essentially, semiotics refers to the systematic study of signs, their possible uses, their classification and their role in social contexts. Umberto Eco (1976) distinguishes between *specific semiotics*, describing the organisation of particular systems such as linguistics, proxemics or iconography, and *general semiotics*, a more philosophical approach concerned with the emergence of meaning. The latter constructs schemas and shared categories to describe heterogeneous phenomena, and a common ground for IDN theory should be understood in this context. Programmatically, this semiotic contribution aims at being:

1 abstract and logical, providing generalisable models. In other words, it looks beyond the single example and its particular characteristics and it concentrates on finding more general similarities and differences across a wide corpus of data;

2 technologically agnostic, independent from specific implementations or platforms—to allow evaluations across different IDN systems without excluding future developments;

3 scalable, allowing the description of simple or complex activities regardless of their size or of the number of interactors taking part;

4 capable of giving useful insights to practitioners. While not intended as design tools, semiotic categories can inspire practitioners by highlighting relevant differences and points of view.

When comparing interactive and noninteractive storytelling, there is a risk of taking an ideological position and assuming the implicit superiority of one of the two sides. This contribution neither wishes to affirm a specific method over others, nor to present IDNs as superior over traditional arts. Quite the opposite, an agreement on a shared ground will strengthen different theoretical approaches by having fewer concerns about misunderstandings on terms, categories and analytical tools. Opposing new and legacy media is not the objective here: the overall intent is to reduce fragmentation by introducing broader concepts that can be adapted to diverse objects.

As with the majority of semiotic approaches, this contribution is mainly descriptive. However, it is important to stress how an analytical approach can bring additional benefits:

1 it complements, and not substitutes, prescriptive design methodologies;
2 it facilitates the understanding and the formalisation of IDNs, their assessment beyond quantitative parameters, their evaluation and their comparison;
3 it helps in opening an interdisciplinary dialogue by suggesting a common metalanguage.

The result of this process will not be another specific tool that adds up to theoretical fragmentation of this field, but three general concepts applicable to digital and nondigital objects. In this sense, the objective here is to complement existing analytical methods with a comprehensive frame accounting for meaning-making across media.

1.2 Early Literary Approaches

In previous decades, literary studies and criticism paid relatively little attention to interactive storytelling. At the same time, researchers and practitioners at the crossroad between IDN, narratology and HCI integrated formal and structural theories for describing and designing computer-mediated narrative experiences. Such formalisations were explored as descriptive and productive tools—in other words, as methods for analysis and as blueprints to follow in the implementation of narrative algorithms. The rationale for this approach was to model storytelling machines according to the processes that guided human narration and understanding. While this is not the place to trace a genealogy of narratology within the IDN field, two outstanding tendencies will be mentioned for the purposes of establishing a context.

A first research strand reinterprets Vladimir Propp's early formalist work *Morphology of Folktale* (1928). In his original work, Propp concentrated on the actions, called functions, of the main characters in folk tales and examined the sequential order in which they are collocated within a narration. He represented each narrated action by mapping it onto a specific function, such as *Departure, Villainy* or *Struggle*, each representing different concrete acts within the narrative: for instance, 'villainy' could stand for kidnappings, thefts, plunders or injuries. In the corpus, he observed that the order of those logical functions always remained constant—with the exception of elements repeated several times or those that were omitted. "The specific act does not matter as long as it contributes to plot progression and makes the next function in the syntagmatic chain emerge," clarifies Budniakiewicz (1978). This way, functions emerged as constants in the text and led Propp to formulate two related hypotheses. The main one is that any tale can be represented by a sequence of 31 functions which always occur in the same, relatively fixed consecutive order and—as a corollary to this—that it is possible to artificially create new plots of an unlimited number using this schema. Already in the 1920s, Propp imagined that:

> All of these plots will reflect a basic scheme, while they themselves may not resemble one another. In order to create a folktale artificially, one may take any A, one of the possible Bs, then a C, followed by absolutely any D, then an E, then one of the possible Fs, then any G, and so on. Here, any elements may be dropped (apart, actually, from A or a), or repeated three times, or repeated in various aspects.
>
> (Propp, 1928)

Following the worldwide diffusion of these concepts, several researchers since Dundes (1965) attempted to implement Proppian algorithms to produce new tales automatically. Post-Proppian approaches to IDN aimed—through different Artificial Intelligence techniques—at implementing functions, plot moves and spheres of action within interactive environments with computer-generated characters.

Brenda Laurel, in her important work *Computers as Theatre* (1991), has been one of the first scholars to explicitly draw a parallel between traditional humanities and interactive systems, between drama and computer-generated experiences. Her heterogeneous background, with academic training in performance studies and work experiences in HCI and game design, put her in a privileged position to formulate her famous metaphor aligning digital environments with theatrical representations—a suggestion that would spur much research, debate and criticism in subsequent years. Starting from this, Laurel proposes a set of notions for describing human-computer activities derived—with a more practical than strictly philological rationality—from Aristotle's Poetics and its rereadings in literary theories of theatre (Freytag, 1895) and in professional playwriting handbooks (Smiley, 1971). On one hand, she argues for her "computers as theatre" metaphor, adapting critical and analytical tools from performance studies to study digitally mediated interactions. On the other hand, Laurel attempts to shift the descriptive system she outlines towards a more prescriptive one, with operational design instructions and criteria for the evaluation of individual user experiences. Her foundational work, written in 1991, has been instrumental in opening the field of computational expressions to discussion in the humanities. However, her reliance on a neo-Aristotelian epistemology isolated her—and those who followed her trajectory—from a more current narratological and semiotic research community.

The two above-mentioned research directions—neo-Proppian and neo-Aristotelian—leave open some crucial questions. Are IDNs texts? In what sense are IDNs narrations? How do interactivity and procedurality relate to commonly accepted narrative schemata? Exploring the implications of these three questions is fundamental for a broader reframing of IDNs, and revisiting their common definitions will make a better shared framework possible. In the following sections, the argumentation will proceed first by examining current classifications of these terms within a semiotic view of noninteractive texts and then by comparing and adjusting it for describing IDNs and other digital texts.

2. FROM TEXTUALITY TO INTERACTIVE MATRICES

The procedural and interactive nature of software seems to be irreducibly at odds with classical definitions of text. The term '*text*' is sometimes used in a narrow sense, referring to static sequences to be interpreted or analysed. They can be verbal, either written or oral: in other words, a text can be constituted by signs—words or ideograms, for example—or by any other system able to convey meaning, such as symbols, rituals or works of art. The relevant condition is that they are concretely realised, existing in the world and not only in the virtual possibilities of a grammar. In this sense, texts are often considered as given and preexisting any analysis. In other words, novels, letters and movies are real whether someone perceives them or not, and they have definite, concrete boundaries in that the identification of any single text is possible through examination of a single part. IDNs, however, do not fit this narrow sense of textuality since such stability is not available—in IDNs, the output changes with each interaction.

A reductive approach could consider each output, each walkthrough, as a closed text by itself; such a minimalistic method would certainly be logical but not fully productive, as it would entail an exponential amount of texts to be considered for analysis. In other words, if we focus only on the great number of narrow texts produced by an IDN, we risk losing the general perspective on the system that produces them. Let us refer to Greimas and Courtés for a possible way out: "We already know," they argue, "that analysis always presupposes the choice of a level of pertinence and seeks to recognise only certain types of relation, excluding those which could just as well be determined" (1979). Since, within semiotics, analysts have control over the object and the scope ("the level of pertinence") of their inquiry, one could frame as text a complete novel or the narrative developments in a single chapter or in a series of interrelated books. To put it another way, the Paris school of Semiotics understands textuality not as *a priori* but as the result of strategic choices functional according to desired objectives, and each analysis pursues its own sets of objectives and requires different methods and framing for the analysed object. "The outcome of this is a new definition according to which a text is made up only of those semiotic elements fitting the theoretical goal of the description" (Greimas and Courtés, 1979). We have now arrived at a broader definition of textuality. Therefore, we can accept that the level of textual pertinence when analysing the output of an IDN is a collection of several instances generated by the same system. IDNs can enter the domain of textuality when framed appropriately by understanding texts not only as static, linguistic entities but also as objects the textuality of which is strategically constructed within analysis.

When considering textuality, there is a common misunderstanding that must be avoided. A semiotic approach shows how part of an IDN—the sum of all its outputs—could be framed textually, but IDNs are not entirely texts. So far, I have argued for a broader definition of textuality when applied to IDN, but at the same time the structuralist roots of the Paris school of semiotics view texts as static forms of expression and, thus, are in contrast with interactivity. Instead, the experiential part of an IDN must be understood together with a dynamic, algorithmic system that precedes the enunciation of any output. The two cannot be separated and need to be understood together. To address this problem, IDNs will be conceptualised here as interactive matrices (Ferri, 2007; Meneghelli, 2007): complex systems that can alter their appearance at run-time and react to user inputs by executing algorithmic rules. In other words, while the sum of all gameplay sessions can be understood as a text, the underlying system lacks stability in its expression, with the ability to enunciate different outputs as determined by the user's choices, software rules or simple probabilities. Moving past early narratological or structuralist formulations (Todorov, 1966; Greimas, 1970), matrices can be formalised as semiotic devices for the creation of a multiplicity of single textual occurrences. In other words, story-generation systems, as well as computer games, will be considered as matrices of possibilities that output a single, well-formed audio-visual text each time a player interacts with it. In this context, a matrix is a semiotic agglomerate existing before the formation of any single output and containing all the semantic, narrative and figurative resources that could possibly be actualised during its activity. It is a complex semiotic object comprising of different functions and different instances, such as victory-conditions, interfaces, links or semantic, procedural, figurative and strategic repertories.

3. BUILDING BLOCKS FOR DIGITAL NARRATIVITY

Are interactive systems narrative? Is storytelling an effect of an interactive system, or are IDNs programs that incidentally happen to be narrative? And how do IDNs compare to noninteractive narrations such as movies or novels? In this section, I will outline a general description of some logical components that are necessary for a narrative semiotic description of IDNs. In particular, a broader, more abstract and general notion of narrativity will be addressed. A promising model will follow a descriptive procedure common in narrative semiotics where three layers are considered: elements from deep semantic structures (abstract, logical organisations) are selected and converted into semi-narrative structures (a skeleton of actants) and, then, into discursive structures (with concrete, figurative and thematic elements). This schema is an analytical guideline for understanding how abstract concepts are articulated in concrete texts. In other words, such a model describes how different meaningful objects are interpreted: abstract concepts (e.g., good vs. evil) turn into narrative roles (e.g., protagonist vs. antagonist) and are made concrete with figurative elements (e.g., a hero with specific qualities vs. an equally detailed antihero). Narrativity constitutes the deepest, most general and abstract identifiable level of any text and the common layer for any meaningful artefact regardless of the medium adopted. In this sense, it should be intended as the logical baseline of every form of expression, and it can be described in highly abstract terms. Narrativity does not refer to 'having a narrative' or 'being a narrative' in the ordinary or literary sense of the term, but it is defined as the quality of every text to be formulated as a network of semantic oppositions and of actantial roles that change over time following a canonical schema. If we adopt this broad logical definition, as Compagno and Coppock remark:

> [E]very meaningful artefact or activity is then narrative in this abstract theoretical sense, and all cultural productions specify the way in which they determine how an interpreter is able to understand and respond to them (thus integrating these interpretations into his/her prior cultural knowledge base). If we agree on this notion of narrativity, then computer games cannot but be narrative.
>
> (Compagno and Coppock, 2009, p. 2)

Actants, actors and automata—crucial for a semiotic analysis—are part of a general narrative grammar (Greimas and Courtés, 1979) and are described as mutually defined positions to be filled during the course of a narrative. Actants do not always correspond to characters (actors) in the traditional sense of the term: an actor occupies a Subject actantial position when it is characterised by agency, competences, and desires; it occupies an Object position when it is acted upon; and it is in a Sender actantial position when it is defined by the transfer of knowledge, aims and tasks to a Subject. While actants are positions in an abstract network, actors are concrete entities occupying them; this way, actors are defined figuratively and thematically, as well as being situated in specific narrative programs. In addition to these general notions employed in all narrative semiotic analyses, the concept of automaton is specific to algorithmic media. An automaton is

> a neutral operator subject in possession of a group of explicit rules and an order requiring the application of these rules or the carrying out of instructions. The automaton is thus ... a simulacrum [that] can be used as a model either for the human subject carrying out a reproducible scientific activity, or for the construction of a machine.
>
> (Greimas and Courtés, 1979)

In general, automata are autonomous actors with some algorithmic programming capable of reacting to outer stimuli, such as a user's behaviour (Ferri, 2012). Drawing from logic and from computer sciences, an algorithm can be described as a well-defined computational procedure or a tool for solving a well-specified computational problem describing a specific procedure to achieve the desired input/output relationship.

To better understand narrativity in IDNs, let us now reconnect actants and automata to the interactive matrix model and imagine several different sessions within the same interactive system. In all likelihood, some items—the behaviour of computer-controlled characters, the narrative development, but also figurative elements such as animations in a video game—will appear in some instances but not in others. With regard to narratives, an interactive matrix does not contain only one plot, but it can generate a large number of actual narrative developments that cannot coexist in a single textual instance. In other words, a single textual output will contain a single plot determined by the user's actions, but the following session will generate a different one if other choices are made.

A matrix does not produce any text without a user, whose choices, strategies and actions select the instantiated elements and cause the automata's reactions; the generated plot is the direct effect of those choices and of the reactions of the system. This way, an interactive matrix can be understood as the place where the user's and the automata's actions converge and interact.

4. PAST A SINGLE CANONICAL NARRATIVE SCHEMA

Having introduced structuralist and poststructuralist definitions of textuality and narrativity, Greimasian semiotics has been useful by allowing a better comparison and differentiation between IDNs and other objects. In this respect, interactive matrices, automata and algorithms have extended the poststructuralist model to account for variability and interactivity in IDNs. However, this leads us to another issue that has its roots in Greimas' Canonical Narrative Schema, an invariant model the conventional formulation of which is at odds with the situated flexibility of IDNs. Greimasian theory assumes that readers have already read through the whole text and have a complete and full view of it; in other words, it theorises a closed, linear and manageable structure for meaning-making that leads to a *post hoc* perspective on narration. Such a perspective—while it can produce interesting analyses of linear media—is impractical and limiting when considering interactive systems. How can we have a full, complete and coherent understanding of a system that changes in response to the user's actions? The relevant part of experiencing an IDN is not a retrospective recollection but the situated experience of interacting with it.

As we already mentioned, the Paris school of semiotics assumed narrativity to be a constitutive component of any meaningful experience and developed a very articulate descriptive method to give an account of this fundamental narrative dimension in all possible domains of application. Starting from formalist studies of folktales, the constant repetition in the same order of three specific phases—first a qualifying test, then a decisive one and finally a glorifying test—across many narrative texts suggested to Greimas and his colleagues the existence of a narrative schema that is pervasive and universal. This "internal structure which assigns a general form to the action and which distributes a limited number of general roles to be played by the protagonists" (Bundgaard, 2007) constitutes the core of narration within the structuralist framework: the Canonical Narrative Schema (CNS), a "cultural grid of narrative organisation sedimented in the collective memory by tradition as a primitive" (Bertrand, 2000). Greimas and Courtés described it as

> constituting a kind of formal framework [in] three essential domains: the qualification of the subject, which introduces it into life—its "realisation," by means of which it "acts"—and finally the sanction—at one and the same time retribution and recognition—which alone guarantees the meaning of its actions and installs it as a subject of being. This schema is sufficiently general to allow for all variations upon the theme: considered on a more abstract level and broken down into trajectories, it aids in articulating and interpreting different types of cognitive as well as pragmatic activities.
>
> (Greimas and Courtés, 1979)

In its recent formulation, the CNS is composed by three phases— manipulation, action, and sanction—that give an account of the emergence and of the articulation of any signification (not only verbal). These phases are not only able to promote narrative performances but also to articulate the different forms of the discursive competence. The CNS aims for a straightforward narration and a stable skeleton of roles. As it has already been argued, "what the schema does not consider is the constitutive instability of human actions ..., the openness of meaning-construction processes, the inextricable mixture of the story and the practice that constructs it" (Ferri and Fusaroli, 2009). In other words, using a canonical narrative schema seems to make an abstraction of the continuous flow of meaning in which human beings are immersed.

If, instead, we consider a situated experience with coexisting interpretations and open hypotheses—such as playing with an IDN—without positioning the reader at the end of the narrative, it is almost impossible to give structure to a well-formed skeleton of actantial roles. Interactors formulate open questions, try to validate interpretive hypotheses and are often surprised by unexpected developments. This position is particularly uneasy, as several schools of narratology and literary criticism have proposed general schemata and diagrams to conceptualise the way narratives unfold: from neo-Aristotelian models, to Propp's sequence of functions, to the CNS. In their standard forms, such diagrams are indeed very difficult to apply to describe interactive experiences for several reasons, the principal of which is their constitutive multilinearity. Yet, canonical schemata are also cultural constructs, sedimented in society and well-known to readers: In other words, the tendency to follow certain storytelling structures may be expected by users due to their competences with other narrative experiences. How is it possible to reconcile the socially shared expectation for a relatively standard narrative unfolding with interactivity, multilinearity and agency?

4.1 Towards Multiple Narrative Schemata

A different approach may yield results that are more general and contribute to reducing this current sense of fragmentation. Let us open this conclusive section by examining briefly a few examples of narrative structures in digital experiences. Narrative development in the well-known IDN *Façade* closely follows Aristotelian drama:

> There is unity of time and space—all action takes place in an apartment—and the overall event structure is modulated to align to a well-formed Aristotelian tension arc, i.e. inciting incident, rising tension, crisis, climax, and denouement, independent of the details of exactly what events occur in any one run-through of the experience.
>
> (Mateas and Stern, 2005)

Other titles, however, show opposing approaches. For instance, the authors of *Breaking Points* describe their piece as

> partly inspired by time-loop stories like the movie Groundhog Day ... where a nameless heroine is indeed trapped ...—everyday she follows the same routine: she ... repeats the same actions at work and returns to her apartment alone ... On this backdrop, the narrative explores a rich amount of variations in her daily life ... and tracks her progress and mood between hope and desperation.
>
> (Koenitz, Sezen and Sezen, 2013)

Furthermore, the successful video game series *The Sims* (2003) takes yet another direction, providing players with an open space without explicit narrative constraints where they can develop—to whatever extent they desire—stories with their characters. All three of these examples present narrative structures—particularly if we accept the broad semiotic notion of narrativity discussed before—but we struggle to fit them in the mould of a Canonical Narrative Schema, particularly the last two. Arguing that *Façade* is a well-formed narration while *Breaking Points* and *The Sims* are not is not convincing and would reinforce the current fragmentation in the IDN field. To conclude this section, a different point of view drawing from Pragmatist Semiotics—a framework adopted, amongst other fields, in cognitive narratology—will be presented. An innovative and rich notion of what a sign is occupied the great majority of Peirce's thinking (1931–1958): I will argue that his work on expectations and tendencies can lead to a different basis for describing interactive narratives that is flexible enough to resolve the issues described so far and to synthesise a middle ground amongst the various perspectives.

Peirce developed an abstract framework where thoughts, perceptions and cognitive activities are all semiotic concepts and are understood as relations connecting an entity (a sign, an object, or a thought ...) to a different sign—called the *interpretant*—through the construction of a common ground, or a point of view. In other words, each possible object, thought, action or perception is a sign standing for other signs for an interpreter. A first example: the word *red* stands for the perception of a particular wavelength through the eyes, and then refers to a chain of cognitive actions—all of which are, in Peirce's pragmatism, signs. In his later years, Peirce reflected on the notion of interpretant—the second sign produced by the interpreter from the first sign through the mediation of a common ground. His conception of meaning has continuity at its core and the possibility of passing from one semiotic entity to another. He defines the pragmatic meaning of a sign as the subject's disposition to act in a certain way, to think certain things or to produce certain other signs: it is not a shapeless continuum where everything can be connected in any circumstance to everything else. Continuity has a structure, and the passage from an object to an interpretant is made possible by a habit—either already established or emerging. Now let us go back to the previous example. While driving a car, an interpreter perceives a red light, which stands for a sequence of cognitive activities that culminates with the pragmatic action of stopping at a traffic light. Therefore, the meaning of a sign in this version of pragmatist semiotics is the final, or logical, interpretant: the habit to act, or interpret, in certain ways in specific circumstances.

The pragmatist notion of habit is not just a philosophical speculation but has very concrete applications if we assume that the meaning of a sign is a disposition to act, we could postulate and exemplify that the meaning of a red traffic light is the general tendency for drivers to stop their cars and for pedestrians to cross the road. But—as road accidents sadly remind us—these are not rigid rules. Two features are of particular interest here: what emerges from Peirce's semiotics is a strong focus on similarity and not sameness, as habits are regularities and not algorithmic rules. The second crucial feature is Peirce's surprisingly modern view on cognition. As signs are always situated in a continuum of interpretation, perception and action, habits are constituted and reinforced through interaction and shaped by social and cultural structures:

> [T]he habit is thus a structure of cognition in the distributed conception of the term, it needs the support of a text, the enaction through an interpreting disposition, and the repetition and integration by a culture to exist.
>
> (Ferri and Fusaroli, 2009)

Let us now return to the different narrative schemas exemplified in the three short examples presented above: rethinking them in terms of habits, not as *a priori* universals, allows us to accommodate the dynamicity and the specific traits of digital storytelling. Canonical schemas cease to be *a priori* models and emerge as sets of flexible and culturally situated dispositions. For instance, *Façade* is particularly attuned to Western readers who usually expect narratives with a beginning, a development and an end linked by cause-effect relations but, as *Breaking Points* and *The Sims* exemplify, this is not always the case. Instead of fragmenting the field between seemingly incompatible schemas—such as Aristotelian plots, Proppian fairy tales or structuralist narratological models—Peircean semiotics understands them as different contextual tendencies to expect and perceive narrations in certain ways. As digital narratives are even more malleable than their linear counterparts, different models might not be mutually exclusive if we stop arguing for their universality.

4.2 In Conclusion: Shared Foundations for Specific Models

A simple understanding of narrativity and textuality has proven ambiguous and problematic when applied to IDN, as exemplified by the fact that each IDN session might be completely different. From that standpoint, two directions were possible: we could have either argued for the radical separation of unilinear and multilinear narratives on the ground of their textual differences; or we could have looked past their technical and formal differences and highlighted their points of contact. The three contributions outlined—a broader textuality, leading to a more general narrativity and then to a multiplicity of narrative schemata—went in the direction of a common ground for comparing static and interactive narratives. Should this general and deeply abstract semiotic view replace media-specific, technologically grounded analyses? Eco's subdivision between General Semiotics and Specific Semiotics suggests that the answer is no. This chapter has outlined three general elements shared by IDNs and unilinear narrations without proposing a reductionist thesis, as the many technological and ontological differences between digital and nondigital narratives remain crucial.

Broad textuality, narrativity and a plurality of flexible narrative schemata are abstract concepts that can be part of the foundations over which specific models for different digital artefacts can be built while remaining compatible with each other.

REFERENCES

Bertrand, D. (2000) *Precis de Semiotique Litteraire*. Paris: Hachette.

Budniakiewicz, T. (1978) A conceptual survey of narrative semiotics. *Dispositio*. 7/8. pp. 189–217.

Bundgaard, P. F. (2007) The cognitive import of the narrative schema, *Semiotica*. 165. pp. 247–261.

Coppock, P. and Compagno, D. (eds.) (2009) *Computer Games Between Text and Practice*. AISS.

Dundes, A. (1965) On computers and folk tales. *Western Folklore*. 24(3). pp. 185–189.

Eco, U. (1976) *A Theory of Semiotics*. Bloomington: Indiana University Press.

Electronic Arts (2003) *The Sims* [computer game: PC]. London: Electronic Arts Inc.

Ferri, G. (2007) Narrating machines and interactive matrices: a semiotic common ground for game studies. In *Situated Play, Proceedings of DiGRA 2007 Conference*. Tokyo: University of Tokyo Press.

Ferri, G. (2012) Between procedures and computer games: semiotics of practices as a unifying perspective. In *Proceedings of the 10th World Congress of the International Association for Semiotic Studies*. La Coruña: Universidade da Coruña.

Ferri, G., and Fusaroli, R. (2009) Which narrations for persuasive technologies? Habits and procedures in Ayiti: The cost of life. In *AAAI Spring Symposium: Intelligent Narrative Technologies II*. Stanford: AAAI Press.p

Freytag, G. (1895) *Technique of the Drama: An Exposition of Dramatic Composition and Art*. S. Griggs.

Greimas, A. J. (1970) *Du Sens*. Paris: Seuil.

Greimas, A. J. and Courtés, J. (1979) *Sémiotique. Dictionnaire Raisonné de la Théorie du Langage*. Paris: Hachette.

Koenitz, H., Sezen, T. I., and Sezen, D. (2013) Breaking points—A continuously developing interactive digital narrative. In: Koenitz, H., Sezen, T. I., Ferri, G., Haahr, M., Sezen, D., Çatak, G. (eds.) *Interactive Storytelling*. Heidelberg: Springer.

Koenitz, H. (2014) Towards a specific theory of interactive digital narrative. In: Koenitz, H., Haahr, M., Ferri, G., Sezen, T. I., and Sezen, D. (eds.) *Interactive Digital Narrative: History, Theory and Practice*. London: Routledge.

Koenitz, H., Sezen, T. I., and Sezen, D. (2014) *Breaking Points* [software]. Available at: https://itunes.apple.com/us/app/breaking-points/id839314877?mt=8

Laurel, B. (1991) *Computers as Theatre*. New York: Addison Wesley.

Mateas, M., and Stern, A. (2005) Procedural authorship: A case-study of the interactive drama Façade. In *Proceedings of the Digital Arts and Culture Conference*. Copenhagen: IT University.

Meneghelli, A. (2007) *Dentro lo Schermo*. Milano: Unicopli.

Peirce, C. S. (1931–1958) *Collected Papers of Charles Sanders Peirce*. Cambridge, MA: Belknap Press.

Procedural Arts (2005) *Façade* [computer game: PC]. Procedural Arts Inc.

Propp, V. J. (1928) *Morfologija Skazki*. Leningrad: Academia.

Smiley, S. (1971) *Playwriting: The Structure of Action*. Englewood Cliffs, NJ: Prentice-Hall.

Todorov, T., (ed.) (1966) *Théorie de la Littérature, Textes des Formalistes Russes*. Paris: Seuil.

6 Towards a Specific Theory of Interactive Digital Narrative

Hartmut Koenitz

Interactive digital narrative (IDN) challenges basic assumptions about narrative in the western world—namely about the role of the author and the fixed state of content and structure as the audience takes on an active role and the narratives become malleable.[1] It seems quite clear that narrative theory—as is—cannot fully account for these changed conditions. Many scholars have reacted to these challenges by adapting established narrative theories. This approach has clear advantages as terms, categories, and methods of analysis are already well understood. On the other hand, analysing IDN with theoretical frameworks created to describe narrative in traditional media carries the risk of misunderstanding the nature of the change. In this regard, Espen Aarseth rightfully warns of the danger of "theoretical imperialism" (1997, p. 16). For example, once we focus on similarities with ancient Greek stage play we can become overly wedded to the framework of Aristotle's *Poetics* and prone to disregard aspects that do not fit that particular frame of reference. A more fully developed theory of digital interactive narrative should be careful to avoid such theoretical pitfalls. Before sketching out a specific theoretical framework for IDN, I will analyse several existing theoretical perspectives to foreground the scope and focus of earlier contributions and investigate which aspects are not fully covered yet.

1. CONSTITUENTS OF IDN

A prerequisite for the analysis in this chapter are definitions of the key terms *digital media*, *interactivity*, and *narrative*. Brenda Laurel first recognised the expressive potential of digital computers as an interactive, representational medium (1991) on equal grounds with electronic media and print. Janet Murray (1997) delivers the next important step by describing *procedural*, *participatory*, *spatial* and *encyclopedic* affordances—the essential characteristics—and *agency*, *immersion* and *transformation*—what users experience during the interaction. Together, the *procedural* (the computer's ability to execute a set of rules [p. 71]) and *participatory* (the ability to react to user input) affordances describe the phenomenon of interactivity. The *spatial* affordance denotes the ability of computers to represent space, while *encyclopedic* describes the computer's ability to represent huge amounts of data.

Murray then defines the phenomenological categories of agency, immersion, and transformation. She sees *agency* as the experience of affecting a meaningful and intelligible change in the digital artefact, while *immersion* describes the ability of a digital artefact to hold our interest. The resulting experience, Murray notes, would be *transformative* in the sense of a kaleidoscope, which recombines its elements into new forms with every turn. Murray's definitions provide a well-defined framework for understanding digital media artefacts. The next task is to find a suitable definition of narrative.

Gerald Prince defines narrative as the representation of events that include both the functions of narrator and audience: "the recounting ... of one or more ... events communicated by one, two or several ... narrators to one, two or several ... narratees" (Prince, 2003, p. 58). Prince's definition leaves room for the procedural quality in the process of recounting but does not cover the participatory element in digital media. The *narratees* as receivers of the narrative cannot have agency—make meaningful changes in the course of the narration; therefore, this stance is not compatible with IDN.

Gérard Genette's definition also emphasises the act of narration and the temporal location of narrative in the form of a story: "I must necessarily tell the story in a present, past, or future tense" (Genette 1983, p. 215). This assumption is challenged in IDN, since the *narrating act* (p. 215) is transformed into an act of creating and designing an environment (we could call that the *designing act*) that lets the user experience a narrative by participating in it (the *participating act*). Furthermore, the procedural quality of digital media complicates the temporal relationship Genette refers to—it is at least conceivable that the position in time could change during the course of the experience.

Moving beyond these earlier perspectives, David Herman (2000, 2002) augments narrative theory with additional aspects drawn from cognitive science. What Herman describes is narrative as a cognitive structure that can be evoked by different manifestations, a "forgiving, flexible cognitive frame for constructing, communicating, and reconstructing mentally projected worlds" (Herman, 2002, p. 49). This definition decouples narrative from established forms and therefore delivers a suitable definition of narrative. IDN can now be characterised as a form of expression enabled and defined by digital media that tightly integrates interactivity and narrative as a flexible cognitive frame.

2. TRAJECTORIES IN IDN THEORY

Several broad trajectories exist in the application of narrative theory to interactive digital narratives. An initial milestone was set by Brenda Laurel who adopted Aristotle's *Poetics* to explain interactive drama (Laurel, 1986,

1991). Laurel's model is based on two major concepts in relation to the Poetics—first, that Aristotle's six elements of drama (Action, Character, Thought, Language, Melody, Spectacle) are related by causal chains, and second, that human-computer interaction should be understood as a complete action in the sense of the treatment of plot in the Poetics. Laurel's perspective has certainly proven to be fruitful since it served as the basis for practical experiments by Carnegie Mellon University's OZ group under Joseph Bates, which eventually led to the first fully realised interactive drama, Michael Mateas' and Andrew Stern's *Façade* in 2005. However, the Aristotelian notion of the well-formed plot—which is perfect if nothing is missing and nothing can be removed—is in conflict with the concept of interactive, changeable narrative that must contain additional options to function. Indeed, Laurel herself tacitly corrects her model in the second edition (Laurel 1993) where she describes a change away from structure and towards the creation of evocative digital environments.

An approach based on the structuralist and poststructuralist concepts of Roland Barthes (1973, 1974, 1977, 1979), Jacques Derrida (1982), Michel Foucault (1972, 1977), Umberto Eco (1984, 1989), Jean Baudrillard (1983, 1987, 1993), and Jacques Lacan (1977) and their idea of a narrative that is free of the direct control of the author and open to interpretation led to Hypertext fiction works like Michael Joyce's *Afternoon, A Story* (1991) and Shelley Jackson's *Patchwork Girl* (1995).

Many theorists and practitioners of Hypertext Fiction (HF) understand IDN as an opportunity to reflect aspects of poststructuralist positions. In this vein, George Landow describes hyperfiction as challenging "narrative and all literary forms based on linearity" (1997, p. 181), a position echoed by Jay David Bolter (2001, p. 3). HF has certainly been successful in creating web-like narrative structures and invite exploration by its users. Yet, it is difficult to reconcile claims of the interactor's freedom of choice and his/ her role as a cowriter (Moulthrop, 1991) with a fixed structure of predetermined hyperlinks. Indeed, Michael Joyce himself considers this form of exploratory HF deficient (Joyce 1995, p. 143) and therefore states the need for further development towards "constructive hypertext" that "aspires to its own reshaping" (p. 12).

A third approach has drawn on nonliterary and nonwestern concepts of narrative as a theoretical basis of IDN. Pamela Jennings' work *The Book of Ruins and Desire* (1996b), Nisi and Haahr (2004) and Fox Harrell's *GRIOT* system (2008) implement this approach. Pamela Jennings suggests a model that combines African oral narrative traditions with Umberto Eco's concept of the Open Work (Eco, 1989). Jennings starts by explicitly rejecting Laurel's Neo-Aristotelian perspective as an "inadequate narrative model for the creation of computer interactive art" (Jennings, 1996a, p. 347). Instead she points out how African oral storytelling accommodates interaction in the form of call and response between narrator and audience; but also it accommodates interaction by means of the narrator's active reshaping of the narrative. Later applications show that Jennings' approach is productive. Fox Harrell applies concepts from orature, grounded in "African diasporic ... traditions" in the architecture of his GRIOT system. (Harrell, 2008) He argues that elements "of interactivity and generativity" in orature support the "expressive affordances of computational media" (Harrell, 2008).

While the move towards oral storytelling is significant, it is not clear that highly structured and culturally determined African oral tradition provides a more adequate and flexible model for IDN. Indeed, the role of the audience on the periphery comes with very limited agency.

Finally, an approach based on narratological theory as developed by Gerard Genette (1980, 1983), Seymour Chapman (1980), Gerald Prince (1982, 1987, 2003), and Mieke Bal (1997) is proposed by Espen Aarseth (1997, 2012), Nick Montfort (2003a, 2003b), Henry Jenkins (2004), and Marie-Laure Ryan (2005, 2006).

Aarseth (1997, 2012) centres his investigation on *cybertexts*, machines that can produce a variety of different expressions and as *ergodic* works require nontrivial effort on the part of the user. By casting his perspective on cybertext as a study of functionality across different media, he limits his investigation to aspects shared between digital and nondigital manifestations and therefore risks overlooking particular features of digital media narratives. In a more recent perspective, Aarseth (2012) identifies shared elements between traditional narrative and video game narrative, but again he asks for scholarly scrutiny before any application of established narratological concepts.

Marie-Laure Ryan (2001, 2005, 2006) is concerned with a more general application of narratology to IDN. She reminds us that both Barthes and Bremond originally conceived narratology as transcending discipline and media (Ryan, 2006, p. 4) and points out how contemporary narratology sees narrative as a media-independent, basic cognitive construct (see Herman, 2000, 2002).

From this perspective, Ryan engages the narratology/ludology debate that centered on the argument from games studies scholars (Frasca 1999, Aarseth 2001, Eskelinen 2001, Juul 1999) that interactivity and narrativity are almost mutually exclusive. Juul initially explicitly rejects the connection between games and narrative:

> [T]he computer game for all practicality can not tell stories—the computer game is simply not a narrative medium.
>
> (Juul 1999, p. 1)

In Ryan's view, the ludologists take Prince's original (1987) (and later modified, see Prince, 2003) definition of narrative as the central tenet of narratology since it can be denounced as not applicable to computer games for seemingly excluding mimetic forms of narrative. Ryan's solution to this proclaimed conflict is an extension of Roger Callois' (1961) distinction between two kinds of play—*paidia* and *ludus*. Ryan takes *paidia* to describe playing games of make-believe (Ryan, 2005) that require participants to play a role and thus actively use their imagination. In contrast, *ludus* denotes engagement with games that are played in a competitive spirit (Ryan, 2005), for example sports games. This means that computer games that invite make-believe activity—like *The Sims* (Wright, 2000)—can be described as narratives regardless of strong ludic elements.

Ryan's application of narratology results in a rich methodological toolkit for the analysis of IDN. Her crucial introduction of *paidia* as a dimension of computer games offers a perspective that reconciles narrative and games. However, Ryan preserves a dichotomy on the core level that depicts interactivity as a distraction to narrative ("interactivity is not a feature that facilitates the construction of narrative meaning" [Ryan 2006, p. 117]). This view seems premature, given the early stage of IDN as an expressive form. Interactivity might very well be able to evoke the cognitive structures Ryan takes to be the core meaning of narrative.

3. BEYOND ADAPTATION

Henry Jenkins (2004) insists that narrative in interactive media will not work in the same way that narrative in other media functions, and we should therefore expect different properties. This important insight is the starting point from which he considers four possible modes for the integration of interactivity and narrative: *evocative, enacted, embedded* and *emergent*. The *evocative* mode describes narratives that reference prior stories in other media. An example would be a Star Wars Game that refers to the movie series. *Enacted* narratives allow the user to act out specific roles within an existing narrative universe, for example the career of a Star Wars star fleet fighter pilot. *Embedded* narratives convey information by means of spatially distributed narrative-infused encounters, as exemplified in the game *Myst*. Finally, *emergent* narratives appear in unstructured but rule-based game worlds like *The Sims* that provide players with the tools to construct stories of their own.

Jenkins' narrative modalities supersede the adaptive strategies outlined so far. However, his understanding of *transmedia storytelling* requires the traditional narrative to point back to, for example, any Star Wars game that implies the movies as a reference. In this sense, Jenkin's perspective stays centred on the traditional narrative, with the new modes relegated to the periphery.

Nick Montfort (2003a, 2003b) provides an important stepping stone for a more adequate theory. In his investigation of Interactive Fiction (IF) works such as Zork (Blank & Lebling, 1980), he emphasises the differences that exist for artefacts in legacy media regarding the key narratological terms of narrative and story: "A work of IF is not itself a narrative; it is an interactive computer program" (Montfort, 2003a, p. 25). Similarly, he rejects Prince's narratological definition of story: "[I]nteractive fiction is not a story in the sense of the things that happen in a narrative" (Montfort, 2003b). However, Montfort still considers narratology a useful framework for the analysis of IF works. This apparent conflict is solved by his observation that IF contains the potential to output narratives. In this way, Montfort establishes an important distinction between the IF/IDN artefact as a computer program and narrative as the output. The two categories are no longer mapped onto each other but are subject to a complex relationship.

4. A SPECIFIC THEORY OF IDN

As the analysis in this chapter has shown, legacy theoretical frameworks—through the connection to earlier narrative forms—are limited in their capacity to understand new phenomena. The poetics provide a perfect toolset for understanding ancient Greek tragedy, but the world that Aristotle tried to understand did not involve computation, or practically limitless memory facilities. It seems almost as archaic to assume that theories of narration developed for the era of the typewriter will be adequate to explain interactive digital narratives. This aspect is at the core of the ludologists' critique of narratological approaches to digital media—traditional narratology has little to say about digital procedurality. While terms and categories can be adapted, this practice clearly has its limits; terminology loses its specific meaning and becomes fuzzy when it is continuously redefined. At the same time, there is the danger of overlooking important aspects when they do not fit the established framework.

For a better understanding of IDN, it is necessary to move beyond legacy notions of what constitutes narrative expression while further developing our analytical toolset to include aspects not covered so far. The way forward, I suggest, is in the development of a specific theoretical framework for IDN, building on earlier work especially by Laurel, Murray and Herman.

4.1　A Theoretical Model for IDN

As a starting point, Nick Montfort's distinction between the material artefact (the computer programme) and its output (the narrative) is especially productive (Montfort, 2003a). The relationship between the two categories is another important aspect. IDN requires an interactive process to produce the output. This product of an IDN work—a recording of a single walkthrough—might be understood as a narrative in a more traditional sense and analysed with the tools and methods of classical narratology. However, this established theoretical framework does not account for the digital computer system (software and hardware) and the participatory interactive process that result in a story output (Figure 6.1). On the side of more traditional narrative forms—for example literature—only the output in the form of a book is available for analysis, while we can merely speculate about the author's thoughts and her writing process (dotted lines). On the side of IDN, we can of course record and analyse the output. However, there are two additional elements: the software/hardware combination and the process of interaction. For a work like *Gone Home* (Gaynor, 2013), this means we could look at the programming code (provided we have access to it) and the hardware that the software is executed on. Additionally we can observe a participant explore the virtual house and react to the scattered objects. Finally, we can analyse a recorded walkthrough and see how particular interactions shaped the outcome.

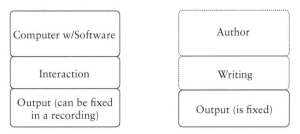

Figure 6.1 Comparison IDN and (literary) narrative in traditional media.

A new theoretical framework is needed to overcome the output-centred view of legacy theoretical frameworks. The crucial first step is to recognise all elements of IDN works including the computer system (software and hardware) and the participatory process. This means to understand IDN as comprised of system, process, and product (see Figure 6.2).

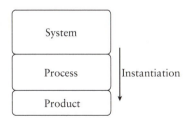

Figure 6.2 High-level view of IDN.

This model takes into account the procedural nature of IDN as a reactive and generative system. The process of interaction with one or several participants is reflected and the output is identified as the instantiated[2] product.

Roy Ascott's theory of cybernetic art (1964, 1990, 2003) provides inspiration for this perspective. Ascott specifically urges artists to look at cybernetics (Wiener, 1948) and change the artistic focus from product to process, from structure to systems. Cybernetics introduced the idea of feedback loops, of actions influencing and changing complex systems. Espen Aarseth explicitly draws the connection when he describes a "cybertextual process" (Aarseth, 1997, p. 1). Ascott's definition improves upon Wiener's mechanistic concept by merging it with artistic sensibility. Furthermore, many similarities exist between Ascott's definition of cybernetic art and IDN in the focus on process, the importance of interaction, and the concept of the recipient as a participant.

In this context, I use the term *system* to describe the digital artefact, the combination of software and hardware on which the software is executed. This includes the executable programming code and virtual assets. Additionally, system refers to the connected hardware—keyboards, mice, displays, and other hardware (e.g., sensors) used in a digital installation. The sum of what the IDN system contains is "potential narratives," following Montfort's (2003b) use of "potential literature."

Once a user starts to engage with the system, a process is created that is defined by the opportunities the system provides and shaped by the user's actions. The resulting product of interactive digital narrative—a single walkthrough—represents an instantiated narrative.[3] Given the participatory process and the procedural nature of IDN, very different narrative products can originate from the same system—any concrete product represents only one particular instantiation. In terms of theoretical analysis, the product alone is therefore severely limited as a representation of an IDN work. A full analysis needs to include process and system. Therefore, theoretical approaches based on theories for unchangeable, static narratives are problematic since they foreground the analysis of the product of IDN.

A potential criticism of this view is the argument that IDN's process substantially overlaps the cognitive process of understanding literature and other narratives, as described for example by reader-response theory (Iser, 1976) and more recently in perspectives related to cognitive science. The model proposed here does indeed consider the creation of meaning in the mind of a recipient as an active process. However, there is an additional cognitive/pragmatic plane that distinguishes IDN from legacy noninteractive forms. More concretely, the interactor's speculation about the consequences of his/her own actions for the narrative, together with an assessment of her/his level of control, results in the formulation of plans and the execution of a strategy of interaction. While this plane of speculations does also exist to varying degrees in participatory theatre, 'improv' performances, nondigital story games, and 'choose your own adventure books, these interactive forms differ from IDN in their respective affordances.

As a result, IDN can now be defined as an expressive narrative form in digital media implemented as a computational system containing potential narratives and experienced through a participatory process that results in products representing instantiated narratives.

4.2 Protostory, Narrative Design and Narrative Vectors

Given the dynamic and malleable quality of IDN afforded by procedurality and participation, neither story/histoire nor plot/discourse can adequately describe an IDN work, as the static story of legacy media gives way to a space containing potential narratives. At the same time, plot/discourse as the fixed material manifestation is replaced with a flexible presentation of narratives while they are being realised through instantiation. A neat distinction between the two categories is no longer possible, since the IDN system contains and encodes aspects of story and discourse by supplying both content and structures of the concrete expression.

To describe these phenomena, I introduce several new terms—*protostory*, *narrative design* and *narrative vectors*. *Protostory* denotes the concrete content of an IDN system as a space of potential narratives. Any realised narrative experience is related to the respective protostory through a process of instantiation. Protostory can most easily be understood as a *pre* story containing the necessary ingredients for any given walkthrough. Conceptually it is derived from the computer science idea of prototype-based programming, where not only the content in a computer program can change while the code is running, but also its behaviour and structures (see Noble, Taivalsaari, Moore, 1999).

This model more adequately describes the flexible relationship between an IDN system and a particular realised narrative. The protostory then is a prototype, or a procedural blueprint, that defines the space of potential narrative experiences contained in one IDN system. Protostory describes both concrete programming code and interactive interfaces, and in this way embodies the artistic intent that enables a participatory process of instantiation resulting in the realisation of potential narratives.

The concept of plot as separate from protostory is problematic given the compound nature of potential narratives, which contain both structure and content. Instead, I introduce the term *narrative design*[4] to describe the structure within a protostory that describes a flexible presentation of a narrative. This includes the segmentation and sequencing of elements as well as the connections between them. Additionally, the procedural logic applied in the presentation of elements is part of the narrative design (Figure 6.3).

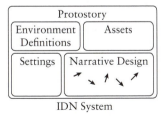

Figure 6.3 Protostory and Narrative Design.

The term *narrative vectors* describes substructures within a narrative design that provide a specific direction. Narrative vectors work not as isolated structures, but rather in connection with the preceding and the following parts of the narrative. The purpose of such structures is to convey important aspects to the interactor, to prevent an interactor from getting lost and to aid authors in retaining a level of control. For example, in an IDN murder mystery, a narrative vector could be the occurrence of a murder or the disappearance of an important witness, but it could also be a breakdown of the interactor's car that prevents him/her from leaving the crime scene before all clues are gathered. Narrative vectors are roughly functionally equivalent to plot points in legacy media (Field, 1988).

Protostory, narrative design, and narrative vectors—together with the triad of system, process, and product—describe a specific theoretical framework for IDN. I will now apply the new terminology and the overall framework to two disparate examples, with the hope of highlighting some advantages of this approach.

4.3 New Terminology Applied: *Afternoon, A Story* and *Façade*

In Michael Joyce's hyperfiction narrative *Afternoon, A Story* (Joyce, 1991), the narrative design embedded in the protostory contains the space of all lexias and hyperlinks together with the possible paths an interactor can take. The protostory is the manifestation of a fragmented, psychotic state the interactor is meant to experience. An interactor instantiates a particular realised narrative by reading lexias (short pieces of text that do not exceed a single screen) and following hyperlinks. The narrative design in *Afternoon* defines the segmentation of lexias as well as the hyperlinks connecting them and the procedural element of guard fields that enable conditional links. Narrative vectors in *Afternoon* are combinations of lexias and links that are designed to create specific experiences, for example the revisiting of a particular passage after the interactor has gathered additional knowledge (see Figure 6.4). In the concrete case, this could for example be a return to a description of a car accident after the interactor has learnt that the protagonist suspects his son to be involved.

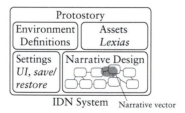

Figure 6.4 Protostory, narrative design and narrative vectors in *Afternoon*.

Mateas' and Stern's work *Façade* (see Mateas & Stern, 2005a) applies sophisticated artificial intelligence algorithms to create a wide range of narrative possibilities. The protostory in *Façade* contains the space of possible stories described by the contents of the narrative units (beats), the drama manager's goals and preconditions, as well as the artist's intent to let the interactor experience a marriage falling apart and have her/his attempt to save it. In addition, *Façade*'s protostory contains the definitions of the user interface and the virtual space, the built-in physics system, as well as the props and the characters Grace and Trip. An interactor instantiates a particular realised narrative by communicating with Grace and Trip, the two other characters in *Façade*, by moving within the space of their apartment, and by using the available props. These actions have consequences and can for example lead to the couple breaking up or to the interactor being thrown out.

The intricate narrative design in *Façade* is in the combination of several distinct elements. An Aristotelian story arc provides the overall structure, and individual narrative units—beats—supply the content (Figure 6.5). Beats come with pre and postconditions to help retain narrative consistency. Finally, a drama manager component controls the flow of the narrative, in accordance to previously authored goals and distinct phases in the story and by taking the interactor's actions into account. Narrative vectors in *Façade* determine if an interactor is kicked out or if she/he reaches the therapy part in which Grace and Trip are able to rescue their marriage.

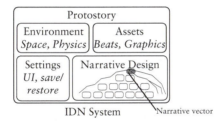

Figure 6.5 Protostory, narrative design and narrative vectors in *Façade*.

Understanding the two works in this way facilitates the examination of aspects which so far has been mostly overlooked, as they are outside of the focus of traditional narrative studies. In the case of *Afternoon*, the aesthetics and participatory possibilities provided by the Storyspace authoring system and its playback component can now be analyzed as part of the protostory in the form of environment definitions and settings. In the case of *Façade*, the virtual space of the couple's apartment and the possibilities afforded by the physics engine become an integral part of the examination of the protostory and allow a more complete understanding of the work.

In both examples, the notion of narrative design as comprised of narrative vectors enables a classification independent of legacy story structures. Consequently, *Afternoon* no longer has to be understood as a poststructuralist rhizomic narrative and *Façade* can be classified independently of legacy dramatic structures. This move signifies that the analysis is no longer constrained by the need to adapt legacy theoretical positions and can instead fully focus on describing the particular narrative strategies of *Afternoon* and *Façade*.

5. SUMMARY: A SPECIFIC THEORETICAL FRAMEWORK FOR IDN

The theoretical framework described in this chapter overcomes the limitations inherent in approaches that adapt and redefine existing theories of narrative grounded in legacy media. Instantiation is identified as a crucial distinction from nondigital forms of narrative. The triad of *system*, *process*, and *product* describes the entire phenomenon of IDN. Together with the terms *protostory*, *narrative design*, and *narrative vectors* the framework captures specific aspects of IDN. This move makes aspects like the user interface or rule systems finally available to enquiry from a narrative perspective. The advantage of this new vocabulary is in its explanatory power in comparison to legacy-derived terms such as story and plot/discourse that do not account for the specific affordances of digital media. This theoretical framework forms the foundation of a more fully developed theory. Further work in this area should analyse the primitives and the segmentation of protostories and create a taxonomy of narrative designs to identify forms and genres. More work is also necessary to investigate the process; in this particular area, a look at performance studies should be productive.

In practical terms, the clear departure from legacy narrative opens up a space for bold experiments in IDN that do not need traditional narratives as a yardstick to measure against and help avoid a pattern of *interactivisation* that Jennings eloquently denounced in 1996: "It is a waste of energy and resources to make applications that merely imitate media that exist in other forms, such as print, television, and film" (Jennings 1996a, p. 349).

NOTES

1. Aspects of this chapter have been covered previously in Koenitz (2010).
2. The term instantiation – as used in this chapter – is derived from computer science. I would like to acknowledge the usage of the same term in narratology that differs conceptually.
3. Noah Wardrip-Fruin (2009) shares the concern for process; however, his major interest is in describing the aesthetics of "expressive processes."
4. In contrast, Michael Mateas uses the same term to describe narrative segmentation (Mateas & Stern, 2003).

REFERENCES

Aarseth, E. (1997) *Cybertext: Perspectives on Ergodic Literature*. Baltimore, Maryland: Johns Hopkins University Press.
Aarseth, E. (2001) Computer Game Studies, Year One. *Game studies*, 1(1), 1–15.

Aarseth, E. (2012) A narrative theory of games. In *FDG '12 Proceedings of the International Conference on the Foundations of Digital Games*. New York, NY: ACM. pp. 129–133.

Ascott, R. (1964) The construction of change. *Cambridge Opinion*. 41. pp. 37–42.

Ascott, R. (1990) Is there love in the telematic embrace? *Art Journal*. 49(3). p. 241.

Ascott, R. and Shanken, E. (eds.) (2003) *Telematic Embrace: Visionary Theories of Art, Technology, and Consciousness*. Berkeley: University Of California Press.

Bal, M. (1997) *Narratology: Introduction to the Theory of Narrative* (2nd ed.). Toronto: University of Toronto Press.

Barthes, R. (1973) *Mythologies* (selections from this and other works). New York: Noonday Press.

Barthes, R. (1974) *S/Z*. (R. Miller, trans.). New York: Hill and Wang.

Barthes, R. (1977) The death of the author (R. Howard, trans.). In: *Image, Music, Text*. New York: Hill.

Barthes, R. (1979) From work to text. In: Harari, J. (ed.) *Textual Strategies: Perspectives inPoststructuralist Criticism* . Ithaca: Cornell University Press.

Baudrillard, J. (1983) *Simulations*. New York: Semiotext.

Baudrillard, J. (1987) *The Ecstasy of Communication*. New York: Semiotext.

Baudrillard, J. (1993) *System of Objects*. New York: Verso.

Bolter, J. D. ([1991] 2001) *Writing Space: Computers, Hypertext, and Remediation of Print*. Hillsdale, NJ: L. Erlbaum Associates.

Caillois, R. (1961) *Man, play, and Games*. University of Illinois Press.

Chapman, S. (1980) *Story and Discourse: Narrative Structure in Fiction and Film*. Ithaca: Cornell. University Press.

Derrida, J. (1982) *Margins of Philosophy*. Chicago: University of Chicago Press.

Eco, U. (1984) The role of the reader. In: *Explorations in the Semiotics of Texts*. Bloomington: Indiana University Press.

Eco, U. (1989) *The Open Work*. Cambridge, Massachusetts: Harvard University Press.

Eskelinen, M. (2001) The Gaming Situation. *Game studies*, 1(1), 68.

Field, S. (1998) Screenplay: The Foundations of Screenwriting; a Step-by-step Guide From Concept to Finished Script. New York: MJF Books.

Foucault, M. (1972) *Archaeology of Knowledge*. New York: Pantheon.

Foucault, M. (1977) What is an author? (D. F. Bouchard and S. Simon, Trans.). In: Bouchard, D. F. (ed.) *Language, Counter-Memory, Practice*. Ithaca, New York: Cornell University Press.

Frasca, G. (1999) Ludology Meets Narratology: Similitudes and Differences Between (Video)Games and Narrative. Originally published in Finnish as Ludologia kohtaa narratologian in, Parnasso, 3 (1999).

Gaynor, S. (2013) *Gone Home* [video game]. Portland, OR: The Fullbright Company.

Genette, G. (1980) *Narrative Discourse: An Essay in Method*. Oxford: Blackwell.

Genette, G. (1983) *Narrative Discourse Revisited* (J. E. Lewin, trans.). Ithaca, NY: Cornell University Press.

Harrell, D. F. (2008) *Second Person: Role-Playing and Story in Games and Playable Media*, Noah Wardrip-Fruin and Pat Harrigan, eds. Cambridge, Massachusetts: MIT Press, 2007, pp. 177–182. Peer-reviewed and republished in Electronic Book Review, February 19, 2008. http://www.electronicbookreview. com/thread/firstperson/generational

Harrell, D. F. (2009) Toward a theory of phantasmal media: An imaginative cognition- and computation-based approach to digital media. *CTheory.* rt006.

Herman, D. (2000) Narratology as a cognitive science. *Image & Narrative.* 1(1).

Herman, D. (2002) *Story/Logic: Problems and Possibilities of Narrative.* Lincoln, Nebraska: University of Nebraska Press.

Iser, W. (1976) Der Akt des Lesens. Theorie ästhetischer Wirkung. München; Jauß.

Jackson, S. (1995) *Patchwork Girl* [Hyperfiction]. Watertown: Eastgate Systems.

Jenkins, Henry (2004) Game design as narrative architecture. In: Wardrip-Fruin, N. and Harrigan, P. (eds.) *First Person: New Media as Story, Performance, and Game.* Cambridge, MA: MIT Press.

Jennings, P. (1996a): Narrative structures for new media: Towards a new definition. *Leonardo.* 29(5). pp. 345–350.

Jennings, P. (1996b) The book of ruins and desire [Description of Interactive installation]. Available at: http://www.pamelajennings.org/PDF/Jennings-ruins%20 and%20desire.pdf

Joyce, M. (1991) *Afternoon, a Story.* [Hypertext fiction]. Watertown: Eastgate Systems.

Joyce, M. (1995) *Of Two Minds: Hypertext Pedagogy and Poetics.* Ann Arbor: University of Michigan Press.

Juul, J. (1999) A Clash Between Game and Narrative. *Danish literature.*

Koenitz, H. (2010) Towards a theoretical framework for interactive digital narrative. In: R. Aylett et al. (eds.) *Proceedings of the ICIDS Conference 2010.* Berlin: Springer-Verlag.

Lacan, J. (1977) *Écrits: A Selection* (A. Sheridan, Trans.). New York: W.W. Norton & Company.

Landow, G. (1997) *Hypertext 2.0.* Baltimore: Johns Hopkins University Press.

Laurel, B. (1986) *Toward the Design of a Computer-Based Interactive Fantasy System.* Doctoral Thesis. Drama Department, Ohio State University.

Laurel, B. (1991) *Computers as Theater.* Reading: Addison-Wesley.

Laurel, B. (1993) *Computers as Theater* (2nd ed.). Reading: Addison-Wesley.

Mateas, M. and Stern, A. (2003) Façade: an experiment in building a fully-realized interactive drama. In *Game Developers Conference (GDC '03).* San Jose, CA, USA, March 4–8, 2003.

Mateas, M. and Stern, A. (2005a) Structuring content in the facade interactive drama Architecture. In: Young, R. M. and Laird, J. (eds.) *Proceedings of the First Artificial Intelligence and Interactive Digital Entertainment Conference* (AIIDE 2005). Menlo Park, CA: AAAI Press. pp. 93–98.

Mateas, M. and Stern, A. (2005b) Façade [Software]. Available at: http://www.interactivestory.net/

Montfort, N. (2003a) *Twisty Little Passages: An Approach to Interactive Fiction.* Cambridge: The MIT Press.

Montfort, N. (2003b) *Toward a Theory of Interactive Fiction.* Available at: http://nickm.com/if/toward.html

Moulthrop, S. (1991) You say you want a revolution? Hypertext and the laws of media. *Postmodern Culture.* 1(3).

Murray, J. (1997) *Hamlet on the Holodeck: The Future of Narrative in Cyberspace.* New York: The Free Press.

Murray, J. (2011) *Inventing the Medium: Principles of Design for Digital Environments.* Cambridge, MA: MIT Press.

Nisi, V. and Haahr, M. (2004) Weird view: Interactive multilinear narratives and real-life community stories. *Crossings: Electronic Journal of Art and Technology.* 4(1).

Noble, J., Taivalsaari, A., Moore, I. (eds.). (1999) Prototype-based Brogramming: Concepts, Languages and Applications. Berlin: Springer-Verlag.

Prince, G. (1982) *Narratology: The Form and Functioning of Narrative.* Amsterdam: Mouton Publishers.

Prince, G. (1987) *A Dictionary of Narratology.* Lincoln: University of Nebraska Press.

Prince, G. (2003) *A Dictionary of Narratology* (2nd ed.). Lincoln: University of Nebraska Press.

Ryan, M.-L. (2005) Narrative and the split condition of digital textuality. *Dichtung-digital: Journal für digitale Ästhetik.* 5(34).

Ryan, M.-L. (2001) *Narrative as Virtual Reality: Immersion and Interactivity in Literature and Electronic Media.* Baltimore: Johns Hopkins University Press.

Ryan, M.-L. (2006) *Avatars of Story: Narrative Modes in Old and New Media.* Minneapolis: University of Minnesota Press.

Wardrip-Fruin, N. (2009) *Expressive processing.* Cambridge, MA: MIT Press.

Wiener, N. (1948) *Cybernetics, or, Control and Communication in the Animal and the Machine.* Cambridge, MA: MIT Press.

Wright, W. (2000) The Sims. [Computer game]. Emeryville: Maxis.

7 Emotional and Strategic Conceptions of Space in Digital Narratives

Marie-Laure Ryan

In 1997, and again in 2011, Janet Murray identified spatiality as one of the four major distinctive properties of digital media, along with being procedural, participatory and encyclopedic. Espen Aarseth concurred: "[W]hat distinguishes the cultural genre of computer games from others such as novels and movies, in addition to its obvious cybernetic differences, is its preoccupation with space" (Aarseth 2001, p. 161). These pronouncements, which relegate time to a secondary role in digital media, fall in line with Fredric Jameson's claim (1984, p. 64) that late twentieth century culture is characterised by a 'spatial turn' Yet the notion of space is too broad a category to provide a sharp analytical tool. The human mind deals with the immensity and abstractness of space by dividing it into subcategories. In this chapter, I propose to look at two conceptions of space that are particularly relevant to interactive digital narrative: emotional and strategic space.

The term of emotional space speaks for itself: it is an experience of space associated with affective reactions. These reactions can be either positive, such as a sense of belonging, of security, of being home, or negative, such as repulsion, fear, or a sense of being lost. Emotional space is best represented by pictures taken from a horizontal perspective—an elevation view—because this perspective captures the perception of the human body, and therefore comes closest to the lived, embodied experience that produces emotions. In emotional space we relate to space—or to certain places within space—not in a utilitarian way, not to get somewhere, but rather for the sake of what it evokes in the imagination. Emotional space has a special affinity with stories and with memories—it is because it is linked to stories that it matters to us, either positively or negatively. For instance, legends relating to a certain landscape create an interest in this landscape that can lead to emotional attachment.

While the emotional conception of space constructs the self as a relation to its environment (or as the failure to establish such a relation), the strategic conception constructs the self as possibilities of action. Insofar as it uses space as a way to reach personal goals, this attitude can be represented by a chess board. The squares on a chess board have no intrinsic emotional value for the player: they only matter because of the actions that they allow to perform. Chess players want to move their rook to a certain square because by doing so they can capture one of their opponent's pieces, not because they like the square. Strategic space is best represented in map view, as a vertical projection in which no object hides any other, because it is very important for strategic planning to see how objects relate to each other.

The concepts of strategic and emotional space entertain close relationships with the two terms of a dichotomy that is frequently invoked in human geography, the dichotomy of space vs. place (Tuan 1977). Here it is how I personally conceive space vs. place:

Space	Place
Movement: to be traversed	Rootedness: to be lived in
Freedom, adventure, danger	Security
Container for objects	Network of interrelated objects
Open and infinite	Limited by boundaries
Anonymous	Associated with community
Timeless	Shaped by history
Abstract concept	Concrete environment with which people develop emotional bonds (positive or negative)

Yet despite their obvious affinities, the two pairs are not completely equivalent, and we can cross-classify them:

Emotional places are locations that evoke either positive or negative feelings. The French philosopher Gaston Bachelard (1969) has compiled a catalogue of happy places in a book titled *The Poetics of Space*, which should really be titled a *poetics of place*. His places are the *house*; the *corner*; *drawers*, *nooks and crannies*, *nests* and *sea-shells*. They are all closed and protective; they are the places where a cat would like to curl up. One type of place that Bachelard does not describe, though it is equally important for the mapping of affective geography, is places that restrict people's freedom, such as the *cage* and the *prison*.

Emotional space is a space that permits movement; once again, this movement can be either positively or negatively valued. An example of euphoria-inducing movement is the experience of a skier who moves at great speeds, making beautiful tracks in powder snow, or of a nomad who finds pleasure in the journey itself rather than in the destination. An example of a type of space allowing only futile, frustrating movement is the *labyrinth*, a space where one gets lost. Disorientation, a major theme in 20th-century literature, is typical of a negative emotional relation to space.

Strategic space is the space you have to cross to reach a certain goal, and in order to cross it you need to solve certain problems. Take a computer game where you receive a quest: you have to get through closed doors by finding password, avoid a ferocious dog by putting it to sleep, move past a watchman by distracting him, and kill a boss to get to the next level. You use keys, weapons, spells, magic potions—whatever is in your inventory. When space is strategically planned toward you, it erects barriers and boundaries between you and your goal, and you have to demonstrate considerable skills to cross these boundaries.

Strategic places are locations that need to be controlled in order to gain some advantage, especially military or economical. Examples are the Bosporus in World War I or the Straights of Ormuz in the current oil situation. In the game of baseball, the field as a whole is a strategic space, but the bases are strategic places. As long as players stay on base they are safe; but once they venture onto the path between bases, they can be thrown out. Home plate is the ultimate strategic place: when players get there they become invulnerable, until they're next at bat.

Literature has a rich tradition of developing and pitting against each other emotional and strategic experiences of space. A good example is Homers' *Odyssey*. Odysseus' sense of identity is defined by his place of origin and by his love for those he left behind; hence his obsessive desire to return home, even when a beautiful goddess, Calypso, offers him immortality in a pleasant environment. But after his return to Ithaca, Odysseus the strategist knows exactly how to take advantage of the particular configurations of the great room of his palace, which serves as battlefield in his fight against Penelope's suitors. Another example of a dual relation to space is found in *The Metamorphosis* by Franz Kafka. Transformed into a giant insect, Gregor Samsa must learn to use space in a way that fits his new body. Objects that were previously useful to him become useless, and vice-versa. For instance, he is now able to climb the walls and to spend time on the top of the windows, and the area below the bed offers a convenient hiding place, but he does not dare use the top of the bed for fear of being seen, since he has become a repulsive object. However, he is also emotionally attached to his room, and he is very upset when his sister removes the furniture and the picture he loves to make it easier for him to crawl on the walls.

1. EMOTIONAL SPACE

As an example of digital narrative that expresses an emotional relation to space, consider the web site Memory Maps, which offers an opportunity for users to tell their own story through a different mode of organisation than the chronological order that is typical of autobiography. It offers, instead, a spatial mode through which stories are associated with specific locations. The map serves here as a mnemonic device that activates personal memories. Looking at (or thinking of) a place, narrators remember episodes from their childhood that took place in this precise location. These narratives create a sense of place that is unique to the writer.

Figure 7.1 is a map that recounts the childhood of a narrator named Angus McDiarmid in the Scottish town of Carnock. While the Google Earth photo that serves as a map records impartially every feature visible from the air, the narrative map created by the annotations is highly selective in its choice of locations: some areas are places, because memory associates them with a story, and others are empty nonplaces. As the user moves the cursor over the white squares that are sites of memories, text relating to these places appears. The annotations deal mainly with the mischief of the boys of the town. One annotation signals the place of the narrator's most memorable mischief: "The bridge into the park, site of the worst crime of my childhood—which involved a group of boys, a schoolmate's forgotten schoolbag, and the inviting waters of the burn." Because of the space limitations, it is told in a very elusive fashion that leaves the story to be mostly guessed by the reader. Another annotation marks the second-worst crime; a third commemorates the place where the boys of Carnock hid during wars with the boys of the next village. Horror plays a prominent role in these memories; among the places that are singled out is the house of a woman with a gun who shot at kids, the house of drug dealers, and a field where the boys make a grisly discovery: "Former site of bloated, decaying corpse of a cow, about which children were sworn to secrecy, having been led to it by a child who had been sworn to secrecy about it by another child." The whole of the memory map project can be regarded as a secret geography created by the boys of the town as a challenge to the adult organisation of space and its centres of authority, the school that, according to the narrator, is a site of "incessant humiliations" and the church, which is left "largely unvisited."

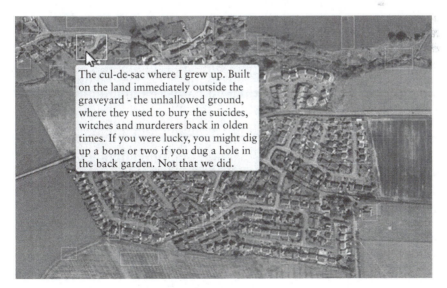

Figure 7.1 Memory maps: Carnock.

An important part of these childhood recollections consists of stories that reach much further back in time than personal memories. For instance, a field is said to be the site where suicides, witches and those who died of the plague were buried in the Middle Ages, a tree marks the site where John Knox gave sermons, and stones in a field are said to be part of an extinct volcano. This kind of annotation suggests that our sense of place comes as much from folklore tradition and second-hand information as from lived experience and genuine recollections.

Not all the stories represent enjoyable experiences; there are stories of being scared and stories of being humiliated, such as as being beaten by a girl. Yet the locations where these negative experiences took place contribute to what is, on the whole, a geography of happiness because the narrator enjoys revisiting, narrating and sharing these memories. The pleasure of remembering spells the difference between bad experiences that turn with the passing of time into treasured memories and truly traumatic experiences.

Another example of a use of digital technology that encourages an emotional construction of place is the online world *Second Life*. As Tom Boellstorff writes, "placemaking is absolutely fundamental to virtual worlds" (2008: 91). More precisely, placemaking is fundamental to the kind of virtual world represented by *Second Life*. Unlike competitive online worlds, such as *World of Warcraft*, *Second Life* does not give tasks to the user and does not involve a system of advancement; it is rather a sandbox environment where users can meet other people and freely engage in a variety of activities. Two of the major activities of *Second Life*, besides socialising, are building things (through a construction kit rather difficult to master) and buying commodities for the player's avatar. *Second Life* is basically a game of self-creation, and building a space that reflects the virtual self's identity is an essential part of this creative process. Literalising the saying "my home is my castle" (but also inverting it, since castles become homes) many players buy a plot where they can build their dream house, often spending considerable time and real-world money to furnish it with beautiful things. Once the home has been built, players can invite their friends to admire it, but just as kids may want only their friends to be allowed in their bedroom, in *Second Life* players can restrict access to their place to a few selected guests.

The players' pursuit of happiness is not limited to the design of a space strictly their own; it also involves the building of neighbourhood communities held together by common values, lifestyle and aesthetics. Boellstorff (2008, pp. 89–91) demonstrates the attachment inspired by these virtual neighbourhoods when he mentions the case of players who became upset when somebody built a huge neon-lighted store in a low-key, small-town area called Green Acres. The players organised a boycott by placing "do not support" signs around the offending structure. The new building violated the spirit of the place—what the Romans called *genius loci*.

2. STRATEGIC SPACE

As one may expect, the most dominant form of a strategic conception of space in interactive digital narratives is computer games. Early games, for instance *Pac-Man* (Figure 7.2) looked like a map and their space was not really a world; it was a playfield with an abstract design. By playfield I mean something like a soccer field. On a soccer field, the lines correspond to rules, which mean that they are strategically significant, but they do not represent anything external to the game. With the improvement of graphics and processing speed, the space of computer games has evolved from abstract playfield represented in map view to concrete worlds seen from the perspective of a human body (Figure 7.3). This new type of game space has great advantages from a player's point of view. When a game is played on an abstract playfield, players must learn the rules before playing the game; but when it is played in a concrete world, they can use their real-world experience. For instance, when they see a car in *Grand Theft Auto* they know right away what they can do with it—they know its affordances.

The space of games no longer looks like an abstract playfield, and it is no longer represented in map view, but there cannot be games without some kind of strategic design. Borrowing terminology from Henri Lefebvre, Espen Aarseth writes: "[A]s spatial practice, computer games are both representations of space (a formal system of relations) and representational

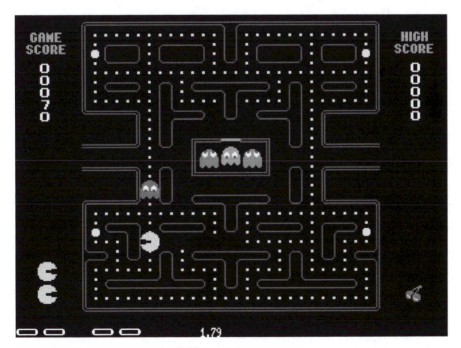

Figure 7.2 Game space as playfield: Pac-Man.

Figure 7.3 Game space as world: World of Warcraft.

spaces (symbolic imagery with primarily aesthetic purpose)" (Aarseth 2001, p. 163). I find the terms *representation of space* and *representational space* rather opaque, and I prefer to call them strategic and mimetic design. While the mimetic design presents the player with a world full of familiar features, such as mountains, deserts, cities, castles, cars, airplanes, and swords, the strategic design, which is invisible to the player and must be discovered during gameplay, organises game space into distinct areas where specific events can happen. At least two types of diagram are necessary to represent strategic design: one of them is a flowchart that shows the tasks given to the player and the successions of steps necessary to fulfill them (with separate branches when there are multiple solutions), and the other is a map that shows the location in the game world of the objects that the player must collect. Nitsche (2008, p. 180) shows a design document for the game *Zanzarah* that combines the flowchart and the map.

The invisibility of the strategic design is due to the procedural, code-driven nature of games. As players venture into the landscapes of the game world, they don't know what code is attached to their various features. To adopt a pair of concepts made famous by Deleuze and Guattari (1987), the mimetic design deploys a smooth space to the eye of the player, while the strategic design creates a striated space that subordinates travel to the points to be reached and to the tasks to be performed in order to progress in the game.

Since the advent of mobile computing a new trend in gaming has developed, known as location-specific games, that uses the real world as the play-field. These games, which are usually based on traditional games, include geocaching, a variation on the old treasure hunt that uses GPS technology to locate the treasure, games of tagging (such as Humans and Zombies) in which cell phones allows players to recognise who is a participant and who must be tagged, and alternate reality games (ARGs), a genre that offers a combination of game and storytelling, and that I will discuss in greater detailbecause it represents a new kind of IDN.

The purpose of ARGs is to reconstitute a fictional story—a story that takes place in an alternate reality, hence the name—by following a trail of clues, much in the way a detective puts together the story of a case. The structure of ARGs, basically, is the structure of the treasure hunt. The first clue is called the 'Rabbit Hole,' an allusion to *Alice's Adventures in Wonderland*, because it takes players to another level of reality. The story is fictional, but the clues are located in the real world or on the Internet: you may find a clue on a poster that advertises a movie (this happened in the first ARG, nicknamed 'The Beast,' which was designed to advertise Steven Spielberg's movie *AI*), or you may find clues on a web site that looks like a regular commercial web site but was in fact designed for the game. The clues can be provided by a variety of delivery systems. For instance, a web site may contain a phone number to call, and the person who answers the call may indicate a real-world location to visit where a message will be intercepted. In addition, the player may receive e-mails or SMS messages on his/her cell phone and may get clues from live actors positioned in certain locations. The riddles are usually so difficult that people cannot solve them on their own: in order to progress in the game it is necessary to communicate with other players—in other words, to form communities.

ARGs have been described by Jane McGonigal (2011), a leading developer, as chaotic storytelling. The clues may be connected in multiple ways, rather than in a linear order, which means that the fragments of story are not necessarily discovered in an order that corresponds to the chronological sequence of the narrative. When the game is completed, the web sites that contain clues and the wikis on which players exchange information are usually taken off-line so that there is no permanent written documentation of the plot. The story only exists in the mind of the participants.

Location-based games involve a strategic design of space, but many of them are conceived in such a way as to take players to interesting locations. A game of geocaching may for instance lead players to places they would never visit otherwise; a game of tagging may be an incentive to explore a campus, and an ARG may ask players to look closely at a building and to notice some architectural details that constitute a clue. When games lead to such discoveries, the journey becomes more important than the destination, and players develop a new appreciation of cultural and natural features, an appreciation that we may call an emotional relation to space and place.

3. DUAL EXPERIENCE OF SPACE

Let's return to screen-based computer games. There are basically two types of game design: the *journey* and the *world*. In a journey design, the player enacts a story with a prescribed beginning, middle and end, or in the case of a branching pattern, a story with multiple endings. The actions of the player make the game world pass from one state to another until the prescribed narrative arc is completed. Most adventure and shooting games follow this formula.

In the world design, there is no global narrative arc that the player must enact, no linear trail that the player must follow, but there are a number of individual tasks, or quests, which can be performed in a relatively free order. Henry Jenkins (2004) calls this design "environmental storytelling," while others compare it to a theme park because it is a space that offers a variety of activities. The geography of the game world is diversified into distinct regions that allow different activities. For instance, you can dig for gold in the mountains, you can fish in the stream, you can buy and sell items in the city, and you can fight ferocious beasts in the forest. In the world design, there is no overarching story but a variety of little stories that relate to the various regions of the world's geography. For instance, if you wander near a certain village, you will meet an NPC (non-player character) who will gossip about the people of the village. Further down the road, another character will tell you about a serious problem that plagues the area and will give you a quest to perform. If you fulfill this quest's objectives, you will gain experience points and become a more respected member of the game world.

But in a world design you do not have to accept all the tasks given to you by NPCs. In other words, you do not have to strive for achievement. The world of the game provides ample opportunities for socialising with other players, for exploring its diversified landscapes, and above all for engaging in the kind of relation to space that the French poet Charles Baudelaire called *flânerie*. While a quest is a deliberate search for specific objects, *flânerie* is a free wandering open to chance meetings and random discoveries. In a quest, space only exists to be traversed, which means to be negated; in *flânerie*, it is enjoyed for its own sake and becomes the object of aesthetic pleasure, which should be considered an emotional experience. In an online world, players can spend hours fishing in a calm stream if they are so inclined, rather than trying to progress in the game.

What I am getting at with this contrast between pursuing quests and indulging in *flânerie* is that the space of computer games can be experienced both strategically *and* emotionally. And this, it seems to me, is one of the distinctive features of computer games as opposed to traditional board games such as chess or sports games such as soccer and baseball. The space of digital game worlds is not only an arena where players demonstrate their skills; it can also become a place and a community that inspires loyalty and a sense of belonging, a sense of being at home. The dual experience of space inspired by some computer games is illustrated in Figures 7.4 and 7.5. Figure 7.4 is a user-generated, strategic map of Liberty City, the setting of *Grand Theft Auto*, that shows the locations that players must visit in order to fulfill certain quests. It tells players how to *use* space to their advantage. The map in Figure 7.5 is not a tool that helps players to solve problems. Rather, it is a geographic map that shows the spatial configuration of the game world; but, by showing the shape of this world, it symbolises the pride that players take in being a citizen of a virtual nation. While players will consult a map like Figure 7.4 to play the game efficiently, they will put a map like Figure 7.5 on their wall to display their emotional attachment to the *World of Warcraft* culture and community.

Figure 7.4 Strategic game map: Liberty City from *Grand Theft Auto IV.*

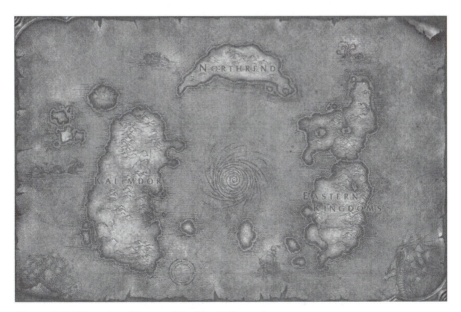

Figure 7.5 "Emotional" map: *World of Warcraft.*

To illustrate the case of a game that inspires an emotional relation to space, in addition to involving a strategic design, I will rely on the work of Celia Pearce (2009), an ethnographer of digital media who has studied the diaspora of an online community. The original homeland of this community was the world of *Myst*, one of the most popular games of all time and a landmark in video game history. In order to complete the game of *Myst*, players have to travel through several worlds, and in order to move through these worlds or to pass from one world to another they have to solve puzzles, find keys, locate secret codes, and so on. The gameplay of *Myst* relies on a highly strategic conception of space, since it divides the game world into useful objects, i.e., objects that present possibilities of action, and inert objects that fulfill a function comparable to descriptions in a novel, such as the function of providing a rich image of the story world. However, the popularity of the game also came from the surreal beauty of the graphics, a beauty both realistic and dreamlike which is unique to computer-assisted graphics. The aesthetic pleasure that the players take in the landscape does not focus on specific objects at the expense of others, as does the strategic approach. It embraces the whole of the game world.

In the early 2000s an online world based on *Myst* was created, called *Myst Online: Uru Live* (pronounced 'you-are-you'). However, in 2004 it was closed due to a lack of subscribers. This traumatic event resulted in a diaspora for the faithful players. Many of them migrated to other worlds—among them *Second Life*—where they founded communities in exile. In *Second Life*, the members of *Uru* used the building tools of the system to recreate the landscape of the lost world, creating a virtual world within a virtual world. They used this landscape as the setting for regular gatherings of *Uru* expats, and they created an *Uru* culture in exile very similar to what immigrants from a certain country do in American cities. The recreated world of *Uru* is expanding with new islands full of puzzles and legends in the style of *Myst*. There is also a blog devoted to keeping the *Uru* community together until the Second Coming of *Myst* Online (which indeed happened in 2011).

The lesson to learn from this example is that people can feel the same kind of attachment to virtual worlds as they do to real world countries. (I mean the same in kind, but not necessarily the same in intensity). This attachment links the virtual world to memories of happy times, to a corpus of stories—in this case the legends of the *Myst* games—to a supportive community, and above all to a sense of cultural identity.

In my next example, the purpose of the game's strategic design is to induce an emotional experience of space. This example is *The Path* (2009), an independent art game based on the fairy tale of *Little Red Riding Hood* (Figure 7.6). In this game you choose one of six girls. You are told that you must go to the grandmother's house, and in order to find it you must stay on the path. The path is a good example of strategic space, since its function is to take you straight to the grandmother's house. But the advice given to the player is deceptive. If you stay on the path and see nothing of the world that surrounds it, you won't be able to enter the grandmother's house. The game wants you to stray off the path, and to experience space for its own sake by exploring the woods, where many surprises await you. At first the woods seduce you with their misty landscape, with their weird vegetation, and with their strange and slightly scary atmosphere. But after a while you feel lost, you get tired of not getting anywhere, and you develop an antagonistic relation (still emotional, but now negative) to the woods. The more you progress, the more the woods look the same. But if you look around carefully, you may see a faint light on the horizon. When you get close, you will discover some kind of landmark. Within the undifferentiated space of the woods, you have discovered a place. It is the anticipation of the pleasure taken in finally arriving somewhere that keeps the player moving through the nowhere of the woods.

Figure 7.6 Screenshot from *The Path*.

In most of these places, there is something different, something interesting to see, but nothing really happens. After inspecting the area, your avatar resumes her wandering through the woods. But for each avatar-girl game creates a fateful place where she meets the wolf (represented in most cases by a human predator). The scene is shown in a cut scene that leaves a lot to the imagination, so it is not clear what exactly happened. After the conclusion of the cut scene the girl is transported to the gate of the grandmother's house, and she walks through hallways, rooms and staircases, getting a glimpse of a fabulous interior that looks like a Cabinet of Wonders until she gets to the grandmother's bed. How long it takes her to reach the grandmother, and how much she sees of the house depends on how many places she has visited before meeting the wolf, and on how many objects she has collected; this is an index of how well she (or rather the player) knows the game world. It can be argued that the grandmother represents death, and that the girl must meet a tragic end in the woods or at least have a traumatic experience in order to finally get to the grandmother. The fulfillment of the player's desire to reach a final destination, rather than wandering forever, has ambiguous consequences, since on one hand it spells the doom of the avatar, but on the other it means success for the player. The game presents death as inevitable, but if there is nevertheless a positive moral to *The Path*, it is that life is a journey, and the more you learn about the space that you traverse during the journey, the most you make of life.

4. DIGITAL MEDIA AND THE EXPERIENCE OF SPACE

Why is spatiality so widely considered a distinctive property of digital media, while their temporality has attracted little critical attention? The computer has certainly done much more for our use of time than for our actual mobility through space. Just think of email vs. snail mail, of the speed at which news reaches us on the Internet, or of all the time we save as scholars by accessing documents online rather than consulting them at the library. However, we tend to take these services for granted, and whenever the computer makes us think about time, it is because it frustrates us with lag and slow downloads. Yet computer games and digital art make a highly strategic use of time that deserves more attention; many computer games—war games, shooters, sports games—operate in real time, which means that the player and his/her opponents make their moves in the same time frame. It is therefore necessary to act quickly and precisely to kill your enemy before your enemy kills you. As for digital artworks, many of them animate text and image and coordinate them with sound in a way that makes timing an absolutely crucial artistic dimension. In their artistic and entertainment applications, digital media play with time as much as they play with space.

Yet, I believe that digital media are much more efficient at giving us an experience of space than at intensifying our awareness of time. The reason is that time is much more abstract than space. We experience time with our mind, and we do so mostly retroactively. We may think "how time flies" when we look at the calendar and find out that a deadline is now close, or when we see a child having turned into an adult, or when we see a friend having grown old—but we do not experience the passing of time itself, nor do we see the child grow, nor the friend age. Time in fact is so abstract that millions of pages have been written about its nature and, as St Augustine observed, we still cannot tell what it is.

While we experience time by thinking about it, we experience space with our senses and with the movements of our body. We relate to space proprioceptively and kinetically. Space, unlike time, is visible, and we see space gradually unfold as we move, especially when we move at high speed. The taming of the horse, and later the invention of the bike and of the car, must have had a crucial impact on how people experienced space.

Before the advent of digital media, we had art forms such as painting, theatre and film that presented space to our senses in its visual aspect, but with the exception of architecture, these art forms addressed an immobile body, even when the camera was mounted on a moving support. The great innovation of digital media with respect to our experience of space lies in their ability, due to their interactive nature, to display space from the point of view of a moving body and a moving eye. Digital media can display the virtual body of an avatar in games and simulations or the real body of the user with mobile technology and augmented reality. Even though digital media use time as a resource, they do no more than old media to make us aware of its passing. But they *do* do more than any other art form and any other medium to make us aware of our spatial surroundings because they are able to update our perception of space according to the changing position of an actual or virtual body.

REFERENCES

Aarseth, E. (2001) Allegories of space: The question of spatiality in computer games. In: Koskimaa, R. (ed.) *Cybertext Yearbook 2000*. Jyväskylä, Finland: University of Jyväskylä.

Bachelard, G. (1969) *The Poetics of Space: The Classic Look at How We Experience Intimate Places*. Boston: Beacon Press.

Boellstorff, T. (2008) *Coming of Age in Second Life*. Princeton: Princeton University Press.

Deleuze, G, and Guattari, F. (1987) *A Thousand Plateaus: Capitalism and Schizophrenia*. Minneapolis: University of Minnesota Press.

Jameson, F. (1984) Postmodernism, or, the cultural logic of late capitalism. *New Left Review*. 146. pp. 53–92.

Jenkins, H. (2004) Game design as narrative architecture. In: Wardrip-Fruin, N. and Harrigan, P. (eds.) *First Person: New Media as Story, Performance, and Game*. Cambridge, MA: MIT Press.

Lefebvre, H. (1991) *The Production of Space*. Oxford: Blackwell.

McDiarmid, A. (2013) *Carnock*. Available at: http://www.flickr.com/photos/angusmcdiarmid/4557625632/

McGonigal, J. (2011) *Reality is Broken*. London: Penguin.

Memory Maps. (2013) Available at: http://www.vam.ac.uk/page/m/memory-maps/

Murray, J. H. (1997) *Hamlet on the Holodeck: The Future of Narrative in Cyberspace*. New York: Free Press.

Murray, J. H. (2011) *Inventing the Medium: Principles of Interaction Design as Cultural Practice*. Cambridge, MA: MIT Press.

Nitsche, M. (2008) *Video Game Spaces: Image, Play and Structure in 3D Worlds*. Cambridge, MA: MIT Press.

Pearce, C. (2009) *Communities of Play: Emergent Cultures in Multiplayer Games and Virtual Worlds*. Cambridge, MA: MIT Press.

Tales of Tales (2009) *The Path* [video game]. Tales of Tales.

Tuan, Y. (1977) *Space and Place: The Perspective of Experience*. Minneapolis: University of Minnesota Press.

8 A Tale of Two Boyfriends

A Literary Abstraction Strategy for Creating Meaningful Character Variation

Janet H. Murray

1. DERIVING A "WOMAN TWO PARTNERS" (W2P) FORMALISM

In early 1990s Joe Bates, one of the first researchers to apply artificial intelligence techniques to the creation of fictional characters, made an important but often forgotten distinction between believability and realism (Bates, 1992, 1994). Noting that computer scientists looked to realism as the standard for virtual reality, Bates pointed out that the great animators did not mimic actual motions but abstracted and exaggerated them, creating artificially expressive conventions (such as the unrealistically distorted 'squash and stretch') that were more persuasive than literal depictions. As interactive narrative has become the focus of artificial intelligence experimentation, computer scientists have again been excited by the possibility of creating detailed simulations of the real world. For example the impressive social simulation *Prom Week* (McCoy, 2013) offers eighteen multi-parameterised characters whose interactions are controlled by a social physics that is 'based on a set of over 5,000 sociocultural considerations.' The highly detailed back end does not necessarily make for more engaging storytelling. For example, the authors offer this exchange as a representative interaction:

> ZACK (whom the interactor has directed to seek a change in relationship to Monica): Do you want to date or whatever?
> MONICA (who is cold and honest): I kinda only should be seen dating you know popular people.

It is hard to care about Zach and Monica and the other sixteen characters because they are both under-dramatised and over-specified. The emphasis on simulation over storytelling can create a kind of uncanny valley that is neither game nor fiction, a problem that the developers addressed by switching their focus from open-ended storytelling to the setting of goal-directed puzzles in the form of social games. Despite the very impressive social modelling of *Prom Week*, the characters do not engage us as the developers originally intended them to because there is a mismatch between computational abstraction and dramatic abstraction.

How can we identify the appropriate level of abstraction for creating engaging characters within a coherent storyworld? One way to answer this question is to look for durable abstractions—the equivalent of the animator's 'squash and stretch'—in existing story systems. In Western culture much of the classical canon, from the Greek epics to chivalric ballads, to Shakespearean comedy and tragedy, to Restoration drama, to 18th–21st-century novels, through the last one hundred years of storytelling in movies and television series, has focused on romantic triangles. Although gender roles and social values vary tremendously within this tradition, the basic situation of multiple rivals for the same partner is identifiable across nations and time. This essay offers a preliminary formalism for describing character relationships within this tradition, and more particularly character relationships within the story pattern in which one woman is positioned between two potential partners.

I call this pattern 'W2P,' and I offer it as an alternative to the familiar formalisms for fairy tales (Propp, 1928) and hero stories (Campbell, 1949), which have been extensively exploited by game designers and researchers in computational narrative systems. The W2P interpretation is also meant to be a corrective to dominant story traditions in which the woman is the hero's prize and monogamous marriage is heroine's reward. My approach to this pattern privileges the female position by evaluating the male figures as potential choices, or alternate boyfriends, even though the original source material may not offer much agency to the women. In contrast to the conventional Western male positioning of women as divided between Madonna and Whore, this proposed W2P pattern divides male characters into Boyfriends of ObliGation (BOGs) and Boyfriends of Desire (BODs). I am focusing on a heterosexual pattern because it is the predominant one in the mainstream canon, but this pattern can also accommodate same-sex and bisexual love stories as long as they fit the triangle structure of a desirable and obligated person romantically positioned between desire and obligation.

This essay deals with characters only, though a complete formalism would also include an integrated schema for events. Rather than simulating the reality of romantic relationships, or the psychological or sociological or historical interpretation of romantic relationships, the W2P formalism is a purposeful interpretative exaggeration of traditional story patterns. It is meant to be a model for a more general method that could be applied to other common story patterns in order to expand the expressivity of the emerging practice of parameterised, interactive story systems by exploiting the abstraction and variation techniques of age-old narrative traditions.

I have discussed elsewhere (Murray, 2011a, 2011b) two early examples of the two boyfriends pattern. The first is Helen of Troy, wife of Menelaus, King of Sparta, whose seduction or capture by Paris, a son of the King of Troy, precipitates the Trojan War. The other is Guinevere, wife of King Arthur of the Camelot, who is seduced by Lancelot, a knight of the Round Table who is betraying his own allegiance to Arthur, thus precipitating a civil war, the death of Arthur, and the end of the idealised chivalric world of Camelot. I have pointed out that the depiction of characters within these stories exemplifies the key narrative design value of dramatic compression, in which elements are clearly defined and selectively presented to intensify our focus on the central plotline. I also have emphasised that in successful narratives, characters and events reflect a consistent moral physics (Murray, 1997) that orients us to what is at stake in the characters' actions.

Although in both stories the partnering woman is relatively powerless, she is held responsible for dishonouring a legitimated partner and ruler with an illicit, politically disruptive lover. We can therefore use these two classic stories to identify contrasting attributes of the BOG and BOD characters as potential partners for a GWEN character (as we will call the focal female figure, after Guinevere). We can express these attributes as binary oppositions (see Table 8.1).

Table 8.1 Binary Attributes of the BOG and the BOD

THE BOG, or Boyfriend of Obligation Exempla: Menelaus, Arthur	THE BOD, or Boyfriend of Desire Exempla: Paris, Lancelot
Husband, sacramental and civically legitimised	Lover, violating sacred and legal order
Power of control	Power of rescue
Security, Protection, Confinement	Risk, Vulnerability, Mobility
Pleasures of Position (Queen, wife)	Pleasures of Love

However, there are other attributes that are distributed across the BOG and BOD categories, which could be expressed in relative rather than binary form. In particular there are positive attributes that are important in the originating storyworlds, and these attributes together make up heroism (see Table 8.2).

Table 8.2 Scalar Heroic Attributes of the BOG and the BOD

Heroic Attributes	THE BOG (Boyfriend of Obligation) Menelaus, Arthur	THE BOD (Boyfriend of Desire) Paris, Lancelot
Potency in battle	Arthur: High Menelaus: Medium	Lancelot: High but below Arthur Paris: Low
Charisma	Menelaus: Average with men and women Arthur: Higher than Lancelot with men	Paris: Only with women Lancelot: Higher than all other knights with men and women but below Arthur with men
Honourableness/ Chastity/Faithfulness	Menelaus: Good standing Arthur: Gold standard	Paris: Negative Lancelot: Very high until fall
Handsomeness	Menelaus: Average Arthur: High	Paris: Highest Lancelot: Very high

2. THE BOYFRIEND OF DESIRE (BOD)

To create a formalism for describing or generating characters of the BOD type, one could start by combining the Helen and Guinevere scenarios. It could arrange the characters as exemplars on a spectrum and assign values to the prototypically heroic and villainous figures of Hector and Mordred, and then place Paris and Lancelot in relation to them (see Table 8.3). We could use a system with these distinctions to create foils for the main character or to create different versions of the same character for successive instantiations of the same scenario. We could also use these differences in scalar values to calibrate the moral trajectory of a single character—such as Lancelot's decline from chastity and loyalty into lust and betrayal. It is important to identify a limited number of attributes and to limit ourselves to qualities that have clear dramatic behaviours associated with them.

Table 8.3 Spectrum of Classic BOD Moral Qualities

	Mordred	*Paris*	*Lancelot*	*Hector*	
Treason	−5	−3	−2	+5	Loyalty
Self-interest	−5	−5	+2	+5	Sacrifice
Villainy	−5	0	+4	+5	Heroism
Lustful violence	−5	−3	+2	+5	Chastity

It is also useful to think in terms of qualities that can be transposed across time and social contexts. For example, an updated version of these characters might involve treason against a powerful benefactor or employer, as in Season Four of the HBO TV series *The Sopranos* when Carmela, the neglected wife of Mafia capo Tony, has a flirtation with the tempting BOD Furio, a Mafia soldier bound by loyalty to her husband just as Lancelot was bound to King Arthur. The situation creates a dramatic tension in which Carmela and Furio, like Guinevere and Lancelot, are risking their lives by flirting with one another, a scenario that would be productive for interactive narrative because it creates a choice with powerful opposing incentives and clear dramatic possibilities.

Creating a limited matrix of attributes forces an author to concretise the moral physics of the story, to identify what kinds of choices will be important dramatically and how they will be operationalised so that they make for a consistent worldview. For example, in specifying the attribute of chastity in a modern story, an author would have to decide whether to imagine it as serial monogamy, faithfulness to one's current partner, or as having a limited number of lifetime partners. Faithfulness might be particularly important in a twenty-first century BOD character if paired with an adulterous husband in the BOG role, but the author would have to decide if male adultery was going to be given the same dramatic weight and consequence as female adultery.

3. THE BOYFRIEND OF OBLIGATION (BOG)

We can similarly refine the BOG Character Class by drawing on contrasting prototypical examples from the husband figures in the Helen and Guinevere stories and their many foils. In the *Iliad,* our view of Menelaus is regulated by comparison with the other heroes around him, his brother Agamemnon who commands the fleet (and whose wife, Clytemnestra, will later kill him), Achilles, who kills Paris' braver brother Hector (and who experiences the loss and return of his concubine Briseis as a parallel to Menelaus' loss of Helen), and Odysseus, who was once one of Helen's unsuccessful suitors and whose wife is the proverbially faithful Penelope (and thus a foil to Helen). The world of *Camelot* offers fewer potential foils for Arthur. Mordred is relevant here as a prototype of the illegitimate king and husband, since he briefly holds the throne and he aspires to be Guinevere's husband (and in some versions of the tale he succeeds). In addition, when we think of both stories as part of the same story system, we can also see the wronged King Priam, sorrowful but dignified in defeat, as a parallel figure to King Arthur, who more heroically manages to deal a mortal blow to Mordred even as he is vanquished (see Table 8.4).

Only the potency value can be easily quantified here, but the other attributes could be linked to specific behaviours. Some of these attributes could also be directly transposed into surviving patriarchal structures within the modern world, such as the royal families, the Mafia, the military or perhaps a large corporation.

We can find more variety of BOG figures in plots from later eras where the model of marriage is companionship and love rather than obligation. For example, the conventional but boring suitor is a staple of romantic fiction from Mr Collins, the dull curate in Jane Austen's *Pride and Prejudice,* to the rejected businessman fiancé in many classic Hollywood romantic comedies. In *His Gal Friday* (1940), for example, the BOG is a stolid fiancé, played by Ralph Bellamy, who wants to take the snappy newspaper reporter GWEN character, played by Rosalind Russell, off to wedded bliss in Buffalo and away from her career in New York City and her ex-husband and BOD, a fast-talking, devious, but irresistible Cary Grant. Throughout the film, the GWEN character is given a choice of continuing to report on an exciting story for her devious ex-husband editor or meeting her reliable but less exciting fiancé to take the train out of town. Such choices would also be appropriate for interactive storytelling.

Another familiar BOG figure is the dependent, unworthy whiner who has somehow wed the more passionate GWEN character despite her attraction for a more energetic and transgressive BOD. There are two such figures in *Wuthering Heights* (1847), the fastidious Edgar Linton who marries Cathy Earnshaw though she is in love with the romantically rugged Heathcliff, and Linton Heathcliff, a sickly boy whom Heathcliff maliciously weds to Cathy's daughter Catherine instead of to the roughly

Table 8.4 Comparative Attributes of Boyfriends of Obligation (BOGs)

Attribute	Mordred	Achilles	Agamemnon	Menelaus	Arthur	Priam	Odysseus
Authority	Bastard and usurper, menacing potential captor-husband	Unruly, but gods are on his side	Absolute but oversteps (takes Briseis)	Rightful husband of Helen, pact-maker among young Helen's suitors	Ideal King	Doomed king of besieged city	Charismatic leader, challenged but rightful husband and king in Ithaca
Potency: Heroism to Villainy scale	-5 Treason	+5 Defeats Hector	+4 Needs Achilles to win	+3 Wins battles but goddess swoops Paris away	+5 A hero when young; even in defeat, kills his enemy Mordred	+2 Figure of pathos	+5 Wins battles, leads men home through many dangers, defeats Penelope's suitors
Patriarchal Privilege	Bastard and captor of Guinevere	Possessive of concubines, spoils of war	Absolute patriarch. Sacrifices his daughter Iphigenia to get to Troy, for which he is killed by his wife, Clytemnestra and her usurping lover, when he returns home	Helen is the emblem of his patriarchal authority—he wins her, loses her, goes to war to bring her back to Greece	Patriarchal but not hierarchical with men (Round Table)	Defeated patriarch	Most legitimate patriarch whose wife is true to him when he is away, and who defeats would-be usurpers when he returns home
Temperament (Kind of attachment)	Murderous envy	Hot-headed possessiveness	Murderous control	Legalistic possessiveness	Judicial (willing to burn Guinevere at stake)	Forgiving	Coolheaded but relentless in general; fiercely loyal but wandering

treated but much more vital and worthy BOD, Hareton Earnshaw, whom she eventually takes for her second husband. Cathy is the exception, being granted a second marriage by the death of the first husband. More commonly, nineteenth century GWENs wind up committing suicide as the inevitable result of transgression against their BOGs. In Tolstoy's *Anna Karenina* (1877), the husband is not a King but works for the government, and he has the authority of the patriarchal laws and the weight of public opinion behind him. As a BOG, he is devoid of attraction but impossible to leave. In Flaubert's *Madame Bovary* (1856), Charles, the cuckolded husband, is cluelessly devoted to a woman he completely misunderstands. The bourgeois life he offers bores her by its lack of resemblance to her fantasies of romantic heroes, the BOD she seeks repeatedly in secret love affairs. Edna Pontellier in *The Awakening* (1899) is seeking a more feminist autonomy in her love affairs, but the boring businessman husband is once again the fate she can only escape from by suicide. An interactive story system could offer more agency to the woman, and could accentuate the conflict between one's love for one's children and attraction to the BOD, which many of these stories introduce.

The expanded social opportunities of women in 20th-century Western countries gave rise to another version of the undesirable BOG, the disapproving, discouraging authority figure, often robotically analytical and opposed to new ventures. For example, the impeccably proper fiancé in *Pat and Mike* (1952) has only to show up in the grandstands to cause the spunky athlete heroine to miss her swing or drop the ball; she trades him in for Spencer Tracy as her lower class but encouraging BOD-as-coach. An interactive narrative could further dramatise the tensions of crossing social classes or the pressure of athletic performance and build up the pathos of disappointing the committed fiancé. Or it could exaggerate the comic contrast between the two potential marriages and allow the interactor to switch between visions of the heroine swinging a golf club in a championship round, or smashing a formal table setting out of boredom with her privileged life.

Another familiar modern stereotype of the undesirable husband is the self-absorbed, unfaithful sexist who is often portrayed in late 20th-century films as the first husband whom the heroine has to leave in order to begin her journey to self-fulfilment. For example, in the film *Heartburn* (1986) based on an autobiographical novel by the feminist writer/director Nora Ephron, the BOG is a D.C.-based philandering journalist not unlike Ephron's ex-husband Carl Bernstein, and the heroine, like Ephron, finds professional success and a more suitable partner in New York City. The BOG can also be more menacing, like the gangster husband whose jealousy is dangerous, or the abusive husband who holds the heroine captive with violent threats and actions, or the wealthy fiancé who tries to murder the rival lover in *Titanic* (1997). A menacing BOG character also can be a comic figure, as in the classic Judy Holiday comedy *Born Yesterday* (1950) where a bookish journalist steals the heart of a corrupt and bullying junkman's showgirl mistress.

Drawing on all of these unlovable BOGs, we can create an attribute table based on summary prototypes that would work particularly well for stories where the GWEN-BOD relationship is positioned, not as a transgression against legitimate order as in the Helen/Guinevere pattern, but as an empowering escape from a confining, joyless individual (see Table 8.5).

Table 8.5 Attributes of the negative modern BOG

Attribute	Wimp	Robot	Chauvinist	Scary Gangster	Evil Captor
Authority	Manipulative	Rule-based	Conformist	Dictatorial	Menacing
Potency	Impotent	Withholding	Controlling	Despotic	Violating
Patriarchal Privilege	Exploitative	Snobbish	Unfaithful	Abusive	Tyrannical
Attachment	Cloying	Cool	Objectifying	Jealous	Sadistic

We could choose one of these five familiar prototypes as our BOG or create a more composite BOG figure drawing from multiple columns, such as a conformist who is faithful and withholding but highly jealous. We could also provide some positive BOG or BOD characters, aligning their virtues to make explicit contrasts with the vices of the oppressive BOG figure (see Table 8.6).

Table 8.6 Benevolent BOG / Rescuing BOD Prototypes

Attribute	Hippie	Scientist	Marshall	Knight (BOD)	Sugar Daddy
Authority	Communitarian	Rational	Legal	Physical	Financial
Potency in	Sexuality	Knowledge	Legal System	Fighting	Wealth
Patriarchal	(anti)Pacifist	(anti) Egalitarian	Protection / Punishment	Macho gallantry	Sheltering
Attachment	Supportive	Encouraging	Impersonal	Amorous	Indulgent

Depending on the moral physics of the story, we could choose to populate the world with only negative BOG and BOD examples, leaving GWEN to ally with other women or to rescue herself.

4. THE GWEN FIGURE

The classic GWEN figures cannot be seen outside of the ideology of patriarchy that defines them in relationship to men, so a feminist presentation of their stories might contextualise their limited agency by presenting their stories as part of a wider spectrum of female roles. Instead of limiting the characters to traditional GWENs (women with two suitors), we can make the patriarchal social structure explicit by including Briseis and Iphegenia as the mute victims of male power, Clytemnestra and Penelope as prototypes of active resistance to male aggression, and the Sirens who tempt Odysseus as male fantasies of women's sexuality divorced from patriarchal control (see Table 8.7).

The patriarchal structure allows little room for agency. In the patriarchal story world, there is often little difference between the BOD and the BOG, both of whom may have an attitude of exploitation. The violent women do not triumph in the end, and the sexually adventurous are punished. This pattern can persist, even in explicitly feminist popular narratives, such as *Thelma and Louise* (1991). We could nevertheless use this taxonomy to create an interactive narrative with agency for the protagonist by creating a GWEN who is in constant danger of exploitation and violation but who can use the power of seduction or withholding sexuality, or the resourceful cunning of a Penelope, as survival strategies. Or with a more feminist moral physics, we could create a world in which women unite to help one another to escape from patriarchal power.

We could also give the GWEN figure more agency by taking the W2P story into other genres where women's adultery does not lead to catastrophe. For example Chaucer's "Miller's Tale," one of the *Canterbury Tales* (ca.1395) belongs to the genre of the fabliau, which is comedic and vulgar. It takes a sympathetic view of the adulterous couple, Alisoun, the wife of a carpenter who has an affair with Nicholas, a student who is a boarder in their house. Nicholas concocts a scheme to trick her husband into sleeping in a tub hanging out the window thinking that Noah's flood is coming again, while the lovers spend the entire night together. There is a foil to Nicholas, another student Absalon, who is also trying to sleep with Alisoun. His attempts to get into the room are comically foiled with some bathroom humour, causing a ruckus that sends the carpenter crashing to the ground. His neighbours see him as a madman and a cuckold, a fate he deserves according to the logic of the story because he is a fool. Although the Chaucerian story is told from Nicholas' point of view, we can appropriate Alisoun as another reference point on the GWEN spectrum, a woman who is frankly sexual and whose sexual transgression is celebrated and unpunished within the moral physics of the fabliau. We could make the comic arrangements to fool the husband into active choices in the story, while separately programming the interventions of the rival Absalon to make him more or less of a threat. The moral physics of the story would work to reward adultery by making it the hard to achieve a winning ending.

However, to imagine a system in which women have agency, we need to move to narrative traditions that take the woman's choice of sexual partner as the focus of dramatic action. Jane Austen is a pivotal figure here, and her revitalised popularity, evidenced by book club discussions, derivative novels, film and television adaptations and interactive narratives in

Table 8.7 GWEN Characters within a Patriarchal World

Patriarchal Role	Woman as Danger		Woman as Possession		Woman as Commodity		
Narrative function	Man-killer	Femme Fatale	Beauty	Queen (Courtly love object)	Trophy-captive	Sacrifice	Captive to be rescued
Exemplum	Clytemnestra Circe Avenging Furies	Sirens	Helen	Guinevere	Briseis	Iphegenia	Penelope
Status	Queen, God	Illicit Temptress, outside the norm	Singular beauty that is out of reach	Contingent on her position and virtue; she is adored but out of reach	Defenceless after husband is killed (as will be all the women of Troy when their men are defeated); pawn between Agamemnon and Achilles	Daughter, Virgin	Wife of absent lord, target of predation because of her wealth
Agency	Murder, Castration	Irresistible deadly sexuality, seduction to transgress moral boundaries	Beauty—her presence is rapturous to others but does not bring her happiness	On a pedestal where she receives gestures of adoration and can bestow tokens of recognition on knights	None—praised for her love for her captor Achilles, totally in the power of men	None—deceived and betrayed by father—must obey and be sacrificed	Uses cunning to delay sexual violation while awaiting rescue
Contemporary Examples (in news stories and fictional stories)	Nurse Ratchet in One Flew Over the Cuckoo's Nest; Tony's mother in The Sopranos	Vampires Con artists The Postman Always Rings Twice, To Die For	Princess Diana after divorce Betty Draper, the ex-model and remarried first wife of Don Draper on TV series Mad Men	Princess Diana before divorce Mrs Ramsay in To the Lighthouse	Real life stories: Schoolgirls kidnapped in Nigeria, women raped as a war tactic; war brides of invading soldiers from conquered countries.	Real life stories: Girls sold into marriage or slavery by impoverished families; expectation of self-immolation of widows in rural India.	Stories of predatory suitors and husbands such as Henry James' Washington Square and Portrait of a Lady; Reversal of Fortune

our own era, make her a particularly appropriate source for prototypical characters for W2P system. Although Austen's world can be rendered as a social simulation governed by clear rules of behaviour, the novels owe their appeal to the specificity of the dramatic characters and to their place in a world with consistent moral physics that give their actions meaning.

Austen's most-adapted novel, *Pride and Prejudice* (1813), is a rich source of prototypical female characters, with two sisters as protagonists (Elizabeth Bennett, the main focus, and Jane) and their three younger sisters, the bookish Mary, and the flighty Kitty and flightier Lydia, as well as Elizabeth's neighbour and close friend Charlotte Lucas, as clearly defined moral foils (see Table 8.8). Elizabeth is a Penelope character, remaining self-possessed in a situation of relative powerlessness by virtue of her sharp mind. Jane is almost a Briseis character in her complete dependency on the good will of more powerful men; she never does anything wrong, but she is without any direct agency in her own destiny. The novel traces Elizabeth's courtship by Mr Darcy and Jane's by Mr Bingley, who is led by Darcy to temporarily abandon Jane. Jane's social conformity and ladylike accomplishment are made less wimpy through juxtaposition with the pretension of her sister Mary, who is as eager to perform as she is talentless. Mary's pedantic conversation is also a contrast to Elizabeth's easy intelligence. Lydia and Kitty are two giddy young teenagers, boy-crazy for the local soldiers. The most telling foil is Charlotte Lucas, who marries the odious curate Mr Collins, who will one day inherit the Bennett's house because of its entailment to male heirs. Elizabeth rejects his proposal in a comic scene that mocks his stupidity, pomposity, and sense of entitlement. Charlotte acts out of economic necessity, a sensible decision that dooms her to life with an insufferable fool who is also a slave to his snobbish patroness (see Table 8.8).

Table 8.8 GWEN Exemplars and Foils in *Pride and Prejudice*

	Lydia/ Kitty	Elizabeth	Jane	Mary	Charlotte
Social Behaviour	Reckless Flirtation	Witty, Confident	Modesty, Warmth	Affected, Tactless	Practical, Circumspect
Intelligence	Cunning	Smart	Smart but Emotional	Bookish but idiotic	Strategic
Autonomy	Shameless/ easily led	Conscientious, Responsible	Gentle, Dutiful	Oblivious to others	Self-protective

The main action in *Pride and Prejudice* is the eliciting and acceptance or rejection of marriage proposals. The protagonist Elizabeth has three suitors, her true love Mr Darcy, who is handsome, intelligent, rich, but too prideful and against whom she is prejudiced because of his snobbish attitude toward her family; the horrid Mr Collins, a clergyman whose stupidity and fawning attendance on his snobbish patron, Lady Catherine DeBourgh, makes him one of the most odious characters in the novel; and the handsome, charming, intelligent, but secretly corrupt Mr Wickham who ultimately elopes with Lydia and has to be bribed to marry her. Since Mr Darcy is the hero, the other men can be seen as foils to him. Collins' snobbery makes Darcy's seem less offensive, and the upstart Wickham's treachery makes Darcy's hereditary superiority seem justified (see Table 8.9).

Table 8.9 Attributes of Suitors in *Pride and Prejudice*

	Wickham	*Collins*	*Bingley*	*Darcy*
Honesty	Deceitful	Hypocritical	Frank	Blunt
Selfishness	Exploitative	Selfish	Caring	Responsible
Intelligence	Cunning	Pedantic	Reliable	Superior
Manners	Smooth	Smarmy	Congenial	Entitled

These attributes are related to the BOD qualities of Loyalty, Sacrifice, Heroism and Chastity, but they are tied to the social practices of the drawing room rather than the tribal battlefield. Wickham is a Paris-figure whose seductive charms lead to ruin and the threat of social chaos. Mr Darcy can be seen as a Lancelot figure (his counterpart in *Emma* is actually called Mr Knightley) who comes to the rescue of the maiden with his wealth and good character, despite being forbidden to her by their difference in social status. However, Darcy is also clearly the socially approved but undesirable husband, like Collins, whom a GWEN might choose to marry purely for economic security. This is the figure he presents in his first proposal to Elizabeth, the figure whom she is clearly right to reject. In his second proposal, he is the positive BOG figure, the husband who is protective and supportive rather than oppressive. By creating all these parallels that reinforce a common moral distinction—class snobbery versus civilised respect, economic self-interest versus true love—Austen increases our belief in the fictional world and our appreciation of the happy ending.

Emily Short and Richard Evans have had significant success in reproducing the texture of the Austenian world in a simulation-based story system (Short, 2013a, 2013b; Evans and Short, 2013), and the *Lizzie Bennett Diaries* (2012) was similarly successful in transposing the storyworld of *Pride and Prejudice* to a contemporary story told in social media. I envision a somewhat similar digital adaptation, further from the particular plot of any existing novel but more closely based on Austenian methods of character abstractions. Such an interactive story would present the interactor with an array of potential suitors, and invite her to use appropriate social rituals to uncover clues to the underlying selfishness, intelligence and honesty of each of them. The suitors would not be based on any existing characters, but they would differ from one another in ways similar to the ways in which Mr Collins, Mr Bingley and Mr Wickham differ from Mr Darcy. The plot need not be set in the Regency period, but it would emulate the

Austen novels by presenting a central female protagonist who would elicit and respond to proposals of marriage while indulging in matchmaking of supporting characters, who would differ to her in ways similar to the ways in which Jane and Charlotte differ from Elizabeth. The moral physics of the story would determine whether marriage was desirable (as in Austen) or not (as in many 21st century stories) and what actions would be good evidence of a suitable partner.

One way to think about the creation of characters from the Austen template who live in a very different moral physics is to compare the sexually adventurous women characters on two 21st century HBO television series, *Sex and the City* and *Girls,* with the women in *Pride and Prejudice.* All three storyworlds are based on one observant single female protagonist surrounded by contrasting girlfriends, all of whom are engaged in looking for male partners (see Table 8.10). Unlike Austen's world, the TV protagonists can earn a living on their own and suffer no ill consequences from having sex before marriage. As a result, hedonism is treated as just another way to go through life, similar to rationalism or social conformity. Social conformity remains an issue for all these women, but conformity changes to reflect changing value structures. Jane Bennett's modesty and dutifulness reflect the norms of her society, as do Charlotte's WASPy preppiness in *Sex in the City* and Shoshanna's fashion obsessions in *Girls.* The sister/best friend is specifically designed to provide clear contrasts with one another and to exaggerate or complement aspects of the protagonist's personality. For example, Charlotte Lucas accepts the proposal that Elizabeth rejects; Miranda has a baby as a single mother (the only character to become a mother); and Marnie's absurd sense of entitlement provides a strong contrast to Hannah's profound self-doubt (see Table 8.10).

Table 8.10 Parallels between GWEN characters in *Pride and Prejudice, Sex in the City,* and *Girls*

	Hedonist	*Rationalist*	*Everywoman*	*Conformist*
Pride and Prejudice	Lydia	Charlotte Lucas	Elizabeth Bennett	Jane
Sex ... City	Samantha	Miranda	Carrie Bradshaw	Charlotte
Girls	Jenna	Marnie	Hannah Horvath	Shoshanna

Although the contemporary stories of young women in search of romance often feature multiple sexual partners, they tend to focus major storylines on W2P rivalries. Both *Sex in the City* and *The Good Wife* sustained multi-season plots around a choice between a BOG and BOD character. On *Sex in the City,* as in *Pride and Prejudice,* wealth is appealing, and so the hard-to-get, adulterous older rich guy called Mr Big is the BOD and the faithful young carpenter-artist is the BOG fiancé whose heart gets broken when Carrie betrays him. On *The Good Wife,* the main character, a lawyer, is married to a philandering politician (played by the same actor who played

'Mr Big') and is in love with a younger lawyer. She has an affair with the lawyer but breaks his heart when she returns to her kingly husband (now governor) because of her allegiance to her children. The *Good Wife* W2P romance is paralleled by a professional rivalry plot in which the protagonist betrays the law firm that has made her a partner—a partnership of obligation—to create a start-up with younger associates—the partnership of desire. A feminist interactive story might create a similar professional parallel to the underlying romantic triangle with similar trade-offs in status versus risk.

5. CULTURALLY SITUATED STORY PATTERNS

The W2P pattern, like the fairy tale or hero's quest, is not an objective, empirical taxonomy. It is a product of culture, in Geertz's sense of a semiotic system (Geertz, 1973), a shared set of symbols and relationships efficiently compressed by millennia of human experience, whose meanings are being constantly renegotiated (Vigotsky, 1962) and whose use is always situated (Suchman, 1987) within particular times, places, traditions and particular storytellers and audiences. It is one of many such culturally situated story patterns that are familiar to us when we encounter them, even across great differences in media and moral code.

The practice of storytelling, in contrast to simulation-building or game design, is primarily focused on exploring highly charged emotive and moral contradictions within these culturally situated patterns. A satisfying fictional story is not an objective recording of the world, a solvable puzzle or a winnable contest. It is a highly compressed sequence of actions among characters whose fate we care about because they have been engineered to exemplify meaningful emotional and moral contrasts within particular traditions of human culture. The W2P pattern is open to multitudinous interpretative frameworks, which in turn could produce countless authorially honed instances of internally consistent storyworlds with dramatically meaningful variations for the interactor to explore. It is offered as just one example of how a culturally situated narrative abstraction schema might serve as a resource for interactive digital narratives.

In a culture with a strong narrative tradition, elements of stories such as character types and plot events form open systems of signification, always growing and changing and capable of infinite combinatorics. It is not surprising that game designers and simulation-makers have made use of this age-old system of abstraction, nor is it surprising that storytellers are increasingly drawn to the digital medium in order to create formal structures that allow for a similar fluidity of recombination. As these three distinct but overlapping traditions continue to grow in ambition and expressive power, it is important that we distinguish the aesthetics of storytelling from those of gaming and systems engineering, and that we create computational structures that allow us to focus on the abstraction layer in which traditional narrative creativity takes place.

REFERENCES

Bates, J. (1992) Virtual reality, art, and entertainment. *Presence: The Journal of Tele-operators and Virtual Environments.* 1(1). pp. 133–138.

Bates, J. (1994) The role of emotion in believable agents. *Communications of the Association for Computing Machinery.* 37(7). pp. 122–125.

Campbell, J. (1949) *The Hero with a Thousand Faces, The Bollingen Series, 17.* New York: Pantheon Books.

Evans, R. and Short, E. (2013) Versu—A simulationist storytelling system. *IEEE Transactions on Computational Intelligence and AI in Games.* 6(2).

Geertz, C. (1973) *The Interpretation of Cultures.* New York: Basic Books.

McCoy, J., Treanor, M., Samuel, B., Reed, A., Mateas, M., and Wardrip-Fruin, N. (2013) Prom week: Designing past the game/story dilemma. In *Proceedings of the 8th International Conference on the Foundations of Digital Games* (FDG 2013), Chania, Crete, Greece May 14–17.

Murray, J. (2011a) Mapping seduction: Traditional narrative abstractions as parameterized story systems. In *ACM Creativity and Cognition Conference*, November 2011, Atlanta, GA.

Murray, J. (2011b) Why Paris needs Hector and Lancelot needs Mordred: Using traditional narrative roles and functions for dramatic compression in interactive narrative. In *International Conference on Interactive Digital Storytelling (ICIDS)*, Vancouver, CA.

Murray, J. (1997) *Hamlet on the Holodeck: The Future of Narrative in Cyberspace.* New York: Simon & Schuster/Free Press.

Propp, V. (1928) *Morphology of the Folktale.* Austin: University of Texas Press.

Short, E. (2013a) *An Introduction to Society* [software]. Versu interactive storytelling system.

Short, Emily (2013b) *The Unwelcome Proposal* [software]. Versu interactive storytelling system.

Suchman, L. A. (1987) *Plans and Situated Actions: The Problem of Human-Machine Communication.* Cambridge [Cambridgeshire]; New York: Cambridge University Press.

Vigotsky, L. S. (1962) *Thought and Language.* Cambridge MA: MIT Press.

9 Reconsidering the Role of AI in Interactive Digital Narrative

Nicolas Szilas

1. HIGHLY INTERACTIVE NARRATIVE: WHAT IS THE PROBLEM?

In this chapter, I will present Highly Interactive Digital Narrative (HIDN) as a vision for future IDNs offering a higher degree of interaction possibilities and more reactive/generative narrative potential than currently possible. In particular, I will discuss some issues of relevance to the application of artificial intelligence to interactive narrative, with the objective of pointing at possible future developments of the IDN field. However, numerous signs indicate that the problem of developing an HIDN is in itself highly problematic. We are not mentioning here the well-discussed "interactive narrative paradox" (Aylett, 1999; Crawford, 1996), but the fact is that the research problem itself, as it is currently formulated, may be a dead end. The research directions presented here constitute a proposal for moving this field forward.

First, how can highly interactive narratives be defined in the context of IDN? For years, the field of study has not been clearly delimited. For example, Brenda Laurel defines interactive drama via the use of an expert system responsible of driving the story "in a dramatically interesting way" (Laurel, 1986; Weyhrauch, 1997). This definition raises two issues:

1 What constitutes a dramatically interesting experience is open and a matter of degree. Is playing *The Sims* a dramatically interesting experience? If not, what is the threshold of interest for interactive software to be a valid HIDN?
2 The field is delimited by the use of specific technologies: why should the use of a specific kind of technology be a necessary feature of interactive drama?

Most alternative definitions would share similar difficulties. For a long time, the field has been narrowed in a negative form (Portugal, 2006): it is not branching narrative; it is less linear than videogames; it is not scripted, etc. More recently, *Façade* was released (Mateas and Stern, 2003), followed by *Balance of Power: 21st* Century,[1] Versu (Versu, 2012) and *Nothing For Dinner* (Szilas, Dumas, Richle, Habonneau and Boggini, 2013). Each of the above examples can also be criticised: are they really solving the interactive narrative conundrum/paradox? However, the lack of clear boundaries is not critical and it has not prevented scientific research in the field to be productive. Interestingly, artificial intelligence (AI) in general is suffering a similar issue: most of its definitions rely on the concept of intelligence that is not clearly defined either.

Second, since Brenda Laurel introduced this concept in mid-80s, very few examples of highly interactive narrative have been created, which led some observers to conclude that it was in fact a chimera (Portugal, 2006). The lack of interactive narrative examples may be only transitory, but only the future will tell. It is also a hard task to build a fully realised interactive narrative with enough quality and gameplay to be made available to a large audience. The procedure involves developing a fully functional interactive narrative engine, filling (fuelling) this engine with meaningful narrative content, developing an appealing rendering (text, 2D, 3D) and solving the challenging issue of capturing player's choices among dozens of possibilities without ignoring debugging (which is increasingly difficult in nonscripted works), distributing and advertising. Most of these works are out of the scope of academic research.

Third, as a consequence, most researchers tended to focus their study on goals other than HIDN. For example, many AI-based interactive narrative researches address story generation rather than interactive storytelling. More recently, some researchers have been studying various means to provide an illusion of agency rather than agency itself (Fendt, Harrison, Ware, Cardona-Rivera and Roberts, 2012; Figueiredo and Paiva, 2010; Yu and Riedl, 2013). At last, in the narrative emergence approach, the focus is more on the psychological and social simulation of characters than on the resulting narrative experience. For example, comparing *Façade* (Mateas and Stern, 2003) and *Prom Week* (Mccoy et al., 2010), a shift from the narrative to the social can be observed as *Prom Week* is often presented as a social simulation game.

Fourth, the kind of user experience that is targeted by HIDN remains largely unknown. The pioneering work of Janet Murray led to the definition of three categories of experiential qualities—immersion, agency and transformation (Murray, 1997)—however, these qualities are still too general to enable a strict formulation of the research problem and they are often subject to debate (Knoller, 2012; Szilas, 2004). Our goal is not to enter the debate but to point out that the type of user experience targeted in HIDN is still open.

Fifth, after a five-year building of *Façade*, the first and emblematic playable interactive drama, the authors conclude that game design, in particular interactive storytelling game design, is a wicked problem, meaning that "there exists no theoretical framework that allows one to formally define the problem and solution criteria" (Mateas and Stern, 2005).

Taken individually, each of the above-mentioned issues may be seen as a temporary and solvable problem whereas taken together, they strongly call for a reconsideration of the way we have been using technology, mainly AI, within interactive storytelling. In the rebuilding process that follows, we will attempt to stay concrete by providing suggestion of approaches and methods for better tackling HIDN. General philosophical considerations that do not help taking concrete decisions will be avoided. As we know that the domain of IDN is not only technical, rethinking the role of AI involves focusing on the human actors and processes in IDN (next two sections) before redefining the problem and providing propositions for future research. The final section will synthesise the rebuilding of HIDN that is envisioned in this chapter.

2. RETHINKING ACTORS IN AI SYSTEMS

In its early days, AI was thought in terms of modelling intelligent human functions, such as reasoning or learning. For example, the General Problem Solver created in the late 1950s aimed at solving general problems in a way that may be compared to a human problem solver (Newell, Shaw and Simon, 1959). We define this usage as 'one-actor AI' because, once developed, the intelligent system is facing its environment as an autonomous agent. This is in line with the modern definition of AI in terms of a rational agent acting to reach its goals (Russel and Norvig, 1995).

In some AI applications, the intelligent system is in direct interaction with a user: automatic recommendation systems, intelligent tutoring systems, interface agents, search engines and of course interactive storytelling. If it is possible to see these systems within the one-actor view, considering that the user is part of the system's environment, it is more fruitful to consider that both the system and the end-user are collaborating to perform a task together. We define this usage the 'two-actor AI.' The end-user may intervene either in input or output. In input, it provides data necessary to perform the intelligent task. In output, it receives the result of the intelligent task. The communication between the user and the system often occurs iteratively, the task being progressively refined collaboratively, as illustrated in search engines. In this setting, AI algorithms cannot be judged only according to their computational performances but also, and often firstly, according to the user satisfaction when interacting with the algorithm. This leads to the concept of 'usable AI' (Jameson, Spaulding and Yorke-Smith, 2009) that combines goals and methods of AI and Human Computer Interaction (HCI). Various strategies may be adopted in usable AI. In the case of IDN, the novelty of the targeted user experience calls for an integrated perspective, where the usability constraints intervene early in the design process. Therefore, the two-actor AI often uses user-centred design methodologies involving user participation and iterative design (Spaulding and Weber, 2009; Weber and Yorke-Smith, 2009).

In the field of IDN, a third actor intervenes: the author. Over the years, the role of the author appeared more and more critical in highly interactive narrative (Louchart, Swartjes, Kriegel and Aylett, 2008; Si, Marsella and Riedl, 2008; Spierling, Grasbon, Braun and Iurgel, 2002; Spierling and Szilas, 2009; Szilas, Marty and Réty, 2003). Advanced algorithms for dynamic story generation, such as rule-based systems, intelligent agents, planning systems, etc., are useless if they are not provided with narrative content. Adapting an existing nonlinear narrative to an interactive system is indisputably a convenient solution for getting meaningful content, as illustrated in several research prototypes (El-Nasr and Horswill, 2003; Hsueh-Min Chang, 2009;

Pizzi, Charles, Lugrin and Cavazza, 2007). However, these approaches do not dismiss the role of the author because successful adaptations also need a creative rearrangement and rewriting of the original work. For example, *The Unwelcome Proposal* on the Versu system, adapted from *Pride and Prejudice*, has been written by Emily Short, a skilful writer of text-based interactive fictions. The three-actor AI makes the design of highly interactive narrative systems considerably more complex, as it doubles the above-mentioned difficulties of usable AI. Systems must satisfy needs of both the end-user and the author. More fundamentally, it redefines the very goal of HIDN: the problem is no longer to combine narrativity and interactivity for creating a new playing experience, but to provide authors with expressive tools for them to create meaningful narrative and procedural experiences. This new definition does not solve in any way the above-mentioned difficulties (e.g., we are still facing a wicked problem), for the reason that the user experience is still unspecified and possibly not yet discovered. Nevertheless, it has two consequences regarding the role of AI technology in HIDN. First, it deemphasises the computational challenge of automatic/intelligent narration in favour of other aspects of IDN: usable authoring tools, the authoring processes and methodologies, the interaction modalities (see Chapter 10 by Ulrike Spierling in this volume). Second, it impacts the computational models themselves. In addition to internal representations of human intelligent processes (reasoning, learning, etc.), they become external representations of narratives, to be handled by authors. As external representations, computational models of narrative need to be meaningful (making sense for authors), usable (providing clear affordance on how to alter the narrative) and learnable (making it possible for moderately computer-skilled authors to learn how to use these models).

The evolution from one-actor AI to two-actor AI to three-actor AI, illustrated in Figure 9.1, is not specific to IDN. Other fields could be fruitfully analysed in the same way, such as Intelligent Tutoring Systems, Medical Expert Systems, Computer Animation, etc.

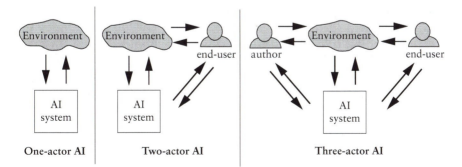

Figure 9.1 Three kinds of Artificial Intelligence, from one-actor to three-actor. The environment can be either physical (robotics) or computational (virtual world, Internet, etc.).

3. RETHINKING HUMAN PROCESSES: FROM END TO END TO INTERWOVEN

User-centred design brings the idea that the process of designing a system should not occur before the process of using it; it should occur concurrently. In an iterative manner, the system is designed, tested, redesigned, retested, etc. The above-mentioned difficulties in HIDN call for such an iterative approach because its final goal remains fuzzily defined. User-centred design usually involves circumscribing the functionalities of a system and optimising their usability. Rarely does such an approach redefine the AI models and processes *per se*. In the three-actor framework discussed above, this is nevertheless the case. Indeed, because the model needs to be designed according to the author's needs and abilities, he or she intervenes as an intermediate user for evaluating and shaping the computational models of narrative.

More precisely, three human processes can be distinguished: *design* (by the engine designer), *authoring* (by the creative author) and *playing* (by the end-user). These three processes produce respectively the *system*, the *artefact* and the *interactive narrative experience* (Spierling, Hoffmann, Szilas and Richle, 2011; Szilas, 2005). Furthermore, the system can be further decomposed into the *narrative engine*, which is the software that is needed to run the interactive narrative, and the *authoring tools* that authors use to enter content into the engine. Figure 9.2 depicts these entities and processes according to two perspectives. The linear perspective consists of chaining processes end to end. Historically, it corresponds to the cinematographic model: the camera is invented and then it is used to create films that are finally viewed by an audience. However, in the case of IDN, this linearity needs to be broken and all four human processes ideally occur almost simultaneously, in a participative perspective.

Practically, the linear perspective dominates: rarely are authors involved early enough in a project to be able to really shape the computational models. This may be explained by various reasons, including institutional ones. We claim however that the participative perspective would enable one to discover new design spaces for HIDN more suitable to the three-actor AI view. We will illustrate this via concrete examples. In the TBI-SIM project (2010–2013), which produced the interactive drama *Nothing for Dinner*, we worked closely with a creative author (Urs Richle), from the very beginning of a project. Nevertheless, the narrative engine (IDtension) was already available as a result of previous research (Szilas, 2007), which posits the project in a linear perspective. However, some modifications of the engine were made afterwards, following the observation of concrete and intensive authoring activity with the engine. For example, the narrative engine, IDtension, originally chains goals via the concept of obstacles: an obstacle hinders a character to reach a goal; it contains a special precondition named 'cause' (Szilas, 2003, 2007). If a cause is known by the character facing the obstacle, the character looks for another goal whose consequences invert

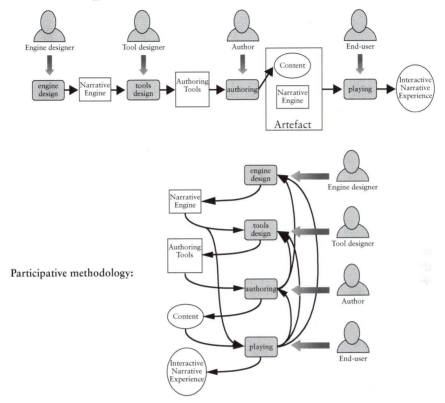

Figure 9.2 Comparison between the linear and participative methodologies. The latter repeats elements of former, but additional arrows denote the bottom up influences from playing to authoring and design, and from authoring to design. The thick arrows from actors to processes denote that the actor is responsible for the process.

the cause. Although the author grasps easily the concept of precondition, it appears particularly cumbersome to design a goal (e.g., "Paul_motivated") with a specific consequence (e.g., "IS(paul,motivated)") that inverts the cause ("~IS(paul,motivated)") of an obstacle ("paul_refuses") for the sole purpose of providing a way for the character to move forward in the story. In fact, the creative author would spontaneously draw an arrow from the obstacle to the subgoal, although no IDtension object corresponded to such an arrow. Therefore, we have decided to implement a simplified description of the stories that would include such direct relations between an obstacle and its subgoal. The subgoaling relation activates the subgoal when the obstacle is encountered. Though it is a new component of IDtension, the subgoaling relation does not bring new possibilities to the narrative generation. It just simplifies the authoring process. Moreover, this simplification comes with a price to pay: the subgoaling relations do not cover all cases covered by the initial mechanism (considering the case when several goals could solve the obstacle). But in practice, the advanced features of the original mechanism are never used. Note that the simplified mechanism does not replace the original one: the two mechanisms coexist in the engine. Other simplified relations have been similarly implemented: the *counter-goal relation* (when a goal triggers an obstacle instead of solving it) and the *chaining relation* that triggers a goal when a first goal is reached. It should be noted that the chaining relation, contrary to the two other relations, has no equivalent in the original model but is needed by the author. More recently, we have designed but not implemented a new computational model of narrative that extends the above-mentioned ideas and therefore is informed by the practical authoring activity (Szilas, Richle and Petta, 2012; Szilas and Richle, 2013).

For future research, the three-actor based AI suggests to systematise such an early intervention of the author by interweaving closely the following activities: *authoring*, the *computational model design*, the *authoring tool design* and *playing*.

4. RETHINKING THE PROBLEM: FROM PROBLEM-SOLVING TO CREATIVE

Why is the core problem of HIDN ill-defined, or wicked? On the one side, the concept of 'highly interactive' is explicit and measurable. It consists in counting, during the unfolding of a story, how many choices were offered to the user. For example, in *The Mutiny* (Mutiny, 2011), made with IDtension, the user had, on average, 93 choices (Szilas, 2007). In other systems, such as Façade, such a measurement is more difficult to establish because of the free text entry. However, the freedom at the interface level is filtered at a later stage. In Façade, for example, there exists a list of around 40 acts that the system interprets from the textual entry. On the other side, the concept of dramatically or narratively interesting is more problematic. In general, there is a large variety of criteria to qualify a narrative or drama as interesting: causality, unity of action, suspense, conflict, etc. Measuring the quality of the narrative experience according to such criteria is always sensitive because no consensus exists regarding which criteria are necessary and sufficient to state that a narrative is an interesting narrative. In the case of interactive narrative, the problem is even more difficult because the nature of narrative is different. The fact that the player intervenes in the story changes the conditions of narrative perception. The narrative is no longer a story—a sequence of events that can be analysed afterwards—but an interactive narrative experience resulting from the coupling of the player's actions and the events given in return (Aylett and Louchart, 2007; Szilas, 2010). According to this view, it is not known what kind of experience is better than another.

Some researchers have investigated nondigital interactive narrative (role playing games, theatrical improvisation) to identify characteristics that may apply to the interactive narrative experience targeted by HIDN (Louchart and Aylett, 2006). However, these nondigital interactive narratives are social whereas IDN is computer-assisted. Therefore, both classical narrative theories and nondigital interactive narrative theories only provide hints of what the targeted interactive narrative experience is.

In this context, it seems difficult to formulate HIDN in terms of a problem to solve and then to apply AI algorithms to solve this problem. In fact, researchers tend to define a different problem and attempt to solve it, which may lead to relevant scientific results but may not serve the purpose of HIDN. Rather, HIDN should be fundamentally formulated as a design activity, aiming at building a series of software products that satisfy the author and then, consequently, the end-user. Our claim is that this way of exploring the design space is more likely to lead to significant advances in HIDN at both practical and theoretical levels.

5. RETHINKING REPRESENTATIONS

In this design-based view, the concept of intelligence and its related processes (learning, reasoning, planning) do not even appear necessary, which may question the role of AI in such systems. Nevertheless, AI uses concepts that seem appropriate to the kind of processes and representations at work in HIDN. Notably, there are evidences that HIDN requires some abstract representation of narrative (Szilas et al., 2003; Szilas, Richle and Dumas, 2012), and AI has developed many ways of dealing with abstraction: separation of knowledge and rules for the modelling of reasoning (compared to simple procedural reasoning); use of generic elements (variables, slots) to generically describe an operator or state; hierarchical representation of knowledge from concrete objects to abstract categories, etc.

The above notions, classically used in AI to solve problems, should be seen in HIDN as processing blocks that the IDN engine designer and the author may use to create new artefacts. Beyond this option, the shift from a problem solving view to a creative view may lead to the foundation of a new subfield of computing, a sibling of AI, where core concepts would be both narrative and authorable; they would be represented in a way that is meaningful for an author. It is important to note that our claim is *not* to provide a simplified and accessible AI that nonprogramming authors would be able to use effortlessly, such as visual programming. Authorable and narrative concepts need to be the first-hand concepts handled by both the author and the engine designer. In current AI-based approaches, AI core concepts are used to describe narrative principles. For example, an operator, or a predicate, is used to describe an action; a list of atomic logical states conditions is used to describe a narrative goal; a planning goal is used to describe a dramatic conflict, etc. The creative view of AI fosters the development of a new logic that handles concepts such as action, narrative goals or dramatic conflict directly, not as *applications* of known AI algorithms. In other words, the computational models become natively narrative, as illustrated in Table 9.1.

Table 9.1 Comparison between the classical view on HIDN and the novel view that is suggested in this chapter.

Classical View	Novel View
One-actor AI	Three-actor AI
Problem-solving oriented	Creativity oriented
AI models applied to narrative	Natively narrative computational models
Theoretical expressivity (what can be represented)	Authorability (ability to be handled by an author)
Internal focus (compactness, speed, etc.)	External focus (expressivity towards the end-user)
Logical concepts: state, operators, rational agents, etc.	Narrative concepts: action, narrative act, dramatic tension, inter-character relation, beat, etc.
Focus on a tangible product (the generated story)	Focus on a psychological process (the interactive narrative experience)

We have initiated, albeit in a primitive way, such a rethinking of core AI concepts. In IDtension (Szilas, 2003) and subsequent theoretical models (Szilas, Richle and Petta, 2012; Szilas and Richle, 2013), the notion of obstacle, for example, does not come from AI. We have implemented it as a concept of its own, in relation to other concepts such as a task or a goal. The obstacle mechanism is used to determine the success or failure of a task, propagate related information among characters (including the risk of occurrence), trigger subgoals in order to remove the obstacle, etc. Each of these mechanisms can be implemented with classical AI concepts, but the use of the concept of obstacle enables the author to straightforwardly reason at the narrative level. For creative authors in particular, who have often read some literature on screenwriting and dramaturgy (Field, 1984; McKee, 1997; Vale, 1973), this concept is appealing. Another attempt to move AI models towards more narrative representation has consisted in getting rid of the omnipresent concept of state, used in particular as preconditions and consequences of actions or events. In fact, although using states seems rather obvious for programmers, it is not straightforward for creative authors. Furthermore, in many cases when authoring with states, one has to add a state as a consequence of some element and then add the same state as a precondition of another element, which is cumbersome. Therefore, we proposed to replace such states with meaningful *relations* between possible actions (enabling relations, relevance relations, etc.) (Szilas and Axelrad,

2009). On a small-scale simulation, we could demonstrate that this alternative representation generates simple stories, similarly as classical state-based representations.

These two examples only provide some hints of what could be a novel form of knowledge representation dedicated to HIDN and more generally to narrative. Reformulating computation in narrative terms is a difficult and long-term enterprise. We, the researchers, were born in the problem-solving AI, and now narrative-based AI requires us to break out of the mould by defining new axioms and rules that will generate a new sort of computation.

6. SYNTHESIS AND CONCLUSION

We have claimed so far that significant progress in HIDN may be achieved if we are able to rethink not only the processes and goals of research and design, but also the actors and the basic types of knowledge representations. In practice, it means that we need to bring together HIDN researchers (engine designers), creative authors and software engineers around three common goals:

- a model for HIDN,
- a playable artistic piece,
- a set of authoring tools and methods.

In terms of methodology, none of these three goals come first in time—they are pursued concurrently. This goes against the classical software engineering practices, notably because authoring tools need to be developed whereas the underlying model is not even specified. Therefore, agile and iterative methodologies are mandatory in this context. It should include the paper prototyping approach (Fullerton, 2008) that is widely used in game design. Other recent software development trends and ideas should also be investigated, such as real-time coding (ability to change your program while the code is running), authoring while coding (the ability to semiautomatically build the authoring tool while coding), generic authoring tools, tangible interfaces, etc.

The computational models should be progressively refined not only to reach well-known computational criteria (variability, genericity, simplicity, tractability, etc.); but also they should satisfy expressivity constraints such as the ability to produce an effect to the player (Mateas, 2000) and authorability constraints such as the ability to be conceptually usable by an author (Szilas, 2007). This latter constraint should also benefit to the system designers because it will guide the design process towards simpler models, avoiding a tendency of gratuitous sophistication: developing clever and complex computational features that seem useful but that are not. More generally, expressivity and authorability constraints should help prioritising the developments and find the optimal narrative representations for building a HIDN.

Since these computational models are designed for human users (authors and players), the user interface is essential. Following the HCI principle that the interface is the software, the computational models will be designed at the same time as the corresponding authoring tools. This requires thinking right away in terms of graphs, schematics and other visualisation tools and techniques. On the player side, a proper way to visualise the narrative and making it interactive should be available right at the beginning of the project. This seems unfeasible given the difficulty of handling a graphical representation of characters' actions, in particular in 3D. A possible solution lies in simpler modes of representations of characters' actions, either as work in progress or target work (Szilas, Wang and Axelrad, 2008).

To conclude, the core challenge of highly interactive digital narrative, which is merging narrative coherence and user intervention, has been analysed from various perspectives leading to the simple conclusion that the problem is fundamentally ill-defined; therefore, its current solutions need to be rethought. Moving from a problem solving to a creative perspective, we redefined the priorities for future research in the domain. It consists of shifting the research focus from the technical realm to a deeply interdisciplinary realm in which researchers, authors and software developers work collaboratively and concurrently towards their respective goals (creative, scientific and technical).

This kind of research setting is rather incompatible with academic organisation, systematically divided into disciplines, branches and sections. Even if, since the 1990s, researchers and institutions praise interdisciplinary research, we could observe how it is difficult to introduce a creative author within a technical team. The game industry constitutes a more appropriate environment for such collaboration, but they are naturally inclined towards short-term research which is not suited to interactive narrative research. Not surprisingly, practically all successful projects in our domain are often the fruit of game engineers who moved in an academic or independent setting, being thus able to combine the best of both worlds.

Beyond the domain of interactive narrative, the new natively narrative models that we are calling for fall within the scope of Narrative Intelligence: they may lead to novel human-like ways of storing and processing data, with applications ranging from interactive entertainment to knowledge management and interactive marketing.

NOTE

1. Released by Chris Crawford in 2009 at http://www.swatbugs.com/play-bop2k-launch.php but later closed down and no longer available.

REFERENCES

Aylett, R. (1999) Narrative in virtual environments—Towards emergent narrative. In: Mateas, M. and Sengers, P. (eds.) *Proceedings of the AAAI Fall Symposium on Narrative Intelligence.* The AAAI Press.

Aylett, R. and Louchart, S. (2007) Being there: Participants and spectators in interactive narrative. In: Cavazza, M. and Donikian, S. (eds.) *Fourth International Conference on Virtual Storytelling (ICVS 2007). LNCS 4871.* Berlin, Heidelberg: Springer.

Crawford, C. (1996) *Is Interactivity Inimical to Storytelling.* Available at: http://www.erasmatazz.com/library/Lilan/inimical.html

El-Nasr, M. S. and Horswill, I. (2003) Real-time lighting design for interactive narrative. In: Balet, O., Subsol, G., and Torguet, P. (eds.) *Virtual Storytelling, Second International Conference (ICVS 2003). LNCS 2897.* Berlin, Heidelberg: Springer.

Fendt, M. W., Harrison, B., Ware, S. G., Cardona-Rivera, R. E, and Roberts, D. L. (2012) Achieving the illusion of agency. In: Oyarzun, D., Peinado, F., Young, R. M., Elizalde, A., and Méndez, G. (eds.) *Fifth International Conference on Interactive Digital Storytelling (ICIDS). LNCS, 7648.* Berlin, Heidelberg: Springer.

Field, S. (1984) *Screenplay—The Foundations of Screenwriting.* New York: Dell Publishing.

Figueiredo, R. and Paiva, A. (2010) I want to slay that dragon!: Influencing choice in interactive storytelling. In *Proceedings of the Third Joint Conference on Interactive Digital Storytelling (ICIDS 2010). LNCS 6432.* Berlin, Heidelberg: Springer-Verlag.

Fullerton, T. (2008) *Game Design Workshop: A Playcentric Approach to Creating Innovative Games.* Burlington, MA: Morgan Kaufmann.

Hsueh-Min Chang, V.-W. S. (2009) Planning-based narrative generation in simulated game universes. *IEEE Transactions on Computational Intelligence and AI in Games.* 1(3). pp. 200–213.

Jameson, A., Spaulding, A. and Yorke-Smith, N. (2009) Introduction to the special issue on "usable AI". *AI Magazine.* 30(4). pp. 11–14.

Knoller, N. (2012) The expressive space of IDS-as-art. In: Oyarzun, D., Peinado, F., Young, R. M., Elizalde, A. and Méndez, G. (eds.) *Fifth International Conference on Interactive Digital Storytelling (ICIDS). LNCS, 7648.* Berlin, Heidelberg: Springer.

Laurel, B. (1986) *Towards the Design of a Computer-Based Interactive Fantasy System.* PhD Thesis. Ohio State University.

Louchart, S. and Aylett, R. (2006) Investigation théorique sur le récit émergent. In: Szilas, and Réty, J.-H. (eds.) *Création de Récits Pour les Fictions Interactives: Simulation et Réalisation.* Paris: Hermes and Lavoisier.

Louchart, S., Swartjes, I., Kriegel, M., and Aylett, R. (2008) Purposeful authoring for emergent narrative. In: Spierling, U. and Szilas, N. (eds.) *First Joint International Conference on Interactive Digital Storytelling (ICIDS). LNCS 5334.* Berlin / Heidelberg: Springer.

Mateas, M. (2000) Expressive AI. In *SIGGRAPH 2000 Electronic Art and Animation Catalog.*

Mateas, M. and Stern, A. (2003) Integrating plot, character and natural language processing in the interactive drama Façade. In: Göbel, S., Braun, N., Spierling, U., Dechau, J., and Diener, H. (eds.) *Proceedings of the Technologies* for *Interactive Digital Storytelling and Entertainment (TIDSE) Conference*. Darmstadt: Fraunhofer IRB.

Mateas, M. and Stern, A. (2005) Build it to understand it : Ludology meets Narratology in game design space. In *Transactions of the DiGRA Conference 2005*.

Mccoy, J., Treanor, M., Samuel, B., Tearse, B., Mateas, M., and Wardrip-Fruin, N. (2010) Authoring game-based interactive narrative using social games and comme il faut. In *Proceedings of the 4th International Conference and Festival of the Electronic Literature Organization: Archive and Innovate (ELO 2010)*.

McKee, R. (1997) *Story: Substance, Structure, Style, and the Principles of Screenwriting*. New York: Harper Collins.

Murray, J. (1997) *Hamlet on the Holodeck: The Future of Narrative in Cyberspace*. New York: Simon & Schuster/Free Press.

Mutiny (2011) *The Mutiny*. Available at: http://tecfa.unige.ch/perso/szilas/IDtension/installIDtension_beta3.jar

Newell, A., Shaw, J. C., and Simon, H. A. (1959) *Report on a General Problem-Solving Program*. Report P-1584. Available at: http://bitsavers.informatik. uni-stuttgart.de/pdf/rand/ipl/P-1584_Report_On_A_General_Problem-Solving_Program_Feb59.pdf

Pizzi, D., Charles, F., Lugrin, J., and Cavazza, M. (2007) Interactive storytelling with literary feelings. In: Paiva, A. C. R., Prada, R., and Picard, R. W. (eds.) *Affective Computing and Intelligent Interaction. LNCS 4738*. Berlin / Heidelberg: Springer.

Portugal, J.-N. (2006) L'avenir dira ce que nous aurons créé. In: Szilas, N. and Réty, J.-H. (eds.) *Création de Récits pour les Fictions Iinteractives: Simulation et Réalisation*. Paris: Hermes and Lavoisier.

Russel, S. J. and Norvig, P. (1995) *Artificial Intelligence: A Modern Approach*. Englewood Cliffs, New Jersey: Prentice Hall.

Si, M., Marsella, S. C. and Riedl, M. O. (2008) Integrating story-centric and character-centric processes for authoring interactive drama. In: Darken, C. and Mateas, M. (eds.) *Fourth Artificial Intelligence and Interactive Digital Entertainment Conference (AIIDE)*. Menlo Park, CA: AAAI Press.

Spaulding, A. and Weber, J. S. (2009) Usability engineering methods for interactive intelligent systems. *AI Magazine*. 30(4). pp. 41–47.

Spierling, U., Grasbon, D., Braun, N. and Iurgel, I. (2002) Setting the scene: playing digital director in interactive storytelling and creation. *Computers and Graphics*. 26(1). pp. 31–44.

Spierling, U., Hoffmann, S., Szilas, N., and Richle, U. (2011) *Educational Material for Creators on AI-Based Generative Narrative Methods*. Deliverable D3.2 for the FP7-ICT-231824 EU Project. Available at: http://ec.europa.eu/information_society/apps/projects/logos/4/231824/080/deliverables/001_IRISFP7ICT-231824Deliverable32.pdf

Spierling, U. and Szilas, N. (2009) Authoring issues beyond tools. In: Iurgel, I., Zagalo, N. and Petta, P. (eds.) *Second Joint International Conference on Interactive Digital Storytelling (ICIDS 2009). LNCS 5915*. Heidelberg: Springer.

Szilas, N. (2003) IDtension : a narrative engine for interactive drama. In: Göbel, S., Braun, N., Spierling, U., Dechau, J. and Diener, H. (eds.) *Proceedings of the Technologies for Interactive Digital Storytelling and Entertainment (TIDSE) Conference*. Fraunhofer IRB.

Szilas, N. (2004) Stepping into the interactive drama. In: Göbel, S., Spierling, U., Hoffmann, A., Iurgel, I., Schneider, O., Dechau, J., and Feix, J. (eds.) *Technologies* for Interactive Digital Storytelling and Entertainment (TIDSE 2004). LNCS 3105. Berlin, Heidelberg: Springer.

Szilas, N. (2005) The future of interactive drama. In *Proccedings of the Second Australiasian Conference on Interactive Entertainment (IE'05)*, pp. 193–199.

Szilas, N. (2007) A computational model of an intelligent narrator for interactive narratives. *Applied Artificial Intelligence*. 21(8). 753–801.

Szilas, N. (2010) Requirements for computational models of interactive narrative. In: Finlayson, M. (ed.) *Computational Models of Narrative, Papers From the 2010 AAAI Fall Symposium*. Menlo Park, California: AAAI Press. pp. 62–68.

Szilas, N. and Axelrad, M. (2009) To be or not to be : Towards stateless interactive drama. In: Iurgel, I., Zagalo, N., and Petta, P. (eds.) *2nd International Conference on International Digital Storytelling (ICIDS 2009)*. LNCS 5915. Berlin, Heidelberg: Springer.

Szilas, N., Dumas, J., Richle, U., Habonneau, N., and Boggini, T. (2013) *Nothing For Dinner*. Available at: http://tecfalabs.unige.ch/tbisim/portal/

Szilas, N., Marty, O., and Réty, J. (2003) Authoring highly generative interactive drama. In: Balet, O., Subsol, G. and Torguet, P. (eds.) *Virtual Storytelling, Second International Conference (ICVS 2003)*. LNCS 2897. Heidelberg: Springer Verlag.

Szilas, N. and Richle, U. (2013) Towards a computational model of dramatic tension. In: Finlayson, M. A., Fisseni, B., Löwe, B., and Meister, J. C. (eds.) *2013 Workshop on Computational Models of Narrative*. Dagstuhl, Germany: Schloss Dagstuhl—Leibniz-Zentrum fuer Informatik.

Szilas, N., Richle, U., and Dumas, J. E. (2012) Structural writing, a design principle for interactive drama. In: Oyarzun, D., Peinado, F., Young, R. M., Elizalde, A., and Méndez, G. (eds.) *Fifth International Conference on Interactive Digital Storytelling (ICIDS)*. LNCS, 7648. Berlin, Heidelberg: Springer.

Szilas, N., Richle, U., and Petta, P. (2012) *Structures for Interactive Narrative: An Authored Centred Approach*. Technical Report TECFA-TR-12-01. 2.

Szilas, N., Wang, J., and Axelrad, M. (2008) Towards minimalism and expressiveness in interactive drama. In *DIMEA 08 Proceedings of the 3rd International Conference on Digital Interactive Media in Entertainment and Arts*. pp. 385–392.

Vale, E. (1973) *The Technique of Screenplay Writing*. New York: Grosset and Dunlap.

Versu (2012) Versu—Living Stories. Available at: http://www.versu.com

Weber, J. S. and Yorke-Smith, N. (2009) Designing for usability of an adaptive time management assistant. *AI Magazine*. 30(4). pp. 103–109.

Weyhrauch, P. (1997) *Guiding Interactive Drama*. PhD Thesis. Carnegie Mellon University.

Yu, H. and Riedl, M. O. (2013) Toward personalized guidance in interactive narratives. In *8th International Conference on the Foundations of Digital Games (FDG 2013)*.

Section III
IDN Practice

Introduction

Beyond the Holodeck: A Speculative Perspective on Future Practices

Hartmut Koenitz, Gabriele Ferri, Mads Haahr, Diğdem Sezen and Tonguç İbrahim Sezen

Interactive Digital Narrative is an ever-growing field that encompasses a number of diverse practices, from avant-garde art to interactive documentaries, electronic literature, video game design, applications of artificial intelligence (AI) research and ubiquitous computing. To provide a context for understanding today's practices, in this introduction we will trace some of the exciting directions in the field of interactive digital narrative (IDN) by examining characteristics and current applications in three areas. In addition to that, as an exercise in futuring, we also hypothesise on possible developments. More concretely, we will examine how interactive narratives are used in the context of creating compelling game experiences and suggest possible future directions in that field. We will then consider some relationships between interactive narrative and place-specific digital experiences, from current geolocalised apps to upcoming developments. Finally, the application of IDN technologies to news reporting and documentary practices will be discussed, along with possible perspectives for its developments in the next years.

USING IDN TO CREATE COMPELLING GAME EXPERIENCES

Narrative components are emerging as increasingly relevant for today's video games to complement and support game mechanics. Current titles are adopting a wide range of narrative structures. These structures range from the long, overarching narratives often found in single-player cinematic games such as the *Assassins' Creed* (2007–present) series, to the chains of quests driving the exploration in massively multiplayer online roleplaying games such as *World of Warcraft* (2005–present), to the more emergent structures that can appear in sandbox games like the *Grand Theft Auto* (1997–present) series. The fact that narrative genres and subgenres in video games are quickly differentiating themselves from and diverging from their original inspirations is a testament to how mature this medium has become in a surprisingly short time. Some specific forms have already emerged; for example, games like *The Wolf Among Us* (2013) and *The Walking Dead* (2012) have appropriated forms of episodic storytelling typical of graphic novels or television series and essentially constitute short video game episodes where play and narrative cliff-hangers complement each other. Similarly to independent filmmakers, video game auteurs have experimented with narrative in pieces such as *Dear Esther* (2012), *Gone Home* (2013) and *The Stanley Parable* (2013) to bring tropes such as the unreliable narrator or the role reversal into contemporary digital narratives. Finally, new narrative experiments are bridging the gaps between different IDN forms—another case of hybridisation and cross-fertilisation within the field that testimonies its vitality. For this last group, we can mention examples such as *CAVE! CAVE! DEUS VIDET* (2013), an art piece blending elements from interactive visual novels with graphic adventure games, or the many text games made with Twine, a highly accessible authoring system for interactive fictions that was used for influential and provocative titles such as *Howling Dogs* (2012).

A plausible future trend in video games concerned with storytelling would be an even tighter integration between narrative components and game design elements leading to a more central role of computer-controlled characters in video game narratives and, at the same time, to a more conscious and varied use of dramatic compression. Years after the heated debate on the compatibility (or lack thereof) between gameplay and narrative elements, the two sides not only coexist but complement and enhance each other in current titles. Indeed, it is not difficult to foresee a more refined use of in-game constraints, rules and objectives to serve narrative purposes and, vice versa, dynamic quests and backstories to support gameplay. Advances in AI for computer-controlled characters might be particularly beneficial for providing narrative coherence in online games, to orient players' actions, and to provide narrative hooks and closure. Today, narrative in multiplayer or the sandbox game is relatively rudimentary, principally because of the technical and logistical challenges in orchestrating a coherent experience for a multitude of players at once. More advanced AI routines might solve this problem in the future, improving the narrative experience in these types of games. Finally, more refined computational algorithms and narrative structures could enable dynamic dramatic compression and eventually be able to detect whether a player would like to skip some gameplay parts to reach the next narratively relevant one or, if the player prefers, to spend more time in an action phase before reaching the following chapter.

USING IDN TO CREATE LOCATION-BASED NARRATIVE EXPERIENCE

Micronarrations that react to their user's physical location are another recent trend. Location-based applications are, generally speaking, applications running on mobile devices that detect the device's current location through Wifi triangulation and/or GPS satellite tracking. Today, these technologies allow users to associate narrative microcontents to specific places and to retrieve contents tied to a specific location. Currently, the Foursquare app is one of the best-known examples in this category: in addition to game-like mechanics, Foursquare (2009–2014) can be used "as a recording device (in the fashion of a travelogue, to share written notes on places, routes, episodes) [and] as a factitive device, similar to the use of a bottom-up guide book" (Caruso et al., 2011). However, Foursquare adopts a very simplistic cooperative narrative structure—leaving tips on specific venues—that could be greatly refined. A range of other apps follow Foursquare's model of linking recommendations and comments to specific physical locations, but only a handful of them are specifically designed for storytelling—amongst them Broadcastr (2011) and MapSkip (2007–2013).

The combination of interactive digital narratives with location-based technology and pervasive gaming has resulted in playful travel guides, interactive museum experiences and even geolocalised fitness apps. In their influential book *Pervasive Games: Theory and Design*, Markus Montola, Jaakko Stenros and Annika Waern described 'pervasive gaming' through a corpus of playful practices that share "one or more salient features that expand the contractual magic circle of play spatially, temporally, or socially" (Montola, Stenros and Waern, 2009, p.12). For example, *Whaiwhai* is a framework for digital urban game experiences (Log607, 2009–2011); currently, *Whaiwhai* apps are available for the cities of New York, Florence, Rome, Milan, Venice and Verona. *Whaiwhai* is partly a remediation of traditional travel guides, as it challenges players to explore historical areas of specific cities; yet the framework brings in game elements in the form of missions users need to fulfil by visiting specific places. The system tracks players throughout their game, offering new challenges as they progress. Whaiwhai aims to make the travel experiences more game-like by offering an objective and a set of quests to solve while blending a fictional narrative with the participants' explorations.

Fitness apps like *Zombies, Run!* (2012) and *The Walk* (2014) feature complex, nuanced narrative structures in addition to other ludic elements. These titles, developed by British studio Six to Start with funding from the UK Department of Health, are among the first to rely on interactive storytelling to entice users to start training and to keep them going. Both of these examples are realised as mobile apps accessing the GPS sensor in mobile devices and offering a rich storyline through the headphones, as if it were an interactive radio drama where users proceed in the story only when physically moving.

Future developments in this specific area of IDN practice would rely on more advanced techniques for geolocalisation, especially following recent developments in in-door tracking for an even tighter integration between narrative and physical places. The combination of interactive narrative and ubiquitous computing—for example with complex narratives that react specifically to the place, time and social context in which they are experienced—is indeed promising and could open a new field for IDNs to develop.

USING IDN TO CREATE DOCUMENTARIES AND NEWS ITEMS

Adopting IDN elements and technologies to present news and other journalistic contributions is a relatively new tendency in this field. Partially overlapping with the fields of news gaming, serious gaming and interactive documentaries, some recent digital narrative projects aim to inform their audience or present political messages. As we have mentioned before in our sketch of the historical development of IDNs, interactive documentaries have existed since the 1980s as exemplified by Glorianna Davenport's piece *A City in Transition: New Orleans 1983–86* (Davenport, 1987). However, only recently with the widespread diffusion of fast broadband connections, interactive documentaries are becoming a more established genre of IDN that brings together interactivity, a documentary perspective and—in some cases—game elements. *Inside the Haiti Earthquake* (2010), an online companion to the *Inside Disaster: Haiti* (2011) documentary film, is a recent example that casts the user variously in the role of journalist, aid worker or survivor of the January 2010 Haiti earthquake. The piece is designed to challenge assumptions about relief work in disaster situations, allowing interactors to try various strategies and experience their consequences. As an extension of a high-production value documentary series, *Inside the Haiti Earthquake* integrates video footage in a branching structure presenting different perspectives selected through audience choices. *Fort McMoney* (Dufresne, 2013) discusses the Canadian oil industry and lets players explore the small town of Fort McMurray and the consequences caused by the get-rich-quick mentality of its inhabitants. This piece is more explicit than many others in blending typical video game structures and design tropes with a documentary objective. Instead of presenting an open space to be freely explored, *Fort McMoney* creates a quest-like system; participants need to search for information by exploring interviews and their progress is tracked using points and credits on a dashboard. Finally, *1000 Days of Syria* presents three narratives set in the Syrian civil war that began in 2011; users can follow a foreign photojournalist, a mother of two living in Daraa or a rebel youth living in Aleppo. In stark contrast with *Inside the Haiti Earthquake* and *Fort McMoney*, *1000 Days of Syria* (Swenson, 2014) renounces graphics in favour of a text-only hypertextual structure in an attempt to force users to empathise more with the characters' internal struggles without being distracted by visual elements.

Future developments for this specific IDN practice might follow different paths. One could be tied to more realistic virtual environments—with similarities to open-world video games—for players to explore, interacting with relevant computer-controlled virtual characters. This way, users could experience far away or dangerous places and interact with specific characters within these environments. Another possibility would be related to new developments in three-dimensional displays. Today, an app named

Condition One (2011–2014) is already available on smart phones and tablets to present video footage in which users can rotate their point of view by physically turning the device. One of the demonstrations for this system was a short interactive documentary in which the participant was situated in a trench during a battle in Libya. An improved version of the same system is currently under development for the Oculus Rift virtual reality headset, promising a true immersive experience in documentary footage. Finally, documentary IDNs might become closer to the news game genre, adopting more ludic characteristics such as providing players with objectives to achieve, and leaving them to explore the different consequences and the effectiveness of various tactics.

A VIBRANT FIELD OF HETEROGENEOUS PRACTICES

Foregrounding these three perspectives in our introduction is meant to convey the impression of a lively and growing field, but we wish to remember that they are not the only ones, as the essays that comprise the last section of this volume will show. Given the vitality of IDNs, we are confident that in the next years we will see further growth and diversification.

REFERENCES

Blizzard Entertainment. (2005–2013) *World of Warcraft*. [video game]. Vivendi.

Broadcastr Inc. (2011) *Broadcastr*. [software].

Caruso, G., Fassone, R., Salvador, M., and Ferri, G. (2011). Check-in everywhere. places, people, narrations, games. *Comunicazioni Sociali Online*.

The Chinese Room. (2012) *Dear Esther*. [video game].

Condition One Inc. (2011–2014) *Condition One*. [interactive documentary].

Davenport, G. (1987). New Orleans in transition, 1983–1986: The interactive delivery of a cinematic case study. In *The International Congress for Design Planning and Theory, Education Group Conference Proceedings*. Boston, MA. pp. 1–7.

Dufresne, D. (2013). *Fort McMoney*. [interactive documentary].

Foursquare Inc. (2009–2014) *Foursquare*. [software].

The Fullbright Company. (2013) *Gone Home*. [video game].

Galactic Café. (2013) *The Stanley Parable*. [video game].

Log607. (2009–2011) *Whaiwhai*. [video game series]. Padova, Italy: Marsilio.

Mapskip.com. (2007–2013) *Mapskip*. [software].

Montola, M., Stenros, J., and Waern, A. (2009) *Pervasive Games. Theory and Design*. Burlington, VA: Morgan Kaufmann Publishers.

Porpentine. (2012) *Howling Dogs*. [video game].

PTV Productions, Inc. (2010) *Inside the Haiti Earthquake*. [interactive documentary]. PTV.

Rockstar Games. (1997–2013) *Grand Theft Auto*. [video game series]. BMG Interactive.

Six to Start. (2012) *Zombies, Run!* [video game]. Six to Start.

Six to Start. (2014) *The Walk*. [video game]. Six to Start.
Swenson, M. (2014). *1000 Days of Syria*. [interactive documentary].
Telltale Games (2012–2013) *The Walking Dead*. [video game series]. Telltale Games.
Telltale Games. (2013) *The Wolf Among Us*. [video game series]. Telltale Games.
Ubisoft. (2007–2013) *Assassins' Creed*. [video game series]. Ubisoft.
We Are Muesli. (2013) *CAVE! CAVE! DEUS VIDET*. [video game].

10 Interaction Design Principles as Narrative Techniques for Interactive Digital Storytelling

Ulrike Spierling

1. INTERACTIVE STORY CREATION

The various tasks of creation in the domain of Interactive Digital Narrative (IDN) are often referred to as *authoring*. At annual research meetings like the International Conference of Interactive Digital Storytelling,[1] several kinds of solutions to authoring problems are addressed by technical papers, such as the development of authoring tools. Along the lines of easy-to-learn multimedia authoring tools for point-and-click interactions, content programming for interactive story engines should be eased accordingly. The notion of *the author* used in this context often implies the existence of a single user of a tool, suggesting the idea of one exclusive author similar to a traditional view of literary writing. In the following, we will see that this image needs some adaptation for interactive narrative.

1.1 Perspectives on Authoring

Computational IDN research began in the early 1990s with the formulation of high-level mission statements about interactive drama as a new media form. Examples of such visions are the notion of highly interactive drama (Kelso et al., 1993), enabled by real-time computer graphics, and the concept of the Holodeck (Murray, 1997), a fictional reality simulation platform invented in the American science fiction TV series *Star Trek: The Next Generation* (1987–1994). Both ideas reach beyond point-and-click hypertext in that readers become active participants in a simulated world of life-like inhabitants, technically immersed in a fictional experience. The goal is a feeling of natural interaction, where participants are talking and moving around freely—like in the real world—while other (simulated) agents behave as if they were humans.

Easy-to-learn multimedia authoring tools do not seem to be progressing enough to support the authoring tasks involved in highly interactive storytelling. In order to give end-users a feeling of participation, virtual characters need to respond believably to user actions. Crafting the full set of possible consequences of all possible event sequences is a tedious problem to solve manually, and therefore complex algorithms and story engines based on Artificial Intelligence (AI) are deployed. This situation results in a crisis for creative authors. Traditional writing of dialogue has been a form of artistic expression performed by writers who empathise deeply with their invented characters, letting each line express personality, emotional state and thematic coherence. However, for example with dialogue engines that undertake the task of rendering a suitable reaction, it is necessary to code precise conditions for answers and grammatical templates of sentence parts, which mostly cannot be done intuitively by creative writers.

Hence, in a recent European research project called IRIS,[2] one objective was to make contemporary engine concepts more accessible to authors. Going beyond an investigation of the expectations and requirements of traditional authors, we wanted to identify general design principles for interactive storytelling.

1.2 Design Principles

By means of practical authoring experiments involving several different story engines, we tried to identify general design principles independent of a specific technical approach. We suggested a list of principles that we tested as being useful within educational material for authors (Spierling et al., 2011). We also discussed them in practical case studies in which authors with various professional backgrounds were involved (Spierling et al., 2012). These are briefly summarised below.

One of the major conclusions from the experiments was that in order to achieve dynamic behaviour that can be controlled by an engine, it is essential to approach the task of interactive story creation as the modelling of a storyworld. *Modelling* in this context means the construction of a dynamic world model of all story elements, along with rules for agents' behaviour and for selecting actions and events. In this model design process, authors need to anticipate potential story states to occur during interaction. It is crucial that we distinguish a logical model of story as separate from a plot-like structure that details the concrete reactive scene rendering and the order of events. In that sense, different aspects of narrative structure may be addressed, similar to a distinction that Seymour Benjamin Chatman (1978) proposed by separating the story as the content of narrative expression from what he referred to as its form, the narrative discourse. In our experiments (IRIS, 2012), we tested several approaches, such as knowledge engineering for planning, conversational modelling and modelling with state machines. Practical experiments showed that it is difficult to draft interactive story experiences solely based on an abstract model; therefore, creators probably want to intertwine logic modelling phases with writing concrete scene content and testing of the results, thus going back and forth between these different activities (Spierling, 2011).

For the modelling phase, the two proposed design principles, *abstraction* and *conditional thinking*, are most important. By abstracting events, we can generalise potential system reactions and achieve a metaphorical understanding of the underlying system behaviour. By thinking in terms of conditional actions and events and considering the effects of each possible action, we make explicit the underlying acting situations for story characters as well as for end-users, thus laying the ground for a logical progression. On the one hand, this perspective makes the behaviour of virtual characters situation-dependent; on the other, it means creating interesting affordances for situations the end-users can act in. This led to a third principle: to always include the user from the start, defining possible players' actions as an inherent part of the abstract storyworld model. Rather than trying to script the player's decisions, this means to consider the scope of possible changes that players can effect within the storyworld. It is more difficult to account for all possible user influence at a later stage of story design than at the beginning. Finally, such a model needs to be 'debugged,' or refined, in an iterative process of model-building and experiencing because it is unlikely that optimal behavioural rules will be guessed right from the start. In this sense, *debugging* (a storyworld) should also be seen as an authoring principle.

These design principles were evaluated with several case studies of a size typical for research projects, which usually do not cover extensive content creation tasks—ranging from summer school results to half-year media projects (Spierling et al., 2012). Without practical evaluation, another design principle has been included in the list as a hypothesis, namely to *externalise the internal*. We mainly acknowledged this principle as a quality we miss when it is not realised properly. The principle has been adopted from screenwriting. David Howard and Edward Mabley (1993) described it as a tool to show in film what is going on inside a character at any given time. The obvious solution—to let the characters just talk about their thoughts and plans—is rarely regarded as satisfactory. Rather, it is an artistic challenge to invent a set of scenarios that allow or facilitate the expression of hidden feelings. What is difficult in film is all the more challenging for AI-based storytelling.

NoahWardrip-Fruin (2007) called a related phenomenon "the Tale-Spin-Effect." He referred to the *Tale-Spin* system (Meehan, 1977) that was able to compute complex psychological processes, such as an internal plan of a character. But nothing of this showed up at the interface level apart from a blunt chosen action that was the result of all the digital considerations. To relate plot elements calculated from abstract story models to the user, some surface realization at the user interface is needed that realises abstract messages as perceivable text (Wardrip-Fruin, 2009). Wardrip-Fruin discussed the difficulty to achieve this realisation by computational linguistic processing. Regardless of the chosen process, this interface to the user/player/audience needs to be created—either written, configured or otherwise defined during authoring.

1.3 Graphics and Multimedia in Computer Games: A Feedback System

Independent of these aspects of story modelling, we can also take a look at the related area of interactive games. Guides to video game writing stress the importance of designing for a feedback system. They consider player agency as a basic concern, even if an 'illusion of agency' is also admitted (DeMarle, 2007). This implies that audiovisual or textual display of a narrative, which is the result of all the game writers' and artists' efforts, is mostly considered feedback that is triggered by the actions of players, giving them guidance and meaning. "The more your story can be told through gameplay, the better. Much like the film axiom 'Don't say it, show it,' you should be thinking in a similar fashion for the game: 'Don't show it, play it'" (Dille and zuur Platten, 2007).

Interface design is hardly considered a distinct discipline separate from game design. According to Kevin Saunders and Jeannie Novak (2007), the term *interface* "refers to anything that helps the player interact with the game." Thus, it includes not only hardware and graphical components such as menus and health bars, but "[e]ven the game characters can be considered interface elements" (Saunders and Novak, 2007, p.3). Translated to our field of interactive narrative, the design of such interface elements representing, for example, a character's health or other inner value, correlates with the definition of narrative elements. The more a player gets to participate as a member of a storyworld, the more its interface and narrative become the same thing, distinguishing highly interactive drama from hypertextual narratives or other forms with less player involvement.

2. INTERACTION DESIGN AS A NARRATIVE TECHNIQUE?

Interaction design and similar tasks, such as interface design or user interface engineering, are professional disciplines (Preece et al., 2002). Experts create the shapes and behaviour of human-computer interfaces to make interactive digital products usable, which can mean more accessible, efficient and/or safe, as well as enjoyable or at least less frustrating. This branch of design affords to take the perspective of the human in the interactive loop and to go through several iterations of eliciting user requirements, designing and user testing.

2.1 Interaction is Content

This chapter is not about this kind of user-friendliness, nor does it tackle usability testing or user requirements analysis. These are tasks that may still need to be added once a modelled story is brought towards its realisation. Instead, we pose that conceptual authors in interactive storytelling are actually responsible for a whole experience, orchestrating narrative processes with interaction, while a complex interactive storyworld is created. A similar orchestration was already demanded by Brenda Laurel (1993) in her influential book *Computers as Theatre*. It is necessary to elaborate on this again, as in many discussions about authoring, only the narrative side of interactive narrative seemed to be of interest, while the interactive component of the discipline was not seen as that relevant for authors. This exclusive perspective may fit the concept of hypertextual narrative with default user interfaces for following links. Our storyworld model—since it is interactive—needs to contain information about the acting situations of users/players. Therefore, there is interaction design involved in the very construction of that storyworld. It can be stated that in highly interactive narrative; interaction design is not just another task besides the storytelling but can be an inherently narrative task. Therefore, below we will explore theoretical concepts of interaction design in order to apply them to interactive narrative contexts.

2.2 Affordances, Feedback, Mapping, Constraints

For shaping acting situations for end-users, Don Norman's high-level principles of designing everyday things (Norman, 1988) can be applied to novel designs, as they are general enough and independent of the chosen interface styles. In the future, they may lead to concrete IS design guidelines based on necessary heuristics that need to be established. Norman's metaprinciple is the design of a conceptual model, or mental model or metaphor, guiding all concrete actions. Further relevant principles include *affordance*, "*feedback*, *mapping* and *constraints*. Perceived *affordances* provide strong clues for users about their possibilities for action in each situation. Immediate *feedback* occurring after users' actions is a prerequisite for feeling in control and gaining confidence. While natural *mapping* between visible parts of an interface and their supported actions support the easy learning of an application, physical or logical *constraints* limit interaction possibilities to only appropriate actions. When technical interface constraints are loosened (for example, by allowing natural language interaction or free gestures), affordances and feedback are important design aspects (Norman, 2010) for guiding users.

2.3 Four Levels of Interaction Design

In early computer graphics (CG) research, James D. Foley et al. (1995, p. 394) described the design of Human-Computer dialogues as a CG discipline. They divided the tasks of dialogue design into four levels, where decisions at the top level affected design decisions at lower levels (Table 10.1, left column). Ben Schneiderman and Catherine Plaisant (2010) suggest that this division into levels is convenient for interface designers because it breaks the whole task down into modular concepts and allows for a top-down design approach.

Although originally intended for graphical user interfaces on desktop systems, this model is universal, as are Norman's principles described above. Applied to interactive storytelling, the conceptual level—which corresponds to Norman's necessary mental model—can refer to the design of the principal narrative interaction metaphor and genre, while the level of functional design corresponds to the construction of possible story events to be influenced by players, including their achievements and failures. Technically, these two upper levels define the abstract story logic with rules as a foundation for calculating the plot progress or discourse in response to user actions, which then results in sequences of abstract story states. These states—at this stage expressed by mere technical messages—need to be made perceivable for members of the audience to let them interpret the upper levels. Comparable to the required authorial decisions on the text as surface realization mentioned by Wardrip-Fruin (2009) for interactive literature, the two lower levels of this model explain authorial decisions of how the story is actually told or—rather—experienced interactively. These levels require decisions about the fictional story's natural mapping to real-world symbols and hardware.

Table 10.1 Four-level model; left column: as described by Foley et al. (1995); right column: its application to Interactive Digital Narrative

	Human-Computer Dialogue	Interactive Narrative
Conceptual Level	**Application Concept and Design** Definition of the principal application concepts that a user must master. It builds the user's mental model and is sometimes described in a 'real world analogy' (for example, a spreadsheet). This conceptual level defines the typical objects, their properties and relationships, as well as possible operations of an application.	**Story, Metaphor** Overall narrative story logic including the player's assigned role in the diegetic world, which gives a reason and foundation for what can be done and what story attributes can be influenced by players. It can include 'fictional world analogies' (for example, having to use 'magic equipment' to speak to ghosts).
Semantic Level	**Functional Design** Definition of the functionality of the system, including the 'meaning' of user-initiated functions, or 'user actions' and their results, specification of possible errors and error handling.	**Narrative Function of Action** Definition of 'acting situations,' of narrative conditions for actions, and of the effects of actions and happening events on the narrative progress in a storyworld. This applies to actions of players and fictional characters (story agents).
Syntactic Level	**Sequencing Design** Definition of the order of input and output as part of the 'form' of the interface. This comprises rules of forming sequences of user actions or of 'units of meaning,' which cannot be further decomposed without losing meaning. This level affects the graphical layout of information display, and its sequencing.	**Form, Patterns and Sequences** Definition of a (possibly 'natural') mapping of the functional level (actions and events) to symbols and patterns at the user interface. Design decisions for 'surface realisation' of told events using graphics or sound, as well as for user actions, their affordances and their immediate feedback, including turn-taking with virtual characters.
Lexical Level	**Hardware Binding Design** Definition of the most basic form of the interface. The design includes the specification of input and output devices, display primitives and their attributes, and the precise mechanisms with which users specify input (for example, keystrokes, mouse clicks, body movement, etc.).	**Hardware Binding Design** Definition of the most basic form of the interface, just as described in the original model (left column). Choice of hardware, its use and possible functions, which constrain the surface realisation of the above level of narrative and user actions.

By applying this model to interactive story design, we can construct ideal cases in which story content and interaction are perfectly integrated. Ideally, an overall narrative story logic, including the player's assigned story role defined at the uppermost level, embraces all lower level design decisions. In the sense of Norman's conceptual model, it provides guidance and a general metaphor for the actions that a user can do in accordance with it. Through abstract story modelling, we construct a strong metaphor and a network of logical dependencies, including rules governing how all actions affect the narrative (upper two levels). This should justify all decisions at the lower levels concerning the symbolic layers of narration as elements of the discourse (or surface).

2.4 Simulation and Interface Stats

The imagination of a fully dynamic interactive storytelling system implies that story events will be generated ad-hoc by a digital and/or social process, as in a simulation. Modelling such an underlying dynamic system is a nontrivial task if the goal of a simulation is a certain desired outcome defined by authors. This is not only known in the domain of computer-based simulations, but it is also known in the design of nondigital gaming simulations, such as for training, learning or organisational change, as discussed for decades within the gaming simulation discipline (Duke, 1974). For the design of such a serious (nondigital) simulation game, high-stress situations, intercultural encounters, or organisational issues are often analysed to inform the design, mostly by the search for critical incidents and other effects of mostly intertwined factors. According to Willy Christian Kriz (2000), it is important to maintain a level of abstraction and not to model too many parameters in an endeavour to be faithful to reality because a communicated simulation depends on pragmatic issues to be effective. Similarly, for modelling dynamic worlds, John H. Holland (1998) motivates the discovery of selected building blocks that are at work in a complex system at a high level of abstraction. The challenge is to creatively construct or find unchanging laws that generate the changing configurations. Hence, finding a simulation model with an effective choice of parameters for a dynamic storyworld is a matter of storytelling because creative selections need to be made that are motivated by story goals. Authors need to be aware of the underlying message or moral of a story, including the most important attributes of characters and situations that they want to convey, and they must ensure that these features are effectively communicated.

A computational simulation that calculates new situations in response to story events is at first invisible to end-users because it runs beneath an interface that would communicate those processes. Internally, the simulation may need more parameters than those necessary to convey a plot or enable end-user interaction. Therefore, it is also an authoring decision to define a selection of those attributes that need to be exposed to convey the intended story to the audience. Further, decisions about the symbolic kinds of display are part of the representation layer of the interface and narrative design. For example, an emotional state can be expressed as a facial expression, as spoken text or as a varying value of a gauge on a dashboard, thus 'looking into the brains' of characters. The particular implementation is a design decision at the symbolic levels.

3. EXAMPLES

Implementing the interaction design principles mentioned in the above section, especially integrating all levels, can lead to long and intense conceptual development processes for interactive narrative projects. Although Table 10.1 suggests that a top-down approach could make sense, experiences have shown that there is no right starting point. In some projects, we may test innovative hardware interfaces or settings and let their affordances or limitations inspire narrative ideas bottom-up. Frequently, we search for potential high-level narratives that can then provide mental models that guide *a priori* conceived interaction styles. Putting it all together has often been perceived as a holistic task involving all team members and many disciplines.

3.1 Modelling with Different Systems

To better understand the creation of dynamic (and simulation-like) narrative models, several story modelling activities have been analysed within the IRIS project. Most of these examples started out as authoring case studies to create new content for previously conceived AI-based story engines, each of which afforded different structural modelling approaches (such as for plan structures, finite states, conversation structures or engine-specific narrative structures). The engines' main functions were the sequencing of authored actions and events at runtime according to rules or statements that also needed to be specified during authoring. One subsequent question was to what extent the characteristics of a resulting story model depended upon a given underlying system including its engine affordances. First, it was remarkable that, independent of the chosen AI-based engine approach, the easiest way to start was to model something linear and controllable in order to get a grip on the behaviour of a targeted system. Next, exercises in abstraction (e.g., generalisation/grouping of single actions) and conditioning events upon variable states followed. This approach led to story models that were more general in the sense that they showed at least one or several defined story-determining attributes that could be affected by a story's (non-player) characters as well as the player/end-user.

In the following, we discuss examples designed for different platforms and interaction paradigms.

3.2 Conversational Story Modelling

Offering free text input to let users chat with digital characters has been a creative goal for several authors; however, it is a challenging exercise in input recognition. So far, even the most convincing examples in interactive drama, such as *Façade* (Mateas and Stern, 2004), which required extensive effort in natural language processing, do not guarantee meaningful reactions to the many possible choices of free user utterances (Dow et al., 2010). With the Scenejo project (Weiss et al., 2005), we explored possible conversations within a similar interaction paradigm as in *Façade*, in that ongoing conversations of two chatbot characters can be interrupted by one user typing text utterances. In several projects of designing content (Spierling, 2008), we found we were able to improve our design of the interactive experience by thinking about each utterance as a narrative action. Beyond just chatting, giving players certain objectives to "do things with words" (Austin, 1962) motivated them to enter text with a goal-oriented perspective, awarded by narrative feedback and progress. Player objectives need to be embedded in a narrative frame, starting with an assigned role for the user to play. Other created story characters need to be equipped with roles, traits and missions that relate to the player's designed task. Important attributes of these traits or of other story elements need to be made perceivable and variable, depending on interactions and/or the narrative leading to certain outcomes. In other words, it means modelling the whole conversation in narrative terms.

One of the narrative experiments considered in the project, *Office Brawl* (Scenejo, 2013) will be briefly analysed by applying the interaction design principles mentioned in the previous section. The story is about an ironic (and self-referential) argument between a designer, Lucy, and a programmer, Ben, who have a fight over the right approach in their current interactive storytelling project. The user plays the project manager with the task to lead the discussion. Ben and Lucy mostly do not use good arguments for their position, but they react to each other with insults unless the user reacts first by typing cautionary remarks. Figure 10.1 shows the interface after the user has failed to moderate the discussion and the situation escalated. Technically, *Office Brawl* is based on authored chatbots (Spierling, 2011) and an ad hoc concatenation of video snippets, one for each utterance (Müller et al., 2013).

When applying the above-mentioned four-level model of interaction, initial design tasks for the uppermost level consisted of defining the two characters, their traits and the user's mission. The kinds of endings for the conversation had to be determined, too, for example, by asking what is at stake (to escalate the discussion) and what can be achieved (to let the characters continue their work). The upper design levels were not completely independent because the intended interface style—defining the lower levels to a great extent—was given by the adopted system following the paradigm

[Lucy]: You have no clue about aethetics.
[Ben]: A beautiful game without any working technology will not sell either. So we should continue to focus on the technology.
[Lucy]: You freak just do not get it, do you?
[Projectmanager]: Lucy, please explain what you mean.
[Lucy]: Alright. Well, if the player is to find himself in a real situation, the look will have to be more believable and professional.
[Ben]: Why is it that everything always has to be all colourful and flashy?
[Lucy]: It is always the same bullshit.
[Ben]: All you ever care about is the look. Could you please grow up?
[Lucy]: Yeah, right, why dont we offer players a command line? Or better yet, shoot ourselves right away?
[Ben]: What a load of crap!
[Lucy]: There is no point in continuing this discussion. If you were not such a lousy project manager, we might have come to some kind of agreement. But you are not exactly good in your job.
[Ben]: Yeah, Lucy is right, for once. You are a dork.

0 Ben   1 Lucy

[Projectmanager]:

Figure 10.1 Interface of Office Brawl. End of the interaction with a negative outcome.

of typed language conversation. There is also a strong connection to the next level, at which level we had to decide on actions and events that could happen. The first drafts of the written dialogue were analysed for possible actions (dialogue acts) that could arithmetically influence story states. It was also necessary to find attributes that could be influenced by user actions. For this level, we worked in iterations on paper prototypes, for example, playing dialogue pieces as cards. The result was a simple model of how qualitative arguments influence a counter (Figure 10.2). Each dialogue act in the conversation was written three times, once as a strong argument explaining a point of view, once as a weak argument and once as an interjection, insult or no argument. In the abstraction, during authoring the resulting sentences were tagged accordingly.

Figure 10.2 Argument types influencing a counter.

User actions/utterances influence the counter indirectly. For example, after the user reacts to an utterance tagged as no argument, the characters are more likely to respond with strong arguments, including a repetition of the last argument using different phrasing. Apart from that, argument types are chosen randomly during the flow of the conversation, with the tendency to allow the conversation to escalate when no interaction occurs. After one of the values reaches zero, the escalation sequence is initiated (as in Figure 10.1). Thus, the high-level conception includes a simple rule-based simulation at the action level.

Further design decisions had to be made about how to represent different story states for the user at the lower interface levels. Replacing the initial realistic representation of the characters with cartoon-like and wiggly photo animations made it easier to include other interface elements without breaking stylistic consistency. In this way, facial expressions and gestures of the characters could be exaggerated. The amount of accentuation was then associated with the type of the actual argument (most exaggerated for negative effects). At the same time, we found it necessary to indicate the overall state of the progressing escalation in the form of a mood barometer for each character. This can be seen as a design choice at the symbolic narrative level to externalise the internal states of a character that are selected from all internal simulation states for narration at the surface. The barometer also provides a consistent visual reaction as immediate feedback to user actions, indicating the success of each intervention.

(a)   (b)

Figure 10.3 Changing barometer levels on the left and right give feedback on conversational progress and the user's influence.

As soon as the user clicks into the text input window, the logical progress of the conversation is paused, but the video presentation is not. The two characters appear to listen to the user—displayed by looping feedback videos showing the characters waiting—until the Enter key is hit.

3.3 Framing Narratives

The technical concept of *Office Brawl* contains video output as well as preauthored utterances of the characters. Therefore, the interaction design could not include ad-hoc verbal generation of unprepared content, which is similar to the approach used in *Façade* (Mateas and Stern, 2004). This implies that during interaction, non sequitur responses may occur if the user does something unexpected. The design of the piece does not cater to all possibilities imaginable, but it tries to anticipate interactions in accordance with the narrative frame. Because of a lack of constraints at the lowest interface level, any framing story in this interaction paradigm needs to present clear objectives along with some hints on how to interact, where giving these objectives and hints can be justified by events in the story. In addition, there should be a story-intrinsic reason why it is impossible for the player's fictional role to always get a suitable answer. Our solution for *Office Brawl* was capricious characters that hardly listen and would just continue fighting if user input is not registered properly.

Consequently, in many examples of interactive narrative, giving the player/user more agency means that either we have to provide additional appropriate reactions, or that there should be an acceptable reason for the limited possibilities.

In another IRIS example, a framing story forced the player to pretend to be somebody else and act like this person. This has been called the *undercover story device* by one of its authors (Struck, 2013). For example, the player character needs to convince a gangster community on a cruise ship that she/he is a long-missing member of the group. If the player then uses words that disclose him/her as a stranger, the player will be thrown overboard. Here, potential difficulties with interaction are fully integrated in a framing story.

A further example is that of the on-going project SPIRIT, in which we design magic equipment for interacting with ghosts in a location-based mobile augmented reality setting (Spirit, 2014). The lowest interaction level in this case is the choice of hardware—mobile devices—and the use of their sensors (camera, accelerometer, GPS, Bluetooth, etc.). In a serious game setting turning history lessons into an adventure, the user is given the task to walk across a cultural heritage site, meet spirits of the past and have conversations with them. Designed as magic equipment, the mobile interface is an intrinsic part of the story. At the highest narrative level, the metaphor of contacting and visualising ghosts with the equipment implies that it is not easy to hold the connection, which playfully challenges the game player to use the interface the right way. This constrains further design decisions on other levels.

Framing of possible user interactions with a high-level narrative is considered useful in more areas than just in digital environments. In an experimental example of live interactive theatre in the project *Game on Stage* (Game on Stage, 2014), members of the audience and actors share the same space, and apparently all kinds of interactions are possible. The piece *Right of Passage* is set in a theatre room transformed into a refugee camp. All members of the audience are refugees trying to leave the camp and cross the border to the neighbouring republic. However, the piece is not designed as a freeform role-playing game allowing any kinds of experiences. The authors want to convey typical stories of refugee camp life and succeed to do so by actually taking agency away from the players. Because of the strong high-level narrative turning players into refugees, there is a natural mapping of restrictions that are forced upon participants, allowing them to feel frustration and even other negative emotions towards the actors.

In all examples mentioned, the design of interface components providing concrete affordances and feedback, integrated with a strong metaphor and action possibilities at the higher levels, has been a holistic process that involves all team members and many iterations through all levels.

4. CONCLUSION

This chapter explored areas of interaction design that are relevant for authors of interactive narratives. Depending on the chosen genre and system, as soon as interaction goals go beyond a standardised hypertext or small set of fixed variations, the design of an interactive storyworld may turn end-users into participants of a story. Their goals and role as well as their possible acting situations and effects need to be considered during conception of the storyworld as much as those of nonplayer characters. Such integrated interaction design is deemed successful narrative design if it finds solutions that embrace all levels—from conceptual levels such as metaphors down to lexical levels of symbolic choices for input and output, graphics and media.

However, interaction design of course cannot be reduced to the narrative concept. After all, participants of storyworlds are users as well. As with all interactive systems, storyworlds will need to be evaluated for several target usability goals. In contrast to the understanding of usability in consumer products, these goals may not be mere efficiency, but they should probably include the learnability of the metaphor and effectiveness of user actions. Iterations of design and testing are needed to perfect the narrative flow. This is especially true when the interactive narrative concept includes experimental interaction styles for which we cannot rely on traditional interface rule sets.

We have shown that for many forms of interactive narrative, participant interaction is an aspect of the narrative content. Therefore, authors who enter the field with a background in so-called linear writing profit from acquiring knowledge about interaction design because it can influence narrative choices at several levels of abstraction. Most likely, authoring and conception is performed by interdisciplinary teams in which tasks are distributed, and in which each role contributes to the resulting interactive narrative experience. In the established field of game design, this is nothing new. However, in the area of interactive narrative, for too long the interface has been considered transparent and therefore neglected as relevant for narrative authoring.

ACKNOWLEDGMENTS

All mentioned examples, projects and story modelling exercises have been compiled collaboratively. For complete lists of credits including all contributors, please see the respective references.

NOTES

1. http://icids.org/
2. Integrating Research in Interactive Storytelling (IRIS) ran from 2009 to 2011.

REFERENCES

Austin, J. L. (1962) *How to Do Things with Words*. Oxford: Oxford University Press.
Chatman, S. (1978) *Story and Discourse. Narrative Structure in Fiction and Film*. Ithaca: Cornell University Press.
DeMarle, M. (2007) Nonlinear game arrative. In: Bateman, C. (ed.) *Game Writing: Narrative Skills for Videogames*. Boston: Cengage Learning.
Dille, F. and zuur Platten, J. (2007) *The Ultimate Guide to Video Game Writing and Design*. New York: Lone Eagle Publishing Company.
Dow, S., Mehta, M., MacIntyre, B., and Mateas, M., (2010) Eliza meets the Wizard-of-Oz: blending machine and human control of embodied characters. In *Proceedings of ACM CHI 2010*, ACM, New York, pp. 547–556.
Duke, R. D. (1974) *Gaming: The Future's Language*. New York: John Wiley & Sons.
Foley, J. D., van Dam, A., Feiner, S. K., and Hughes, J. F. (1995) *Computer Graphics, Principles and Practice*. 2nd Edition in C. Reprint with corrections 1997. Reading, MA: Addison-Wesley.
Game on Stage, 2014. *Project Description*. Available at: http://www.gameonstage. blogspot.de/ and http://machinaex.de/project/right-of-passage/
Holland, J. H. (1998) *Emergence: From Chaos to Order*. Oxford: Oxford University Press.
Howard, D. and Mabley, E. (1993) *The Tools of Screenwriting: A Writer's Guide to the Craft and Elements of a Screenplay*. New York: St. Martin's Press.
IRIS, 2012. *Interactive Story Creation. IRIS Repository: Authoring Tools and Creation Methods*. Available at: http://iris.interactive-storytelling.de/
Kelso, M. T., Weyhrauch, P., and Bates, J. (1993) Dramatic Presence. *Presence: Journal of Teleoperators and Virtual Environments*. 2(1). pp. 1–15.
Kriz, W. C. (2000) *Lernziel: Systemkompetenz. Planspiele als Trainingsmethode*. Vandenhoeck und Ruprecht.
Laurel, B. (1993) *Computers as Theatre*. Reading, MA: Addison-Wesley.
Mateas, M. and Stern, A. (2004) Natural language understanding in *Façade*: Surface-text processing. In: Göbel, S. et al. (eds.) *TIDSE 2004 Proceedings. LNCS 3105*. Berlin, Heidelberg: Springer.
Meehan, J. (1977) Tale-spin, an interactive program that writes stories. In *Proceedings of the Fifth International Joint Conference on Artificial Intelligence*, Cambridge, MA, USA, pp. 91–98.
Müller, W., Spierling, U. and Stockhausen, C. (2013) Production and delivery of interactive narratives based on video snippets. In: Koenitz et al. (ed.) *Interactive Storytelling, Proceedings of ICIDS 2013. LNCS 8230*. Berlin, Heidelberg: Springer.
Murray, J. H. (1997) *Hamlet on the Holodeck. The Future of Narrative in Cyberspace*. Cambridge, MA: Free Press.
Norman, D. A. (1988) *The Design of Everyday Things*. New York: Basic Books.

Norman, D. (2010) Natural user interfaces are not natural. *Interactions.* 17(3). pp. 6–10.

Preece, J., Rogers, Y., and Sharp, H. (2002) *Interaction Design: Beyond Human-Computer Interaction.* New York: John Wiley & Sons.

Saunders, K. and Novak, J. (2007) *Game Development Essentials: Game Interface Design.* New York: Thomson Delmar Learning.

Schneiderman, B. and Plaisant, C. (2010) *Designing the User Interface. Strategies for Effective Human-Computer Interaction.* 5th Edition. Reading, MA: Addison-Wesley.

Spierling, U. (2008) 'Killer Phrases': Design steps for a game with digital role-playing agents. In: Z. Pan et al., (eds.) *Transactions on Edutainment I. LNCS 5080.* Berlin, Heidelberg: Springer.

Spierling, U. (2011) Introducing interactive story creators to conversation modelling. In *Proceedings of the Eighth International Conference on Advances in Computer Entertainment Technology* (ACE 2011), Lisbon, Portugal, ACM Digital Library.

Spierling, U., Hoffmann, S., Struck, G., Szilas, N., Mehlmann, G., and Pizzi, D. (2012) *Integrated Report on Formative Evaluation Results of Authoring Prototypes.* Deliverable 3.4, IRIS-Project (Integrating Research in Interactive Storytelling [NoE]), EU FP7-ICT-231824.

Spierling, U., Hoffmann, S., Szilas, N., and Richle, U. (2011) *Educational Material for Creators (Non-Computer-Scientists) on AI-based Generative Narrative Methods.* Deliverable 3.2, IRIS-Project (Integrating Research in Interactive Storytelling (NoE)), EU FP7-ICT-231824.

Spirit, 2014. *Spirit Project Website.* Available at: http://spirit.interactive-storytelling.de/

Struck, G. (2013) *How to Build the Holodeck with Undercover Games.* Available at: http://static.researchinggames.net/2013-struck-holodeck.pdf

Wardrip-Fruin, N. (2007) Internal processes and interface effects: Three relationships in play. In *Proceedings of Electronic Techtonics: Thinking at the Interface,* HASTAC.

Wardrip-Fruin, N. (2009) *Expressive Processing.* Cambridge, MA: MIT Press.

Weiss, S., Müller, W., Spierling, U., and Steimle, F. (2005) Scenejo–an interactive storytelling platform. In: Subsol, G. (ed.) *Virtual Storytelling. Using Virtual Reality Technologies for Storytelling. LNCS 3805.* Berlin, Heidelberg: Springer.

11 Posthyperfiction
Practices in Digital Textuality

Scott Rettberg

Web hypertext fiction works never really had an operable business model, nor a significant cultural apparatus. They were pure artistic experiments in that sense. Perhaps because no models really existed to qualify a hypertext novel as successful, more hypertext narratives were created in short forms than as long novels. The early 2000s saw other important examples of web hypertext novels, such as Caitlin Fischer's 2001 Electronic Literature Award-winning *These Waves of Girls*. However, as electronic literature began to develop as its own field in the 2000s, short forms, in particular digital poetry, would for a time dominate the field.

Web hypertexts were part of a larger global experiment in digital textuality. As much as the Web now seems second nature, an at-hand information landscape crowded with social networks, streaming video and online commerce, the late 1990s and early 2000s were more of a Wild West. No one knew precisely what 'Web Content' should be or would become. It made just as much sense to think of the Web as a new platform for writing and reading literature as anything else. It is fair to say that the ubiquitous adoption of personal computers, mobile devices and the Internet has been the most profound technological shift in the way that human societies produce and interact with writing since the Gutenberg press. Works of electronic literature will not only continue to help us explore the novelty of new forms, but also—and this might be even more fundamental—changes in everyday textuality are taking place so rapidly in this environment that we might otherwise miss them.

Since the turn of the millennium, writers working with digital narrative have been decreasingly interested in the poetics of the hypertext link and network story structures and more interested in evolving network styles of writing. Each new communication platform adopted—e-mail, blogs, Wikipedia, social networks, Twitter and so forth—in some sense generates a new genre of writing practiced on the Web. Of these communication platforms, each offers its own affordances for narrative, and each shapes the language produced within it in distinctive ways, whether it be the particular epistolary forms of e-mail, the reverse-chronology unfolding of weblogs or the rapid-fire 140-character-limited lines of Twitter.

Many of the early web hypertext fictions explored some of the material aspects of the early hand-coded HTML Web. Shelley and Pamela Jackson's

The Doll Games (2001) is a hypertext that documents a complex narrative game that Shelley and Pamela Jackson used to play when they were prepubescent girls, and the game frames that documentation in faux-academic discourse. In their DAC 2001 presentation of the project, the authors described *The Doll Games* as sitting "uneasily between fiction nonfiction, serious inquiry parody."[1] In 'sitting uneasily between' different styles of discourse, the work enlists the reader to differentiate between authoritative knowledge and play. Throughout, the project plays with constructions of gender and of identity. *The Doll Games* is a network novel in the sense that it uses the network to construct narratives in a particularly novel way. *The Doll Games* is also consciously structured as a network document and plays in an ironic fashion with its network context. A portmanteau work, it takes formal cues both from the playful tone of childish obsession of the games themselves as they were enacted by the girls as children and from academic discourse. Taking a page from Vladimir Nabokov's *Pale Fire*, the work includes a complex scholarly academic apparatus and features J. F. Bellwether, PhD, a scholar who has allegedly made the study of a "ground-breaking series of theatrical performances by Shelley and Pamela Jackson that took place in a private home in Berkeley, California, in the first half of the 1970s" a focus of his scholarly work. Structurally, the content of *The Doll Games* is assembled as a kind of cross between a play-set of materials. The material includes photographs and profiles of the dolls, narratives written by and about them, interviews between Shelley and Pamela, and an academic case study. Thus, a great deal of narrative material is presented and made available for play, without the provision of any sort of comprehensive narrative lines.

Just as they were using and exploring other forms to disperse the materials for a storyworld, Shelley and Pamela Jackson were also exploring some aspects of the materiality of the network itself. The first page past the title page includes a small grey footer with the keywords "doll sex, doll mutilation, transgender dolls, prosthetic doll penises, doll death, doll dreams." These keywords may be intended to cue readers as to the content that will follow, but they also serve a function in how this particular HTML page will be read *by the network*. The Jackson sisters likely knew how search engines operate and placed these keywords conspicuously on the front page in order to draw a particular readership for the work. Indeed for a time, *The Doll Games* was the first site returned by a Google search for *doll mutilation*. The savvy placement of phrases such as these by the Jackson sisters was used to draw readers to the network fiction, in this case readers who are prequalified as interested in *The Doll Games* by virtue of their interest in doll mutilation. The project also solicited and integrated doll game stories provided by readers who responded to a call for e-mail submissions. The use of keywords and meta-tags and the authors' consciousness of how the work fit into the search engine ecology, as well as the integration of user-generated content, are in keeping with an emerging awareness during this period that the network was not simply another means of distribution for hypertext. It was a materially distinct writing platform that itself affects and shapes work developed there.

Talan Memmott's *Lexia to Perplexia* (2000) and other hypertext works produced during this period continued to develop the philosophical and theoretical concerns of network consciousness first emerging as fodder for fiction in Amerika's *Grammatron*. Memmott's works explored what he called "network phenomenology" and the effects of hybridised human/machine/ network intelligence, essentially providing the literary work as an objective correlative for a posthuman state of being.[2] *Lexia to Perplexia* was also notable for its relation to what would become known as *codework*—a strand of electronic literature interested in exploring the relation of human and machine language and the various poetic possibilities emergent from those relations. The other lasting contribution of *Lexia to Perplexia* was its sophisticated use of graphic design and web programming. The graphics, user interface and programmed behaviours of *Lexia to Perplexia* are as essential to the story it is trying to tell as is its text.

Rob Wittig's *The Fall of the Site of Marsha* (1999), *Friday's Big Meeting* (2000) and *Blue Company* (2002) were each narrative experiments that explored the potential of a different communications platform for fiction. *The Fall of the Site of Marsha* was at play with the conventions of the phenomena of *home page*—that early web genre of website in which individuals would roughly hack some HTML and fill a page with a few biographical details, hobbies they were obsessed with, links they were interested in, animated gifs, crazily mixed typography, pictures of their cats, etc., for little apparent purpose other than to claim a space on the Web as their own. Wittig's fiction included three iterations of a home page dedicated to angels (the particular obsession of Marsha, the title character in *The Fall of the Site of Marsha*). One of the sites was provided as Marsha first published it, and two further hacked versions revealed a story behind the scenes. Marsha's husband, who wanted to get out of the marriage, had hacked the page to make it seem as if the angels were after Marsha. His infidelities are revealed comically in the clues left in the vandalism of the site itself. *Friday's Big Meeting* similarly explored a new medium—a corporate bulletin board—to unfold a story of workplace intrigue, deception and romances. Wittig's *Blue Company* was an e-mail novel about an advertising writer who had been recruited to travel though space and time to 14th century Italy as part of a campaign to change the course of history to make it more profitable for a contemporary corporate client. Told through a series of e-mails to a potential lover in the present day (on a smuggled laptop), the novel used a classic epistolary structure and themes adapted to the particular modalities of contemporary e-mail. The novel was also distributed to its initial subscribers in serial form in e-mail messages over the course of a month. Thus, the story transpired on a real-time basis in relation to the time scale in which it was read. Here we can again identify a trend in posthypertext digital narrative. The text is not to be understood only as a singular work or artefact bound by printed space, but as a performance that unfolds over time.

Rob Wittig's recent projects, particularly his 'netprov' projects, developed in collaboration with Mark Marino, continue to develop his interest in network styles of writing and the affordances of particular communication technologies, as well as his interest in network writing as performance. Wittig and Marino's netprov projects, such as *Grace, Wit & Charm* (2012), *Occupy MLA* (2012) and *@Tempspence* project (2013), have taken place on Twitter and other social media platforms, though they have sometimes also extended onto websites and into the physical world. The netprov projects have integrated elements of contributory collaboration, social media discourse and online hoax in developing online performance fictions. While *Blue Company* was an e-mail novel written by one author for a subscribing audience, the netprov projects have typically not been announced to readers until they are underway or finished. Instead, the characters present themselves on Twitter accounts as real people. In the case of *Occupy MLA*, the characters were a group of adjunct humanities faculty, who over the course of a year struggled to cope with the demands of excessive teaching loads, job interviews and the typical trials and tribulations of faculty in tenuous underpaid positions. The three main characters then proposed to start a labour protest movement which would culminate in an action at that year's Modern Language Association (MLA) conference. They even named specific sessions at which the protest was to take place. Only the authors themselves knew that their identities were false and that the Twitter accounts were representing parodic characters rather than real people. When the hoax was finally revealed, a good deal of controversy surrounded it, even drawing chastisement from Michael Bérubé, the outgoing president of the MLA, in the *Chronicle of Higher Education*.[3]

While it is a long way from *Afternoon, A Story* in 1990 to *Occupy MLA* in 2012, I mention the project not because it is a hypertext but because it illustrates one of the directions in which the narrative side of digital media writing has moved in the past decade or so. It is not the case that the majority of authors who were working in hypertext in the 1990s and 2000s have abandoned digital writing altogether, but that they have continued to experiment with and invent new forms that have become possible in contemporary network contexts.

Nonlinear interactive narrative also moved from the web browser to other spatial environments, including the physical world. The hypertext project *34 North 118 West*, produced by Jeremy Hight, Jeff Knowlton and Naomi Spellman in 2003 is one notable example of locative narrative. Using consumer technologies—a tablet computer with a Global Positioning System card—that at the time were in their infancy, the project layered historical stories of Los Angeles during earlier eras, such as the turn of the 19th to 20th century, onto physical spaces in a four-block area of Los Angeles. As the user explored the area with the tablet computer, wearing headphones, he or she encountered narratives set in those environments. Some elements of the narrative apparatus at work are very similar to screen-based hypertext—the user triggers narratives just as readers of the earlier hypertext fictions activated links, and the narrative is nonlinear in the sense that one can encounter narrative nodes in different order, depending on how one moves through the streets. The important difference is that settings in a locative narrative are not merely described, but they are experienced as embodied space. The city was treated in *34 North 118 West* as a sort of palimpsest on which stories could be written, erased and recovered. The voices of imaginary ghosts served to specify memories of a place. There is an important ontological distinction here in the situation of the reader; the reader is not at a remove from the diegetic world of the story but is instead embedded and immersed in the same environment. The physical world that the user and the story share becomes part of the material of the story. As Jeremy Hight wrote in an artist's statement accompanying the RadioELO audio archive of the project,

> A story could be told using walls, buildings, streets, trees, a dry river bed, a lake edge etc. It was now possible to write with [the] physical world. This was the initial realization of the possibilities of locative narrative.
>
> (Hight et al., 2003)

As awkward as it may have been to lug an early 2000s tablet computer around the streets of Los Angeles, *34 North 118 West* represented an important decoupling of hypertextual narrative from the situation of sitting in front of a computer screen. The narrative was not a distant object for the reader to interpret, but it was something the user could walk inside.

A focus on the relation of the reader's body to the body of text is indeed one of the notable recurring interests of digital narrative after hypertext. If Talan Memmott's *Lexia to Perplexia* was in large part a meditation on the sort of post-human consciousness framed by the relations between person and screen, individual identity and network, more recent digital narratives are more likely to reconfigure the reading situation more generally. Readers are not necessarily sitting in a chair in front of a screen. They are just as likely to be moving through a narrative situated in physical space, or moving through the virtual space of an augmented reality environment, or experiencing the narrative in a 3D CAVE environment, or encountering a digital narrative in a communal experience of a performance.

Around the same time that *34 North 118 West* was 'narrativising' the streets of Los Angeles, the development of another sort of embodied narrative immersion was taking place in Robert Coover's CAVE Writing workshops at Brown University. The CAVE (Computer Assisted Virtual Environment) is a room-sized virtual reality display. In this particular implementation of a CAVE, participants wearing 3D glasses with attached sensors can enter a text in the virtual space. In 2002 the work *Screen* was developed by Noah Wardrip-Fruin, Josh Carroll, Robert Coover, Shawn Greenlee, Andrew McClain and Ben 'Sascha' Shine. The work begins as a simple listening and reading experience. Narrative 'memory text' appears on the walls and is read in voiceover. This initial experience is much like listening to a story being read, and the walls of the CAVE seem very much like the two dimensional space of the page. After the initial narration of the piece is complete, however, the words on the walls become unsettled and begin to move, eventually peeling off the walls and floating in three-dimensional space. The user discovers that it is possible to interact with the words, as material objects can be knocked around the room or split in two with the wave of a hand. The words are hypertextual in that they can be activated and interacted with in ways that extend the text; but rather than functioning as links to other nodes of narrative, they are made literalised objects that the reader confronts in space and then returns to the walls in new configurations. The result of this interaction in the third stage of the piece is a poem, formed from the words the reader has interacted with, and serves as a meditation on the nature of memory and forgetting.

The 2014 CAVE2™ narrative developed by Roderick Coover, Arthur Nishimoto, Scott Rettberg and Daria Tsoupikova, *Hearts and Minds: The Interrogations Project* (Coover et al., 2014) at the Electronic Visualisation Lab at the University of Illinois Chicago also uses hypertextual narrative strategies to present a difficult set of materials in an immersive and affective virtual reality environment. The CAVE2™ is the next generation of CAVE technology, described by its creators as "a hybrid system that combines the benefits of both scalable-resolution display walls and virtual-reality systems to create a seamless 2D/3D environment."[4] *Hearts and Minds* is a project based on interviews of American soldiers who participated in acts of battlefield torture and abusive violence during their service in Iraq. The interviews were conducted for John Tsukayama's 2013 doctoral dissertation *By Any Means Necessary: An Interpretive Phenomenological Analysis Study of Post 9/11 American Abusive Violence in Iraq*. The project presents the audience with a narrative environment that begins in a reflective temple space with four doors opening to ordinary American domestic spaces: a boy's bedroom, a family room, a suburban back yard, a kitchen. While exploring each of these rooms, a user is tracked through the space via motion tracking sensors, and the 3D view of the scenes is shown from the user's perspective. Using a wand with a trigger, the user triggers individual objects, such as a toy truck, a Boy Scout poster, a pair of wire cutters, etc. When each object is activated, the walls of the domestic space fall away and a surreal desert landscape is revealed in 2D surrounding panorama, and one of the four voiceover actors is heard recounting particular acts and memory related metaphorically to the object selected. Just as in earlier hypertext narratives, there is a movement through narrative space, in this case a stereoscopic virtual space as well. The objects also function very much like hyperlinks in moving us from one narrative element to another. The project attempts to extend and make accessible difficult narratives based on the actual testimonies involved. The immersion the system provides allows for a different type of affective experience of the narrative, activated through the visceral immersion afforded by the visual and auditory environment, but in structure and form it is essentially a contemporary hypertext.

The two *Electronic Literature Collections* published by the Electronic Literature Organisation—volume one in 2006 and volume two in 2011—evidence the great diversity of literary forms that fall under the broader umbrella of electronic literature and the general movement of the field after the turn of the millennium. In the collections, hypertext fictions appear alongside kinetic poetry, generative poetry and fiction, cinematic digital narratives, interactive narrative animations, interactive fiction, interactive drama, new media performance, locative narratives, hypermedia documentaries and a variety of other forms. If in the 1990s digital writing communities tended to fall into a few identifiable camps that rarely interacted with each other—hypertext authors over here, IF authors over there, e-poets there, etc.—the electronic literature communities represented by the *Collections* and the ELO conferences and e-Poetry Festivals are much more inclusive and diverse in terms of form and genre. The crowd of writers who participate in the Electronic Literature Organisation have more of a cultural affiliation than a generic one. What they have in common is more an interest in exploring and exploiting the capabilities of the programmable networked computer and the network context for creative writing (and more generally, creative media) than an affiliation to any particular form therein.

All of this is not to say that the potentialities of the hypertext novel have been fully exhausted, or that it has not had a lasting impact on the other digital media narrative forms that have followed. Some essential components of hypertext—breaking the narrative line; structuring stories into small segments, episodes or nodes; enabling readers to interact with or arrange the presentation of narratives in various ways; weighing the user interface, graphic presentation, and navigational apparatus as poetic elements of the work—have carried through into a variety of other digital narrative forms. Hypertext and hypermedia remain elements of many contemporary digital media narrative projects. Complex and ambitious digital writing and performance projects, such as Judd Morrissey and Mark Jeffrey's *The Last Performance* (2007) and *The Operature* (2013), for instance, include hypertext elements within a more baroque poetic architecture—though it could no longer be said that the hypertext novel itself is an area of much contemporary activity.

In 2011, Paul La Farge published *Luminous Airplanes* with Farrar, Strauss and Giroux. The main character and narrator of the novel is a web developer, a graduate of Bleak College and a former history PhD student at Stanford. After the internet bubble has burst, he has moved back to his hometown of Thebes to sort through the belongings of his deceased grandfather and to prepare the family home for sale. In the process, he is sorting through his own past in an attempt to sort out his own identity. The novel functions as a sort of *Bildungsroman* as the narrator moves us through different periods of his life. The novel as it was printed is a kind of cut of a larger hypertext project published online. Though the "immersive text" version of the novel (La Farge's editors at FSG did not want him to call it hypertext because they felt the word had negative connotations) is presented as an expansion of the novel, it is clear from reading La Farge's commentary within the hypertext that the writing and development of the hypertext actually preceded the printed book. What essentially occurred, then, is that an editor came to the hypertext with a sharp knife and whittled away about two thirds of the material included in the hypertext.

The 'immersive text' version of *Luminous Airplanes* includes a great deal more material than there is in the printed book. The segments or episodes of the novel that appear there include both the material found in the book and other stories, episodes and texts that expand on the context of the novel. On the one hand, much of the material in the online hypertext version of the story fleshes out the reader's understanding of the characters and their relationships, but on the other, some of the material such as the long section "Summerland" (about half a novel,—a manuscript written by the main character) does not add much to the experience of reading the work. There is a quality of everything-and-the-kitchen-sink-ism to the immersive text, and some gems appear alongside pages that might have been better left in the author's drawer.

> Reviewing the project in *The New York Times*, Kathryn Shultz (2011) wrote:
> [T]he whole thing feels like a kind of literary 52-card pickup—i.e., a lot more fun for the thrower than the throwee. The most generous take on this Web project is that it reads like a rough draft of a very good novel—which this is.

My own experience of reading both the book and the hypertext version of *Luminous Airplanes* was similar. La Farge clearly included material written over the span of many years. The sections written earlier in his career, such as the "Summerland" and "Bleak College" sections, are simply not as engaging on a sentence-by-sentence level as the material he wrote later, such as the "Thebes" section about his homecoming, reconnection and interaction with old friends and uncovering of family secrets. I suppose it is not surprising that in a project written over the course of more than a decade, the nature and quality of the writing would change. The good news is that La Farge's writing style and his sense of character and plot improved immensely over the course of those years. The bad news is the hypertext includes all of the evidence of that improvement.

Luminous Airplanes has problems from a user interface standpoint. An apparatus that offers the reader logical, or interesting, or satisfying ways of traversing the text is essential to the reading experience of hypertext fiction. While many hypertexts (including *The Unknown*) suffer to a degree from over-linking, the use of hypertext in this work is actually quite conservative and somewhat limiting. In-text hyperlinks are used infrequently and generally only in a referential style. Large episodes are held together with previous/next buttons, but when you reach the end of a section, links are not always used to offer the reader narrative progression or an associative logic. While an interactive visual map is provided dividing the narrative into different subthemes and periods of time, most of the offshoots from the main narrative are connected only to the *previous section* read or the narrative hub from which they originated. This leaves the reader to do a great deal of clicking back to texts he or she has already read. These loops often seem more repetitive, incidental and time-consuming than generative. It would have been useful to be able to click from any text being read back to its position on the map and to navigate more directly from there.

There has always been a metafictional impulse to hypertext fiction, and La Farge indulges in this as much as any of the early hypertext novelists, commenting and situating his technical effects while he uses them and throwing shout-outs to his chosen antecedents, for example in a two-page comment about his use of photographs being preceded by the work of W.G. Sebald. Within the hypertext, La Farge offers an extensive commentary. These sections, identifiable by a light blue background tint, are among the most interesting in the project, as we see La Farge struggling with the form of hypertext and his relationship to it as author (a relationship curiously tinged with what he describes as *guilt*). At one point in a discourse on constraint, La Farge muses: "What I want to know is, what happens if you take these restrictions away? Beginning, I guess, with the idea of a definite beginning, or a fixed end. And then also: what happens if you let everything in?"[5]

I could not help but identify with La Farge there, as these were the same kind of questions my coauthors and I were asking while we were writing *The Unknown*. The answer to his question, unfortunately, is 'something bad happens if you let everything in.' The potential for the hypertext author to cast all constraints aside and to make connections across time, space, theme and different types of texts—the temptation to simply keep going, to let the narrative expand and move and change and grow, endlessly—is both wonderful and terrible. In some sense, this limitlessness is more fundamentally at odds with the form of the novel than any of the other subversions of story structure, or character development, or point of view or causality enabled by the use of the hypertext form. Once you let everything in, perhaps you no longer have a novel but some other type of textual creature whose growth will eventually become malignant.

No story is boundless. The story must eventually cease, and the author—a pathetic mortal—must eventually die. In some ways it does seem as if the American hypertext novel is a kind of ghost town—a narrative genre that after being quickly discovered, developed, evolved and was then abandoned in pursuit of new territories before ever reaching its full potential. Of course, while stories end and writers expire, once invented literary forms do not ever really perish. They merely go into hibernation and, in dormancy, await their rediscovery and reinvention. And so it may be with the hypertext novel. We have seen how many of the theoretical underpinnings, structural elements, and narrative techniques of hypertext have migrated into other forms of digital narrative. This is not, however, to say that the hypertext novel has simply been raided for spare parts. La Farge's experiment, if not entirely successful, is evidence that the form is not completely moribund. It is entirely likely that authors will return to the hypertext, embrace its comparative computational simplicity which while driven towards excess is also in its own way austere, and will develop its future even as they learn from its past. Hypertext is dead. Long live hypertext.

NOTES

1. From abstract http://cds.library.brown.edu/conferences/DAC/abstracts/jackson. html.
2. A connection explored in detail by N. Katherine Hayles in her 2002 *Writing Machines*.
3. In a reply to the authors' post about the project in the Prof. Hacker column of the *Chronicle*, Bérubé wrote "I can say that *Occupy MLA* had no influence on my agenda whatsoever. It was merely annoying ... *Occupy MLA* came to 'the crisis of the moment' a good while after the MLA did. I followed the Twitter feed in late 2011, though, and now I think it's really regrettable that anyone would try to advance the cause of NTT faculty by making adjuncts appear so—what is the word?—'cartoonish.'"
4. http://www.evl.uic.edu/cave2
5. http://www.luminousairplanes.com/section/constraint/

REFERENCES

Borrás, L., Memmott, T., Raley, R., and Stefans, B. K. (eds.) (2011) *The Electronic Literature Collection, Volume Two*. Cambridge: The Electronic Literature Organisation. [online] Available at: http://collection.eliterature.org/2/

Coover, R., Nishimoto, A., Rettberg, S., and Tsoupikova, D. (2014) *Hearts and Minds: The Interrogations Project*. [Interactive virtual reality installation and performance] Chicago: University of Illinois, Electronic Visualisation Lab. Documentation at: http://retts.net/documents/hearts_minds_art_vis2014.pdf and https://www.youtube.com/watch?v=jJFgsFXMF_s

Fisher, C. (2001) *These Waves of Girls: A Hypermedia Novella*. Available at: http://www.yorku.ca/caitlin/waves/

Gillespie, W., Marquardt, F., Rettberg, S., and Stratton, D. (1999) *The Unknown*. Available at: http://unknownhypertext.com

Hayles, N. K, Montfort, N., Rettberg, S., and Strickland, S., (eds.) (2006) *The Electronic Literature Collection, Volume One*. College Park: The Electronic Literature Organization. [online] Available at: http://collection.eliterature.org/1/

Hight, J., Knowlton, J., and Spellman, N. (2003) *34 North 118 West*. Documentation at: http://www.radionouspace.net/radioelo-hight.html

Jackson, P. and Jackson, S. (2001) *The Doll Games*. Available at: http://ineradicablestain.com/dollgames/index.html

Jackson, S. (1995) *Patchwork Girl*. Watertown, MA: Eastgate Systems.

Jeffrey, M., Morrissey, J. et al. (2007) *The Last Performance [dot org]*. Available at: http://thelastperformance.org/title.php

Jeffrey, M., Morrissey, J. et al. (2013). *The Operature*. Available at: http://atom-r.tumblr.com/

Joyce, M. (1990) *Afternoon, A Story*. Watertown, MA: Eastgate Systems.

La Farge, P. (2011) *Luminous Airplanes*. New York: Farrar, Straus and Giroux.

La Farge, P. (2011) *Luminous Airplanes*. [online] Available at: http://www.luminousairplanes.com/

Marino, M. and Wittig, R. (2012) *Occupy MLA*. Available at: http://markcmarino.com/omla/

Marino, M. and Wittig, R. (2013) Occupying MLA. *The Chronicle of Higher Education*. ProfHacker column. January 14 [online] Available at: http://chronicle.com/blogs/profhacker/occupying-mla/45357

Marino, M. and Wittig, R. (2012) @*Tempspence*. [Twitter feed] Available at: https://twitter.com/tempspence

Memmott, T. (2000) *Lexia to Perplexia*. Available at: http://tracearchive.ntu.ac.uk/newmedia/lexia/index.htm

Shultz, K. (2011). A novel of flying machines, apocalyptics and the San Francisco Internet boom. *The New York Times*. Oct 7. [online] Available at: http://www.nytimes.com/2011/10/09/books/review/luminous-airplanes-by-paul-la-farge-book-review.html?_r=0

Tsukyama, J. (2013). *By Any Means Necessary: An Interpretive Phenomenological Analysis Study Of Post 9/11 American Abusive Violence In Iraq*. PhD dissertation, University of St Andrews, St Andrews, UK.

Wardrip-Fruin, N., Carroll, J., Coover, R., Greeley, S., McClain, A., and Shine, B. (2002) *Screen*. Documentation at: http://www.noahwf.com/screen/

Wittig, R. (1999) *The Fall of the Site of Marsha*. Available at: http://www.robwit.net/MARSHA/

Wittig, R. (2000) *Friday's Big Meeting*. Available at: http://www.robwit.net/MARSHA/

Wittig, R. (2002) *Blue Company*. Available at: http://www.robwit.net/bluecompany2002/

Wittig, R. (2012) *Grace, Wit & Charm*. Available at: http://robwit.net/?project=grace-wit-charm.

12 Emergent Narrative

Past, Present and Future of An Interactive Storytelling Approach

Sandy Louchart, John Truesdale, Neil Suttie and Ruth Aylett

1. RESEARCH BACKGROUND

The Emergent Narrative (EN) concept is a developing Interactive Storytelling (IS) approach, which aims to investigate the implications of an interactive user within the context of a narrative environment. The EN approach has thus far followed both a theoretical and practical evolution; and in this chapter we aim to discuss the context in which it initially took shape, share our vision for what it could mean for the community at large and discuss the current ongoing developments: specifically Distributed Drama Management (DDM), Relevant Context Modelling (RCM) and Intelligent Narrative Feedback (INF) for authoring EN.

The EN approach was first conceptualised at the turn of the century in the wake of booming interest in Interactive Storytelling (IS) from the Artificial Intelligence (AI) research community (Aylett, 1999). In particular, Janet Murray had previously just published her seminal *Hamlet on the Holodeck* work (Murray, 1997) and Michael Mateas and Andrew Stern were in the process of developing the ground-breaking work *Façade* (Mateas and Stern, 2003) on the back of earlier research into Interactive Drama (ID) in the Oz project (Mateas, 1997). With IS research still in its infancy, the notion of the Narrative Paradox (Louchart and Aylett, 2003) was rightly identified as a core though complex priority issue. How could IS authors and a system's artificial intelligence (AI) reconcile the demands of a carefully structured story experience with the necessary freedoms (movement, decisions) one would expect to grant an interactive user?

Most approaches, particularity at the time, tended to favour some level of top-down (story to interaction) interventions or mechanisms through which a story's plot could be modified or articulated and react accordingly to a user's inputs. Whilst there existed clear benefits in such approaches (Riedl, 2004; Szilas, 2003; Cavazza et al., 2002), Sandy Louchart and Ruth Aylett put forward the position that a top-down approach would always lack flexibility and prove difficult to scale, particularly when ensuring the consistency of interactive non-player characters (NPCs) within a narrative environment (Aylett and Louchart, 2003).

The EN concept put forward a radical hypothesis in which it was argued that characters, and not the plot, should be central to the development of an interactive and dramatic user experience; in essence, the story would emerge from the interactions between NPCs, the storyworld and the interactive user (Louchart and Aylett, 2003). From the outset, the development of EN took inspiration (and continues to do so) from the already well-established framework and traditions of Role-Playing Games (RPGs) and Live Action Role Play (LARP) in which the bulk of an interactive narrative experience lies in the interactions between characters, often with conflicting goals and motivations, in a narrative environment (Louchart and Aylett, 2005).

The release of the *FearNot!* demonstrator (Aylett et al., 2005), and Fearnot Affective Mind Architecture (FAtiMA) (Dias and Paiva, 2005), provided a glimpse of an EN implementation in its most primitive form; it features emotionally based, and thus emotionally-driven, intelligent agents as NPCs that also serve to enable user interaction. While highly successful in its specific project aims, the *FearNot!* EN integration did not fully reflect the breadth that EN envisioned. *FearNot!* was developed within the highly restrictive domain of antibullying coping mechanisms, and thus the evaluation scenarios were carefully and necessarily constrained within a narrow set of pedagogical and psychological boundaries to ensure success. A relative weakness for EN at this point in time was that these affect-driven agents were mainly focused on providing a high degree of simulative fidelity and subsequently simulated human beings rather than dramatic characters. Robert Scholes, Robert Kellogg and James Phelan (Scholes et al., 2006) described characters in a narrative in terms of aesthetic (i.e., they serve the plot of the narrative), illustrative (i.e., they represent themes in the narrative), and mimetic (i.e., they simulate human beings). Characters are thus only self-aware of their mimetic components while their aesthetic and illustrative components tend to exist outside of the fictional world (i.e., author, audience). EN FAtiMA agents thus emphasised the mimetic component of character but were, as such, unaware of their narrative responsibilities. While these would act believably, it would not guarantee that they would perform dramatically interesting actions. The Double-Appraisal (DA) FAtiMA modification proposed by Louchart and Aylett (Aylett and Louchart, 2008) partially addressed this point of concern by embedding the notion of character intelligence within an emotion-based agent architecture. In line with their developing EN theory, Louchart and Aylett incorporated an additional loop into FAtiMA's appraisal mechanism so that the agents would systematically select from their available goals and actions those that offered the highest emotional impact.

Whilst still needing further developing work, DA introduced the core of a metanarrative layer in which a character agent was aware of the implication(s) of its actions on other characters, including the player character, but not that of the developing core narrative. A similar metanarrative approach is widely in use in collaborative LARP, and to a certain extent in improvisational theatre (Improv), from which players act not only towards developing their own character but, through collaborative opportunities with other characters, allow for further development through interaction.

1.1 Distributed Drama Management

While DA was advantageous in terms of narrative coherence and provided characters with a flexible method of responding to user interaction, it was not without weaknesses and only represented one step towards integrating a complete metanarrative layer to the EN concept. Initially, DA only selected the action with the highest emotional impact; but it did not consider which emotion this was, thus not controlling the range of emotions being considered. As a result, actions with opposite emotional impact could be considered of equal dramatic value and be selected irrespective of the context or structure of the user experience. Additionally, DA was implemented as a constant action-selection mechanism (ASM) and aimed to select the action with the most emotional impact at all times, meaning that it aimed for a constant high rather than a more desirable narrative structure comprising of highs and lows (Figure 12.1).

With reference to Aristotelian structure (Aristotle 330BC), such as rising action, climax and falling action, the most dramatic actions should occur only at the climax and not at any arbitrary point in the story, thus affecting the ability for an EN system to control the pace of a user experience. Subsequently, Sandy Louchart and Allan Weallans investigated how pace and structure could be represented within a bottom-up EN approach (Weallans et al., 2012). The notion of a character's narrative experience, the affective impact of events that shape its own narrative actions, is central to this approach. Distributed Drama Management was developed around the notion of a metanarrative representation at character level by which the agent character is aware of its role as a character in the story as well as its relationship with the player character. In other words, since some characters in an interactive narrative are controlled by intelligent agents, the idea of DDM is, first, that such agents reason both about the actions that are possible in character (i.e., within the role played by their character) and, second, about the impact their chosen narrative actions will have upon other characters. Since we cannot know exactly what the 'players' themselves experience, the agents specifically reason about the narrative experience of the 'character' driven by the player. The DDM implementation thus integrated a feedback mechanism based on the internal representation of the player character. This mechanism consisted in assessing the player character's likely emotional state as a basis for predicting the potential impact of decisions made by NPCs on the player and his/her character. A player experience could thus be defined

Colonel - Let's be clear about what we are all about to do! No one has ever been down there! Our intelligence reported this site has a potential threat to our land security! We all know why we are here today! The technology possibly hidden in there is all that matters to us. In the unlikely event of an encounter of any type, we are to wipe this place down and make sure no one or nothing ever come out of this temple! Dead or alive!

Colonel - God bless you all. Military personnel in formation, the others behind me, keep an eye for traps, and do not loose sight of each other. All right, let's go!

Character actions	Lieutenant - Yes Sir!
	Sergeant - Following your order Sir!
	Professor - Yes Sir, yes!
	Doctor - OK Sir!
	Researcher - Following your order Sir!
	Colonel - Explores temple
	Lieutenant - Explores temple
	Sergeant - Explores temple
	Professor - Explores temple
	Doctor - Explores temple
	Researcher - Explores temple
Dialogue actions	Doctor - Colonel, everyone, I have something strange there. There are some writings on this stone. A strange drawing and some hieroglyphs!
	Doctor - Oh my god, this is fascinating. my grand father was right all along!
	These are the four element guardians, they represent ancient gods, prior to the ones to which most of Egyptain mythology is based upon!. If the predictions are right they shall return within & days of their temple being penetrated! By entering this chamber we have provoked their return! The infidels will all die and I shall trust them my life! This family talisman should revive the sacred guardians!
	Statues are starting to be animated and move towards the party
	Colonel - In the chest. Fire at the red light in the chest! Fire! Fire!
	Statues are not stoppable Statues kill Lieutenant
	Colonel - You stupid weirdo! (to Doctor)
	Colonel - Kill Doctor
System actions	Statues stop and break into pieces
	Colonel - Ok nothing to worry about here!. Come on everybody; remember what we are looking for, a sort of entrance to another chamber!
	Colonel - Here!, Here come here..Hell man, I think this thing might be real after all.
	Colonel - Professor! Are these hieroglyphs there above the door say anything of what might be behind it?
	Professor - Hum Yes Colonel!. Well, this is strange, these do not appear to be conventional hieroglyphs! There are actually two sets of text there. One that can be interpreted as a death threat to any mortal disturbing the lizard gods, no idea whose these can be! The other one although looks like Egyptain hieroglyphs contains many symbols I have never encountered and does not make any sence to me I am afraid!
	Colonel - This is a door, therefore it should open one way or another, look for clues on the structure of the door and the wall!
	Colonel accidentally orients the light beam onto the door and trigges the opening of the door - End of scene!

Figure 12.1 A Double-Appraisal agent scenario example where each agent selects the most dramatic action available.

through the emotional arc of the player character. As such, the DDM incorporated a feedback mechanism, which allowed characters to act in role but—more importantly—within the remit of a predetermined player character experience.

Agent characters in the DDM make decisions based on their contextual availability (characterisation) in order to maintain character coherence, but also in relation to a predetermined emotional trajectory initially set by an author. In the DDM, agent characters include both a character and an actor layer. Both layers are integrated within the agent's ASM and represent a dual cognitive process in which decisions are selected with regards to both in-character and out-of-character considerations.

In this context, in-character decisions are decisions made within the remit of the character's set of actions, goals and emotional range; and out-of-character decisions are decisions made in consideration of the storyworld and the user experience. Thus out-of-character decisions, while still in character, might not represent the most optimal decision from the character perspective, but they may be a necessary concession towards facilitating higher story goals for the user experience. The character layer, in the DDM, is responsible for simulating the agent character according to its own beliefs, desires, intentions and emotional state. The actor layer, on the other hand, is responsible for mediating actions in terms of their dramatic appropriateness with respect to the player character. In the DDM, dramatic appropriateness is determined by simulating the hypothetical impact of action choices on the virtual user (VU), a dynamically updated inactive agent representing the player character controlled by the user (Figure 12.2).

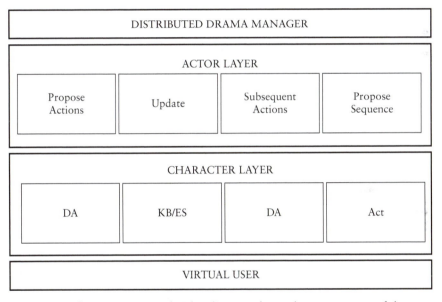

Figure 12.2 The DDM approach. This diagram shows the components of the DDM along with the DA represented at character level.

Whilst not acting in itself, the VU represents the hypothetical intentions and emotional state of the player character and serves as the basis for determining which agent character action is likely to achieve the predetermined emotional trajectory. The development of the DDM represents a stepping stone towards producing a series of tools which will allow for character-based IS to be explored from the basis of intelligent, affect-driven narrative agents with metanarrative capabilities (Figure 12.3).

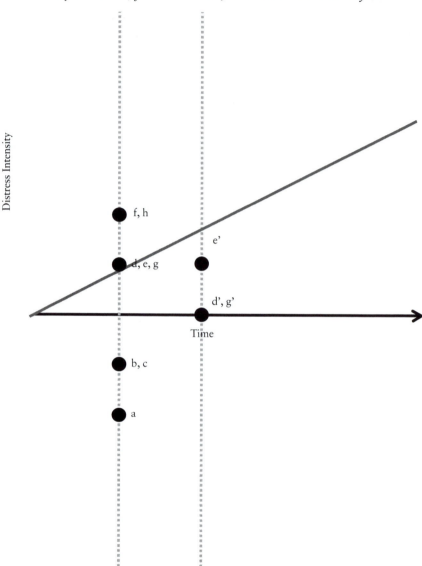

Figure 12.3 Example of a DDM mechanism. The target for the DDM agent is
to generate a level of distress for the player character. The agent
could thus choose from actions *d*, *e* and *g*. However, *e* is closer to the
targeted distress emotion for the follow up action than *d* and *g* are,
and thus it represents a better option.

The EN concept should not be regarded as a different take on the typical
open world gaming approach in which characters are placed within a virtual
world and a story experience automatically emerges. DDM characters are

developed for user interaction, and some level of story facilitation is necessary for any meaningful narrative to emerge. In order to overcome this, the Game Master (GM) takes on the role of a story facilitator in the space of the RPG setting, and thus manages the intended and perceived plot, the fictional characters (NPCs) and the overall environment that represents the player experience. A crucial role for the GM is to provide the player(s) with the means to understand the game world and authorial intent in real-time via representations of the overall setting, scene sequence, direction of events, objects and NPCs in the fictional world. Beyond this, the ability to monitor the creative tension and integrate a social consideration of the player's experience when participating in the game session (Tychen et al., 2009) is required.

The GM's considerations go beyond ensuring dramatic story arc and narrative consistency and also include considerations related to the specific participation and experience of the player in the game in real-time. The player experience (social, participative, narrative) represents the determining element through which story facilitation is conducted. The aim is to deliver a good storytelling experience to participants, and the requirements for story facilitation are partly determined by monitoring the participants' activities and behaviour. Based on this conceptual backdrop, Weallans and Louchart proposed for the DDM to include an integration of GM activities directly within the action selection mechanism of the EN character agent in the DDM (Weallans et al., 2012).

1.2 Research Vision and Future Proceedings

Given the central role played by characterisation in EN, its concrete deployment has been conditioned by the technical implementation of synthetic acting capabilities. This is not trivial, and the addition of preliminary metanarrative capabilities to the FAtiMA agent architecture should be regarded as an enabling technical breakthrough. The DDM represents a technical platform through which higher-level narrative components such as pace, context, authoring and intelligent narrative feedback can now be investigated from a simulated perspective. The long-term vision for EN is the development of an authoring framework through which characters and story settings can be authored, designed and tested, and that would allow the simulation of interactive story-based practices such as LARP, RPG and Improv. Current ongoing work (i.e., Relevant Context Modeller, Intelligent Narrative Feedback) focuses on both authoring and coherence of narration.

The EN concept aims to be inclusive and provide a practical tool for practitioners and to position the EN IS approach as a creative medium. This can only be achieved if writers and artists are allowed to bridge the substantial gap between creative writing and technological mastery. The EN has been conceived as an enabling approach towards a novel way of expressing creativity. The relationship between context and narration is a question of form and relates to the notion that many real-life interactive drama interactions rely heavily on identifying and exploiting narrative opportunities. In a LARP setting, for instance, a substantial amount of the perceived story emerges from narrative opportunities and affordances provided by character or story-world interactions. From an EN perspective, this is a powerful affordance that can be directly applied to synthetic characters so as to orchestrate climaxes and context-related behavioural changes without retreating to a static rule-based approach.

2. RELEVANT CONTEXT MODELLING

The ability for agent characters to make believable decisions within a loose narrative setting is a solid advantage for future EN research. This lies in their ability to make decisions reflective of themselves and other characters, the high-level narrative, and the player character whilst adhering to an authored, sequence-orientated emotional trajectory. In essence, these agent characters need access to more information than is coming in from the local world state. Approaches to this global narrative state include Agent Omniscience (AO) (where every agent character is aware of the entire world state, including the minds of other characters) (Dias and Paiva, 2005) and Drama Management (DM) (where omniscient agent characters manage the way the narrative unfolds) (Weallans et al., 2012).

Both DA and the DDM are affect-driven architectures in which hypothetical scenarios are simulated in order to obtain emotional responses and thus select the most appropriate action for any given situation. AO projects the complete mental states of all agent characters and DM is fully aware of everything that could possibly happen. While necessary, AO and DM pose a threat to character consistency and coherence. There is a risk that characters might no longer act on their own beliefs and intentions but aim to serve the DM instead and thus not conform to the EN ethos. Consistency, in this case, relates to whether or not the sequences of decisions made by the character are consistent with its definition. Coherence relates to the user and whether or not he/she perceives the character decisions as coherent from a behavioural point of view.

The application of a metanarrative concept must differentiate between that of the character layer (provided by the DDM for character consistency) and the necessity for a structural metanarrative layer (for character coherence). The demand for affect-driven characters to provide a sense of dramatic tension has been explored extensively (Murray, 1997; Laurel, 1991; Ryan, 2009) and stipulates the need for relevant character-to-character interactions. Additionally, these interactions should adhere to a typology of narrative structure, which in the context of EN could be simplified to both the static story background and the dynamic set of hypothetical events. As discussed earlier, a character in a LARP environment will participate in the development of a narrative through interactions but additionally needs to understand and adhere to a metanarrative layer, which is outside of the character's control. Thus the requirement for a link between a proposed metanarrative layer and the character layer becomes absolute. Additionally, this notion implies that there must exist a way in which to translate meta-narrative events into data that is understandable, consistent and coherent to emotional dispositions and goals of affect-driven EN agent charac-ters. The initial EN concept explicitly opposed dynamic story facilitators or global management systems built upon traditional plot mechanics. It favoured an approach allowing for each agent character to monitor and manage themselves internally with respect to other agent characters and the metanarrative, whilst remaining consistent and coherent. Essentially this range of data represents context and the DDM thus represents a crucial advance in EN.

Currently, the DDM only selects an action based on its correlation with the current emotional trajectory. It does not consider whether the most emo-tionally relevant action is the most contextually appropriate. For example, the desire for one character to yell at another may be emotionally correct but not politically correct in certain contexts. Thus the need for the inclu-sion of a contextually-weighted aspect to the DDM is clear. Yet this context must be proportionate to the context of the ASM, where only the most rel-evant data is simulated. Thus, the desire to yell may be the best action for the situation, and yet it should not be constrained due to the character gender, for instance, as that is irrelevant for consideration of the yell action. The DDM is a complex decision-based system and would benefit from averaging out both emotionally- and contextually-based factors.

2.1 Adaptability and Suitability of Context

The concept of *context* can potentially strengthen some of the foundations of the EN approach. Yet it does come with its own share of issues; amongst them is ambiguity. Such ambiguity would imply that if the definition—and thus the role—of context is not addressed, it will subsequently lead to an exponential data conundrum, such that if context is everything, how would we selectively choose what information is most relevant? In effect, the how and why of a context-based system's decision that the colour of a character's hair is relevant to another character for consideration within their ASM needs to be identified. John Truesdale and Sandy Louchart proposed (Trues-dale et al., 2013) that *context* could be defined within the realm of EN by addressing such a problem.

We propose that the key to contextual integration lies in reducing the scope of the definition to that of emotionally relevant data. The formation of relationships between higher-level data sequences could then connect the emotional attributes of an agent character's schema(s) and reflect their dis-position accordingly. For instance, a character will not care if the curtains in the living room are blue and will not consider it context unless blue happens to be the character's favourite colour and inherently affects an emotional threshold—for instance, lowers his/her stress level.

The addition of a context-based layer would act as a mediator between the metanarrative layer (character coherence) and character layer (character consistency). It would allow for both global-narrative and private-character knowledge bases to coexist with the DDM, thereby locating the DDM in between strong character systems and strong story systems as described by Mateas (Mateas and Stern, 2003).

A contextual DDM would dynamically manage the allocation of different schema(s) relevant to the player character's emotional trajectory. This stipulates that a high-level narrative event, such as the death of Caesar, could have an indirect, yet profound effect on a Roman farmer character; essentially influencing both his/her emotions and motivations at character level.

Additionally, a contextual integration could do more than simply aiding the DDM with inferences about unobservable aspects of the environment (metanarrative events, character to character interactions). Identifying context is only half the solution, the other half lies in how to attribute environmental data (contextual events such as character interactions and hypothetical plot instances) to emotional values in relation to individual character schemas.

2.2 Consistency and Emotional Attribution

Characters must be able to exhibit the ability to adapt dynamically at run-time, whilst not risking compromising consistency (by changing too much) or coherence (by changing too little). There is an essential need for continuous consistency checks when working with affect-driven agents because agent autonomy might be unduly compromised should their personalities be affected too much, for example if context increases an agent's threshold to crying constantly instead of just occasionally. The proposal for contextual integration is that by allowing agents to reflect upon themselves, others, their surroundings and the context of a situation, it enables them to make the most internally coherent narrative decision possible—consistent with their agent core and coherent with their character.

Agent characters in EN have unique personalities that determine their emotional dispositions and moods (mindset). These personality building blocks define how an agent will react to events and make decisions based on his/her goals and associated actions; however, current DDM implementations do not include any form of personality management. The concern is that without a form of dynamic personality adjustment, an agent character will not have the ability to adapt to changing situations, as his/her mindset will be unchanged from the beginning of the simulation. Introducing a contextual layer, and thus the inherent ability to manage and adapt contextual data would allow for agents to consider their surroundings, thus providing for a greater degree of narrative depth and coherence. Relevant Contextual Modelling (RCM) would adapt preauthored static narrative events dynamically at run-time. The desired outcome is for an agent character to maintain a sense of self whilst emotionally adjusting to the situation at hand. For instance, without the proposed RCM mechanism, a character that has a history of being bullied and has failed at fighting back in the past will always refuse to attempt it again in the future. Yet if a narrative event should occur that makes fighting back a viable and contextually consistent option in the narrative for the character, the conditions for the goal 'fight back' must be adjusted to reflect this change in both the character and scenario. This decision must reflect the internal disposition of the bullying event being associated with sadness, as well as the desired emotional trajectory to be happy, and it will place a higher value on the importance of fighting back. RCM would allow changes that are consistent with the character's personality and would provide the means for a character to maintain coherence with future events. The DDM enforces a level of character consistency, whereas RCM would additionally achieve character coherence by authorising interactions nearest to the targeted emotional trajectory in line with narrative events, while not inhibiting the free will of the agent character.

The proposed integration of RCM into the EN framework is currently under development and aims to provide a creative approach towards developing a unique dynamic experience in a highly sensitive, narrative environment. The end result would be for a player to experience the illusion of scripted authorial coherent narrative in a fully dynamic, satisfying experience, with dramatic agents that exhibit free will and reflect the world, narrative and player realistically and emotionally.

3. INTELLIGENT NARRATIVE FEEDBACK

With the EN concept based on an affect-driven model, its character-based approach would be much more efficient if it could develop a sense of narrative structure at authoring time, where an ordering of sequences of narrative artefacts (events, actions, staging) could take place in an interactive narrative environment.

It is therefore necessary to author agent characters in the role they would play within a given scenario rather than the role they would play from a narrative perspective (or traditional plot-first approach)—a subtle yet important difference. This stipulates that actions cannot be forced upon agent characters, but it argues that EN scenarios be orchestrated in such a manner that increases the chances for dramatically interesting events— arising from the character's own personalities and goals. Thus, authoring EN scenarios is not just a matter of simply building and simulating agent characters but one of crafting characters that possess the potential to produce dramatically interesting narratives.

3.1 Authoring Emergent Narrative

The development of both DA and the DDM, whilst providing a preliminary foundation for dramatic adaptability (by aiding the author in ensuring that dramatically interesting actions could be presented at run-time), failed to assist the author at authoring time. The DDM enables an author to determine if a possible scenario corresponds to a specific player character's emotional target. It thus relies on the author's technical ability to write characters that would display a behaviour in line with the authorial intention in an interactive drama environment. In essence, the authors must be able to visualise how the scenarios may play out at run-time if they are to craft characters through whom their target emotional experience can be accomplished.

This is by no means an easy task because the dynamic nature of the approach prevents the true depth and diversity of the narrative space from being fully observable prior to simulation at run-time. It becomes apparent that in order to facilitate a form of EN authoring, a new method is required. Essentially it must be one in which the final state, or elements of the final state, at run-time can be visualised during authoring. This would provide a platform from which to manage the visualised, hypothetical narrative structure and assist in crafting a consistent, coherent narrative experience for all characters involved.

3.2 Approach and the Feedback Loop

Neil Suttie and Sandy Louchart proposed the concept of Intelligent Narrative Feedback (INF) (Suttie et al., 2013) as a means of exposing this hypothetical narrative space to the author and putting forward potential solutions to problems illustrated within the dramatic representation. In order to be both efficient and effective, INF must provide the author with a clear representation of the hypothetical narrative space at a dramatic level and facilitate an understanding of potential narratives at run-time from the perspective of the character's actions and motivations. The practical consequences are:

1 Feedback must be based on a run-time simulation (Kriegel et al., 2007).
2 Feedback must address problems inherent to an EN approach, such as lack of authorial certainty and visibility at authoring time and narrative dead ends (i.e., an agent is inactive due to a lack of narrative option).
3 Feedback must assist in solving these issues in a manner consistent with the metanarrative considerations.

Thus, INF would provide the author with intelligent feedback, collected via the run-time simulation, towards developing a compelling, consistent and coherent EN experience. Thus INF forms the backbone to an iterative approach to authoring EN. Prior to authoring, it is the author's task to determine the high-level narrative, and thus the experience targeted for the proposed scenario beforehand. Eventually, abstract yet dramatic concepts must be translated into low-level instructions required by the ASM and DDM integral to all agent characters in an EN environment (Figure 12.4).

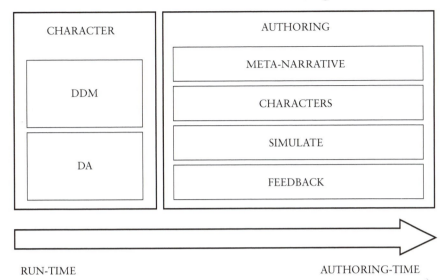

Figure 12.4 The authoring components for creating EN character agents.

The proposed result of INF is a generic scenario template (i.e., LARP structure) from which an author may interactively construct his/her scenario and characters bit by bit. As each element is added, the developing scenario will be simulated and adjusted in a manner that it remains semantically correct (free from error), and it will be both consistent and coherent with the experience targets defined. For example, while a scenario definition may be semantically correct, variations at run-time may result in character goals failing to activate or actions never being used. The INF feedback mechanism would then expose these faults to the user and, by providing appropriate suggestions, prompt them to modify or remove the respective actions or goals. In order to bridge the gap between the author and the AI engineer, a new generation of authoring tools based on a new approach to authoring and IS is required. Tools must be capable of enabling the author to understand and develop scenarios without requiring an understanding of the inner workings of a complex agent goal structure (Suttie et al., 2013; Spierling and Szilas, 2009; Louchart et al., 2008). INF will provide the first step towards developing a set of authoring tools that serve to abstract the purely functional authoring of EN characters towards a drama-oriented, non-functional authoring process.

4. CONCLUSION

In this chapter we looked back at the origins of the Emergent Narrative concept and discussed its iterative evolution over the last decade. EN represents a theoretical approach towards IS born out of existing practices in nondigital domains such as Improv and LARPs. It also represents a technical quest towards developing agent characters with a level of emotional and narrative intelligence that could act, in an interactive setting, for the benefit of both the story and the player experience. In developing such an approach, new and exciting questions arise and new avenues need to be investigated from both a theoretical and technical perspective. Our current research work aims to further past development (e.g., context modelling builds on DDM) and orient the technology towards greater inclusivity (e.g., INF for authoring synthetic characters for EN).

REFERENCES

Aristotle (330 B.C.) *The Poetics of Aristotle.* Transl. Halliwell, S. (1987). London, UK: Duckworth.

Aylett, R. S. (1999) Narrative in virtual Environments: Towards emergent narrative. In: Mateas, M. and Sengers, P. (eds.) *Narrative Intelligence: Papers From the 1999 AAAI Fall Symposium.* Menlo Park, CA: AAAI Press.

Aylett, R. S. and Louchart, S. (2008) If I were you: Double appraisal in affective agents. In *Proceedings, Autonomous Agents and Multi-agent Systems*, AAMAS.

Aylett, R. S. and Louchart, S. (2003) Towards a narrative theory for virtual reality. *Virtual Reality Journal.* 7(1).

Aylett, R. S., Louchart, S., Dias, J., Paiva, A., and Vala, M. (2005) FearNot!—an experiment in emergent narrative. In: Panayiotopoulos, T. et al. (eds.) *Intelligent Virtual Agents: 5th International Working Conference. LNAI 3661.* Berlin, Heidelberg: Springer.

Cavazza, M. O., Charles, F., and Mead, S. J. (2002) Planning characters' behaviour in interactive storytelling. *The Journal of Visualization and Computer Animation.* 13(2). pp. 121–131.

Dias, J. and Paiva, A. (2005) Feeling and reasoning: A computational model. In: Bento, C., Cardoso, A., and Dias, G. (eds.) *12th Portuguese Conference on Artificial Intelligence.* Berlin, Heidelberg: Springer.

Kriegel, M., Aylett, R. S., Dias, J., and Paiva, A. (2007) An authoring tool for an emergent narrative storytelling system. In: Magerko, B. and Riedl, M. (eds.) *AAAI Fall Symposium On Intelligent Narrative Technologies*, Technical Report FS-07-05. Menlo Park, CA: AAAI Press.

Laurel, B. (1991) *Computers as Theater.* Reading, MA: Addison-Wesley.

Louchart, S. and Aylett, R. S. (2003) Solving the narrative paradox in Ves—Lessons from RPGs. In: Rist, T. et al. (eds.) *Proceedings for the IVA Conference.* Berlin, Heidelberg: Springer.

Louchart, S. and Aylett, R. S. (2005) Managing a nonlinear scenario—A narrative evolution. In: Subsol, G. (ed.) *Virtual Storytelling: Using Virtual Reality Technologies for Storytelling.* Berlin, Heidelberg: Springer.

Louchart, S., Swartjes, I., Kriegel, M., and Aylett, R. S. (2008) Purposeful authoring for emergent narrative. In: Spierling, U. and Szilas, N. (eds.) *Proceedings of the First Joint International Conference on Interactive Digital Storytelling (ICIDS 2008).* Berlin, Heidelberg: Springer.

Mateas, M. and Stern, A. (2003) Integrating plot, character and natural language processing in the interactive drama Façade. In: Göbel, S. (ed.) *Proceedings of the Technologies for Interactive Digital Storytelling and Entertainment (TIDSE) Conference*. Berlin, Heidelberg: Springer.

Mateas, M. (1997) An oz-centric review of interactive drama and believable agents. *Technical Report CMU-CS-97-156*, Pittsburgh, PA: Carnegie Mellon University.

Murray, J. (1997) *Hamlet on the Holodeck: The Future of Narrative in Cyberspace*. New York: The Free Press.

Riedl, M. O. (2004) *Narrative Generation: Balancing Plot and Character*. PhD Dissertation, Department of Computer Science, North Carolina State University.

Ryan, M. (2009) From narrative games to playable stories. *StoryWorlds: A Journal of Narrative Studies*. 1.

Scholes, R., Phelan, J., and Kellogg, R. (2006) *The Nature of Narrative, Fortieth Anniversary Edition*. Cambridge: Cambridge University Press.

Spierling, U. and Szilas, N. (2009) *Authoring Issues Beyond Tools*. In: Lurgel, I. A., Zagalo, N., and Petta, P. (eds.) *Proceedings of the ICIDS 2009 Conference. LNCS 5915*. Berlin, Heidelberg: Springer.

Suttie, N., Louchart, S., Aylett, R., and Lim, T. (2013) Theoretical considerations towards authoring emergent narrative. In: Koenitz, H., Sezen, T. I., Ferri, G., Haahr, M., Sezen, D., and Çatak, G. (eds.) *Interactive Storytelling. Proceedings of the 6th International Conference, ICIDS 2013. LNCS 8230*. Berlin, Heidelberg: Springer.

Szilas, N. (2003) IDtension: A narrative engine for interactive drama. In: Göbel, S. (ed.) *Proceedings of the Technologies for Interactive Digital Storytelling and Entertainment (TIDSE) Conference*. Berlin, Heidelberg: Springer.

Truesdale, J., Louchart, S., Hastie, H., and Aylett, R. S. (2013) Suitability of modelling context for use within emergent narrative. In: Koenitz, H., Sezen, T. I., Ferri, G., Haahr, M., Sezen, D., and Çatak, G. (eds.) *Interactive Storytelling. Proceedings of the 6th International Conference, ICIDS 2013. LNCS 8230*. Berlin, Heidelberg: Springer.

Tychsen, A., Hitchens, M., Aylett, R., and Louchart, S. (2009) Modelling game master-based story facilitation in multi-player role-playing games. In: *AAAI Spring Symposium Interactive Narrative Technologies II*. Technical Report vSS-09-06. Menlo Park, CA: AAAI Press.

Weallans, A., Louchart, S., and Aylett, R. S. (2012) Distributed drama management: Beyond double appraisal in emergent narrative. In: Oyarzun, D., Peinado, F., Young, R. M., Elizalde, A., and Méndez, G. (eds.) *Fifth International Conference on Interactive Digital Storytelling (ICIDS). LNCS, 7648*. Berlin, Heidelberg: Springer.

13 Learning Through Interactive Digital Narratives

Andreea Molnar and Patty Kostkova

1. INTRODUCTION

One of the most effective ways of conveying information and learning is through storytelling and narratives. Thus, naturally, narratives have generated great interest and are being incorporated into educational computer games. They are seen as a valuable support for learning, allowing players to "make sense of experience, organize knowledge, sparking problem-solving skills and increase motivation" (Hodhod, Cairns and Kudenko, 2011). The story can provide a context for learning (Kapp, 2012), and interaction allows the player to actively participate in the construction of the story, stimulates curiosity and imagination, and leads to unintentional learning (Hodhod, Cairns and Kudenko, 2011). Integrating the narratives in the context of a computer game is seen by some authors as one of the elements that could determine the success or failure of a game (Göbel et al., 2009). In educational games, this adds another layer of complexity. The successful integration of educational content into the ludic component could determine its motivational nature (Padilla-Zea et al., 2014) and predict the students' engagement with the game. Narratives in an educational game are considered especially important for games aimed at children because their attention span is short and the games must keep them engaged while they are playing and learning (Padilla-Zea et al., 2014). It also shows how games could help teenagers improve their cognitive skills (Gaeta et al., 2014). This chapter aims to explore the research undertaken to integrate educational content into games that make use of narratives. We then examine how a predefined set of Learning Objectives (LOs) are integrated into an interactive detective story using the Storytelling for educAtional inteRventions (STAR) framework, and we present the results of evaluating explicit knowledge acquisition (Rowley, 2007) through the gameplay of the Global Hamdwashing Day (GHD) game.

The rest of this chapter is organised as follows. First, a review of the existing approaches to integrating interactive narratives in educational games is presented. Then, we describe our approach to integrating the educational content in an interactive digital narrative (IDN) game. This will be followed by an evaluation of the game, as well as some concluding remarks.

2. EDUCATIONAL CONTENT INTEGRATION IN THE EDUCATIONAL GAME STORY

Storytelling in educational games is used as a method for improving students' motivation and is considered an important component of learning (Padilla-Zea et al., 2014). One way educational storytelling can be used to motivate students is as a reward, where parts of the story are only shown to the player as a result of overcoming a challenge in the game (Bopp, 2008). Despite the potential of storytelling, most educational games have focused on simulations, thereby ignoring the actual storytelling aspect (Padilla-Zea et al., 2014). In order to motivate students, the challenge for games is to integrate the educational content into the ludic component of the game. Properly integrating the interaction methods in the story is of particular importance, as this can lead to the success or the failure of a game (Göbel et al., 2009).

Despite the recognised potential of educational games that make use of narratives (Gobel et al., 2009; Hodhod, Cairns and Kudenko, 2011; Molnar and Kostkova, 2013c; Padilla-Zea et al., 2014), very little research has been done on the integration of the educational content in the narrative of an educational game (Hodhod, Cairns and Kudenko, 2011; Molnar, Farrell and Kostkova, 2012; Padilla-Zea et al., 2014). According to Matthias Bopp (2008), a video game should define the game goal, divide the main goal into subgoals, and the subgoals should be related to the final goal of the game such that the player finds the task that provides her/him with a rewarding experience. Stefan Göbel et al. (2009) consider three elements essential in any educational game: learning, play and story, and they emphasise the importance of finding a balance between them. Their proposed scheme comprises of an introduction and a set of missions that act as game levels. Natalia Padilla-Zea et al. (2014) propose the division of the storytelling into scenes, sequences and chapters.

3. STAR FRAMEWORK

In our approach we used the Storytelling for educAtional inteRventions (STAR) framework (Molnar, Farrell and Kostkova, 2012). This framework (Figure 13.1) focuses on the level of the mission and proposes five characteristics of a successful interactive digital storytelling experience: an engaging story plot; conveying different sets of LOs and reinforcing the important ones; flexibility in adding or removing the LO; and having an interactive story and allowing the user to influence it. The story structure consists of an *introduction*, a set of *puzzles*, a *resolution* and a *debriefing*. The *introduction* will set the scene and define the problem. The set of *puzzles* consists of *clues* and *red herrings* that will either guide the player or move him away from the solution to the main puzzle. The next part is where the player finds the *resolution*, and hence the solution to the game/mission puzzle. The last part consists of a *debriefing*, a layer where the learning objectives are reinforced. Having this last part has facilitated the integration of the evaluation in the game (Molnar and Kostkova, 2013c).

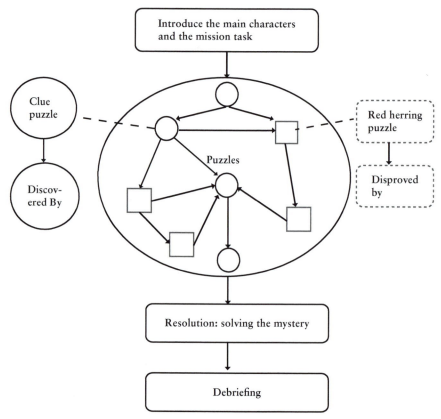

Figure 13.1 Story structure as described in the STAR framework (Molnar, Farrell and Kostkova, 2012).

From a pedagogical perspective, the STAR framework follows a problem-based learning approach (Savery and Duffy, 1995). Also, in every mission, in order to solve the mystery the player has to recall knowledge, comprehend the situation, apply previous knowledge in a new situation, analyse a complex situation and break it out into parts, and synthesise and evaluate the information. These follow the six levels of Bloom's taxonomy (Bloom, 1974) and were initially outlined by Farrell et al. (2011a). Using this approach, several missions were created, as part of the Edugames4all project (Kostkova and Molnar, 2013), including the GHD game. The results of the GHD game evaluation are presented below.

4. CASE STUDY

The Edugames4all initiative (www.edugames4all.org) consists of a set of educational games aimed at increasing children's awareness of important health issues in an enjoyable manner. The games are aimed at children

between the ages of 9 and 15 years. Two types of games were created: platform games (Molnar and Kostkova, 2013b) and interactive digital storytelling games (Molnar and Kostkova, 2013c). The latter consisted of five
missions: one training mission that familiarised the players with the game
mechanics (Molnar and Kostkova, 2013a) and another four missions during which the player became a detective who had to solve a mystery during
which s/he learns about health issues (Molnar, Farrell and Kostkova, 2012).
To solve the mystery, the player has to question possible guilty people
(Figure 13.3), gather evidence and examine it, and draw and evaluate conclusions based on such evidence. The games are created following the STAR
framework described above and have the LOs integrated based on the European curriculum (Lecky et al., 2011), and their development with children in
Europe was published by (Farrell, 2011b; de Quincey, 2011) and translated
to 10 languages (Weerasinghe, 2010). The aim of the games is to have the
children take the message home and lead to awareness about responsible
hygiene and antibiotic use in the family (Lecky and McNulty, 2013).

We will expand on one of the missions, Global Handwashing Day Game
(GHD Game), as this was used during this evaluation, but the other missions follow a similar pattern by presenting a different mystery to be solved,
along with different learning objectives. The plot of the game is as follows:

Introduction: First, the player is placed in the e-Bug/edugames4all agen-
cyvand s/he is introduced to her/his boss, Big C (Figure 13.2). Also here,
the player meets Alyx, who will be the player's partner and will help him/
her during the investigation. After the introductions are made, Big C presents the problem. Hugh Gaego, a famous actor, is allegedly poisoned and
the player has to decipher the mystery: whether it was a case of an alleged
poisoning or not, and who the guilty party is, if any, for poisoning Hugh.

Figure 13.2 The player is welcomed to the agency.

Puzzles: The state space of the game is quite vast, allowing players to explore different parts of the game. The game is nonlinear and allows different options during the investigation. Not all the paths lead to an answer and they are not all mandatory for solving the mystery. The clues should lead the player closer to solving the mystery whereas the red herrings should make the investigation more challenging.

Figure 13.3 The player gathering evidence by talking with the witnesses.

During the investigation, Alyx is always ready to help the player by providing clues, asking questions related to the investigation and assisting with the evidence that was collected. There are six puzzles that integrate the learning objectives from this game, and they are described in detail in Molnar, Farrell and Kostkova's discussion (2012). The game also integrates the game flow questions (possible answers and feedback for assessing the learning objectives taught) (Molnar and Kostkova, 2013c). The questions are seamlessly integrated with most of the players not even noticing that they are evaluated (Molnar and Kostkova, 2013c). As a preknowledge and postknowledge test of the LOs integrated in the game is typically required to evaluate the game's effectiveness at delivering the educational content, the questions are asked at least two times during the game; they are asked once before the player is exposed to the game mechanics and narratives aimed at teaching a LO and once afterwards. Although the questions seamlessly integrated into the narrative flow, the evaluation is done by assessing the abstract and generalisable concepts within the game, as previous research has shown that some of the skills learned through games are not necessarily broad and general, and the player is able to use the skills in the same environment but has problems translating them into a real-world environment (Bavelier et al., 2011).

In order to reinforce the learning value of the game, we designed the LOs to be delivered both in an abstract manner and through fundamental game mechanics. There is a feedback mechanism integrated in the game in order to either reassure the player that his/her answer is correct, or to correct misconceptions (e.g., a nonplayer character provides the player with the answer and explanation of why that is the correct option). The preevaluation is done through the puzzle section, and careful attention has been paid so that the player could be evaluated on all of the learning objectives before being exposed to them, regardless of the path s/he chooses to follow within the game.

Resolution: The resolution is reached when the player has solved the mystery (i.e., has found the guilty party for Hugh's poisoning—Figure 13.4). At this point the player has been exposed to all the learning objectives integrated in the game.

Figure 13.4 Hugh finds out that Heracles (his bodyguard) is the source of his illness.

Debriefing: After the investigation is over, the player returns to the agency for debriefing (Figure 13.5). Because we have a set of pregame and postgame questions to assess the knowledge before and after the LO is delivered, the second round of questions were asked during the debriefing. At the headquarters, Big C asks the player the same set of questions and the player has to select among the same set of options as when the questions were asked for the first time. However, the player feels like s/he is reporting back to the boss rather than actually being asked the same initial questions during the game to seamlessly assess his/her knowledge update. This approach enables us to measure knowledge obtained in a manner that does not decrease the usability or enjoyment of the game (Kostkova, 2012; Molnar and Kostkova, 2013c).

Figure 13.5 Debriefing—Big C asking questions about the investigation.

5. EVALUATION

We have performed an evaluation with school children demonstrating that the players did not feel that they were assessed through the game play, showing that the LOs and the evaluation were seamlessly embedded in the game story (Molnar and Kostkova, 2013c). The aim of the section is to expand upon the evaluation that was done to assess the effectiveness of the learning objectives integrated in the IDN of the GHD Game.

5.1 Method

The study took place either in a controlled environment or online at the participants' convenience. Children and teachers from two schools from London and Glasgow, UK, took part in the controlled environment study. All the participants were given incentives to participate in the study, such as vouchers or prizes that the children could earn by entering in a raffle. To measure the statistical significance of the effectiveness of the overall game in delivering the LOs, a paired t-test was used (Hsu and Lachenbruch, 2008), comparing the players' knowledge about the health issues before and after playing the game. To assess the statistical significance of the effectiveness of the game in delivering each of the LOs included in the game, we used the McNemar test because the answers for the questions used to assess the LOs were nominal (Eliasziw and Donner, 1991).

5.2 Participants

First, the participants were asked to complete a questionnaire through which demographic data was collected, and afterwards to play the game. The questionnaire was online and was displayed immediately before the game started loading. Completing the questionnaire was not mandatory (the participants could skip directly to the game) and the participants could at any time give up playing the game. The people who did not take part in a controlled environment study were mostly people who found the game online. The website containing the questionnaire and the games were relaunched in October 2011, and it was promoted during the Global Handwashing Day (15 October 2011) as well as through mailing lists. Most of the traffic recorded by the website was from English-speaking countries—UK (~60%), US (~10%), Ireland (~9%)—probably due to the fact that at that time only the English version of the games was posted online despite website traffic having come from 73 countries. A total of 145 participants were considered for the evaluation. As the evaluation is integrated in the game and the postknowledge evaluation is done just at the end of the game, the participants were selected based on whether they finished the game or not. Having participants that did not finalise the game would imply not having the results of the evaluation.

5.3 Results

Eleven LOs were assessed, as described in Table 1. The effectiveness of the game at conveying the educational content was performed using a paired t-test (Hsu and Lachenbruch, 2008) on the number of correct answers the players had given for the questions asked before and after playing. The results show that the difference between the players' pregame and postgame answers to the questions assessing the LOs is statistically significant ($p = 0.01$, $\sigma = 2.20$) when a 99 percent confidence interval is considered. The average number of correct answers to the pre-questionnaire was 7.8, while the average score to the post-questionnaire was 8.8. This result shows that the game is an effective way of conveying learning outcomes.

In order to assess whether each LO was efficiently conveyed, we used the McNemar test (Eliasziw and Donner, 1991). The results of the pre- and post-questionnaire evaluation for each of the LOs were analysed. A 95 percent confidence interval was considered statistically significant. The results of the analysis are presented in Table 13.1. The first column shows the LO that the row addresses. The second column presents the number of answers that were right (R) both during the pre- and post-evaluation questionnaires, meaning that the player knew the answer before and after playing the game. The third column displays the answers that were answered wrong twice (W), meaning that the player did not know the answer previously to playing or afterwards. The fourth column shows the answers that changed from wrong to right, meaning that the player did not know the answer before playing, but s/he knew it after the game playing session. The fifth column presents the case when the player initially answered the question correctly, but after the game playing session the answer s/he gave was incorrect. The sixth column is the chi squared obtained as a result of the McNemar test, and in the last column we have the p value. For the LOs written with italics in the table (LO-1, LO-2, LO-4, LO-5, LO-8 and LO-9), the players' knowledge between the post-test and pre-test on that LO had significantly changed. Therefore, the narrative was more effective at delivering certain LOs than others.

Table 13.1 McNemar test results on the players' answers to the Pre and Post LOs evaluation.

LO	R&R[1]	W&W[2]	W&R[3]	R&W[4]	χ^2	p
LO-1: *Microbes found in food can transfer to humans*	109	6	8	22	7.01	0.01
LO-2: *Separate utensils should be used for raw meat and vegetables*	97	6	14	28	5.00	0.03
LO-3: Bacteria from raw meat can make a person sick	103	6	19	16	0.18	0.67
LO-4: *Food cooked properly should be free of bacteria*	59	7	61	10	35.92	0.01
LO-5: *Vomiting viruses are unpleasant but usually not dangerous*	47	15	60	16	24.90	0.01
LO-6: Vomiting viruses can spread through sneezing, coughing or just particles of vomit that are in the air after someone is sick	67	22	39	31	0.80	0.37
LO-7: Vomiting viruses and E. coli can spread through bad hygiene	111	8	16	14	0.08	0.78
LO-8: *It is not always necessary to take medicine when dealing with E. coli and vomiting viruses infections*	60	4	36	20	4.29	0.04
LO-9: *E.coli is commonly found in the lower intestine*	74	29	40	11	15.93	0.01
LO-10: E.coli can spread through the 'faecal-oral' route or poor food preparation hygiene	95	20	30	18	2.76	0.10
LO-11: If eaten, bacteria from raw meat can make a person sick	102	2	22	14	1.57	0.21

Italic text was used to highlight the LOs for which statistical significant difference was obtained between the player knowledge before and after playing the game.

[1]R&R – the numbers of player that provided a right answer for the given LO before and after playing the game.

[2]W&W – the number of players that provided a wrong answer for the given LO before and after playing the game.

[3]W&R – the number of players that provided a wrong answer for the given LO before playing the game and a right answer for the given LO after playing the game.

[4]R&W – the number of players that provided a right answer for the given LO before playing the game and a wrong answer for the given LO after playing the game.

6. CONCLUSION

Although narratives and storytelling are well known methods through which information is conveyed, little research has been done on how to integrate educational content into the narratives of games. The STAR framework proposes to have a sequence of puzzle and red herrings during which LOs are taught (Molnar, Farrell and Kostkova, 2012). Different paths are allowed through the game and the player is free to explore them, but regardless of the path, the player has to cover the core of the LOs aimed to be taught. Evaluation could be seamlessly integrated into the game narratives (Molnar and Kostkova, 2013c). Based on the STAR framework, a game (GHD Game) was implemented. The efficiency of the game in delivering the LOs was assessed with 145 participants. The results showed that the students learned as a result of the game play; however, the players' learning achievements are not evenly distributed across all the LOs.

REFERENCES

Bavelier, D., Green, C. S., Han, D. H., Renshaw, P. F., Merzenich, M. M., and Gentile, A. A. (2011), 'Brains on video games.' *Nature Reviews Neuroscience.* 12. pp. 763–768.

Bloom, B. S. (1974) *Taxonomy of Educational Objectives: The Classification of Educational Goals. Handbook 1–2.* Longmans: McKay.

Bopp, M. M. (2008) Storytelling and motivation in serious games. In: *Final Consolidated Research Report of the Enhanced Learning Experience and Knowledge Transfer–Project* (ELEKTRA, http://www.elektra-project.org/), a project supported by the European Commission (nr. 027986).

de Quincey, E., Kostkova, P., Jawaheer, G., Farrell, D., McNulty, C. A. M., Weinberg, J., Goossens, H., Adriaenssens, N., De Corte, S., Holt, J., Noer, M., Kremastinou, J., Merakou, K., Gennimata, D., Cornaglia, G., Koncan, R., Grzesiowski, P., Olczak-Pienkowska, A., Brito Avo, A., and Campos, J. (2011) Evaluating the online activity of users of the e-Bug web site. *Journal of Antimicrobial Chemotherapy.* 66(44–49, suppl 5).

Eliasziw, M. and Donner, A. (1991) Application of the McNemar test to non-independent matched pair data. *Statistics in Medicine.* 10(12). pp. 1981–1991.

Farrell, D., Kostkova, P., Lazareck, L., Weerasinghe, D., Weinberg, J., Lecky, D. M., Adriaenssens, N., Herotová, T. K., Holt, J., Touboul, P., Merakou, K., Koncan, R., Olczak-Pienkowska, A., Avô, A. B., Campos, J., Cliodna A. M., and McNulty, C. A. (2011a) Developing e-Bug web games to teach microbiology. *Journal of Antimicrobial Chemotherapy.* 66(33–38, suppl 5), v33–v38.

Farrell, D., Kostkova, P., Weinberg, J., Lazareck, L., Weerasinghe, D., Lecky, D. M., and McNulty, C. A. M. (2011b) Computer games to teach hygiene: an evaluation of the e-Bug junior game. *Journal of Antimicrobial Chemotherapy.* Vol. 66. suppl 5. v39–v44.

Gaeta, M., Loia, V., Mangione, G. R., Orciuoli, F., Ritrovato, P., and Salerno, S. (2014) A methodology and an authoring tool for creating Complex Learning Objects to support interactive storytelling. *Computers in Human Behaviour.* 31. pp. 620–637.

Göbel, S., de Carvalho Rodrigues, A., Mehm, F., and Steinmetz, R. (2009) Narrative game-based learning objects for story-based digital educational games narrative. *Narrative.* 14. p. 16.

Hodhod, R., Cairns, P., and Kudenko, D. (2011) Innovative integrated architecture for educational games: challenges and merits. *Transactions on Edutainment.* 5. pp. 1–34.

Hsu, H. and Lachenbruch, P. A. (2008) Paired t Test. *Wiley Encyclopedia of Clinical Trials.*

Kapp, K. M. (2012) *The Gamification of Learning and Instruction: Game-based Methods and Strategies for Training and Education.* New Jersey: Wiley.

Kostkova, P. (2012) Seamless Evaluation of Interactive Digital Storytelling Games: Edugames4All, P. Kostkova, M. Szomszor, and D. Fowler (Eds.): *eHealth 2011, Springer Lecture Notes of the Institute for Computer Sciences, Social-Informatics and Telecommunications Engineering LNICST 91*, pp. 80–84.

Kostkova, P. and Molnar, A. (2013) Edugames4all: Computer games teaching children abstracts about bugs and drugs. In *IPNET-Kenya/ICAN Joint Conference*, 6–8 November, Mombasa, Kenya.

Lecky, D. M., McNulty, A. M. C., Adriaenssens, N., Herotov, T. K., Holt, J., Touboul, P., Merakou, K., Koncan, R., Olczak-Pienkowska, A., Avo, A. B., Campos, J., Farrell, D, Kostkova, P., and Weinberg, J. (2011) What are school children in Europe being taught about hygiene and antibiotic use? *Journal of Antimicrobial Chemotherapy.* 66(13–21, suppl 5).

Lecky, D. M. and McNulty, C. A. (2013) Current initiatives to improve prudent antibiotic use amongst school-aged children. *Journal of Antimicrobial Chemotherapy.* 68(11). pp. 2428–2430.

Molnar, A., Farrell, D., and Kostkova, P. (2012) Who poisoned Hugh?—the STAR framework: Integrating learning objectives with storytelling. In: Oyarzun, D., Peinado, F., Young, R. M., Elizalde, A., and Méndez, G. (eds.) *Fifth International Conference on Interactive Digital Storytelling (ICIDS). LNCS, 7648.* Berlin, Heidelberg: Springer.

Molnar, A. and Kostkova, P. (2013a) If you build it would they play? Challenges and solutions in adopting health games for children. In *ACM SIGCHI Conference on Human Factors in Computing Systems.*

Molnar, A. and Kostkova, P. (2013b) On effective integration of educational content in serious games. In *13th IEEE International Conference on Advanced Learning Technologies*, Beijing, China.

Molnar, A. and Kostkova, P. (2013c) Seamless evaluation integration into IDS educational games. In *Foundations of Digital Games*, Chania, Greece.

Padilla-Zea, N., Gutierrez, F. L., Lopez-Arcos, J. R., Abad-Arranz, A., and Paderewski, P. (2014) Modelling storytelling to be used in educational video games. *Computers in Human Behaviour.* 31(1). pp. 461–474.

Padilla-Zea, N., Sánchez, J. L. G., Vela, F. L. G., Abad-Arranz, A., and Lopez-Arcos, J. R. (2012) Evaluating emotions in educational videogames: The particular case of children. In *13th International Conference on Interacción Persona-Ordenador.*

Rowley, J. (2007) The wisdom hierarchy: Representations of the DIKW hierarchy. *Journal of Information Science.* 33(2). pp. 163–180.

Savery, J. R. and Duffy, T. M. (1995) Problem based learning: An instructional model and its constructivist framework. *Educational Technology.* 35(5). pp. 31–38.

Weerasinghe D., Lazareck L., Kostkova P., and Farrell D. (2010) Evaluation of popularity of multi-lingual educational web games—Do all children speak English? *eHealth.* 2(23). pp. 44–53.

14 Everting the Holodeck
Games and Storytelling in Physical Space

Mads Haahr

1. VIRTUAL REALITY INSIDE OUT

Janet Murray's proposal of the Holodeck as an immersive environment for interactive digital storytelling (Murray, 1997) has served as a guiding metaphor for researchers in interactive digital narrative since it was proposed. At present, a sizeable portion of the entertainment industry is in agreement with the vision of highly immersive virtual environments as a powerful medium for storytelling, and recent AAA titles such as *Heavy Rain* (2010), *L. A. Noire* (2011) and *The Last of Us* (2013) can be seen as serious experiments in this vein. In terms of platform support, Virtual Reality (VR) ideas developed in the 1990s are making a comeback in the form of new head-mounted displays, such as Oculus Rift and Project Morpheus, only this time with support of large industry players like Sony and Facebook. These interfaces, if adopted at the mass scale that their backers are hoping for, are likely to further enhance the use of virtual environments for digital storytelling.

VR may be happening for real this time, made possible by powerful miniaturised graphics processing units, lightweight high-resolution displays and small responsive motion sensors, none of which existed (or were prohibitively expensive if they did) in the 1990s, but which have been developed for the growing smartphone market. Interestingly, the same technologies are also being adopted for a type of storytelling more aligned with the mobile platform for which they were primarily developed: location-based, or locative, storytelling. Where the predominant vision of the immersive interactive digital storytelling environment situates the audience 'inside' a simulation, there is also work going on in which the narrative elements are being placed 'in the physical space' that the audience happens to inhabit. This work is highly aligned with Mark Weiser's famous vision of *ubiquitous computing*, which he characterised as the opposite of VR because the technology is brought out into the real world through device sentience and mobility rather than the user being brought into the virtual world (Weiser, 1991).

In this chapter, we explore the current state of interactive digital narrative practice that relates to physical space. We think of such works as everted holodecks, a series of Weiser-esque attempts to turn VR not on its head but inside out. Rather than inserting the audience into an interactive story simulation, such works construct a story that relates in one way or another to the physical world inhabited by the audience, typically by superimposing or mixing narrative elements on top of or into a real-world environment. Determining location is of course of great importance for such works—indeed so important that the term first proposed to describe them and related works was *locative media*. While locative media projects are not necessarily concerned with narrative, the canon that was established in the early and mid 2000s has been influential for later projects. The term *locative media* was first used by Karlis Kalnins (Albert, 2004) to describe a test-category of work that originated in the now-defunct Locative Media Lab. Albert also offers the following description:

> Locative media art at its best enhances locative literacy. The ability to read, write, communicate is vital for any person needing to act, take power, to have agency. An awareness of how flows and layers of information intersect with and augment a person's locality, and the ability to intervene on this level is a further extension of this literacy, and of their agency.
>
> (Albert, 2004)

Seminal works from the early and mid 2000s were primarily art projects and research projects; they were experimental systems that drew attention to and helped express spatial relationships. Many were performance-driven and some also intended to be hackable, i.e., allowing modification by the participants. Some developed their story through player engagement with high-activity game mechanics, while others were concerned with a slower story-driven development. In the former category, Blast Theory's *Uncle Roy All Around You* (2003) used a fictional character and the players' quest to find him to explore how game mechanics (e.g., puzzle-solving, time-constrained navigation) could be used to link a virtual gameworld with a real, urban environment. In the latter category, history-focused projects, such as *Media Portrait of the Liberties* (Nisi et al., 2008) and *Riot! 1831* (Reid, 2008) explored how media fragments could be situated in locations that were of historical relevance to the story material, while *REXplorer* (Ballagas et al., 2008) and *Viking Ghost Hunt* (Carrigy et al., 2010; Paterson et al., 2010) did the same for game activities.

The widespread adoption of GPS-enabled smartphones that began in the late 2000s allowed locative media to transition from short-lived art and media experiments or pure performance pieces to become a mass medium. Hence, while locative media have existed for well over a decade, it is only within the last few years that they have become available to general audiences. A number of works have been put forward, some of which are concerned with storytelling and some of which have received respectable participant numbers.[1] The analysis presented here focuses on four influential projects that feature an approach to interactive storytelling in which geolocation mechanics play a crucial role: *Parallel Kingdom* (2008), *Shadow Cities* (2010), our own platform *Haunted Planet* (2012) and finally *Ingress* (2013). The titles are deconstructed to show how game mechanics and storyworld, and to a lesser extent aesthetics, are used in the service of narrative. The chapter concludes with a perspective on the types of narratives that can be expressed in location-based games and their general characteristics compared to other digital media.

2. PARALLEL KINGDOM (2008–PRESENT)

Parallel Kingdom by Wisconsin-based game studio PerBlue is a location-based smartphone massively multi-player online role-playing game (MMORPG) in which the gameworld is overlaid on top of the real world. The gameworld is fantasy-themed and features a range of game characters and opponents typical of classic role-playing game (RPG) titles. *Parallel Kingdom* uses GPS to detect the player's real-world location; and when the game starts, their avatar is placed in the corresponding location in the gameworld. The game contains three core movement mechanics, one of which is hard, requiring physical movement in the real world, and two of which are soft, allowing movement in the gameworld without real-world movement.[2]

When a *Parallel Kingdom* player has had their location sampled using GPS, the game positions their avatars within a circle of mobility (around 400m radius, see Figure 14.1) from the sampling point. The game allows them to move their avatar around this area simply by tapping on their screen, i.e., without having to move physically. We call this the *soft micromovement* mechanic. The player can relocate their circle of mobility in a number of different ways, for example by physically moving to a new real-world location and taking a new GPS reading. We call this the *hard macromovement* mechanic. Other options also exist for relocating the circle of mobility without physical movement, such as *walking the dog*, in which the game relocates the circle of mobility to a random unexplored area, or by being invited by another player to travel virtually to their location. We call such movement mechanics *soft macromovement* mechanics. One of the first tasks that a new player encounters is that of mastering these nonspatial modes of transport.

In addition to these movement mechanics, *Parallel Kingdom* contains a series of typical MMORPG mechanics, such as monster combat, levelling up, resource gathering, and crafting of game objects, as well as competitive and cooperative multiplayer interaction. There is a strong territorial aspect to *Parallel Kingdom*, and many of the game objects constructed by players (e.g., flags and houses) serve a territorial purpose. The player chooses where in the world to place such game objects (and most of them remain in these locations afterwards), and while they serve a territorial function (e.g., are worth conquering), they are not strongly linked with the real

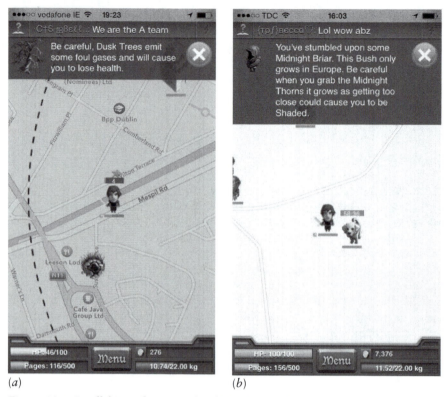

Figure 14.1 Parallel Kingdom's Circle of Mobility and a Region-Specific Game
Object (Screenshots by Mads Haahr).

world. Their virtual location is not linked in any intrinsic/extrinsic way to
the actual location—other than the player's choice in positioning—and the
real-world location's atmospheric and historical qualities are of no consequence to the game, except through direct player knowledge—and perhaps,
for players with a shared context, also a shared meaning.

Parallel Kingdom adopts a typical MMORPG narrative structure, with
the notable difference that it does not propose a main storyline and leaves
players the freedom to construct their own narratives (narratives of their
characters and those of friends and enemies of their characters) through
RPG game mechanics. Characters can be developed using a customisation
system and their abilities advanced through the game's levelling mechanic.
The main game activities include resource gathering, combat and other territorial mechanics: Players may embark on adventures with friends, conquer
nearby lands, tame the wilderness and establish new cities. The absence of
a series of quests forming a main storyline—an otherwise common trait
for MMORPGs—highlights the freeform nature of *Parallel Kingdom*.
Rather than a grand structured narrative arc, it offers a narrative sandbox

environment in which players can shape their characters' stories through play. The game's locative aspect remains at the level of game mechanics (movement and territory) and never directly transcends into the narrative domain. Despite the fact that the gameworld's foundation happens to be the real world, the two worlds are not guaranteed to meet in any narratively cohesive manner—unless players decide to do so by creating game objects of their own that are tied to the physical world.

3. SHADOW CITIES (2010–2013)

Like *Parallel Kingdom, Shadow Cities* by Helsinki-based game studio Grey Area Labs is a location-based MMORPG that uses the real world as its gameworld, and similarly, it is a territorial game where players are shown in real-time and battle for control over different geographical areas. Differently from *Parallel Kingdom, Shadow Cities* divides its player community into two opposing factions, the Architects and the Animators, and territorial battles take place between those two. While the gameworld in *Shadow Cities* contains spells and magic, its gameworld and aesthetics are distinctly modern, almost futuristic in style. Even the way the spells are cast, through gestures (called runes) drawn with a finger on the touch screen, are modern and sleek compared to *Parallel Kingdom's* more traditional button-based User Interface (UI).

On the game mechanics in *Shadow Cities*, the game's lead designer Markus Montola states: "The basic game mechanics are about casting spells, killing enemies, gathering [Experience Points] XP, completing missions, fighting other players, so forth, but what makes it special is that everything is done on a map" (Montola, 2012). The company's CEO, Ville Vesterinen, adds: "Shadow Cities is rather literal when it comes to location. Every game object maps to one exact location in the real world. Every player is in one exact location" (Vesterinen, 2012). *Shadow Cities* includes a hard as well as a soft movement mechanic. Using the hard movement mechanic, the player can change their avatar's location in the gameworld through physical travel in the real world. The soft movement mechanic is implemented through the existence of game objects called *beacons*, which allow players to travel to other parts of the gameworld without moving physically.

Shadow Cities is essentially social, as it is intended to be played with friends exploring and conquering nearby (algorithmically generated) neighbourhoods. To facilitate this, the game contains social features, such as chat and friending. Like in *Parallel Kingdom,* these functions enable the soft movement mechanic, but the strong social aspects of *Shadow Cities* are also in good accord with the territorial game mechanics. Ville Vesterinen observes, "cities and neighbourhoods evoke strong emotions" (Vesterinen, 2012), meaning that emotional investment that players have in their home locality helps amplify the emotional investment in the territorial mechanic. The result is a sociolocative game mechanic.

In terms of story, the conflict between the Architects and the Animators is cast as being a battle of mythic proportions, an eternal struggle that neither side will win. "Hundreds of years ago, an ancient now long-forgotten force pulls through our world. This alternative reality has now returned, using technology as the gateway" (Montola, 2012). Game creatures are inspired by Norse mythology and carry names like Fenrir and Valkyries. This mythological backstory functions as a framing device within which players' individual stories can be constructed. In addition, it is *location* that plays an important role as a catalyst for people's imagination about their game actions. If a player's actions take place in an area that is of particular significance to them (even if they are not there physically), then the actions will take on special significance for them too, be more memorable and hence serve as more important components of emergent stories. Figure 14.2 shows screenshots of play in culturally significant places in Paris and New York. The designers of *Shadow Cities* also observed a considerable amount of emergent play (Juul, 2005), such as the kind described by Markus Montola at GDC in 2012:

> We don't need to put stuff on the map in order for [the players] to find it, for instance here the players are in the Forbidden City in Beijing, they organised these treasure hunts—here they are in the Arc de Triomphe in Paris [Figure 14.2], or Pearl Harbor, or Area 51. Players go into these places, they organise their own competitions, they organise scavenger hunts or whatever, they write fanfic [Fan Fiction] based on what we do, they write fanfic about gathering in Area 51 and going there and doing stuff. The powerful resource we have here is that we have a coherent world, everything in the game is supporting the same fiction because this is not a game, it is your magic device where you draw runes and you cast spells, so everything you have in the real world, you can appropriate into the game. If you have a cool piece of local folklore, you can enter it into the fiction, if you have a mage meet-up cruise you can make that a game event.
>
> (Montola, 2012)

The emergent behaviours observed are evidence of player creativity and evidence of the game's success as a platform for player's to construct their own events and narratives. Anecdotes recounted by Vesterinen (2012) include a protest outside Grey Area Labs when an unpopular change had been made during a game update, and a no-war zone (i.e., no fighting between the two factions) at Ground Zero in New York during a 9/11 anniversary (see Figure 14.2b) in which players constructed skyward beams of light similar to those used in a real-world memorial installation. In this fashion, *Shadow Cities* retains the grassroots feel of the first locative media projects in that it supports emergent play, even if it is not directly hackable.

(a)   (b)

Figure 14.2 *Shadow Cities* at Champs-Élysées in Paris and Ground Zero in New York (Copyright Grey Area Labs).

4. HAUNTED PLANET (2012–PRESENT)

The Haunted Planet games are a series of smartphone-based location-based games by Dublin-based game developer Haunted Planet Studios for which the author serves as CEO and Creative Director. In the Haunted Planet games, the player takes on the role of paranormal investigator, exploring a real-world area for paranormal activity, encountering ghosts and other supernatural entities, documenting their existence with photos and audio recordings and ultimately solving a mystery. In terms of genre, they fall within the categories of "locally staged treasure hunts" (Montola et al., 2009, pp. 32–34) and "urban adventure games" (Montola et al., 2009, pp. 42–44). We think of the games as an attempt to reinvent traditional Gothic storytelling using modern technology and draw upon many Gothic narrative techniques, such as "pretension to veracity," "fragmented narratives," "heavy historical trappings" and the "disturbing return of pasts upon presents" (Botting, 2001). Our analysis will focus on two games, *Bram Stoker's Vampires* (2012), which is a heavily Gothic game based on the novel *Dracula,* and *The Amazing Transfabulator* (2013), which is a lighter, more whimsical time travel adventure loosely inspired by the works of Jules Verne.

Each game has a site-specific mode and a random mode. In the site-specific mode, the game is played in a particular location where the encounter locations are chosen by the game designers to resonate with the story and through site atmosphere and/or history. In site-specific mode, *Bram Stoker's Vampires* is set in Trinity College, Dublin in Ireland where Bram Stoker (the author of *Dracula*) was a student (1864–1870). Founded by Queen Elizabeth in 1592, the College is rich in history and its old buildings provide a powerful backdrop to the game experience, in particular its augmented reality view of the gameworld. In this mode, the player searches the College grounds for characters related to the famous novel *Dracula*, which have mysteriously appeared in the author's old stomping grounds. In site-specific mode, *The Amazing Transfabulator* is set in the Victorian precinct of Oamaru, New Zealand, the historical buildings of which form a similarly powerful backdrop in terms of its aesthetics and history. In this game, the player searches for members of a Victorian time-travel expedition whose time machine (the transfabulator) has malfunctioned, leaving them stranded in interdimensional limbo. In the random mode, each game can stage itself to where the player happens to be, and in this configuration it is suitable for playing in a park or another open area anywhere in the world.

While the two games have different subject matter, they employ identical game mechanics. Each game turns the player's smartphone into a paranormal detection device, through which she/he interacts with the gameworld and the physical environment. The game has four different gameplay modes (Adams, 2009) that enable the game mechanics. The map (Figure 14.3) shows the general area in which the game takes place but does not show the individual encounter locations. The paranormal radar (Figure 14.4) works like a ship's radar, showing the player in the centre and showing relative distance to nearby encounters. Together, these two modes facilitate a search/navigation mechanic in which the player explores his/her physical environment in order to get close to an encounter. The search/navigation mechanic is a hard movement mechanic; there is no in-game travel that does not involve the player traversing the physical space in which the game is staged. When the player gets close to an encounter, layers of audio build up (Paterson et al., 2013) and the ghost view (camera) mode can be activated, allowing the player to engage with the scan/capture mechanic in order to see and photograph the game entity (Figure 14.5). A successful capture enters the photo into the game's casebook where additional visual detail is revealed (a good photo results in more visual detail) and also unlocks a snippet of character backstory (Figure 14.6). The Haunted Planet games do not contain territorial or competitive mechanics; instead they are heavily focused on solving the mystery.

The two games differ slightly in their approach to narrative structure. *Bram Stoker's Vampires* uses a parallel inclusive structure for the first three encounters (the three vampire sisters from Stoker's novel) followed by five sequential encounters (four with Count Dracula and one with the ghost of Bram Stoker). *The Amazing Transfabulator* uses a purely parallel inclusive structure for the

Figure 14.3 Bram Stoker's Vampires (2012) Map Mode (Copyright Haunted
Planet Studios).

Figure 14.4 Bram Stoker's Vampires (2012) Radar Mode (Copyright Haunted
Planet Studios).

first six time travellers followed by a final encounter with the eccentric professor who has created the time machine. Through exploring the environment
and unlocking the characters' visuals and backstory, the player constructs the
narrative in her/his mind. In comparison to *Parallel Kingdom* and *Shadow
Cities*, the Haunted Planet games are discrete story experiences, strongly
curated and allowing for little story development by the players themselves.

Figure 14.5 Bram Stoker's Vampires (2012) Ghost View Mode (Copyright Haunted Planet Studios).

Figure 14.6 Bram Stoker's Vampires (2012) Casebook Mode (Copyright Haunted Planet Studios).

5. INGRESS (2013–PRESENT)

Ingress is developed by Google game studio Niantic Labs and shares many similarities with *Shadow Cities*. Similarly, *Ingress* is a location-based MMORPG in which players take part in a grand struggle between two factions. *Ingress'* backstory states that Earth has been seeded with Exotic Matter (XM) by an alien race called the Shapers. Little is known about the Shapers, but they serve to divide the player base in two based on human beliefs about them: Players belonging to the Enlightened faction believe the Shapers are benevolent, while players belonging to the Resistance believe they are malevolent. Players choose their faction when they begin, but other than providing allegiance to a faction, the choice has little consequence for the gameplay. It is mainly a social decision.

Ingress employs conventional RPG mechanics, such as resource gathering and levelling. The gameplay is centred on the conquest and maintenance of portals (Figure 14.7b), gameworld representations of real-world landmarks of historical or architectural value, such as a public art or historical buildings. The main game resource is XM, which is gathered by walking and can be expended to hack the portals in order to obtain game items (Figure 14.7a), which in turn are used to capture and protect portals from the opposing faction. Game actions, such as hacking enemy portals, is rewarded with Action Points (APs), which trigger the player's level progression. The game contains a clever balancing mechanic in that APs are rewarded for hacking enemy portals, but not friendly ones, meaning that players who find themselves in a region in which their faction is in the minority are likely to level up faster than players from the opposing faction in the same region.

 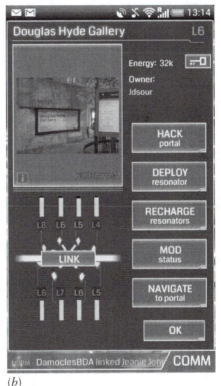

(a)   (b)

Figure 14.7 *Ingress* (2013) Resource Gathering and Portal View (Screenshot by Mads Haahr).

The visuals in *Ingress* (see Figure 14.7) are similar to those of *Shadow Cities,* showing the gameworld as a 3D stylised map view of the player's vicinity. Portals appear as glowing bonfire-shaped game objects that are colour-coded to indicate ownership (grey is neutral, blue is resistance, green is enlightened). XM is shown as small glowing dots scattered across the map.

Similarly to the beacons in *Shadow Cities,* control of portals in a particular area is of territorial significance. While portals do not allow virtual travel in the gameworld, players can use friendly portals to create *control fields* by linking three portals to form a triangular shape across the gameworld. The larger the control field, the greater its effect on the total score for the faction that created it. Figure 14.8 shows a control field created over Ireland by the Resistance on 26 January 2014.

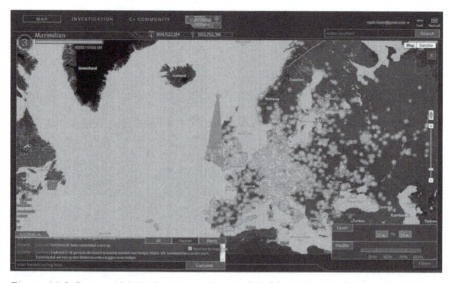

Figure 14.8 *Ingress* (2013) Resistance Control Field over Ireland (Screenshot by Mads Haahr).

Similarly to *Parallel Kingdom, Ingress* overlays the gameworld on top of the real world and creates a circular area around the player's game location within which they can affect the game state. (See Figure 14.7a.) In contrast, however, *Ingress* contains no soft movement mechanics and always requires the player to travel physically in order to move this circle of influence. In fact, *Ingress* does not allow any game actions to be performed if it is not able to acquire the player's precise location. Travelling is also encouraged since it is required to gather XM.

In contrast with most MMORPGs, *Ingress* contains little in terms of crafting/creation mechanics. The developers chose public art to represent portals because it was safe and accessible (Badger, 2013), and they allow players to suggest landmarks as potential new portals by taking photos of candidate landmarks and submitting them through the game. While Badger states that "the player community helps build out the game board" (Badger, 2013) in this fashion, the players have no influence over whether their portal proposals are eventually adopted, and even the submission of photos has the feel of an extra-game activity rather than an in-game action.

Ingress has a highly engaged player community with events in which players gather to hack portals and exchange knowledge and game objects, and like *Shadow Cities,* the community has also produced fan fiction. The social experience of play was an important design consideration for the developers. Like the other MMORPGs that were discussed in this chapter, *Ingress* contains an in-app geo chat to help members of each faction coordinate their efforts; and to create the highest-level portal, a total of eight high-level players must collaborate, resulting in social coordination of game activity as well as social play. Badger explains:

> If you interview players, it's those social connections that add the most fun to the game. So it's not just about shooting your weapons ..., it's really about your friends, it's about that walk you take with your friends.
>
> (Badger, 2013)

The developers also arrange agent meetups, local events in which players from the two factions compete to control a number of specific portals at specified points in time.

While *Shadow Cities* contained a complex mythical backstory, *Ingress* adopts a complex science fiction universe. The backstory is developed through multiple channels, which in addition to the game app includes an online intel map that gives a global view of the game state and an investigation board containing redacted CIA documents and other material. In addition, weekly five-minute news broadcast called *Ingress Report* is transmitted to players as game objects. The report contains material authored by the game developers as well as material sourced from the player community in the form of stories about player exploits and feats. This shows players what other groups are doing and helps motivate them to one-up it.

6. STORYTELLING IN PHYSICAL SPACE

Our analysis of the four titles has revealed some of the different aspects in which location-based mobile games allow the players' physical environments to help tell stories, and it discusses the game mechanics involved. The particular mechanics associated with locative-narrative gaming vary significantly between works. While they always involve a hard movement mechanic, a soft movement mechanic is also sometimes offered. Additional game mechanics can involve exploration, capture, chase, collection and territorial conquest, and there is often (but not always) a social aspect to their use.

In terms of structure, the way the narrative experience is constructed by the games can be classified using a dichotomy. The majority of games (all except the Haunted Planet games) took a sandbox approach to narrative, offering a context absent of any inherent plot progression, and in several instances cast as a never-ending struggle. In these games, the narrative is best characterised as a frame within which players can develop their own stories as a way to remember certain events. Markus Montola, Jaakko Stenros and Annika Waern characterise this as a first person story (Montola et al., 2009, pp. 151–152). The other category contains the Haunted Planet games, which took an *auteur* approach, offering a highly structured (albeit nonlinear) narrative progression that the players explore through the game mechanics. While the players create their own photos through the game experience, it is more akin to following a story trail than creating stories of one's own. The unstructured-structured dichotomy can be compared to the narrative difference between sandbox games like *The Sims* and quest-based RPGs like *Neverwinter Nights*.

A second consideration is the way in which the different experiences map the gameworld and the real world to each other. The approach taken by *Ingress* is perhaps the clearest example of this: The gameworld is attached to the real world through notable features in the urban environment. Farman defines such urban mark-up as follows:

> The various ways that narrative gets attached to specific places in a city. Urban mark-up can be done through durable inscriptions (like words carved into the stone façade of a building or statue) or through ephemeral inscriptions (ranging from banners and billboards to graffiti and stickers).
>
> (Farman, 2013, p. 3)

While *Ingress* allows players to submit their local urban mark-up for possible inclusion as a portal, the decision relies with the game developer and is essentially curated. Even more curated are, of course, the Haunted Planet games in site-specific mode, since the urban mark-up to which they are attached is fixed and no new mark-up is added to the game once it has been published. In comparison, *Parallel Kingdom* and *Shadow Cities* essentially offer uncurated mapping between the gameworld and the real world. In these titles, it is up to the players to decide which structures to place on the game map to represent the features of the real world that they feel are significant. Regardless, whether we are concerned with a curated or uncurated mapping, the act of performing the mapping is of course in service of the story—and vice versa. As Farman writes, "[t]he meaning of a story is affected by the place in which the story is told and, similarly, the meaning of a place tends to be told through stories" (Farman, 2013, p. 8).

The two considerations—general narrative approach (structured/ unstructured) vs. gameworld/real-world mapping (curated/uncurated)—are shown in Table 14.1. In addition to the prior discussion, we have placed the Haunted Planet games in random mode in the uncurated section, because the encounter locations in this mode are chosen neither by the game developer nor the players (other than by virtue of their choosing the general location of play).

Table 14.1 Narrative approach (columns) and gameworld/real-world mapping (rows)

	Unstructured/Sandbox	*Structured/Auteur*
Curated mapping	Ingress	Haunted Planet Games in Site-Specific Mode
Uncurated mapping	Parallel Kingdom Shadow Cities	Haunted Planet Games in Random Mode

We have analysed four significant works in the area of location-based mobile gaming and found that the majority employ unstructured, sandbox-style narrative environments. As the analyses of *Shadow Cities* and *Ingress* have shown, it is clear that considerable audience engagement can be obtained by staging an experience in a neighbourhood that people feel invested in, and there also exists a small body of fanfic constructed on the basis of such play—a clear, if tentative, sign of the games being deployed as story platforms. The Haunted Planet games are in the minority with their auteur-driven, curated approach and serve as a counterpoint to the main trend. Both narrative approaches can be found in earlier (nonlocative) interactive media, but the linking of the gameworld and the real world is unique to the locative medium. As pioneers in locative media observed, this linking is ultimately about control—for us, the curative control of the real/virtual mapping. Fortunately, many simultaneous mappings are possible. As Farman writes:

> What mobile media storytelling projects demonstrate … is that someone can be staring at a mobile device and be more deeply connected to the space and to others in that space than other people might perceive. Storytelling with mobile media takes the stories of a place and attaches them to that place, offering an almost infinite number of stories that can be layered onto a single site.
>
> (Farman, 2013, p. 6)

Where the holodeck (even as an abstraction) promises to create a perfect, brilliant canvas to carry your story, the everted holodeck promises to create (or let you create) a perfect, brilliant story to attach to your canvas. While the realisation of the holodeck might be about to take a big step forward, there is still important work to do in turning it inside out.

NOTES

1. *Ingress* is reported to have had at least 500,000 players (Dalenbert, 2013).
2. The term *hard* in relation to physical location is borrowed from Vesterinen (2012) who discusses *hard location* in the context of *Shadow Cities*.

REFERENCES

Adams, E. (2009) *Fundamentals of Game Design.* (2nd ed). Peachpit.

Albert, S. (2004) Locative literacy. In *Mute*, vol 1, no. 28, Summer/Autumn 2004. http://www.metamute.org/editorial/articles/locative-literacy.

Badger, B. (2013) Ingress: Design principles behind Google's Massively Multiplayer Geo Game. In *Game Developers Conference (GDC) 2013.* Independent Game Track.

Ballagas, R., Kuntze, A., and Walz, S. P. (2008) *Gaming Tourism: Lessons from Evaluating REXplorer, a Pervasive Game for Tourists.* In *Pervasive Computing* 2008, LNCS vol. 5013, Springer, pp. 244–261.

Botting, F. (2001) *Gothic.* Cambridge: D. S. Brewer.

Carrigy, T., Naliuka, K., Paterson, N., and Haahr, M. (2010) Design and evaluation of player experience of a location-based mobile game. In *Proceedings of the 6th Nordic Conference on Human-Computer Interaction* (NordiCHI 2010). Reykjavik, pp. 92–101.

Farman, J. (2013) The Mobile Story: Narrative Practices with Locative Technologies. Routledge.

Juul, J. (2005) *Half-Real: Video Games between Real Rules and Fictional Worlds.* Cambridge: MIT Press.

Montola, M., Stenros, J., and Waern, A. (2009) *Pervasive Games: Theory and Design.* Burlington, MA: Morgan Kauffman.

Montola, M. (2012) Shadow cities and the future of location-based games. In *Smartphone and Tablet Game Summit*, GDC 2012.

Murray, J. H. (1997) *Hamlet on the Holodeck.* Cambridge, MA: MIT Press.

Nisi, V., Oakley, I., and Haahr, M. (2008) Location-aware multimedia stories: turning spaces into places. In *Proceedings of ARTECH Conference.* pp. 72–93.

Paterson, N., Naliuka, K., Jensen, S. K., Carrigy, T., Haahr, M., and Conway, F. (2010) Design, implementation and evaluation of audio for a location based augmented reality game. In *Proceedings of ACM Fun and Games* 2010. Leuven, pp. 149–156.

Paterson, N., Kearney, G., Naliuka, K., Carrigy, T., Haahr, M., Conway, F. (2013) Viking ghost hunt: Creating engaging sound design for location-aware applications. International Journal of Arts and Technology 6(1), pp. 61–82, inderscience.

Reid, J. (2008) Design for coincidence: Incorporating real-world artefacts in location-based games. In *Proc. of ACM DIMEA*, ACM Press.

Vesterinen, V. (2012) Secret sauce for location based games: Learnings from shadow cities. In *GDC Europe*, Cologne.

Weiser, M. (1991) The computer for the 21st century. *Scientific American.* 265(3). pp. 94–104.

15 Narrative Explorations in Videogame Poetry

Diğdem Sezen

Janet Murray calls video games' ability to make players cry the "folk wisdom test for strong narrative involvement" (Murray, 2005, p. 83). How and even whether or not this can be done has been debated from various perspectives over the years (Zyda, 2005; Wallace, 2006; Humble, 2006; Walker, 2006; Ferrari 2008; Bateman, 2008). Several big budget titles such as *ICO* (Team Ico, 2001), *Heavy Rain* (Quantic Dream, 2010) and *The Walking Dead* (Telltale Games, 2012) have been praised by their fans for their narrative and emotional complexity and their ability to make them cry. With the rise of indie games in recent years, similar remarks were made for games developed on much smaller budgets, based on the powerful emotional responses players elicit through specific ludic and narrative aspects. Amongst them, games creatively blending the affordances and abilities of games with aspects of poetry and narrative created a particular niche, which we can call examples of *videogame poetry*.[1]

In this chapter we will focus on such examples of videogame poetry with possible narrative aspects and try to investigate how they combine poetry, gaming and narrative into one coherent system. Due to their poetic nature, these games potentially differ from mainstream narrative-oriented games, as they must do more than just attempt to overcome the difficulties of mixing narrative and games. By adding poetry, two additional areas of complication arise, namely between poetry and games, and between poetry and narratives. The main focus of our investigation in this chapter will be on the latter two, followed by an analysis of individual games as case studies.

1. POETRY AND NARRATIVE

The relationship between narrative and poetry is complicated. In contemporary narrative theory, poetry has been categorised as a blind spot (McHale, 2005; Alber and Fludernik, 2009). Brian McHale sees the acceptance of the short lyric form as poetry's default mode after the 19th century to be a major issue in this regard. Thus the modernist poetics of the *image* interdicted narrative in poetry, which was consequently left to specialists in prose fiction. Yet before the 19th century, the majority of poetry was not only lyric but also narrative or discursive (McHale, 2005). Epic poetry and ballads are narrative genres; in addition, many lyric poems can be read as narratives or at least contain identifiable narrative elements (Alber and Fludernik, 2009; Hühn and Sommer, 2009; Schmid, 2010). Discussing the evolution of narratological perspectives on poetry, McHale defines three main theoretical problems which are essential to understanding the workings of narrative in poetic form:

1 World-building: Do narrative poems project fictional worlds in the same way prose fictions do, and if not, how do poetry's worlds differ?
2 The counterpoint of narrative and verse form: How does the unfolding of story in poems relate to the formal articulation of poetry in stanzas, lines, metrical feet, etc.?
3 The relation between narrative and figuration: Granted the special affinity between poetry and figuration, what relations exist between narrative logic and the logic of poetic metaphor? (McHale, 2005, p. 358)

Importantly, these theoretical questions show similarities with the basic questions of the field of interactive digital narratives (Koenitz et al., 2013) in relation to noninteractive narratives with regard to form, composition and analysis. Looking at Interactive Digital Narrative (IDN) through poetry's perspective also liberates the IDN researcher from the necessity to align critical perspectives and experiments in form with prose. By understanding a narrative game in the frame of poetry with all its ambiguities and possibilities, we can reroute the patterns of thought in the field and see even familiar IDN examples in a new light.

2. POETRY AND GAMES

Since the mid-20th century, poets have used the analogy of machinery to describe their work. In 1939, Paul Valéry wrote in his essay "Poetry and Abstract Thought" that "a poem is a kind of machine for producing the poetic state of mind by means of words" (Valéry, 1954, p. 231). Five years later, in 1944, the American poet William Carlos Williams wrote in his introduction to *The Wedge*:

> A poem is a small (or large) machine made of words … It isn't what he [the poet] *says* that counts as a work of art, it's what he makes, with such intensity of perception that it lives with an intrinsic movement of its own to verify its authenticity.
>
> (Williams, 1991 p. 54) (Emphasis in the original)

Similarly, in 1999, German poet Michael Hoffman defined a poem as a "machine for rereading … [and] a line like a mosaic of magnets, charges and repulsion in every word;" he continued: "[T]here is a process called annealment, the heating to a high temperature and slow cooling of glass or metals to toughen them. Making a poem feels like that—writing as yourself and reading it back as someone else" (Hoffmann, 1999, p. 6). In all these conceptions, poets described their creations as finely crafted mechanisms to be operated by someone else. A poet creates a system that waits for the reader's involvement and autonomous movement to elicit meaning. This description shares fundamental similarities with the idea of games as systems.

Gameplay describes free movement within a more rigid structure. In *Homo Ludens*, Johan Huizinga described play as "an activity which proceeds within certain limits of time and space, in a visible order, according to rules freely accepted, and outside the sphere of necessity or material utility" (Huizinga, 1980, p. 132). According to Katie Salen and Eric Zimmerman, play is an expression of the system, one that takes advantage of the space of possibility created from the system's structure. They define a game as a "system in which players engage in artificial conflict defined by rules that result in a quantifiable outcome" (Salen and Zimmerman, 2003, p. 80). Similarly, Jesper Juul defines a game as a

> rule-based formal system with variable and quantifiable outcomes, where different outcomes are assigned different values, where the player exerts effort in order to influence the outcome, the player feels emotionally attached to the outcome, and the consequences of the activity are optional and negotiable.
>
> (Juul, 2005, pp. 6–7)

Both games and poems represent multiple possibilities in a system that determines what outcomes can be generated. Not all readings are possible. Huizinga was one of the first to point out the ludic nature of poetry. Based on his definition of the characteristics of play (see above) he wrote:

> [T]he definition we have just given of play might serve as a definition of poetry. The rhythmical or symmetrical arrangement of language, the hitting of the mark by rhyme or assonance, the deliberate disguising of the sense, and the artificial and artful construction of phrases—all might be so many utterances of the play spirit. To call poetry, as Paul Valery has done, a playing with words and language is no metaphor: it is the precise and literal truth.
>
> (Huizinga, 1980, p. 132)

The playful nature of poetry has also been investigated by contemporary game theoreticians. Mary Flanagan (2009) discussed avant-garde poetry from Dadaist cut-outs to instruction poems as examples of critical 'wordplay' through word meaning, metric and shape. Nick Montfort (2003) argued that the riddle as a poetic form was not only verbal puzzle but also an early ancestor of interactive fiction. Ian Bogost (2010), in his introduction to *A Slow Year: Game Poems,* also emphasised the shared characteristic of games and poems by arguing that good games and good poems are both provocation machines.

3. DIGITAL GAMES AS POETRY

Despite these parallels drawn between poetry and games, not all critiques were optimistic towards the combination of games and poetry in digital form. In his book *Prehistoric Digital Poetry,* Chris Funkhouser wrote that

> poetry in its traditional form may never take the shape of a video game because video games as we know them in popular form (i.e., lots of rapid fire action, to which the player physically responds) are antithetical to the purposes of a certain style of poem.
>
> (Funkhouser, 2007, p. 251)

Yet a mere five years later in his book *New Directions in Digital Poetry,* Funkhouser describes Jim Andrews' *Arteroids* (Andrews, 2002–2007) as one of the primary examples of digital poetry and emphasises the works' dual nature both as a video game featuring fragmented language purporting to be poetry and also poetry in the sense of a game without competitive structure (Funkhouser, 2012). Andrews himself describes *Arteroids* as a "literary shoot-em-up computer game and the battle of poetry against itself and the forces of dullness" (Andrews, 2002–2007). Adalaide Morris classifies *Arteroids* as a *poem-game* and defines poem-games as "rule-driven ritual spaces dependent on an engaged player splicing the appeal conventions of computer and videogames into the critical and creative traditions of poetry" (Morris, 2006, p. 24). The game is based on the 1979 Atari arcade game *Asteroids* (Atari, 1979), and without changing the game mechanics, *Arteroids* replaces the ship and asteroids of the original with words or phrases that fly across the screen and have the abilities of shooting and exploding. In this regard Roberto Simanowski (2001) argues that *Arteroids* appropriates, deconstructs and semantically redefines the rhetoric of shoot-em-up games; and in this way, it alienates the clichés and expectations of the language system in a novel approach to find new possibilities. Yet according to Markku Eskelinen, "*Arteroids* is not a conceptual fusion of game and poetry, but instead a user-friendly compartmentalized hybrid of the two" (Eskelinen, 2012, p. 379). The design of *Arteroids* lets player engage with game mechanics independently from the poetry part. In Eskelinen's words,

> the nonreading player (NRP) can choose to ignore the bits and pieces of sound poetry (by turning the audio off) and also ignore the splintering and exploding words to simply focus on enjoying the borrowed game

mechanics ... while the nonplaying reader might avoid or minimize the game-related challenges.

(Eskelinen, 2012, pp. 378–379)

Compartmentalised hybrid structures are not uncommon amongst video game poems. Jason Nelson's Flash-based titles *Game, Game, Game and Again Game* (Nelson, 2007) and its sequel *I made this. You play this. We are Enemies.* (Nelson, 2008) are basically 2D platformers that use multiple media such as screenshots, animations, sounds, small video clips and texts as backgrounds and pop ups. Even though there is no scoring, one can still play the games to reach the end through the chaotic platform paths; or, as Nelson suggests in the instructions, the player can explore the game elements without trying to get any specific meaning behind them. Similarly, Sandy Baldwin's *New Word Order* (Baldwin, 2003), a mod of the classical first person shooter *Half-Life* (Valve Software, 1998), which features custom maps filled with phrases from a short poem of American poet Billy Collins as shootable objects, can be played either as a (mostly aimless) shooter or in a creative manner suggested by the author. The latter encourages players to explore the game world and break the words as a means of deductive writing (Baldwin, 2011).

The combination of poetry and common game characteristics does not always lead to compartmentalised hybrid structures based on common genres. For example, Ian Bogost's collection of self-described game poems, *A Slow Year* (Bogost, 2010), features four one-kilobyte game poems for Atari VCS. These games are not similar to any typical game genre common in Atari VCS but still use the general constraints of the platform. Based on the seasons of the year and with instructions delivered to the players in haiku form, *A Slow Year* offers symbolical graphic representations with unique details in the visuals and a poetic gameplay based on reflection and observation (Bogost, 2010).

4. NARRATIVE EXPLORATIONS IN VIDEOGAME POETRY

Although most of the game poems mentioned above did not contain easily recognisable narrative contents, in recent years titles with both poetic and narrative features started to gain critical acclaim. These games combined gameplay elements with evocative stories and even stanzas in a way which resembled both the structure and the mood of a poem. The following is a selection of such examples which we think will open up new perspectives on possible directions for interactive digital narratives.

4.1 Passage (2007)

Since its release in 2007, Jason Rohrer's *Passage* has garnered special attention, both from the critics and the public, and has been praised for its simple but emotionally intensive design and poetic nature (Fagone, 2008; Champion, 2008; Trans, 2011). *Passage* is a small and simple game engaging with the concept of the journey of life. The game was inspired by Rohrer's personal observations of an acquaintance's struggle with cancer and thus is described by him as a *memento mori* game (Rohrer, 2007). In accordance with Murray's folk wisdom test metaphor (Does it make you cry?) for strong narrative involvement, many players, including Rohrer himself, reported that *Passage* has made them cry and made them reflect on their priorities in life (Rutkoff, 2008; Benedetti, 2008; Fagone 2008). Rohrer describes *Passage* as follows:

> It presents an entire life, from young adulthood through old age and death, in the span of five minutes. Of course, it's a game, not a painting or a film, so the choices that you make as the player are crucial. There's no "right" way to play *Passage*, just as there's no right way to interpret it.
>
> (Rohrer, 2007)

In the creator's statement, Rohrer also explains that the game mechanics were deliberately selected to characterise the subject. *Passage* was suggested as one of the founding examples of proceduralist games (Bogost, 2011) because of its reliance on computational rules to produce artistic meaning. According to Mike Treanor and Michael Mateas, what makes *Passage* a proceduralist game is that "the ways most players find the game meaningful involves the procedural aspects and these interpretations *happen* to align with Rohrer's stated intentions about how the rules of the game were meant to be metaphorical" (Treanor and Mateas, 2013) [Emphasis in the original]. Miguel Sicart emphasises the role of metaphors in games and claims that games are systems that are communicated to the player through metaphors. Therefore, the meaning of games is a complex interplay between the game system, the metaphors used to communicate with players and the way that players interpret these metaphors (Sicart, 2013, p. 39).

Passage takes place in a maze which, due to the game's screen geometry, can only be seen partially as a narrow slice. The choices Rohrer refers to are mostly navigational decisions within the maze which may lead the player to various treasure chests containing blue stars giving extra points. The most important decision in *Passage* is whether or not to let a female character whom you, the player, meet early in the game to accompany you throughout the journey. Doing so limits the space you can explore since, with the female character on your side, your avatar cannot move through certain passes in the maze. On the other hand, you get more points for each blue star with a companion on your side.

The puzzling aspects of *Passage* are not only the narrow screen and the maze. The game's pixel art visuals are also distorted and hard to decipher. Early in the game, the eastward direction and later the westward direction of the narrow screen gets compressed and thus complicates the perception of the areas in question. Besides strictly controlling the player's knowledge of the game world, these design decisions also have metaphorical meanings: At the beginning of the game, you can see your entire life out in front of you, albeit in rather hazy form, but you can't see anything that's behind you, because you have no past to speak of. As you approach middle age, you can still see quite a bit out in front of you, but you can also see what you've left behind—a kind of store of memories that builds up. At its midpoint, life is really about both the future (what you're going to do when you retire) and the past (telling stories about your youth). Toward the end of life, there really is no future left, so life is more about the past, and you can see a lifetime of memories behind you (Rohrer, 2007). Near the end of the five minutes, characters in the game start to get older until they die. If the player has chosen to have a companion, he/she witnesses the companion's death. The player's now old and slow character follows shortly after. He/she is powerless and cannot prevent this ending; only the memories of the experience can be saved.

Although at first glance *Passage* may seem like a characteristic maze game, neither the avatar nor the obstacles act in a usual fashion. Features like the five-minute time limit, changing colours of graphics and the change of the avatar's physical appearance through time create a strong analogy with life which subvert expectations and repurpose the maze genre. According to Kenny Chow, two levels of conceptual blends take place in *Passage*: "The immediate blend … results in an embodied concept of walking through the virtual passage, and then the metaphorical blend … yields a particular message of how marriage and family commitment limits possibilities" (Chow, 2013, p. 181). Similarly, relying on a polymorphic poetics, Fox Harrell (2013) also analyses how *Passage* provides commentary on real life by means of a subjective computing system. Harrell focuses on metaphorical mappings of *Passage* in parallel to Jason Rohrer's statements about the game and attributes the positive reception of the game to the successful implementation of the metaphor of mortality throughout the gameplay. According to Harrell's analysis, every element and every action in the game is in service of the metaphor involving the passage of time and one's death (Harrell, 2013).

Due to its inherent segmentation, the overall structure of *Passage* resembles a short poem with three stanzas. The first segment bundles events related to youth, the second segment groups midlife experiences and aging, and the last part deals with solitude and death. The interplay of game mechanics and metaphors placed in a storyline with a beginning and an end also provides a sense of coherence for narrative involvement. Due to the time limit, a player can only see a small portion of the maze at any session; thus, every single session holds new potential for exploring different sections of the game map; or, in other words, every new session starts a new life with new potential.

Like all good narratives, *Passage* invites the player to fill in the blanks depending on real life experiences and knowledge of the world. The intense emotional impact of the game is largely based on what we already know in addition to what the game narrative reveals. *Passage* does not answer any questions regarding its message; instead, it is filled with ambiguity: The mechanics do not tell you as player which side of the maze would be better for you or whether what you did throughout the game was right or wrong. Which way would be more convenient, happier, interesting or right? The design does not give a clear answer. The game's mechanics symbolise a human relationship with all its ambiguities and allow the player to contemplate on it.

The most impressive feature of *Passage* is its infusion of powerful metaphors into its gameplay. In addition, the gently crafted design also turns its constraints into meaningful game elements. Subtly changing images, music and inherent rhythm in its segments carry echoes of stanzas. *Passage* is a game which evokes more connotations with a powerful short narrative poem than any other genre.

4.2 Today I Die (2009)

In his 2011 article *Poetics of Game Design, Rhetoric and the Independent Game*, Lindsay Grace claims that the game verb, which is the set of actions executed by the player to accomplish a goal, serves as the atomic unit of game design. According to him, independent games in particular create new verbs for play, and there is an analogy between stanza and game levels:

> Stanzas are often the unit of organisation, binding meter to them. All of the rhythms of game verbs, and all the rests between experiences come in the form of a level. Even when level is less explicit, the stanza reveals itself as a marker of moment. Achievements become stanzas, as progress is formed into stanza through leveling up.
>
> (Grace, 2011)

Probably the most concrete realisations of Grace's analogy are Daniel Benmergui's 2009 Flash-based games *Today I Die* and its extended 2010 iOS version *Today I Die Again*. Described by Benmergui himself as a *game poem* (Graft, 2010), *Today I Die* combines gameplay, a short branching story and literary poetry in one coherent system. The game starts with a girl seemingly drowning, dragged to the ground by a heavy stone tied to her waist. There are dark sharks and several jellyfishes in light colours around her. A short stanza accompanying the scene can be seen above the screen: "Dead world, full of shades, today I die." Next to the girl two words float; 'dark' and 'painful.' The words 'dead, 'dark' and 'painful' are green while all other texts are written in white. There are no other instructions for the player. She has to solve the puzzles based on her intuitions. Right at the beginning, *Today I Die* offers the players two main options. Like playing with magnetic poetry, she can switch between words of the same colour or she can interact with game elements such as the sharks and the jellyfish. While interacting with sharks has no effect at first, interacting with the jellyfish slowly reveals a new word. However, as soon as the word starts to appear, sharks attack the jellyfish to stop the process. The player needs to keep the jellyfish alive until the new word, *shine*, materialises and allows the player to replace the word *die*. This action changes the poetry and thus the girl's state of mind and thereby the scene she is in; consequently, she faces new minipuzzles. Throughout the game, the player has to find the correct combination of words in the stanzas and do the right moves to influence the girl's feelings and state of mind in order for her to reach the surface. Based on the player's actions and the stanzas she has written, the game reaches different endings: The girl may meet a boy or continue swimming alone, etc.

In her critique of *Today I Die Again,* Hilary Goldstein writes that the game and its puzzles were written around the poem and argues that the focus of the game "is clearly on the poem as narrative, with the game merely a medium to deliver Benmergui's message" (Goldstein, 2010). At first glance, the game and poetry may seem separable. However, according to Benmergui, all game elements were designed in an integrated fashion, and he even argues that the poem has a low aesthetic quality by itself if separated from the game (Graft, 2010). Indeed, each level in *Today I Die* is represented by a stanza. Changing the words of the stanza modifies the levels and the mood of the character and the game itself. The rhythm of the game and the accompanying audio also reflect the poem's state. In a way, *Today I Die* is a collection of minigames connected conceptually to the character's inner world represented in the text of the stanzas, and together they tell a story about despair turning into salvation.

4.3 Fatale (2009)

The 2009 game *Fatale* by Tale of Tales is basically an interactive first-person narrative inspired by Oscar Wilde's play *Salome* (1891), which in turn is inspired by the biblical story of Salome, the daughter of Herodias. *Fatale*'s designers Auriea Harvey and Michaël Samyn are also known for their *Real-time Art Manifesto* in which they proclaim the 3D game technology as their artistic medium of choice (Harvey and Samyn, 2006). The duo explicitly rejects plots imposed on players and defends their practice of making short and intense games closer to *haiku* poems than to longer epic forms. Finally, they promote a perspective on games as poetry instead of prose. Their work *Fatale* represents these ideals.

According to Samyn and Harvey (Beech, 2009), Wilde's story is about the passion of Salome, the stepdaughter of the King Herod Antipas. Moreover, it represents her as an evil princess. As John the Baptist does not return her love, she requests his head on a silver platter as a reward from her stepfather for dancing the dance of the seven veils. *Fatale*, as a reimagining of Wilde's text, offers an experience from the perspective of the victim and takes place in the aftermath of the events of the play. According to Samyn and Harvey, this narrative direction was inspired by "the idea of ultimate peace, brought on by death" (Beech, 2009). Throughout his life, John the Baptist rejected earthly pleasures, including love, and cared only for the Messiah. The game, which takes place mostly after his death, offers the player an opportunity to see things from many different perspectives.

Fatale consists of three segments, differing from each other in content and even slightly in mechanics. This first part is about waiting: the player assumes the role of John the Baptist and is placed in a dark dungeon. The player can walk, jump and move objects around, but he/she does not have any tools to use, nor any instructions on what to do. While waiting and exploring the dungeon, she/he finds hidden quotes from Oscar Wilde's *Salome*. Finding the final quote ends this segment with the entrance of armed guards, who will murder John, into the dungeon. The second part starts with the spirit of John floating up through the crenels to the terrace. Eventually, controls are restored and the player gains the ability to move through the terrace of the palace and explore the scene's intricate detail. The moonlit terrace offers more than a beautiful view; it features Princess Salome standing next to John's cut-off head with a pensive look on her face, and also Queen Herodias watching her from a distance. The player is immersed in a crucial frozen moment of the story which can be explored without any rush. Thus the segment is about exploring a moment. The ghost's ability to float gives the player the option to look at every object on the terrace from every angle; but except for the candles, which the player can extinguish, he/she has no power over them.

In accordance with *Realtime Art Manifesto*, *Fatale* allows players to follow their own story path according to their pace and choices of navigation in a virtual environment. The specificity of a frozen moment adds a poetic feature to the game, which Herbert R. Kohl describes "as snapshots that capture a moment and at the same time reveal how connected that particular view is to the larger movement of life on the planet" (Kohl, 1999, p. 11). The virtual environment itself creates a connection between space and narrative by allowing the player to act independently and thus create her/his own narrative. In this respect, Michael Nitsche (2008) describes the relationship between game spaces and narrative as follows:

> Evocative narrative elements encourage players to project meaning onto events, objects, and spaces in game worlds. They help to infuse significance. Their value is not realised on the level of the element itself but in the way players read and connect them. Creating these connections, players can form narratives that refer to the game world.
>
> (Nitsche, 2008, p. 44)

The third part of the game starts after the player (as John's ghost) has extinguished all the candles. In this segment, the player finds herself/himself in a different role, probably as King Herod, on a different terrace in daylight and watching Salome dancing. The player can zoom in and out but cannot perform any other movements or actions. This part of the game is clearly about gazing.

Fatale does not employ the idea of a clearly identifiable plot and instead allows player to start a real-time exploration of a narrative embedded in an ambiguous living tableau through evocative narrative elements. The mood of the narrative can be inferred from the game mechanics. They transform throughout the game, from familiar to unfamiliar and to the almost inactive. Like the changing rhythm of a poem, the game shapes the way the environment is explored.

5. CONCLUSION

Recent approaches in contemporary narratology emphasised the need for a reappraisal of poetry's form, use of metaphors and world-building methods in respect to narrative construction in poems. Parallels between the forms of games and poetry were drawn in some of the earliest philosophical works on games and in recent theoretical perspectives on poetry. In this respect, a combination of the three—games, poetry and narrative—opens up new perspectives for IDN design and analysis.

As a testament to compartmentalised thinking, early digital game poems provided little in terms of narrative. However, recently artists received praise from both the public and critics for game poems following a proceduralist approach with clear narrative aspects. Although quite different in their mechanics, audio-visual aesthetics and fictional content, these artefacts were designed to communicate an emotional experience through a combination of these elements. The examples analysed in this chapter expose several salient characteristics of contemporary game poems. Having no win or lose condition, they urge players to focus on progress and content. When there are multiple endings, none of them can be described as good or bad, and they are equally meaningful dramatically. The use of metaphors to connect game mechanics with real life helps the player to comprehend complex meanings through shared cultural references. The ambiguity of metaphors, on the other hand, leaves enough room for interpretation and thus instigates the participation of the player on a deeper level. In each example there are formal constrains which resemble the structural features of a poem. They evoke continuous acts of discovery and invite a range of interpretations. Finally, videogame poems not only differ from mainstream games but also from IDNs following epic or prose-based approaches and open up new perspectives for future IDN design.

NOTE

1. Similar terms have been used by other scholars to describe specific types and examples of poetry and video game hybrids: 'poem game' (Morris, 2006), 'game poem' (Bogost, 2010), 'digital poetry game' (Funkhouser, 2012) and 'poetic/poetry game' (Ensslin, 2014).

REFERENCES

Alber, J. and Fludernik, M. (2009) Mediacy and narrative mediation. In: Hühn, P., Schmid, W., Schönert, J. and Pier, J. (eds.) *Handbook of Narratology*. Berlin: Walter de Gruyter.

Andrews, J. (2002–2007) *Arteroids*. [Video Game]. Available at: http://www.vispo.com/arteroids/arteroids.htm

Atari, Inc. (1979) *Asteroids*. [Arcade Game]. Atari. Inc.

Baldwin, S. (2003) *New Word Order*. [Half-Life Mod]. Available at: http://collection.eliterature.org/2/works/00_baldwin.html

Baldwin, S. (2011) New word order: Basra. In: Borràs, L., Memmott, T., Raley, R., and Stefans, B. (eds.) *The Electronic Literature Collection Volume Two*. Available at: http://collection.eliterature.org/2/works/baldwin_basra.html

Bateman, C. (2008) A game has never made you cry. *International Hobo*. [blog] 10 December. Available at: http://blog.ihobo.com/2008/12/a-game-has-never-made-you-cry.html

Beech, A. (2009) *Tale of Tales Interview*. Available at: http://venturebeat.com/2009/10/17/tale-of-tales-interview/

Benedetti, W. (2008) When has a video game ever made you cry. *NBC News*. [online] 15 October. Available at: http://www.nbcnews.com/id/27188395/ns/technology_and_science-games/t/when-has-video-game-ever-made-you-cry/

Benmergui, D. (2009) *Today I Die*. [Video Game]. Available at: http://www.ludomancy.com/games/today.php

Benmergui, D. (2010) *Today I Die Again*. [Video Game]. Available at: http://www.ludomancy.com/games/today.php?lang=en

Bogost, I. (2010) *A Slow Year: Game Poems*. Louisville: Open Texture.

Bogost, I. (2011) *How to Do Things with Videogames*. Minneapolis: University Of Minnesota Press.

Champion, E. (2008) The video game as art. *Reluctant Habits*. [blog] 21 January. Available at: http://www.edrants.com/the-video-game-as-art/

Chow, K. (2013) *Animation, Embodiment, and Digital Media: Human Experience of Technological Liveliness*. New York: Palgrave Macmillan.

Ensslin, A. (2014) *Literary Gaming*. Cambridge, MA: MIT Press.

Eskelinen, M. (2012) *Cybertext Poetics: The Critical Landscape of New Media Literary Theory*. London: Continuum.

Fagone, J. (2008) The video-game programmer saving our 21st-century souls. *Esquire*. [online] Available at: http://www.esquire.com/features/best-and-brightest-2008/future-of-video-game-design-1208

Ferrari, S. (2008) A game has made you cry, but … procedural rhetoric's value. *Chungking Espresso*. [blog] 13 December. Available at: http://simonferrari.com/2008/12/13/a-game-has-made-you-cry-but-procedural-rhetorics-value/

Flanagan, M. (2009) *Critical Play: Radical Game Design*. Cambridge, MA: MIT Press.

Funkhouser, C. (2007) *Prehistoric Digital Poetry: An Archaeology of Forms, 1959–1995*. Tuscaloosa: The University of Alabama Press.

Funkhouser, C. (2012) *New Directions in Digital Poetry*. London: Continuum.

Gillen, K. (2006) More than a feeling. *The Escapist Magazine*. [online] Available at: http://www.escapistmagazine.com/articles/view/video-games/issues/issue_41/246-More-Than-a-Feeling

Goldstein, H. (2010) Today I die again iPhone review: Poetry in motion. *IGN*. [online] Available at: http://www.ign.com/articles/2010/11/02/today-i-die-again-iphone-review

Grace, L. (2011) The poetics of game design, rhetoric and the independent game. In *Proceedings of the 5th International Conference of the Digital Research Association*. Hilversum, the Netherlands: DiGRA/Utrecht School of the Arts, 14–17 September 2011.

Graft, K. (2010) Road to the IGF: Daniel Benmergui's Today I Die. *Gamasutra*. [online] Available at: http://www.gamasutra.com/view/news/27036/Road_To_The_IGF_Daniel_Benmerguis_Today_I_Die.php

Harrell, F. (2013) *Phantasmal Media: An Approach to Imagination, Computation, and Expression*. Cambridge, MA: MIT Press.

Harvey, A. and Samyn, M. (2006) *Realtime Art Manifesto*. Available at: http://tale-of-tales.com/tales/RAM.html

Hoffmann, M. (1999) Not even the old rock'n roll. *Poetry Book Society Bulletin*. 181. Summer. p. 6.

Hühn, P. and Sommer, R. (2009) Narration in poetry and drama. In: Hühn, P., Schmid, W., Schönert, J., and Pier, J. (eds.) *Handbook of Narratology*. Berlin: Walter de Gruyter.

Huizinga, J. (1980) *Homo Ludens: A Study of the Play-Element in Culture*. London: Routledge and Kegan Paul.

Humble, R. (2006) Game rules as art. *The Escapist Magazine*. [online] Available at: http://www.escapistmagazine.com/articles/view/video-games/issues/issue_41/247-Game-Rules-as-Art

Juul, J. (2005) *Half Real: Video Games Between Real Rules and Fictional Worlds*. Cambridge, MA: MIT Press.

Koenitz, H., Haahr, M., Ferri, G., and Sezen, T. I. (2013) First steps towards a unified theory for Interactive Digital Narrative. In: Pan, Z., Cheok, A. D., Mueller, W., Iurgel, I., Petta, P., and Urban, B. (eds.) *Transactions on Edutainment X*. Berlin, Heidelberg: Springer.

Kohl, H. R. (1999) *A Grain of Poetry: How to Read Contemporary Poems and Make Them A Part of Your Life*. New York: Harper Perennial.

McHale, B. (2005) Narrative in poetry. In: Herman, D., Jahn, M., and Ryan, M. L. (eds.) *Routledge Encyclopedia of Narrative Theory*. Oxfordshire: Routledge.

Montfort, N. (2003) *Twisty Little Passages: An Approach to Interactive Fiction*. Cambridge, MA: MIT Press.

Morris, A. (2006) New media poetics: As we may think/how to write. In: Morris, A. and Swiss, T. (eds.) *New Media Poetics: Contexts, Technotexts, and Theories*. Cambridge, MA: MIT Press.

Murray, J. H. (2005) Did it make you cry? Creating dramatic agency in immersive environments. In: Balet, O., Subsol, G., and Torguet, P. (eds.) *Virtual Storytelling: Using Virtual Reality Technologies for Storytelling*. Berlin, Heidelberg: Springer.

Nelson, J. (2007) *Game, Game, Game and Again Game*. [Video Game] Available at: http://collection.eliterature.org/2/works/nelson_game.html

Nelson, J. (2008) *I Made This. You Play This. We Are Enemies*. [Video Game] Available at: http://www.secrettechnology.com/madethis/enemy6.html

Nitsche, M. (2008) *Video Game Spaces: Image, Play, and Structure in 3D Worlds*. Cambridge, MA: MIT Press.

Quantic Dream, (2010) *Heavy Rain*. [Video Game] Sony Computer Entertainment.

Rohrer, J. (2007) *Passage*. [Video Game] Available at: http://hcsoftware.sourceforge.net/passage/

Rohrer, J. (2007) *What I Was Trying to Do with Passage*. [online] Available at: http://hcsoftware.sourceforge.net/passage/statement.html

Rutkoff, A. (2008) The game of life. *The Wall Street Journal*. [online] 25 January. Available at: http://online.wsj.com/news/articles/SB120034796455789469

Salen, K. and Zimmerman, E. (2003) *Rules of Play: Game Design Fundamentals*. Cambridge, MA: MIT Press.

Schmid, W. (2010) *Narratology: An Introduction*. Berlin: Walter de Gruyter.

Sicart, M. (2013) *Beyond Choices: The Design of Ethical Gameplay*. Cambridge, MA: MIT Press.

Simanowski, R. (2001) Fighting/dancing words: Jim Andrews' kinetic, concrete audiovisual poetry. *Dichtung Digital: Journal für Kunst und Kultur Digitaler Medien*. [online] Available at: http://dichtung-digital.de/2002/01/10-Simanowski/cramer.htm

Tale of Tales, (2009) *Fatale*. [Video Game]. Tale of Tales.

Team Ico, (2001) *ICO*. [Video Game] Sony Computer Entertainment.

Telltale Games, (2012) *The Walking Dead*. [Video Game]. Telltale Games.

Trans, N. (2011) Video game poetry. *Video Game Expressionism*. [blog] 25 January. Available at: http://mr-wonderfule.blogspot.com.tr/2011/01/video-game-poetry.html

Treanor, M. and Mateas, M. (2013) An account of proceduralist meaning. In *Proceedings of the 6th International Conference of the Digital Research Association*. Atlanta, USA: Georgia Institute of Technology, 26–29 August 2013.

Valéry, P. (1954) Poetry and abstract thought. *The Kenyon Review*. 16(2). pp. 208–233.

Valve Software, (1998) *Half-Life*. [Video Game] Sierra Entertainment.

Walker, J. (2006) Confessions of a crybaby. *The Escapist Magazine*. [online] Available at: http://www.escapistmagazine.com/articles/view/video-games/issues/issue_41/250-Confessions-of-a-Crybaby

Wallace, M. (2006) The crying game. *The Escapist Magazine*. [online] Available at: http://www.escapistmagazine.com/articles/view/video-games/issues/issue_41/251-The-Crying-Game

Wilde, O. (1891) Salome. [Theatre play]. Collected in Ross, R. (ed.) (1909) *Works*. London: Methuen.

Williams, W. C. (1991) *The Collected Poems of William Carlos Williams: 1939–1962*. New York: New Directions Publishing.

Zyda, M. (2005) From visual simulation to virtual reality to games. *Computer*. 38(9). pp. 25–32.

16 Artistic Explorations
Mobile, Locative and Hybrid Narratives

Martin Rieser

1. INTRODUCTION

Ubiquitous technologies have had a profound effect on the design and distribution of mobile narrative experiences. This chapter describes and analyses several significant artistic projects, with a focus on the changes in the relationship between artist and the audience as participant. The author's practice in creating locative, hybrid and mobile augmented reality projects will serve to detail the potentiality for further developments and artistic opportunities.

Amongst these projects described are *Hosts* (Rieser et al., 2006a), a site-specific mobile experience with interactive video in Bath Abbey, in the United Kingdom; *Starshed* (Rieser et al., 2006b), a folksonomic map of the uncanny in Bristol; *Riverains* (Rieser et al., 2008–2013), an exploration of underground spaces in Manchester and London through mobile technology; *The Third Woman* (Rieser et al., 2008–2011), an experiment in multi-linear film narrative and performance for mobiles, reinventing the thematic of *The Third Man* for the 21st century; and finally *Secret Garden* (Rieser et al., 2012), a virtual reality opera.

A major emerging topic in these works is the idea of the *Digital Uncanny*, of mediated reflections that are disturbing for their artificial resemblance to the real world. This chapter will further examine situated and embodied arts in relation to a broader spectrum of ambulant and location-based digital art practice, beyond ludic or Situationist (Debord, 1955) strategies in urban environments. I will analyse how particular artworks that use location-sensing technologies have transformed landscape from a picture to a multi-layered, multi-channel experience, often incorporating multiple-sense modalities and extending beyond the instant into a highly durational, expanded spatio-temporal field.

2. UBIQUITY

The advent of mobile technologies has placed powerful computers in the pockets of more people than have ever possessed a desktop PC. It has created new affordances for creative art out there in real space, dissolving traditional gallery and museum walls, and has allowed new audiences to relate to the spaces of their urban worlds by turning them both into places of possibility, where inner and outer spaces, histories and narratives can be interlocked and explored. It has allowed the user the privilege of co-authorship via social media and other two-way interventions. In a sense we are looking at the very beginning of a new communication form, one that can exist in both the hybrid world, incorporating the new *Hertzian* spaces (Dunne, 2005), and in the imagination of the new audiences.

The melding of two spaces into a combined dualism gives rise to a new space, one where perhaps the *other* (Vardoulakis, 2006) of psychoanalytic theory may find a home. This phenomenon is further complicated when computing becomes ubiquitous and the urban space itself is infused with information-processing capacity. While ubiquitous theorists have welcomed a new age of intelligent urban infrastructure (Graham, 2004), the reality is disappointingly less impressive, with augmented reality often becoming a flashy tool for finding restaurants and friends in one's vicinity. However, location-sensing technologies, in concert with procedural capacities of mobile devices, can create a distinct form of narrative that blends reality and fiction to create a personalised subjective experience that exploits as a narrative strategy the *unheimlich*—or uncanny—in such technologies.

Tversky, Kim and Cohen point out (1999) that mental representations of maps based on object descriptions are in contradiction to the continuous Euclidian space of Google-type GPS maps. The projects examined in this chapter add object descriptions in the form of virtual landmarks and fictional presences to the augmented space.

3. THE DIGITAL UNCANNY

Lisa Bode (2005) points to Otto Rank's (1971) understanding of the earliest connotations of the *double* in Indo-European lore as benign, entailing the immortality of the self. This incarnation stems from animistic beliefs in the manifestation of the soul in shadows, reflections and images and is intimately connected to the magical origins of figurative representation. Bode finds the *doppelgänger* (literally 'double-goer') as a trope of "18th and 19th century European literature ... a sinister likeness, that dogged and shadowed a protagonist," a messenger of impending "death or descent into madness" (Bode, 2005). Schubert's *Der Doppelgänger* (1828) is a further example of this trope in the musical realm.

The *uncanny* and *the double* are connected as Sigmund Freud points out, while emphasising the ominous aspect, characterising *the double* as a thing of terror:

> When all is said and done, the quality of uncanniness can only come from the fact of the double being a creation dating back to a very early mental stage, long since surmounted—a stage, incidentally, at

which it wore a more friendly aspect. The double has become a thing of terror. ...

(Freud, 1919, p. 235)

In literature we see the phenomenon in *Strange Case of Dr. Jekyll and Mr. Hyde* (Stevenson, 1886) and in *The Picture of Dorian Grey* (Wilde, 1891). While the double can be a doppelgänger, a brother or sister, a shadow, or a split personality, Freud believed that the theme of the double was originally insurance against the destruction of the ego. Another powerful example of a device that inspires a sense of uncanniness is what Freud calls animism, which is when an inanimate object moves or speaks. Some such examples which have been well-illustrated in both popular culture and literature are the Jewish legend of the Golem, an animated giant creature of clay, the automaton in the ballet Coppelia, Frankenstein's creature, the replicants in Blade Runner or yet the animated puppet in the Chucky films.

The *uncanny valley* refers to a hypothesis by computer scientist Masahiro Mori (1970), who postulated that when human-like avatars or robots look or move in a manner that is a very close approximation to real human beings, they can cause a revulsion response in the observer. Examples can be found in the fields of robotics, 3D computer animation and in medical fields such as burns reconstruction, neurological conditions and plastic surgery. The *valley* refers to the dip in a graph of a human observer's comfort level as subjects move more closely toward a natural human likeness, described as a function of an exemplar's aesthetic acceptability.

In a recent exhibition (2012) in Germany *Das Digitale Unheimliche*, the curator Brigitte Felderer explored the transfer of the uncanny to the digital realm. In the catalogue we find this statement:

> Media uses fiction to build dimensions—imagined faces, disembodied voices, virtual architecture, objects brought to life. We act in these imaginary realms; we build relationships, make decisions, develop emotions.
>
> (Felderer, 2012)

Felderer considers these creations to be at once both uncanny and reassuring:

> The self that we project to (sic) media consists of selected bits of information that nevertheless remain fragmentary and beholden to technical conditions. These medial doppelgangers are merely the manifestation of technical possibilities, documenting neither truth nor authenticity; they approach us in the guise of revenants that might disclose our secrets, reveal our intimacies, disclose obsessions and other hidden desires or fears.
>
> (Felderer, 2012)

What is interesting is her list of ways that that the uncanny may be revealed as:

> ... shadows that have become independent,
> objects that take on the confusable characteristics of the living,
> interfaces that lead into and not out of real space,
> mirror images in which we no longer recognize ourselves,
> or—last but not least—as virtual doppelgangers and fragments, all of
> which disclose their vulnerability.
>
> (Felderer, 2012)

Freud's famous essay *Das Unheimliche* (1919) explored the origins and meanings of the word *Heimlich*: its first definition of belonging to the house; friendly; familiar; or intimate, comfortable; i.e., secure, domestic(ated) or hospitable is contrasted with the second: concealed, secret, withheld from sight and from others; secretive, deceitful or private. *Unheimlich* is seen as the negation of Heimlich as applied to the first set of meanings listed above: unhomely, unfamiliar, untame, uncomfortable or eerie, weird, etc. That is— the familiar rendered unfamiliar and eerie is the most common meaning of the word in contemporary German usage. The less common variant means unconcealed, unsecret; what is made known; what is supposed to be kept secret but is inadvertently revealed.

Freud assigns to the physical experience of phenomena such as the double, animism, magic and sorcery, the omnipotence of thoughts, man's attitude to death, involuntary repetition and the castration complex—as factors which can turn something merely frightening into something uncanny. We will see in projects such as *Starshed* (Rieser et al., 2006b), *Hosts* (Rieser et al., 2006a) and *Secret Garden* (Rieser et al., 2012), how relevant these ideas of the digital other and the digital uncanny are to the medium and its use in narrative.

4. AUGMENTED REALITY

Augmented reality, is a "field ... in which 3-D virtual objects are integrated into a 3-D real environment in real time" (Azuma, 1997), and is on the verge of becoming a significant cultural and aesthetic phenomenon. Due to the rapid technological evolution of smartphones, video projectors, video game consoles, and other electronics, it is no longer a "slightly futurological domain" (Ryan, 2004). Despite this cultural significance, augmented reality is still a widely uncharted territory for the Arts. A narratological theory of augmented reality is urgently required, since the technology offers enormous potential for unique narrative strategies. Freisinger (2011) provides a first important step in this direction, while Ryan (in this volume) elaborates further on this topic.

The potential for new narrative forms is demonstrated for example in the EU project *Chess*[1] which is particularly user-centric and examines both the affordances of mobile augmented reality for narratised sense-making of culture beyond the gallery or museum; and the unique opportunities for experiencing narratives 'in the wild' in meaningful augmented spaces. This potential for the expansion of the museum and other cultural repositories into the contexts from which artefacts have derived represents a powerful and compelling change in the user-experience.

Recently, David Datuna (Silver, 2014) mixed technology and art to create an immersive experience different from that of viewing traditional paintings. The American artist layers his/her canvases with hundreds of eye-glass lenses, so they appear fractured, with light bending the images in every possible direction. Datuna is most well known for his series *Viewpoint of Millions* (2013), which uses these fractured glass surfaces to explore cultural identity, not as a single profile, but as the sum of many different perceptions and ideas. This was also the first art project to integrate Google Glass. Visitors who viewed Datuna's project through Google Glass also heard audio bites from clips linked to particular areas of his paintings via GPS sensing.

Implementations of augmented reality can merge material and virtual places to create hybrid environments. Due to the mobility of smartphones and new head-mounted displays such as Google Glass, the whole world is a potential setting for interactive environments. Diegetic events in these environments may not only be determined by general topographical features and architectonic details, but also by the historical, social and cultural connotations of a specific place.

As the recipient is able to move freely within the hybrid environment, the construction of the diegesis becomes highly individual and involves a strong feeling of presence. To develop a narratological framework for these and other spatial aspects of augmented reality, one must consider combining narrative theories from computer games, performance art, architecture, alternate reality games, and transmedia storytelling.

Developing a concept of interwoven narrative is more than a matter of simply applying mixed reality techniques. It allows for the unique construction of story for each individual and their dramatic engagement through the use of in situ pervasive media interactions triggered both on and through the user's smartphone.

Recent examples of this approach include *These Pages Fall Like Ash* a project realised in the British city of Bristol by the Circumstance collective. The work

> … is a story told across two books. One is a beautiful, crafted physical artefact, the other a digital text on hard drives hidden across a real city and read on your mobile device (Circumstance, 2013).

The two books are designed to be read in parallel by the participants as they encounter a location-based text snippet on their mobile device. The user constructs memories of two characters represented through locative experiences and a physical book, which becomes a figurative projection surface for another space parallel to the real city at certain locations:

> This is about a moment when two cities overlap. They exist in the same space and time, but they aren't aware of each other. It's a tale about two people who have become separated, one in each world, about their fading memory of each other and their struggle to reconnect.
>
> One of the cities is your own; you become part of the narrative as you travel, moving from place to place. Your version of the story becomes about you and your place in your own city, about what you would hold on to, about what you would fight to remember (Circumstance, 2013).

5. NARRATIVE, SENSE-MAKING AND AUGMENTED REALITY

The use of narrative is long established in many art forms, notably in novels and films. From the beginning of cinema, filmmakers have designed in narratives to help us to make sense of the experience. More recently, films have combined the virtual and the real in ways that convince the real characters in the story and allow them to make sense of their experiences. But this use of narrative works only within the diegesis of the film; the actors—real and digital—are scripted to use and adhere to the narrative created by the filmmakers.

Emerging mobile augmented reality technologies have started to make possible new forms of experience beyond the cinema, in which the real world is combined with digitally constructed objects and experiences in multiple ways and through multiple media. Augmented reality in the wild might be inhabited by actors and experiences that range from the mundane to the fantastical and which may act and interact in unscripted and unpredictable ways, as in the work of Duncan Speakman et al. (2010). Just as they have always made sense of their real world experiences through narrative, people will try to make sense of their experiences in this world through the narratives that they personally construct. Therefore, in developing these technologies and in designing their applications, we should be informed by a deep understanding of narrative, and we should design to support people as they use narrative to make sense of this world of new experiences.

The importance and uniqueness of mobile augmented reality as a medium facilitating personal experiences (and thus could also be called *personal augmented reality*) are the result of three features that combine to distinguish it from earlier media: blending the virtual and physical worlds, continuous and implicit user control of the point of view, and interactivity. While no single feature is unique (except, to some extent, the blending of the virtual and physical worlds), their combination is unique. These features derive from the personal nature of the human-computer interface. Since personal augmented reality displays (e.g., see-through head-worn displays such as Google Glass and Oculus Rift) directly enhance a viewers' perceptions of the world around them, augmented reality techniques can be used to display synthetic information anywhere in the users' environments, at any location or on any object. This fluid blend of the physical and the virtual, and the inevitable tension between them, offers rich dramatic possibilities that are impossible in any other medium. Since the users wear the display, they naturally control the point of view of the experience as they look and move around. Because the users are situated in the physical space being augmented, personal augmented reality systems are inherently interactive; even if the virtual content is non-interactive, the users implicitly interact with the physical space (MacIntyre et al., 2001). A high-profile artistic use of virtually reality has been by the cyberartist group Manifest.AR^2 in their creation of virtual pavilions for the 54th Venice Biennale that extended to the public space of Saint Mark's Square.

People's experiences with interactive computer technology have, like their experiences with cinema, been dominated by a static, screen-based paradigm where the narrative is typically created by others—software designers or filmmakers, for example—and imposed upon the user. There are examples, particularly in the games sector, of sandbox worlds where players are actively encouraged to explore and to create their own experience, e.g., Second Life, in addition to examples of branching nonlinear game play. However, current interactions with mobile augmented reality are often mechanistic, designed and scripted without reference to the individual user. The embodied nature of the augmented reality experience is dependent on understanding the sympathetic process of spatial engagement:

> The painter "takes his body with him," says Valery. Indeed we cannot imagine how a mind could paint. It is by lending his body to the world that the artist changes the world into paintings. To understand these transubstantiations we must go back to the working, actual body ... which is an intertwining of vision and movement, eye and mind.
>
> (Merleau-Ponty, 1993)

Mobile augmented reality has the potential to unlock a more truly interactive and individual relationship with and through interactive computer technology, where users can have previously impossible experiences but can also impose their own narratives on the experiences in order to make sense of them. Scenarios of interaction, driven by specialised knowledge of audience engagement, could repopulate augmented space with specific scenography. Virtual artefacts personalised in accordance with the user's experience, contexts and psychological reactions, construct a sense of aura for the user by applying objects and narratives to their places of origin. In a related perspective, reporting on an augmented reality project at Atlanta's Oakland cemetery, Steve Dow *et al.* locate Walter Benjamin's (1936) concept of "aura," a quality related to the authority of the original, as a singular presence in space and time in the "unique places, objects, and people contained in historic sites ... that intangible aspect of unique objects and places that is felt in their presence" (2005).

Augmented reality also opens social media to the use of metaphor and the concretisation of thought into experience. It can enable a move from the fully scripted diegesis and passive audience of cinema to the projection and sharing of personal narratives within novel visualisations and projections into shared social spaces. One can envisage a personalised cinema that also implies responsive narrative, reacting to user context. While the technologies available to effectively implement this on mobile devices are some years away, we can begin to understand the drivers, structures and syntax of narrative framed for this domain. Consensual narrative (agreeing to play in or enter the same story world) applies both to gaming and to shared or communal narrative; and both require rules, limits and defined affordances to operate safely.

6. HOSTS AND STARSHED: UNCANNY SPACES

The 2006 work *Hosts* (Rieser et al., 2006a) created an embodied audiovisual experience in the historical surroundings of Bath Abbey, in the United Kingdom. The work explored the experience of the *other* and the uncanny through the creation of paired presences for each user.

Figure 16.1 Hosts in Bath Abbey 2006 © Martin Rieser.

Inspired primarily by the ascending and descending stone angels on the Abbey exterior, it formed a reflection on earlier human life and the multitude of the dead and their emergence or absence, which transformed the liminal space into copresence with the audience. Several technologies—including audio position detection and ultrasound badges—were used to trigger the emergence of virtual characters that would address the visitor with a series of poetic aphorisms and accompany her/him from screen to screen. Simultaneously, evanescent figures were continually climbing up and down two ladders on separate screens, mirroring the motif carved on the Abbey frontage. The emotional tone of *Hosts* varied through randomised selection of scripts, while a 3D audio landscape was available via wireless headphones.

Starshed (Rieser et al., 2006b) was a commission for the Electric Pavilion event at the Watershed Media Centre. The Ship of Fools[3] artist group constructed an interactive map of Bristol, and the map related real locations

Figure 16.2 Starshed Map © Martin Rieser.

with a virtual star. Participants could add stories of strange or uncanny encounters found across the city to the map online and via mobile devices. This spatialised log of the uncanny grew rapidly. As one of the first examples of an audience-driven mobile-accessible spatial log, it demonstrated how metaphoric mapping could merge the physical and the imagined in a single interface.

7. THE CITY AS STORY TRAJECTORY

Spatial annotation has emerged in the last few years as a major phenomenon, particularly with the growth of Google Maps, Facebook and social photo-sharing sites such as Flickr and Instagram. In projects like *Yellow Arrow*[4] and *Neighbornode*[5] and in the author's own *Starshed* (Rieser et al., 2006b), cities became surfaces for annotation and repositories of collective memory. In such projects, private narratives become public and allow for reinterpretation and for new social and cultural readings of space.

The interactive mobile film *The Third Woman* (Rieser et al., 2008–2011) revisited motives of the 1949 film noir *The Third Man*. This hybrid narrative successfully merged mobile film and performance in an entity combining diegetic space and the physical location. As an experience designed

Figure 16.3 The Third Woman—Performance at Galapagos Brooklyn © Martin Rieser.

for smartphone-equipped audiences, the project was also instrumental in finding methods for individual and collaborative engagement with mobile-based narratives. The project applied an engine derived from Pia Tikka's Enactive cinema research (2008). *The Third Man* featured three fully realised parallel dramas, each containing three different emotionally toned versions.

In a guided performance that took place in the Viennese underground metro system, the audience moved through varied scenarios and used QR codes as triggers for film clips and text messages. A later version of the work, realised in New York City, featured performers on stage, who demonstrated the use of QR images and invited audience members to play the film-game. Participants could choose different paths by selecting statements related to the characters on their smartphones. These choices could also form a communal vote, which would be displayed on a larger screen.

8. MAPPING AND HISTORY

Spatial annotation storytelling projects allow for new social and cultural readings of space, allowing private narratives to become public and subject to reinterpretation. Cities are increasingly sorted through mapping software and networking, invoking a related political question about the embedding of previous relations of power, class and ownership in the new infra-structures and whether this perpetuates ancient divisions or raises further questions related to the potential for community, memory and individual empowerment. Scott McQuire (2006) reminds us, following David Rokeby (Kwastek, 2013) and Nicholas Bourriaud's (1998) arguments, that "digital aesthetics are about creating relationships" and continues to describe the potential inherent in these social relationships:

> New forms of public interaction which involve sharing and negotiation between individual and collective agency can play a vital role in challenging the dominance of public space by spectacular 'brand-scapes' or its pacification by surveillance.
>
> (McQuire, 2006)

Lev Manovich (2006) reflects on the artistic opportunity and challenge created by augmented spaces by framing the development as continuation in the "trajectory from a flat wall to real space;" instead of filling the empty wall, or gallery space, the artist now places the "user inside a space filled with dynamic, contextual data with which the user can interact."

Riverains (Rieser et al., 2008–2013) used the city as both metaphor and as a multi-layered repository of meanings. The project explored the hidden subterranean presences that connect our cities to the past. To find these presences, participants had to use mobile devices in the manner of a water-diviner. *Riverains* premiered in Manchester, and a second incarnation was developed for the Illumini Festival in the London quarter of Shoreditch.

Both cities posses a plethora of underground spaces including lost rivers, military installations, shelters, Victorian sewers and railway systems. In addition, archaeologic remains go back through medieval to Roman times. The *Riverains* drew from this long historic backdrop to invoke themes of poverty, industrial revolution, immigration, political protest, commerce and innovation, gang warfare and crime.

Riverains at Shoreditch was designed to comprise four elements, offering interaction to users with varying levels of technical requirements; it offered two guided walks, one a QR code reader version and the other a version using Layar[6] augmented reality software for smart phones. The technically more advanced versions could trigger video pieces along the path.

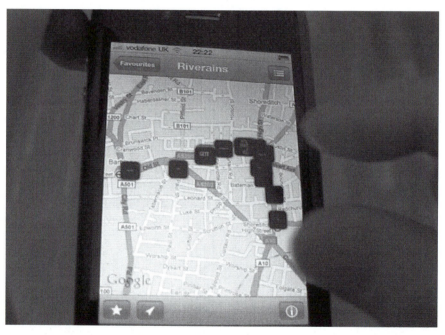

Figure 16.4 Riverains in Shoreditch © Martin Rieser.

The narrative of the *Riverains* explored the rich cultural history of Shoreditch, referencing Shakespeare's early plays, the murder of Mary Kelly by the "Ripper," immigrant voices from the past and present, as well as reflections on the London Plague. The treatment of the Suffragettes at Holloway Prison was echoed in audio-visual sound-image montages. Finally, the work contained reflections of the hidden underground rivers, the Riverains themselves.

The project evoked history through augmented reality and turned audience members into first-person witnesses of the dead's detailed experiences, which became an uncanny co-present, hiding behind the map on user's mobile screens.

9. AUGMENTED REALITY AS MYTHOLOGY

As Catherine Waldby (1997, 2000) has noted, the tendency to project our mythic underpinnings onto technology was particularly pronounced in the famous US National Library of Medicine Visible Human project (VHP) of 1993,[7] where male and female cadavers were sliced and scanned onto the web for medical science students.

> The two imaged figures were referred to as *Adam* and *Eve* ... True to the biblical narrative, Adam was digitalised first, and the rhetoric of the official literature has cast Eve as his companion ... This resort to self-conscious analogies between biblical and medical creation is not exclusive to the VHP ... In the context of the VHP the use of this rhetoric signals the extent to which medicine understands itself to be the master of postnatural life in the virtual garden of Eden, a new domain of representation where new innovations in the simulation of life can be made.
> (Waldby, 2000)

Secret Garden (Rieser et al., 2012) also evokes a biblical narrative by recreating a virtual garden of Eden in the midst of an urban environment. The project, a coproduction between the author and the composer Andrew Hugill, is also one of the first locative mobile digital operas. We created two different versions—a physical installation and as virtual mobile experience. The installation had eleven iPads arranged in a circle. A visitor triggers a view of an idyllic scene in the virtual *Secret Garden* by looking at the iPad screens. The narrative is divided in scenes, distributed to one of eleven different iPad viewports. In each scene, the mythical story of the Fall is told through words, music and other actions. Adam and Eve are represented as humanoid avatars that enact the story, combining sung poetry and video vignettes. Visitors with their own smartphone can see the same content using augmented reality software.

The work explores the burden of adult choice on the backdrop of a story which is shared amongst many of the world's religions, including Judaism, Christianity and Islam. Structurally, *Secret Garden* is inspired by the Kabbalah—an esoteric tradition originated in the Jewish culture—and in particular by the ten paths of the Sephirot, a complex diagram used for the purposes of prayer, study, meditation and divination.

Original poems examining choices in a fallen world comprise the lyrics. An adaptive musical composition features vocal settings and digitally treated percussion. The virtual scenography is inspired by John Martin's 19th century Mezzotints for Milton's *Paradise Lost*. Audience members experience the narrative gradually by visiting the eleven viewports. However, it is not necessary to see the viewports in any particular order, and a partial viewing will also provide a complete experience. The installation is an amalgam of poetry, music and panoramic images. The audience experiences the presentation in 3D vision, with the parallax shift tied to head movements and adjusted in real-time.

The team behind *Secret Garden* is building a mobile phone version for the iPhone and Android smartphone platforms, with a mixture of augmented reality and GPS location technology, using the Empedia Platform[8] and the Layar API. In this way we will create the experience of a locative trail where the scenes are linked to key locations in the area. The resulting work will embody the first spatialised augmented reality (AR) opera ever designed for mobile technologies. The Eden scenes will appear around a user in 360-degree 3D panoramas that will be triggered automatically by GPS location.

Figure 16.5 Scene from *Secret Garden* © Martin Rieser.

By aligning locative technologies with the oldest of mythologies, we built on the notion of the technology offering a portal into the deeper layers of collective cultural myths, revived for a contemporary audience through the uncanny motion of captured avatars. The strange sense of otherworldliness of video game engines combined with smooth animation of the motion-captured avatar creates a contradictory experience that uneasily positions the audience in a physically real sound space and a virtual space quite unlike anything experienced in the real world. Audience reaction to the realistic movement of the avatars was ambiguous, with aspects of the uncanny valley phenomenon actually increasing the sense of mythic space. The spatialised sound was very successful in its creation of a sense of a copresent other world in parallel to the audience's present reality.

10. CONCLUSION

The new mobile technologies have given enormous computing affordances to a broader section of humanity than even the desktop PC. These new affordances are particularly energising for artists, breaking down the boundary between the gallery and real space. They are potentially adding new audiences who can relate directly to spaces and histories of their neighbourhoods or cities, turning them into places and spaces of liminality, allowing inner and outer spaces, histories and narratives to mesh.

The user has also gained the potential for cocreation via social media and other reflexive interventions. I hope that through this interrogation of a range of projects these common properties have been demonstrated—that mobile and digital media can create a new doorway into a space where social, physical and virtual worlds can mix and cross-pollinate. Thus through mobile and digital media, we can enhance our sense of the city as a space of possibilities, augmenting our sense of the mythic, past and present. One could say that we are here at the birth of a new art form, one that lives in the hybrid world of the new 'Hertzian' spaces and in the creative mind of its new audiences; simultaneously addressing both the *heimlich* of place and the *unheimlich* of digital space. It is an art form capable of levering apart the contradictory nature and impact of these new technologies on our lives, our behaviours and our understandings, to reveal their seductive power, their communicative strengths and the challenge to notions of privacy and agency in an increasingly surveyed hybrid public space.

NOTES

1. http://www.chessexperience.eu/
2. Manifest.AR, official website: http://www.manifestar.info/
3. http://www.shipoffools.pwp.blueyonder.co.uk
4. http://yellowarrow.net/index2.php
5. http://www.neighbornode.net
6. Layar was the first augmented reality app launched for the iPhone and Android platforms.
7. http://www.nlm.nih.gov/research/visible/
8. http://www.empedia.info

REFERENCES

Azuma, R. T. (1997) A survey of augmented reality. *Presence*. 6(4). pp. 355–385.
Benjamin, W. (2007, orig. 1936). *Das Kunstwerk im Zeitalter seiner technischen Reproduzierbarkeit*. Frankfurt/M: Suhrkamp.
Bode, L. (2005) Digital doppelgängers. *M/C Journal*. 8.3.
Bourriaud, N. (1998) *Relational Aesthetics*. Dijon: Les Presses Du Reel.
Circumstance (2013) *These Pages Fall Like Ash*. Available at: http://pagesfall.com/
Datuna, D. (2013) *Viewpoint of Millions*. Available at: https://artsy.net/artwork/david-datuna-viewpoint-of-millions-usa
Debord, G. (1955) Introduction to a critique of urban geography. *Les Levres Nues*. 6. September.

Dow, S., Lee, J., Oezbek, C., MacIntyre, B., Bolter, J. D., and Gandy, M. (2005) Exploring spatial narratives and mixed reality experiences in Oakland Cemetery. In *Proceedings of the 2005 ACM SIGCHI International Conference on Advances in computer entertainment technology (ACE '05)*. New York: ACM, pp. 51–60.

Dunne, A. (2005) *Hertzian Tales: Electronic Products, Aesthetic Experience, and Critical Design*. Cambridge, MA: MIT Press.

Felderer, B. (2012) *Das Digital Unheimliche*. Oldenburg, Germany: Edith Russ Haus für Medienkunst, Goethe Institute.

Feyersinger, E. (2011) Transferring narratological concepts of space to augmented reality environments. In *Storyworlds across media*, June 2011.

Freud, S. (1919). The 'Uncanny'. *The Standard Edition of the Complete Psychological Works of Sigmund Freud*. Volume XVII. Norton & Company.

Graham, S. (ed.). (2004) *The Cybercities Reader*. London: Routledge.

Kwastek, K. (2013) Aesthetics of Interaction in Digital Art, MIT Press.

MacIntyre, B., Bolter, J. D., Moreno, E., and Hannigan, B. (2001) Augmented reality as a new media experience. In *IEEE and ACM International Symposium on Augmented Reality (ISAR'01)*.

Manovich, L. (2006) The poetics of urban media surfaces. *First Monday*, special issue 4.

McQuire, S. (2006) The politics of public space in the media city. *First Monday*, special issue 4.

Merleau-Ponty, M. (1993) *The Primacy of Perception*. Evanston: Northwestern University Press.

Mori, M. (1970). The uncanny valley. *IEEE Robotics & Automation Magazine*. 19(2). pp. 98–100.

Rank, O. (1971) *The Double: A Psychoanalytic Study*. Chapel Hill: University of North Carolina Press.

Rieser, M. et al. (2006a) *Hosts*. Available at: http://www.martinrieser.com/Hosts.htm

Rieser, M., Dovey, J., Bacon, T., Milner, L., and Fleuriot, C. (2006b) *Starshed*. Available at: http://www.electricpavilion.org/starshed/

Rieser, M. et al. (2008–2011) *The Third Woman*. Available at: http://www.third-woman.com

Rieser, M. et al. (2008–2013) *Riverains*. Available at: http://www.martinrieser.com/Riverains.htm

Rieser, M. et al. (2012) *Secret Garden*. Available at: http://www.martinrieser.com/Secret%20Garden.htm

Ryan, M. L. (2004) *Narrative Across Media: The Languages of Storytelling*. Lincoln: University of Nebraska Press.

Schubert, F. (1828) *Der Doppelgänger* [song].

Silver, L. (2014) Portfolio review: Google glass artist David Datuna explores perception by painting with lenses. *Complex*, June 19, 2014.

Speakman, D., Anderson, S., and Grenier, E. (2010) *Circumstance* [Software]. Available at: http://wearecircumstance.com/

Stevenson, R. L. (1886) *Strange Case of Dr Jekyll and Mr Hyde*. London: Longmans, Green & Co.

Tikka, P. (2008) *Enactive Cinema—Simulatorium Eisensteinense*. Helsinki: University of Art and Design.

Tversky, B., Kim, J., and Cohen, A. (1999) Mental models of spatial relations and transformations from language. In: Habel, C. and Rickheit, G. (eds.) *Mental Models in Discourse Processing and Reasoning*. Amsterdam: North-Holland.

Vardoulakis, Dimitris (2006) The doppelgänger in Freud's "The 'Uncanny'". *Sub-Stance*, 35.2. pp. 100–116.

Waldby, C. (1997) Revenants: The visible human project and the digital uncanny. *Body & Society*. 3(1).

Waldby, C. (2000) *The Visible Human Project: Informatic Bodies and Posthuman Medicine (Biofutures, Biocultures)*. New York: Routledge.

Wilde, O. (1891) *The Picture of Dorian Grey*. London: Ward, Lock & Co.

17 Remaking as Revision of Narrative Design in Digital Games

Tonguç İbrahim Sezen

1. INTRODUCTION

In his book *Best Before: Videogames, Supersession and Obsolescence*, James Newman argues that game remakes are the result of planned obsolescence imposed on gaming by commercial practices "drawing on notions of 'halfwayness' and hardware and software that is always in forward motion" (Newman, 2012, p. 82). Although this is a valid critical point on industry practices following recent and ongoing studies of fan games (Salter, 2009), 'demakes'[1] (Bogost, 2010), and deep readings of landmark game franchises (Perron, 2012; Pinchbeck, 2013), this chapter asks what we can learn from remaking as a design practice. In their previous work, the editors of this book (Koenitz et al., 2013a) argued for an open-ended theoretical approach for the evolving field of interactive digital narratives (IDNs) in order to recognise and analyse new narrative design approaches and creative possibilities enabled by new technologies. Their observations on the evolution of an interactive digital narrative (IDN) for over half a decade also indicated how an interactive narrative can be improved artistically by adapting technological advances into its design (Koenitz, Sezen and Sezen, 2013). In this respect, remakes provide test cases for analysing the revisions of narrative design in games and IDNs. The term *narrative design*[2] is here used in a broader sense to describe an ideally coherent combination of computational (i.e., artificial intelligence [AI]), interactive (i.e., game mechanics), fictional and other elements constituting the narrative aspects of an IDN or a game. Remakes share a certain amount of components with the originals they are based on, but they also have aspects that are specifically redesigned. A comparative study between the remake and the original thus reveals the effects of elements that their narrative designs do not share.

In order to understand the consequences of remaking, the chapter introduces the concept from film and literary studies and moves it into game studies. After discussing game remakes from several perspectives, including game design, platform studies and user studies, the chapter investigates *realMyst* (Cyan Worlds, 2000), a remake of the classical video game *Myst* (Cyan, 1993), to study the effects of remaking on narrative design.

2. REPETITION AND TRANSFORMATION

Remaking is common in narrative practice—artists and storytellers return to beloved characters, settings and stories for both artistic and commercial purposes. Remaking belongs to a number of forms that institutionalise intertextual relationships such as adaptations, sequels, prequels and series. According to David Wills (1998), remaking is the "precise institutional form of the structure of repetition" (Wills, 1998, p. 148). Constantine Verevis (2005) offers two general, culturally agreed criteria to describe remakes as products "carrying a presold title" and "repeating readily recognizable narrative units" (Verevis, 2005, p. 1). Remakes of digital games and IDNs carrying previous titles and repeating game and narrative design aspects have been a part of the gaming industry since its early days (Kent, 2001; Loguidice and Barton, 2009). In his 1999 article, game designer Richard Rouse III points out the parallels between commercial motivations for remaking games and films, which he calls "extremely commercial art forms" targeting an "expanding youth market" (Rouse, 1999). Indeed, commercial aspects of remaking have almost always been criticised by both scholars and critics in the fields of films and games (Forrest and Koos, 2002; Jess-Cooke and Verevis, 2010; McAllister, 2004; Alexander, 2013). Interestingly, both industries recently started to market extreme forms of remakes as reimaginings or reboots to emphasise the artistic contributions they claim to make to the originals.

The concept of remake indicates a fine balance between repetition and transformation, which can be achieved through different techniques at different levels. In *Palimpsests: Literature in the Second Degree*, Gerald Genette explores such techniques in literary texts. He uses the term *transtextuality* to describe "all that sets the text in a relationship, whether obvious or concealed, with other texts" (Genette, 1997, p. 1). He introduces one particular variety as *hypertextuality*,[3] which he describes as "any relationship uniting a text B (which I shall call the *hypertext*[4]) to an earlier text A (I shall, of course, call it a *hypotext*), upon which it is grafted in a manner that is not that of commentary" (Genette, 1997, p. 5) [original emphasis]. He introduces several subtypes of hypertexts amongst which *serious transformations* or *transpositions* provide the operational definitions of the creative processes behind rewriting and in a general sense remaking.

According to Genette (1997), transpositions can be either be formal or thematic based on what they change in a hypotext: formal transpositions aim to change the mode or the form and include (A) practices like translation, versification and prosification; (B) quantitative transformations like condensation and amplification; and (C) transmodalisations which include changes in the narrative point of view and dramatisation. Thematic transpositions, on the other hand, target both the text and the meaning of an original story and refer either to (D) diegetic transpositions which affect the spatiotemporal world of fiction; or (E) pragmatic transpositions which modify the events or action in a plot.

As critical perspectives have pointed out (Ryan, 2006; Aarseth, 2012; Koenitz et al., 2013b), narrative and literary theories cannot be applied to game and IDN studies directly. However, Genette's observations of remakes in the literary field can still provide a useful pattern for the analysis of IDN remakes, especially in the comparison of fictional and gameplay elements, as long as the crucial differences between traditional and digital forms are acknowledged.

3. HYPOGAMES AND HYPERGAMES

Discussing the graphical aspects of game remakes, Dominic Arsenault asks "what kind of added value can be gained from enhancing a classic game's visual characteristics?" (Arsenault, 2013). This question can be extended to all aspects changed in a game remake. While remaking is generally regarded as enhancement (Camper, 2009) or modernisation (Rouse, 1999) of older games in order to approximate them to contemporary titles, Clara Fernández-Vara argues for an expanded view in her book *Introduction to Game Analysis* (2014). In her view, remakes can create new meaning and even be considered a commentary or critique to an original. Thus, analysing remakes provides valuable lessons on the workings of individual elements in games and IDNs and how game and narrative design is affected by new functionalities and/or content.

Jesper Juul's (2005) and Markku Eskelinen's (2012) works on the relationships between analogue and digital versions of games provide a basis for such an analysis. Their perspectives not only resemble Genette's approach to literary texts but also provide similar operational definitions. Asking whether or not there can be an unambiguous correspondence between all the possible game states in different versions of a game, Juul focuses on remakes of analogue or physical games on digital platforms and vice versa, which leads to a distinction between game implementations and game adaptations. In a game implementation, one can find an exact correspondence between all possible game states in all versions of a game. Most card and board games may be implemented as analogue and digital games. In game adaptation, though, some features of an original cannot be transferred into a new version. Digital versions of sports games are examples of game adaptations because the physical aspects, such as the simple fact that the actions must be performed by the body of the player, cannot be transferred (Juul, 2005, p. 49–51). According to Eskelinen , "in many ways the distinction between implementation and adaptation resembles Genette's hypertextual distinction between imitations and transformations" (Eskelinen, 2012, p. 418); Eskelinen also uses the terms *hypogame* and *hypergame* based on Genette's terminology to describe original and transformed versions of games.

Eskelinen proposes various subtypes of both imitations and transformations and lists some of the possible types as: (A) partial implementation or simplification, leaving out game states which could be implemented;

(B) amplified implementation, implementing original game states while adding new states to them; (C) reductive adaptation, an adaptation containing only game states that could be faithfully adapted; (D) amplified adaptation, an adaptation with qualitative changes in some of the adapted game states; (E) augmented adaptation, an adaptation with new game states compensating for game states that could not be adapted (Eskelinen, 2012, p. 254–255). Eskelinen also emphasises the theoretical impossibility of full game implementations, since there will always be aspects which cannot be translated between different versions, and he concludes that "game adaptations reveal the differences between game elements that move between games with ease versus those that move with difficulty or not at all" (Eskelinen, 2012, p. 256). In this respect, remakes as digital hypergames derived from digital hypogames reveal the differences between elements moved, not moved, added and replaced during their adaptation.

Transformed elements in a remake can be identified on four of the five levels of digital media, as proposed by Nick Montfort and Ian Bogost (2009), while their effects can be observed on the fifth. These four levels are the *interface, form/function, code* and *platform* levels, while the fifth is the *reception/operation* level (Montfort and Bogost, 2009, pp. 145–147). The interface level covers all user-facing aspects of a given piece of software. Changes on this level involve audio-visual features and input modalities. The form/function level covers the functionality of a program itself. Changes in game mechanics, AI and fictional aspects can be observed on this level. The code level covers the source code, while the platform level covers the material and formal aspects of systems on which the games run.

Transformation on any level inevitably affects the whole artefact. Montfort and Bogost's (2009) comparison of several titles ported[5] from arcade machines to Atari VCS provide examples of how the affordances of particular platforms affect game titles. Dennis Jerz's (2007) close reading of the source codes of the two versions of the first interactive fiction *Adventure* (Crowther, 1976; Crowther and Woods, 1977) not only reveals technical changes but also shows differences in the designers' creative approaches; "[w]here Crowther was an efficient minimalist, Woods was comparatively lavish with scenery" (Jerz, 2007). Remakes of Japanese titles such as *Osu! Tatakae! Ouendan* (2005) targeting Western audiences have little left of their original sociocultural contexts due to major changes in their fictional content (Fernández-Vara, 2014). In the context of 3D remakes of 2D arcade games, Rouse (1999) asks whether or not a game may be successful as a remake but a failure as a game. His criterion for a successful remake is maintaining the core gameplay of an original. If this core is not compatible with the transformed elements, such as a 3D map instead of a 2D one, the remake may end up being more confusing than entertaining. The last level of digital media, the reception/operation level, covers all aspects related to user experience. Studies investigating the other four levels need to be complemented by studies of this level in order to understand the reception of changes.

4. REMAKING AND PLAYER EXPERIENCE

In recent years, several IDN researchers studied the effects of different design approaches on players' perceptions of interactive narratives—most prominently the differences between input modalities. To conduct these comparative studies, they created versions of IDNs sharing the same fictional content but differing in other specific aspects. This approach resembles remaking as a practice and provides data on how specific design revisions may affect players' experience. One such experiment (Sali and Mateas, 2011), on the interactive drama *Façade* (Mateas and Stern, 2005), compares gameplay logs of the original natural language input version with a version using a sentence selection system similar to mainstream role-playing and graphic adventure games. While the original dialogue interface allows players to type anything at any time to converse with the characters, the menu-based interface presents players with choices only when their input is required.

The authors wanted to understand "how different dialogue systems affect how players experience the story and how their interaction patterns change" (Sali and Mateas, 2011, p. 285). They note several important differences. First of all, the natural language input system could not understand a considerable amount of utterances, and thus it did not live up to the expectations of players. The menu system, on the other hand, allowed a higher degree of local influence, since the system was aware of the meaning of each predetermined option. However, since in the menu-based version the number of options that can be presented to the player is limited, the NLU (natural language understanding) version allowed the players more global freedom for shaping and creating variations in the story by addressing various mixins, subtopics and objects (Sali and Mateas, 2011, p. 288). The comparison also revealed that the way the players were experiencing the story was more linear in the menu-based version than in the natural language input version, meaning that in the menu-based version, players had little access to narrative branches beyond the ones closely related to the main story line and they could not explore other possible dialogues in the system.

Another study (Mehta et al., 2010) focusing on the same question regarding menu and natural language based input systems used two versions of an IDN based on the 1998 interactive fiction *Anchorhead* by Michael S. Gentry. Both versions had the same gameworld, possible outcomes and possible interactions. To compare these different versions, Mehta collected data using questionnaires and observations of play sessions and conducted a qualitative analysis. The study found that the natural language system increased the engagement with the game and affected players' perception of game characters in a positive way. On the other hand, limitations of the natural language system combined with expectations beyond the system's capabilities created confusion and broke the game flow. In contrast, the menu-based version was perceived as limiting by the players even though the game experience itself was never interrupted.

The results of both studies on two input modalities shows what kind of effects a shift between them has on players. By definition, remakes create such shifts with similar results. For example, Sierra Entertainment's (formerly Sierra On-Line) 1990s remakes of their early adventure games had a similar trajectory to the studies discussed above. After shifting to Sierra's Creative Interpreter (SCI) as the main game engine, Sierra released remakes of its previously successful titles including *King's Quest* (1983; 1990) and *Space Quest* (1986; 1991). The original versions of these games were developed on the Adventure Game Interpreter (AGI) game engine, which offered a text input parser combined with keyboard or joystick controls for the avatars. SCI and its later version SCI1, on the other hand, had an icon-based parser with predetermined actions such as walk, use and talk and also offered predetermined dialogue options instead of textual input (Kalata, 2011). Although there are no empirical studies on the subject, as Bill Loguidice and Matt Barton (2009) note, the shift from one input modality to another was criticised by fans for inhibiting their perceived freedom and creativity. We can say in general terms that all shifts similar to the ones described above may affect players in a similar fashion.

The theoretical and methodological backdrop established so far provides basic grounding for investigating concrete examples. There are many candidates for such a study including complex remakes of classical role playing games such as the Nintendo DS version of *Final Fantasy III* (Square Enix, 2006) and enhanced rereleases of graphic adventure games such as *Broken Sword: The Shadow of the Templars—Director's Cut* (Revolution Software, 2009). We have chosen *Myst* and its remake *realMyst* from the long-running *Myst* (1993–2014) video game franchise as cases for a comparative examination due to the prominence of the original in both game and IDN studies.

5. READING A REMAKE: *MYST* AND *REALMYST*

Developed by Cyan, Inc. (now Cyan Worlds, Inc.) and released in 1993, *Myst* is one of the best-selling (Walker, 2002) and critically acclaimed (GameRankings, 2014) titles in gaming history. It has been ported to many platforms (PlayStation, DS, iOS, etc.) and been rereleased by Cyan Worlds with various improvements several times.[6] Ever since the release of the original version, *Myst* was described by academics as a possible forerunner of future interactive digital narratives (Murray, 1997; Moulthrop, 1999; Wardrip-Fruin and Harrigan, 2004; Jenkins, 2004) and its narrative features have been discussed and analysed from several positive and negative perspectives over the years (Murray, 1997; Manovich, 2001; Moulthrop, 1999; Bolter and Grusin, 2000; Wolf, 2001; Rehak, 2003; Ryan, 2006; Juul, 2005).

The game features two narrative threads, the past and the present. Players cannot change the past but can act in the present with relative freedom, and at the end of the game their choices in the present lead to different outcomes for both themselves and the present versions of the characters from the past. While the present is dominated by navigation and puzzle-solving, the past, which constitutes the main narrative backdrop, is exposed to the player mainly through clues spread throughout the space. Henry Jenkins (2004) called this structure an *embedded narrative* and Celia Pearce (2007) argued that games like *Myst* led players to develop an "ability to read and interpret meaning and narrative embedded in virtual space in a particular way" (Pearce, 2007, p. 311), which she called *spatial literacy*. In this regard, for some scholars (Moulthrop, 1999; Manovich, 2001; Bateman, 2009; Murray, 2011) the main pleasure *Myst* offered to the players was immersion in a detailed and extensive navigable virtual space.

The original *Myst* is based on the hypermedia system *HyperCard* and consists of linked slides containing detailed prerendered first-person perspective images of various objects and locations, ambient sounds, video clips and object animations. The linkage of these elements creates the illusion of movement in a rich 3D world, which can be explored and affected by players, or a 'faux virtual reality effect' (Pearce, 2007, p. 312). The intricate sound design and animations meticulously embedded in still images supported this illusion by adding a degree of liveliness to the scenery (Hutchison, 2008). This technique allowed designers to create a detailed imaginary world represented with high-quality visuals but also limited players' spatial agency compared to early 3D games like *Wolfenstein 3D* (Id Software, 1992) or *Doom* (Id Software, 1993) from the same period, which allowed higher mobility but offered much lower visual detail. Comparing these different approaches of the early 1990s to create navigable virtual spaces, Hutchison describes *Myst*'s aesthetics as "the visual high and slow road," which sacrifices features like the unrestricted, free movement and immediate response (Hutchison, 2008).

Due to its popularity, *Myst* has been ported to various platforms over the years. Most of these ports were more or less unchanged versions of the original. Others had extra features in order to adapt the game to the newer platforms, such as the use of a magnifying glass in the DS version due to the small screen size of the handheld console (Chênevert, 2011). A version called *Myst: The Masterpiece Edition* was released in 1999 using 24-bit rerenders of the original 8-bit images, enhanced sound and offering an additional hint system; in other respects the game was mostly unchanged (Chênevert, 2011).

The version of *Myst* that might be seen as a transposition with adaptive properties is the 2000 version *realMyst*. Unlike the overhauled *Myst: Masterpiece Edition*, *realMyst* was a real-time three-dimensional remake of the original. The game was developed using the Plasma 3D graphics engine (Unity Technologies, 2012) and allowed players to move freely in the world of *Myst* instead of switching from one prerendered static image to another. In order to achieve this, the gameworld had to be remodelled and retextured. Yet the new virtual world was not an exact copy of the original. The new environment was designed to keep "the 'feel' of Myst Island as close as possible to the original" while making necessary changes so that it could "hold up in real-time" (Wolf, 2011, p. 114). In *realMyst,* the general topography and architecture of the world of *Myst* is rescaled in order to create a coherent 3D environment for the players. This new 3D model combined with free movement allowed players to reach previously inaccessible locations revealing new details. In his extensive analysis of *Myst* and *realMyst* in his 2011 book *Myst and Riven: The World of the D'ni,* Mark J. P. Wolf describes the effects of these changes as follows:

> Previously unavailable angles also reveal new objects, like the ceiling fan in the room where the Stoneship Age's linking book resides, and unseen events like the rising of the ship model and the ship in the harbor can now be observed. While *realMYST* strives to keep the feel of the original, the implied size of the spectator and the distances between locations does seem quite different at times from the original. (Wolf, 2011, p. 41)

Additional changes were made in atmospheric elements affecting the mood of the game. These included a lively natural life with birds and butterflies flying around, leaves falling, waving waters, fire and smoke, different weather conditions and a new day and night cycle. While Hutchison (2008) criticises these kinds of visual changes in *realMyst* as window dressing that fails to improve the narrative structure of the game, Wolf (2011) argues that these elements, especially different lightning conditions, gave players much to discover even if they were familiar with the original game. The player's experience of the embedded narrative in both *Myst* and *realMyst* is closely linked to spatial exploration. The changes affecting the geography and the mood of the game mixed with free movement were also affecting this experience. The visually detailed and lively world of *realMyst* could now be explored without sacrificing free look and immediate response features. Compared to *Myst,* this could be described as a very familiar but different and intense spatial experience.

According to Wolf (2011), the original *Myst*'s prerendered images were designed to hide certain details from the player in order to arrange the exposure to the narrative in a certain way. However, in *realMyst*'s 3D world this was not the case. Players' free and mobile point of view allowed them to see and explore what was previously hidden from them (Wolf, 2011). This changed the order in which they discovered and experienced special locations in the gameworld and thus affected the experience of the embedded narrative. Moreover, even though the puzzles and most of the story of the original *Myst* were kept the same, there were subtle additions of new props and various new locations in *realMyst*. Items, like previously nonexisting weapons in the private quarters of a character, underlined certain aspects of nonplayer characters' personalities and thus influenced the player's perception. New locations, referencing to characters and events depicted in the *Myst* prequel novels released after the success of the original game (Miller, Miller and Wingrove, 1995) deepened the story while also creating transmedial[7] links.

The main narrative addition to the game was a new location called the 'Rime Age,' which was accessible only after the player reached the original positive ending. Interestingly, Murray (1997) deems the losing endings of the original game more dramatically satisfying than the positive one because the player reaches a clear and meaningful conclusion—s/he is imprisoned for life. In the positive ending, s/he is told that there are possible dangers in the future but then is left alone on the world of *Myst* without any in-game closure. The Rime Age opens after these events and adds new spaces, puzzles and narrative elements. At the end of the Rime Age—after following the clues, discovering new texts and solving the final puzzle—the player opens a window—through which s/he cannot pass—to a place in the sequel of the original game, *Riven* (Cyan Worlds, 1997) and then once again is left alone without a clear ending. In that sense, the new finale of *realMyst* is no more dramatically satisfying than the original positive ending of *Myst*. Yet it may make more sense if we think about the emphasis on the future in the original. By opening a window to *Riven*, *realMyst* points to this future. The game invites the player to continue the story by playing the sequel. We can interpret this as an attempt to facilitate the delivery of a meaningful conclusion by pointing to a continuation of the narrative akin to a cliff-hanger in a TV series—something which was only hinted at in the original. Thus, the Rime Age expands the original story of *Myst* not only by adding new content but also by establishing what we might call a transtextual (in Genette's terms) link to the next title in the series.

RealMyst is an interesting showcase of how transformed segments in a remake can affect the narrative design of an original. The original *Myst* was trying to create a faux virtual reality effect while *realMyst* offered a free roaming 3D world. In that sense, using Eskelinen's terminology, *realMyst* can be seen as an amplified implementation of the original mechanics. The mood of the game was made livelier and the designers introduced changes in the order of some narrative elements. Maintaining and expanding the fictional content, *realMyst* is a pragmatic transposition in Genettian terms. Transmedial and transtextual relations established in the remake add a new layer of narrative context. Interestingly though, the most prominent point of *realMyst* as a remake was not transformation but repetition. Neither the 3D free movement nor the additional story elements changed the original game's nature of an embedded narrative discovered by spatial navigation. *RealMyst* upgraded the spatial navigation aspect of *Myst* with new content while keeping the original narrative threads intact. In other words, these changes enhanced the original experience and moved *realMyst* closer to the original promise of *Myst*.

6. CONCLUSION

Beyond its negative connotations as a commercial practice, remaking as a concept indicates the pursuit of a balance between repetition and transformation. It offers new creative possibilities by subjecting established works to interpretation and experimentation. This chapter emphasised the benefits of studying remaking as a design practice in IDN research. Remakes and their originals provide comparable case studies, which expose the differences between interchangeable design elements. These differences can be found on each level of the remake; from audio-visual upgrades to changes in the input modalities to revisions of game mechanics to expansion of the fictional contents. Every one of these changes also affects the players' experience on various levels. Therefore, studying remakes provides a deeper comprehension of the internal workings and perception of video games and IDNs.

The comparative reading of *Myst* and *realMyst* represents an introductory example of such a study. The intensification of the original premise in *realMyst* is only one of the many forms the complex relationship between transformation and preservation in remakes can take. The additional examples mentioned in this chapter give a glimpse into other possible directions and their perception by players. Further studies on remakes and other forms institutionalising transtextual relationships will provide new insights on the complex structure of interactive narratives by exposing how they are affected by different design decisions.

NOTES

1. A *demake* is a retro-inspired reimagining or remake of a modern game, as if it had been created on an earlier platform (Bogost, 2010).
2. The terms *narrative design* (Posey, 2008; Dinehart, 2009; Koenitz, 2010) and story design (Mateas, 2002) have been used to describe various design aspects of games and IDNs before. In order to observe the effects of changes in all possible elements made during remaking this chapter uses the term in a very general fashion.
3. The other kinds are *intertextuality*, *architextuality*, *paratextuality* and *metatextuality*.
4. The Genettian term hypertext can be quite confusing in IDN research because of the homonym term *hypertext* coined by Ted Nelson (1965) to describe digital texts interconnected by hyperlinks.
5. Porting: Remaking a game through converting its code and assets from one platform to another (Carreker, 2012). It can be seen as a "translation of a game from one platform to another" (Fernández-Vara, 2014, p. 72).
6. *Myst: Masterpiece Edition* (1999), *realMyst* (2000) and *realMyst: Masterpiece Edition* (2014).
7. Popularised by Henry Jenkins (2006) the term "transmedia storytelling" refers to techniques of telling a single story across media.

REFERENCES

Aarseth, E. (2012) A narrative theory of games. In Seif El-Nasr, M., Consalvo, M., and Feiner, S. (eds.) *Proceedings of the International Conference on the Foundations of Digital Games*, FDG 2012. New York: ACM.

Alexander, L. (2013) Why leisure suit Larry should never have been remade. *Gamasutra*. [online] Available at: http://www.gamasutra.com/view/news/196824/Opinion_Why_Leisure_Suit_Larry_shoud_never_have_been_remade.php

Arsenault, D. (2013) Reverse-engineering graphical innovation: An introduction to graphical regimes. *G|A|M|E Games as Art, Media, Entertainment*. 2/2013. [online] Available at: http://www.gamejournal.it/reverse-engineering-graphical-innovation-an-introduction-to-graphical-regimes/

Bateman, C. (2009) *Beyond Game Design: Nine Steps Towards Creating Better Videogames*. Boston: Cengage Learning.

Bogost, I. (2010) Atari hacks, remakes, and demakes. *Ian Bogost—Videogame Theory,Criticism, Design*. [blog] Available at: http://www.bogost.com/teaching/atari_hacks_remakes_and_demake.shtml

Bolter, J. D. and Grusin, R. (2000) *Remediation: Understanding New Media*. Cambridge, MA: MIT Press.

Camper, B. (2009) Retro reflexivity: La-Mulana, an 8-bit period piece. In: Perron, B. and Wolf, M. J. P. (eds.) The Video Game Theory Reader 2. New York: Routledge.

Carreker, D. (2012) *The Game Developer's Dictionary: A Multidisciplinary Lexicon for Professionals and Students*. Boston: Cengage Learning.

Chênevert, P. (2011) Myst. In: K. Kalata (ed.) *The Guide to Classic Graphic Adventures*. Seattle: CreateSpace Independent Publishing Platform.

Crowther, W. (1976) *Adventure*. [video game] USA.

Crowther, W. and Woods, D. (1977) *Adventure*. [video game] USA.

Cyan (1993) *Myst*. [video game] Brøderbund.

Cyan Worlds (1997) *Riven: The Sequel to Myst*. [video game] Cyan Inc.

Cyan Worlds (1999) *Myst: Masterpiece Edition*. [video game] Cyan Inc.

Cyan Worlds (2000) *realMyst*. [video game] Cyan Worlds.

Cyan Worlds (2014) *realMyst: Masterpiece Edition*. [video game] Cyan Worlds.

Dinehart, S. (2009) Dramatic play. *Gamasutra*, [online] Available at: http://www.gamasutra.com/view/feature/132452/dramatic_play.php?page=4

Eskelinen, M. (2012) *Cybertext Poetics: The Critical Landscape of New Media Literary Theory*. London: Continuum.

Fernández-Vara, C. (2014) *Introduction to Game Analysis*. New York: Routledge.

Forrest, J. and Koos, L. R. (2002) Reviewing remakes: An introduction. In: Forrest, J. and Koos, L. R. (eds.) *Dead Ringers: The Remake in Theory and Practice*. Albany: State University of New York Press.

GameRankings (2014) *Myst*. [online] Available at: http://www.gamerankings.com/pc/89467-myst/index.html

Genette, G. (1997) *Palimpsests: Literature in the Second Degree*. Lincoln: University of Nebraska Press.

Gentry, M.S. (1998) *Anchorhead*. [interactive fiction]. Available at: http://pr-if.org/play/anchorhead/

Hutchison, A. (2008) Making the water move: Techno-historic limits in the game aesthetics of Myst and Doom. *Game Studies: The International Journal of Computer Game Research*. 8(1).

Id Software (1992) *Wolfenstein 3D*. [video game] Id Software.

Id Software (1993) *Doom 3D*. [video game] Id Software.

iNiS (2005) *Osu! Tatakae! Ouendan* [video game] Nintendo.

Jenkins, H. (2004) Game design as narrative architechture. In: Wardrip-Fruin, N. and Harrigan, P. (eds.) *First Person: New Media as Story, Performance, and Game*. Cambridge, MA: MIT Press.

Jenkins, H. (2006) *Convergence Culture*. New York: New York University Press.

Jerz, D. G. (2007) Somewhere nearby is Colossal Cave: Examining Will Crowther's original "Adventure" in code and in Kentucky. *Digital Humanities Quarterly*. Volume 1 (2). [online] Available at: http://www.digitalhumanities.org/dhq/vol/001/2/000009/000009.html

Jess-Cooke, C. and Verevis, C. (2010) Introduction. In: Jess-Cooke, C. and Verevis, C. (eds.) *Second Takes: Critical Approaches to the Film Sequel*. Albany: State University of New York Press.

Juul, J. (2005) *Half Real: Video Games Between Real Rules and Fictional Worlds*. Cambridge, MA: MIT Press.

Kalata, K. (ed.) (2011) *The Guide to Classic Graphic Adventures*. Seattle: CreateSpace Independent Publishing Platform.

Kent, S. L. (2001) *The Ultimate History of Video Games: From Pong to Pokémon and Beyond*. New York: Three Rivers Press.

Koenitz, H. (2010) Towards a theoretical framework for interactive digital narrative. In: Aylett, R., Lim, M. Y., Louchart, S., Petta, P., and Riedl, M. (eds.) *Interactive Storytelling: Third Joint Conference on Interactive Digital Storytelling, ICIDS 2010*. Heidelberg: Springer.

Koenitz, H., Haahr, M., Ferri, G., Sezen, T. I. and Sezen, D. (2013a) Mapping the evolving space of interactive digital narrative—From artifacts to categorizations. In: Koenitz, H., Sezen, T. I., Ferri, G., Haahr, M., Sezen, D., and Çatak, G. (eds.) *Interactive Storytelling: 6th International Conference, ICIDS 2013*. Heidelberg: Springer.

Koenitz, H., Haahr, M., Ferri, G., and Sezen, T. I. (2013b) First steps towards a unified theory for interactive digital narrative. In: Pan, Z., Cheok, A.D., Mueller, W., Iurgel, I., Petta, P., and Urban, B. (eds.) *Transactions on Edutainment X*. Heidelberg: Springer.

Koenitz, H., Sezen, T. I., and Sezen, D. (2013) Breaking points—A continuously developing interactive digital narrative. In: Koenitz, H., Sezen, T. I., Ferri, G., Haahr, M., Sezen, D., and Çatak, G. (eds.) *Interactive Storytelling: 6th International Conference, ICIDS 2013*. Heidelberg: Springer.

Loguidice, B. and Barton, M. (2009) *Vintage Games: An Insider Look at the History of Grand Theft Auto, Super Mario, and the Most Influential Games of All Time*. Burlington: Focal Press.

Manovich, L. (2001) *The Language of New Media*. Cambridge, MA: MIT Press.

Mateas, M. (2002) *Interactive Drama, Art and Artificial Intelligence*. PhD Carnegie Mellon University.

Mateas, M. and Stern, A. (2005) *Façade*. [interactive drama] Available at: http://www.interactivestory.net/

McAllister, K. S. (2004) *Game Work: Language, Power, and Computer Game Culture*. Tuscaloosa: The University of Alabama Press.

Mehta, M., Corradini, A., Ontañón, S., and Henrichsen, P. J. (2010) Textual vs. graphical interaction in an interactive fiction game. In: Aylett, R., Lim, M. Y.,

Louchart, S., Petta, P., and Riedl, M. (eds.) *Interactive Storytelling: Third Joint Conference on Interactive Digital Storytelling, ICIDS 2010*. Heidelberg: Springer.

Miller, R., Miller, R., and Wingrove, D. (1995) *The Book of Atrus*. New York: Hyperion.

Montfort, N. and Bogost, I. (2009) *Racing the Beam: The Atari Video Computer System*. Cambridge, MA: MIT Press.

Moulthrop, S. (1999) Misadventure: Future fiction and new networks. *Style*. 33(2). pp. 184–293.

Murray, J. (1997) *Hamlet on the Holodeck: The Future of Narrative in Cyberspace*. New York: The Free Press.

Murray, J. (2011) *Inventing the Medium: Principles of Design for Digital Environments*. Cambridge, MA: MIT Press.

Nelson, T. (1965) A File structure for the complex, the changing, and the indeterminate. In: Wardrip-Fruin, N. and Montfort, N. (eds.) (2003) *The New Media Reader*. Cambridge, MA: MIT Press.

Newman, J. (2012) *Best Before: Videogames, Supersession and Obsolescence*. London: Routledge.

Pearce, C. (2007) Communities of play: Constitution of identity in persistent online game worlds. In: Harrigan, P. and Wardrip-Fruin, N. (eds.) *Second Person: Role-Playing and Story in Games and Playable Media*. Cambridge, MA: MIT Press.

Perron, B. (2012) *Silent Hill: The Terror Engine*. Ann Arbor: The University of Michigan Press.

Pinchbeck, D. (2013) *Doom: Scarydarkfast*. Ann Arbor: The University of Michigan Press.

Posey, J. (2008) Narrative Design. In: Despain, W. (ed.) *Professional Techniques for Video Game Writing*. Wellesley: AK Peters.

Rehak, B. (2003) Playing at being: Psychoanalyses and the avatar. In: Wolf, M. J. P. and Perron, B. (eds.) *The Video Game Theory Reader*. New York: Routledge.

Revolution Software (2009) *Broken Sword: The Shadow of the Templars—Director's Cut*. [video game] Ubisoft.

Rouse III, R. (1999) Everything old is new again: Remaking computer games. *Computer Graphics*. 33(2).

Ryan, M. (2006) *Avatars of Story*. Minneapolis: University of Minnesota Press.

Sali, S. and Mateas, M. (2011) Using information visualization to understand interactive narrative: A case study on Façade. In: Si, M., Thue, D., André, E., Lester, J. Tanenbaum, J., and Zammitto, V. (eds.) *Interactive Storytelling: 4th International Conference on Interactive Digital Storytelling, ICIDS 2011*. Heidelberg: Springer.

Salter, A. M. (2009) "Once more a kingly quest": Fan games and the classic adventure genre. *Transformative Works and Cultures*. Vol. 2.

Sierra Entertainment (1983) King's Quest. [video game] Sierra Entertainment.

Sierra Entertainment (1990) King's Quest 1: Quest for the Crown. [video game] Sierra Entertainment.

Sierra Entertainment (1986) Space Quest. [video game] Sierra Entertainment.

Sierra Entertainment (1991) Space Quest (SCI remake). [video game] Sierra Entertainment.

Square Enix (2006) *Final Fantasy III—3D Remake*. [video game] Square Enix.

Unity Technologies (2012) *A Classic Adventure*. [online] Available at: http://unity3d.com/showcase/case-stories/cyan-worlds-mystical-properties

Verevis, C. (2005) *Film Remakes*. Edinburgh: Edinburgh University Press.

Walker, T. (2002) The Sims overtakes Myst. *GameSpot*, [online] 22 March. Available at: http://www.gamespot.com/articles/the-sims-overtakes-myst/1100-2857556/

Wardrip-Fruin, N. and Harrigan P. (2004) Cyberdrama. In: Harrigan, P. and Wardrip-Fruin, N. (eds.) *First Person: New Media as Story, Performance, and Game*. Cambridge, MA: MIT Press. p. 1.

Wills, D. (1998) The French remark: Breathless and cinematic citationality. In: Horton, A., McDougal, S. Y. and Braudy, L. (eds.) *Play It Again, Sam: Retakes on Remakes*. Berkeley: University of California Press.

Wolf, M. J. P. (ed.) (2001) *The Medium of the Video Game*. Austin: University of Texas Press.

Wolf, M. J. P. (2011) *Myst and Riven: The World of the D'ni*. Ann Arbor: The University of Michigan Press.

Contributors

Ruth Aylett is a Professor of Computer Science in the School of Mathematical and Computer Sciences at Heriot-Watt University, Edinburgh. She has been an active researcher in Artificial Intelligence for more than 20 years, during which time she has accumulated more than 200 publications— book chapters, journals and refereed conferences. Ruth's research interests include intelligent graphical characters, affective agent models, human-robot interaction and interactive narrative, and she is a founder of the International Conference Intelligent Virtual Agents (IVA). In 2004, she moved to Heriot-Watt as a Professor of Computer Science. She is currently coordinator of the EU project eCUTE and a partner of the EU project LIREC. She is also a PI of the EPSRC project SerenA and led the two networks SPIRES and RIDERS.

Udi Ben-Arie is a Lecturer at the Film and Television Department at Tel-Aviv University and at the Screen-Based Department at the Bezalel Academy of Arts and Design, Jerusalem, where he teaches interactive storytelling, new media production, video cinematography and lighting. Udi has directed and shot several interactive and documentary movies. In 1995, his short film *Second Watch* was nominated for an Oscar for best foreign language student film. In 2003, together with Noam Knoller, Amnon Dekel and others, he created *One Measure of Happiness*, a gesture-based interactive movie on a touch-screen platform. In 2006–2008 he designed, together with MD doctors from Tel Aviv University's School of Medicine, a medical clinic simulation system combining interactive video and networked discussion for a clerkship course in family medicine. Udi currently conducts his PhD research at the Film and Television Department at Tel-Aviv University, concentrating on the user's experience in interactive digital narrative.

Gabriele Ferri is a Postdoctoral Researcher at Indiana University and is currently involved in the Intel Science and Technology Center for Social Computing (ISTC Social), where his research focuses on the interaction between digital media and narrative, playful, satirical and political discourses. He holds a PhD in Semiotics from the University of Bologna, Italy and SUM—Istituto Italiano di Scienze Umane (Firenze, Italy).

Gabriele is a founding member of the Games & Narrative group and brings a humanistic and critical view to the study of digitally mediated interactions, game studies and HCI. He has presented his research in venues such as the World Congress of the International Association for Semiotic Studies, the Designing Interactive Systems (DIS) conference, the International Conference on Advances in Computer Entertainment Technology (ACE) and the AAAI Symposium on Intelligent Narrative Technologies. He is an editor for the G|A|M|E *Games as Art, Media, Entertainment* journal and has been Programme Co-Chair at the 6th ICIDS Conference, as well as recently becoming a member of the ICIDS steering committee. As a practicing urban game designer, he has co-organised location-based performances in London, Barcelona, Bologna and Modena. His publications and research blog are available at http://www.gabrieleferri.com.

Mads Haahr is a true multidisciplinarian, holding BSc (1996) and MSc (1999) degrees in Computer Science and English from University of Copenhagen and a PhD (2004) in Computer Science from University of Dublin, Trinity College. Since 2001, he has worked as a Lecturer at the latter institution, where he gives Masters-level courses in Game Studies, Game Design and Artificial Intelligence for Games and has led nationally funded research projects on sentient computing, self-organising distributed systems and locative media. Mads has published over 50 peer-reviewed papers and chapters on a range of topics, from distributed systems and mobile computing to the art/technology interface and interactive digital narrative, and also reviewed papers for many journals and served on several programme committees. His current research focuses on mobile and ubiquitous computing and is concerned with technology as well as cultural and literary applications. Mads is Founder, CEO and Creative Director of the award-winning game studio Haunted Planet Studios (2010), cofounder of the Games & Narrative international research group (2012) and the online journal *Crossings: Electronic Journal of Art and Technology* (2001) and also created the Internet's premier true random number service RANDOM.ORG (1998).

Chris Hales specialises in the interactive moving image, as practitioner, educator and researcher. His interactive film installations and performances have been presented far and wide, from ARTEC95 in Nagoya to Moscow's *Tactile Cinema* in 2012. His work was included in the landmark 2003 *Future Cinema* exhibition curated by ZKM. In 2008 he exhibited a retrospective of most of his interactive films in a 9-room labyrinth as part of the Prague Triennale. Chris has also published widely, including several book chapters, and has coedited two publications. His 2006 PhD "Rethinking the Interactive Movie" developed the concept of *movie as interface*. In 2003, he carried out primary research in Prague about the development and fate of the Czechoslovak *Kinoautomat* of

1967 (the world's first interactive film) and was able to create, for the first time, a prototype interactive DVD of the entire film, which was used in the first digital reperformance of the film in London in 2006. Recently he has supervised doctoral students at SMARTlab, the Slade School of Fine Art, and at Liepaja University (Latvia) where he holds a Lectureship. He has taught over 150 short workshops in various European universities as well as given numerous conference presentations.

Noam Knoller is a Lecturer in Media Psychology at Amsterdam University College and a PhD candidate at the Amsterdam School for Cultural Analysis (ASCA) at the University of Amsterdam. As part of the Interface Studies group, which he started in 2011, his research centres on the role of interfaces in structuring userly performance in the communicative processes of interactive storytelling. In 2002, together with Udi Ben-Arie, Amnon Dekel and others, Noam designed the InterFace Portrait storyteller system, which invited users to communicate expressively with a storyteller character through affective gestural interaction performed on a touch screen. The installations *One Measure of Happiness* (2003) and *Have I Lost my Plot* (2004), which were based on the system, were exhibited internationally at conferences and new media venues such as Upgrade! and the Netherlands Institute for Media Arts. Noam has also been a creative practitioner in several media, and remains an active documentary film editor and interaction designer.

Hartmut Koenitz is Assistant Professor in Mass Media Arts at the University of Georgia, where he is also a Fellow at the Digital Arts research cluster. He holds a PhD in Digital Media from the Georgia Institute of Technology. His research interests are at the intersection of art, society and technology, with a focus on new forms of narrative expression in video games and other digitally mediated forms as well as serious games and physical computing. Hartmut is the creator of the ASAPS authoring tool for Interactive Digital Narrative (http://advancedstories.net). Recent work produced with ASAPS includes *Breaking Points* (2014) (coauthored with Tonguç İbrahim Sezen and Diğdem Sezen), available via iTunes for iPad, and *Occupy Istanbul* (2013), a serious game about the Gezi park protests, coauthored with Turkish filmmaker Inan Temelkuran. Together with the other editors of this volume he founded the Games & Narrative group (http://gamesandnarrative.net), which is working on furthering the theory and practice of digital interactive narrative through publications, talks and workshops. Hartmut was the Co-Chair of the 6th International Conference for Interactive Digital Storytelling (ICIDS) in 2013, and Programme Chair of the Digital Art section, Augmented Human 2012 conference. As a reviewer he contributes to the ACM *Computers in Entertainment* journal and *Diegesis* journal for interdisciplinary narrative research. Hartmut is also a visual artist, and his works have been shown in Atlanta, Paris and Istanbul.

Patty Kostkova is currently the Principal Research Associate for e-health at the Department of Computer Science, University College London (UCL). In years 2012–13, she held a Research Scientist post at the ISI Foundation in Italy and in June 2014 was appointed ISI Fellow. Recently, she was also appointed a consultant at WHO, ECDC and Foundation Merieux. Patty serves as Advisory Board member at ECDC Knowledge Management Working Group and the NHS National Knowledge Service TB Pilot project. Until 2012, she was Reader and the Head of City eHealth Research Centre (CeRC) at City University, London, UK. With an MSc and PhD degrees in Computer Science and an extensive international experience at public health agencies such as WHO and ECDC, Patty built up CeRC into a thriving multidisciplinary research centre. CeRC piloted a novel model enabling direct technology transfer of a user-driven high impact research through a family of real-world online services for medical professionals, including the National Resource for Infection Control (NRIC), ECDC training resource FEM Wiki and educational games for children (edu-games4all). Patty's activities in research into computer games and Inter-active Digital Storytelling for children include the multilingual e-Bug/Edugame4All project and educational apps. This educational health game project received the Best Student Paper GALA Award at VS-Games 2012 conference, October 2012. Patty has published 100 peer-reviewed papers, several book chapters, edited a number of journals and in 2014 was appointed the Editor in Chief—Speciality Digital Health, Frontiers in Public Health journal. Her research was extensively covered by inter-national media and by the Oxford Internet Institute.

Sandy Louchart is cohead of the Digital Story Lab with the School of Mathematical and Computer Sciences (MACS) at Heriot-Watt University, Edinburgh, where he teaches a number of courses on topics ranging from Interaction Design, Computer Games Design and Programming to 3D Modelling and Animation. Sandy's research interests include intelli-gent agents, Interactive Storytelling, Serious Games, affective computing, physiological monitoring, emergent narrative authoring, and evalua-tion methodologies for interactive dramas. He strives to promote multi-disciplinary research processes and diversify knowledge across adjacent fields such as gaming, digital entertainment, graphical arts and human computer interactions. Sandy's research has investigated the domain of Interactive Storytelling via the development of the Emergent Narrative concept. He was awarded his PhD in 2007 from the University of Sal-ford with his thesis entitled *Emergent Narrative—Towards a Narrative Theory of Virtual Reality*. This research led to the development of the Double Appraisal concept, which represented a novel approach to Syn-thetic Character action selection for affect-driven agents. Sandy has since led projects to develop a number of Serious Games for research and edu-cational purposes. These include a game designed to harness nonexpert human intuition for scientific research in Quantum Physics, a game investigating neural activation during social interactions in children with high functioning autism and a game to explore the biodiversity, culture and people of Scotland. Sandy is currently a coinvestigator on the EU funded Games and Learning Alliance (GaLA) and the EPSRC funded Research in Interactive Drama Environments, Role-play and Storytelling (Riders) research networks.

Andreea Molnar is a Lecturer at University of Portsmouth. Before joining University of Portsmouth she has been a Postdoctoral Research Associate at Arizona State University working on the NSF-funded project Deep Insights Anytime, Anywhere (DIA2). Previously, she was a Research Fellow at in the Business School at Brunel University, UK and she was involved in the European Commission funded research project, Live Video-to-Video supporting Interactive City Infrastructure (LiveCity). Prior to joining Brunel University she worked as a Research Associate at City University London, UK on the edugames4all project and as a Research Intern at Telefonica R&D, Spain, on EducaMovil. She has also been a Visiting Research Student at Warwick University, UK while she was working on the Performance-Aware Multimedia-based Adaptive Hypermedia (PAMAH) project funded by Science Foundation Ireland. She has a PhD in Technology Enhanced Learning from the National College of Ireland (under a scholarship funded by the Irish Research Council for Science, Engineering and Technology) and an MSc in Modelling and Simulations from Babes-Bolyai University, Cluj-Napoca, Romania. During her MSc she was an Erasmus student at the University of Pisa, Italy. Prior to enrolling in the PhD programme she worked as a Software Developer at Silnet Consulting, Italy and Fortech, Romania.

Nick Montfort develops computational art and poetry, often collaboratively. He is on the faculty at MIT in CMS/Writing and is the principal of the naming firm Nomnym. Montfort wrote the books of poems *#!* and *Riddle & Bind*, co-wrote *2002: A Palindrome Story*, and developed more than forty digital projects including the collaborations *The Deletionist* and *Sea* and *Spar Between*. The MIT Press has published four of his collaborative and individual books: *The New Media Reader*, *Twisty Little Passages*, *Racing the Beam*, and *10 PRINT CHR$(205.5+RND(1)): GOTO 10*, with *Exploratory Programming for the Arts and Humanities* coming soon.

Janet H. Murray is the Ivan Allen College Dean's Recognition Professor at Georgia Tech where she teaches in the Graduate Program in Digital Media, within the School of Literature, Media and Communication; and she serves as Associate Dean for Research and Faculty Affairs. She is an internationally recognised interaction designer, educational innovator and media theorist, and the author of *Hamlet on the Holodeck: The*

Future of Narrative in Cyberspace (Free Press,1997; MIT Press 1998) and *Inventing the Medium: Principles of Interaction Design as a Cultural Practice* (MIT Press, 2011), as well as several works in Victorian Studies. Janet is the Director of the Experimental Television Lab at Georgia Tech (http://etv.gatech.edu). She holds a PhD in English from Harvard University and has taught Humanities and led educational computing projects at MIT before coming to Georgia Tech in 1999. She is an emerita member of the Board of the Peabody Awards.

Scott Rettberg is Professor of Digital Culture in the Department of Linguistic, Literary, and Aesthetic studies at the University of Bergen, Norway. Scott was the project leader of "Electronic Literature as a Model of Creativity and Innovation in Practice" (ELMCIP), a HERA-funded collaborative research project, and the founder of the Electronic Literature Organization. Scott is the author or coauthor of novel-length works of electronic literature, combinatory poetry and films including *The Unknown*, *Kind of Blue*, *Implementation*, *Frequency*, *Three Rails Live*, *Toxi-City* and others. His creative work has been exhibited online and at art venues including the Chemical Heritage Foundation Museum, Palazzo delle Arti Napoli, Beall Center, the Slought Foundation, The Krannert Art Museum and elsewhere.

Martin Rieser is Visiting Professor at the DCRC hub of the University of the West of England and Research Fellow at Bath Spa University. Martin's track record as a researcher and practitioner in Digital Arts stretches back to the early 1980s. From a background in English Literature, Philosophy, Printmaking and Photography, he established the first postgraduate course in Computer Arts in London in 1982. His practice in Internet art, interactive narrative and installations, mobile artworks and interactive films has been seen around the world including in Europe, the USA, Canada, Japan, Australia and China. He has delivered papers on interactive narrative and exhibited at many major conferences including ISEA Siggraph and ICIDS. His interactive installations include *Understanding Echo* shown in Japan 2002; *Hosts* Bath Abbey 2006; *Secret Door* Milan 2006; *The Street* Melbourne 2008/ Belfast 2009; *The Third Woman* (2008–2013) Xian China, Vienna, New York, Thessaloniki and Bath; *Codes of Disobedience*, Athens 2011; *Secret Garden*, London 2012 and Taipei 2013. Martin has published in many international journals and edited (together with Andrea Zapp) *New Screen Media: Cinema, Art and Narrative* (2002 BFI/ZKM) and *The Mobile Audience* (2011 Rodopi).

Marie-Laure Ryan is an independent scholar based in Colorado but originally a native of Geneva, Switzerland. Marie-Laure is the author of *Possible Worlds, Artificial Intelligence and Narrative Theory* (1991), *Narrative as Virtual Reality: Immersion and Interactivity in Literature and Electronic*

Media (2001) and *Avatars of Story* (2006). She has also edited *Cyberspace Textuality: Computer Technology and Literary Theory* (1999), *Narrative Across Media: The Languages of Storytelling* (2004), *Intermediality and Storytelling* (2010) (with Marina Grishakova) and, together with David Herman and Manfred Jahn, the *Routledge Encyclopedia of Narrative* (2005). Her most recent books are *The Johns Hopkins Guidebook to Digital Humanties* (coedited with Lori Emerson and Benjamin Robertson) and *Storyworlds Across Media*, coedited with Jan-Noël Thon, both due in 2014. Her scholarly work has earned her the Prize for Independent Scholars and the Jeanne and Aldo Scaglione Prize for Comparative Literature, both from the Modern Language Association, and she has been the recipient of Guggenheim and NEA followships. She has also been Scholar in residence at the University of Colorado, Boulder, and Johannes Gutenberg Fellow at the University of Mainz, Germany. Her website is at http://users.frii.com/mlryan/ and she can be reached at marilaur@gmail.com.

Diğdem Sezen holds a PhD in Communications from Istanbul University. During her PhD, she received the Fulbright scholarship for her doctoral studies, carried out research in the field of interactive storytelling, new media literacies, digital games and experimental TV at Georgia Institute of Technology, School of Digital Media and has presented and published papers and book chapters in many fields across this spectrum. She is a member of Games & Narrative international research group. She is an assistant professor at Istanbul University, Faculty of Communications.

Tonguç İbrahim Sezen is an Assistant Professor at Istanbul Bilgi University, Faculty of Communication. He holds a PhD in Communications from Istanbul University, School of Social Sciences. During his doctoral studies, he visited Georgia Institute of Technology, School of Literature, Media, and Communication as a Fulbright scholar. His research interests include cross-media narration, game design, interactive storytelling and toy studies. He is a member of the Games & Narrative research group.

Ulrike Spierling is Professor of Rich Media Design at the Hochschule Rhein-Main, University of Applied Sciences in Wiesbaden, Germany, since 2010. A designer and researcher active in the field of Interactive Storytelling for over 15 years, she also draws from over two decades of experience in interdisciplinary work, connecting Design and Computer Science. With a degree in Visual Communication Design, Ulrike worked for several years at Fraunhofer Institute for Computer Graphics, Darmstadt, in the areas of Computer Animation, Virtual Reality and Interface Design. From 1998, she served as Department Head in the ZGDV Computer Graphics Institute in Darmstadt and established a research agenda in Digital Storytelling. Later, as a Professor at the FH Erfurt University of Applied Sciences, she cofounded the annual conference series International Conference for Interactive Digital Storytelling (ICIDS, icids.org) in 2008. Ulrike has been teaching animation, game and interaction design, and conducted several international workshops on authoring interactive narrative. She contributed to various national and EU-funded research projects, and she holds a PhD in Interactive Digital Storytelling.

Neil Suttie is currently working towards a PhD in Artificial Intelligence from Heriot-Watt University. He received his BSc with honours in Computer Science from Heriot-Watt University in 2010, with his honours dissertation investigating autonomous story presentation in interactive narrative. His research interests include Artificial Intelligence, Emergent Narrative, Interactive Digital Storytelling, Games Design and Serious Games. During his PhD, Neil has developed several Serious Games including: *Mirror Mirror*—a game developed as a joint project to study positive feedback mechanisms for mirror neuron activation during social interactions in children with high functioning Autism and *Infinite Scotland*—a game commissioned to allow players to discover and explore the biological and cultural diversity of Scotland. He is currently investigating new authorial approaches towards the design of Emergent Narrative characters for applications in Serious Games. Neil is a member of the Games and Learning Alliance (GaLA) and the Research in Interactive Drama Environments, Role-play and Storytelling (Riders) research networks.

Nicolas Szilas completed a PhD in Cognitive Science in 1995 (Grenoble, France), and after two postdoctoral positions (Montreal) started to work at a video game studio in 1997 in order to manage the newly created R&D Programme in AI for video games. Between 1999 and 2001, Nicolas was Chief Scientist at the Innovation Department of a European software integration company. In parallel, from 1997, he conducted his own research programme on Interactive Drama called *IDtension*. He developed this research at the University of Paris 8, then at the Macquarie University in Sydney, before entering the University of Geneva in 2006 as Associate Professor. He has been continuing his research within Switzerland and Europe-funded research projects and has released *Nothing For Dinner*, a 20–40 minute fully playable 3D interactive drama. His current research on interactive narrative includes the creation of computational models and design methods for authoring, which is the exploration of novel artistic forms based on interactive narrative and applications in the domain of learning and training. He also studies games for learning in general—his teaching domain at the University of Geneva—focusing particularly on the issue of integrating learning goals into the game mechanics.

John Truesdale is currently working towards a PhD in Artificial Intelligence at Heriot-Watt University in Scotland. His research interests include Artificial Intelligence, Emergent Narrative, Interactive Digital Storytelling, Narratology, Game Design and Serious Games. He received his MEng in Software Engineering with Distinction from Heriot-Watt University in 2012—his Masters dissertation jointly investigated and developed fundamental and upcoming technical game design considerations, resulting in a prototype game engine. Additionally, his Honours project looked at the implications of integrating affect-driven agents within an interactive narrative environment. During his PhD, John has designed and developed several Serious Games including *Quantum Space*, a casual one-minute game developed to assist research in quantum physics by indirectly invoking players to organically reduce the scope of a quantum search space. Additionally, he was involved with *Infinite Scotland*, an educational game that allowed players to discover and explore the biological and cultural diversity of Scotland, challenging them to both learn and apply their new knowledge. His current research is looking at the role and application of context within the remits of Emergent Narrative; by bridging the gap between traditional top-down story facilitation and bottom up character-first design, context could enhance an interactive narrative environment. John is a member of the Research in Interactive Drama Environments, Role-Play and Storytelling (Riders) research network.

Index